Education Policy and Practice

Bridging the Divide

SUZANNE PLAUT

NANCY S. SHARKEY

EDITORS

Harvard Educational Review
Reprint Series
No. 37

Library of Congress Control Number 2003106676

ISBN 1-916690-40-7

Published by Harvard Educational Review,
an imprint of the Harvard Education Publishing Group

Harvard Educational Review
8 Story Street
Cambridge, MA 02138

Cover design by Anne Carter
Cover photograph by Thinkstock/Getty Images

The typefaces used in this book are New Baskerville and ITC Fenice.

This book is dedicated
to the students and teachers
whom we hope will be served by
effective policy and practice.

Contents

▼▼▼▼▼

Introduction

▼▼▼▼▼

Education Policy and Practice offers educators an exciting opportunity to consider important and often unexamined connections between education policy and teaching and learning practice. Our ultimate aim is to offer insights that could help improve the educational experiences of the estimated 47 million students in our public school system and the professional experiences of the just over three million teachers and administrators (NCES, 2001, 2002) who work with them. It is imperative that practicing teachers, school leaders, policymakers, teacher educators, and graduate students engage in constructive dialogue about effective school structures and teaching practices: that they question one another's assumptions, incorporate one another's unique expertise, and grapple with shared dilemmas. We believe that these articles will inspire readers to do just that. We also urge readers to consider how we might develop what Sonia Nieto calls school *transformation*, a more comprehensive concept of school reform that includes "concomitant changes in educators' attitudes toward students and their families, and the crucial role of power relationships [that] may help rescue current reform efforts from simplistic technical responses to what are essentially moral and political dilemmas."

There has been no lack of school reform, restructuring, and reorganization over the last one hundred years. The causes and effects of these reforms are well documented in the research. Despite persistent efforts, K–12 education in the United States has struggled more with trends and cycles than with sustained improvement (Hess, 1999, Sarason, 1996; Tyack & Cuban, 1995). One potential explanation for this phenomenon is the lack of connection between K–12 policy and practice. Policymakers need to take into account how policy will be interpreted by and implemented in districts and schools (Spillane, 1998). Spillane argues that schools interpret and implement policy differently even within school districts and suggests that the more complex the reform, the greater this variation will be. The extent to which teachers "understand what they are supposed to do" (Berends, Chun, Schuyler, Stockly, & Briggs, 2002), or the extent to which reforms are specific (Clune, 1998; Porter, 1994; Porter, Floden, Freeman, Schmidt, and Schwille, 1988), is a critical determinant of school reform success, yet is one aspect that policymakers often fail to address. Even fewer policymakers address the fact that teachers might be more than simple recipients of these reforms.

The professional cultures and vantage points of practitioners and policymakers differ dramatically, which may be one cause for the persistent disconnection. Policymakers, many of whom may never have taught, work as action executives. They define problems based in part on public opinion, and tend to offer broad guidelines regarding implementation. Practitioners, who have often been neglected in the policymaking process, are responsible for carrying out recommendations and mandates. These include managing day-to-day details such as following curriculum guides, implementing standardized tests, or even tracking student attendance. They also include grappling with the human side of teaching, such as facilitating literature circles in large classes of students from diverse backgrounds, or finding the time for and negotiating political relationships with colleagues and administrators. Using standardized testing as a current example of the disconnection, Graham (2003) writes, "Changing policy is much easier than changing practice. It is easy to mandate tests, but much more difficult to ensure that all children learn and are capable of using that knowledge in a productive manner" (p. 23). She cautions policymakers and teachers alike that, "in education, the issue is not simply to change the policy, but also to change the practice — a tricky translation" (p. 23).

Part of what makes the translation so tricky is that the role teachers should play in effective educational reform efforts is not well defined. Johnson (1990) argues that we must begin to understand the role of teachers in reform efforts. Others stress that teachers need to be sensitive to their moral (Hansen, 2001; Sizer & Sizer, 1999), political (Apple, 1993; Carlson, 1987; Greene, 1986), and cultural (Delpit, 1995) responsibilities to a diverse student population. For instance, as Giroux and McLaren (1986) state, "Questions might be raised about the nature and source of the authority which legitimates a particular type of curriculum, the way school time is organized, the political consequences of tracking students, the social division of labor among teachers . . . highlighting the social and ideological function that educators serve" (p. 225). However, many claim that teachers are unprepared for the complex demands of their work and unsupported when they are asked to implement instructional reforms (Darling-Hammond & Berry, 1988; Darling-Hammond & Greene, 1990), much less educational transformations.

The relationship between policymakers and practitioners has often been hierarchical, unidirectional, and even adversarial — with policymakers "telling" teachers what to do and how to do it. As Carlson (1987) writes, teachers "have been bureaucratically subordinated, rigidly boxed in by a predetermined curriculum, and held accountable for maintaining instructional 'productivity' goals" (p. 284). One purpose of this volume is to highlight the ways that teachers, as professionals, are and should be full partners in this conversation. We are delighted to present ten articles previously published in the *Harvard Educational Review* that serve this aim. Listening to the voices of teachers, students, teacher educators, and both practice-based and academic researchers shows how these perspectives intersect and the role each can play in school reform. By finding the common ground rather than the disconnections, we hope to promote conversation among the groups that will lead to more thoughtful and informed policy *and* practice, and to increased sharing and dialogue between the two. In short, we hope to help with the tricky translation.

The articles in this volume are organized around three major themes that we consider central to school reform and school practice. One article was first published in the *Harvard Education Review* more than thirty years ago; others came out within the past few years. Our selection is clearly limited by the contents of our journal and should be considered within the broader discussion occurring in research organizations, such as the Chicago Consortium on School Reform, the Annenberg Foundation, teacher education programs, and countless faculty rooms and classrooms nationwide. The selected articles can contribute to this broader conversation; they have resonated powerfully with readers and have been used consistently and effectively in graduate courses on teacher preparation, school reform, and educational policy in the context of U.S. K–12 schooling.

Part One, Race, Culture, Power, and Language, offers four articles that challenge current and future teachers to consider how to effectively address issues of race, culture, power, and language in their classrooms, through both their personal presence and their pedagogy. These selections encourage policymakers to consider how teacher education programs need to be structured to address these issues and how to design instructional programs that empower all students. The U.S. public school student population has become increasingly diverse in terms of race, culture, language, social class, and ability, while the teaching population remains predominantly White, female, and middle class (Gomez, 1996; Suárez-Orozco & Suárez-Orozco, 1995; Zeichner, 1996). In her own way, each author in this section questions the middle-class White assumptions that many teachers hold about what, how, and why to teach, and offers a model of how to shift one's stance in order to serve all students' academic and cultural needs with clarity and respect.

Lisa D. Delpit's seminal piece "The Silenced Dialogue" uses the debate over process-oriented versus skills-oriented writing instruction as the starting point to examine the "culture of power" that exists in society and schools. She asserts that issues of power are enacted in classrooms, that there are codes or rules for participating in power, and that these rules are a reflection of the rules of the culture of those who have power. She further claims that those with less power are often more aware of its existence than those with more power, and that being explicitly told the rules of the culture of power makes acquiring power easier. Arguing that "progressive" child-centered, whole language, and process approaches to instruction may leave some students "accountable for knowing a set of rules about which no one has ever directly informed them," Delpit reminds us that "the dilemma is not really in the debate over instructional methodology, but rather in communicating across cultures" in a way that fosters students' own voices while also coaching those voices to be heard clearly in the larger society.

The subsequent articles by Cynthia Ballenger and by Cynthia L. Greenleaf and her colleagues draw on and demonstrate Delpit's ideas in different ways. Ballenger, a veteran early childhood special education teacher, describes how she learned to "control the behavior" of the Haitian students in her preschool classroom. Rather than assume her students had behavioral deficits, Ballenger carefully studied classroom situations and gradually changed her own speech and behavior so it was congruent with students' language patterns and cultural values. Greenleaf et al.'s essay describes reading apprenticeship, an instructional framework based on the premise that "for all students to learn to perform high-level, academically linked literacy tasks, teachers will need to make explicit the tacit reasoning processes, strategies, and discourse rules that shape successful readers' and writers' work." Her findings challenge the current policy push for remedial reading programs for poor readers, offering an alternative that emphasizes inquiry and subject-area expertise.

Part One closes with Marilyn Cochran-Smith's narrative of her experience "unlearning" racism as a teacher educator at the University of Pennsylvania. Cochran-Smith argues that "all teaching (including teacher education) can be regarded as text, that teacher education has both public and implicit or hidden texts, and that the text of teacher education is (in large part) a racial text." Together, the four articles in this first part raise two sets of questions. First, who gets to define the purposes and practices of education, what assumptions are those decisions based on, and how can those decisions be made in ways that are inclusive and empowering of all of our children? Second, how can teachers, teacher educators, and policymakers design programs and prepare professionals to support this work?

Part Two, Teacher Expectations and School Effectiveness, continues to examine the role individual teachers play in students' schooling experiences, and also begins to explore what schools as institutions can do to meet students' needs. Research has consistently shown that teachers' attitudes and beliefs about their students influence the academic performance of students in their classrooms (Brophy & Good, 1974; Irvine, 1990; Oakes, 1985; Ogbu, 1990; Rosenthal & Jacobson 1968). This part opens with Ray C. Rist's classic ethnographic study that describes the social process by which teacher expectations affected achievement and outcomes for one group of "ghetto" children during kindergarten, first, and second grade. Rist poignantly portrays how the kindergarten teacher's judgments about a student's academic potential — based on the extent to which an individual conformed to middle-class norms of attire, demeanor, social skills, and even personal hygiene — determined the child's reading group and tablemates, as well as the quantity and quality of instruction the teacher offered each student.

Following Rist's study are two articles that offer a more hopeful vision of how individual teachers and entire schools can support students' academic and personal growth. Nieto's case studies let us hear the voices of successful secondary school students from a wide range of ethnic, racial, linguistic, and social-class backgrounds. Students describe the policies and practices that helped them succeed: culturally relevant curriculum, empowering and engaging pedagogy, high expectations, and a sense of being known and having a voice. Nieto emphasizes that educators must "look critically not only at structural conditions [of schools], but also at [teachers'] individual attitudes and behaviors." Tamara Lucas, Rosemary C. Henze, and Rubén Donato then describe features of high schools that promote the achievement of language minority students and, most importantly, how these features are operationalized in school policy and practice. The articles in Part Two highlight school designs and teaching practices that make manifest high and constructive expectations for all learners.

Part Three, School Accountability and Teacher Control, explores the role that teachers play in implementing school policy. While the previous articles presented what teachers and schools might do to meet students' varied needs, this section examines the extent to which teachers have the capacity, the will, and the space to do this work, and how policy can best support them. Many researchers have explored issues of teacher autonomy, professionalism, and school reform (see, e.g., Meier, 1985; Newmann, 1994; Sergiovanni & Moore, 1989; Zeichner, 1991); this section touches on all three. It raises questions for teachers about when and how they will support school reform efforts, and for policymakers about how to construct and support reform efforts that penetrate but do not devastate teaching practice.

Johanna Elena Hadden, an elementary school teacher, opens Part Three with a compelling narrative of her conflicts with her school principal over her classroom decisions. Hadden describes her efforts to think independently and critically as a teacher, and to encourage her students to do the same. She argues that teachers are given little space to think independently and critically, and are given even less space to engage in critical pedagogy. They are instead expected to follow district and school mandates without question. Hadden ultimately was deemed insubordinate by her principal and district officials because she did not meet their administrative expectations. The conflict between teaching and training is summed up in a statement made by a district official at a meeting with Hadden: "Although you are obviously an exceptional teacher, this letter [of reprimand] indicates deficiencies as an employee."

Hadden's dilemma — that teachers are expected to train students according to school and district guidelines and that teachers lack the autonomy necessary for critical pedagogy — is the crux of the question explored in the next article in this section. Richard M. Ingersoll explores two common yet conflicting assumptions: that schools are decentralized and teachers autonomous, and that schools are heavily bureaucratized organizations where teachers possess little discretion. Using the Schools and Staffing Survey (a nationally representative survey of districts, school administrators, and teachers) to explore who controls school decisions (including decisions regarding social, sorting, and behavioral activities), Ingersoll finds that teachers have less autonomy —

in both public *and* private schools — than is commonly assumed. The extent to which schools and teachers can, do, and should act independently from centralized policies is at the heart of educational accountability debates.

The section concludes with a hopeful essay describing how to "scale up" school reform in a way that simultaneously meets students' academic needs and teachers' needs to be treated as respected professionals. In "Getting to Scale with Good Educational Practice," Richard F. Elmore describes the problems facing large-scale educational reform, arguing that school organization and structures inhibit successful widespread reform implementation. While school structures (school size, length of school day, etc.) may change, the instructional core remains the same. Elmore concludes with four lessons for policymakers who hope to spread educational reform. He envisions the creation of 1) professional norms for teachers; 2) structures that "intensify and focus" teachers' motivation to improve their practice; 3) processes that allow replication of improvements; and 4) supports for teachers trying to improve their practice. These four recommendations place the responsibility for school reform with teachers and policymakers, recognizing that both have an important role to play if this process is to be successful.

Policymakers and practitioners must learn from one another if school reform is actually to take root in classrooms. In his recently edited volume *A Nation Reformed?* David Gordon states, "Too often, reforms have focused on big-picture issues — school governance, organization, curriculum, accountability, and so forth — without taking into account how decisions affect what happens on the front lines where improvement is most needed" (2003, p. 6). This volume offers a range of articles from a wide variety of voices and perspectives that challenge us to think broadly not only about what happens on the "front lines," but also about how it is done, who gets to decide, and what ultimately is at stake.

Suzanne Plaut
Nancy S. Sharkey
Editors

REFERENCES

Apple, M. (1993). *Official knowledge: Democratic education in a conservative age.* New York: Routledge.

Berends, M., Chun, J, Schuyler, G., Stockly, S., & Briggs, J. (2002). *Challenges of conflicting school reforms: Effects of new American schools in a high-poverty district.* Santa Monica, CA: RAND.

Brophy, J. E., & Good, T. L. (1974). *Teacher-student relationships: Causes and consequences.* New York: Holt, Rinehart, and Winston.

Carlson, D. (1987). Teachers as political actors: From reproductive theory to the crisis of schooling. *Harvard Educational Review, 57,* 283–307.

Darling-Hammond, L., & Berry, B. (1988). *Evolution of teacher policy: Report of the Center for Policy Research in Education.* Washington, DC: Rutgers University, Eagleton Institute of Politics, and RAND.

Darling-Hammond, L., & Greene, J. (1990). Teacher quality and equality. In J. I. Goodlad & P. Keating (Eds.), *Access to knowledge: An agenda for our nation's schools* (pp. 237–258). New York: College Entrance Examination Board.

Delpit, L. (1995). *Other people's children: Cultural conflict in the classroom.* New York: New Press.

Clune, W. (1988). *Toward a theory of systemic reform: The case of nine NSF statewide systemic initiatives.* Madison: University of Wisconsin–Madison, Wisconsin Center for Education Research.

Giroux, H., & McLaren, P. (1986). Teacher education and the politics of engagement. *Harvard Educational Review, 56,* 213–238.

Graham, P. (2003). The long haul. *Education Next, 3*(2), 21–23.

Greene, M. (1986). In search of a critical pedagogy. *Harvard Educational Review, 56,* 427–441.

Gomez, M. L. (1996). Prospective teachers' perspectives on teaching *Other People's Children.* In K. Zeichner, S. Melnick, & M. L. Gomez (Eds.), *Currents of reform in preservice teacher education* (pp. 109–132). New York: Teachers College Press.

Hansen, D. T. (2001). *Exploring the moral heart of teaching: Toward a teacher's creed.* New York: Teachers College Press.

Hess, F. M. (1999). *Spinning wheels: The politics of urban school reform.* Washington, DC: Brookings Institution Press.

Irvine, J. J. (1990). *Black students and school failure: Policies, practices, and prescriptions.* Westport, CT: Greenwood Press.

Johnson, S. M. (1990). *Teachers at work: Achieving success in our schools.* New York: Basic Books.

Meir, D. (1985). Retaining the teacher's perspective in the principalship. *Education and Urban Society, 17,* 302–310.

National Center for Education Statistics. (2001). *Projections of education statistics to 2011.* Available online at http://www.nces.ed.gov/pubs/2001/proj01/tables/table01.asp

National Center for Education Statistics. (2002). *Digest of education statistics.* Available online at http://www.nces.ed.gov/pubs/2002/digest2001/tables/dt065.asp

Newmann, F. M. (1994). *Schoolwide professional communities: Issues in restructuring schools* (Issue Report No. 6). Madison: University of Wisconsin–Madison, Center on Organization and Restructuring Schools.

Oakes, J. (1985). *Keeping track.* New Haven, CT: Yale University Press.

Ogbu, J. U. (1990). Overcoming racial barriers to equal access. In J. I. Goodlad & P. Keating (Eds.), *Access to knowledge: An agenda for our nation's schools* (pp. 19–31). New York: College Board.

Porter, A. C. (1994). National standards and school improvements in the 1990s: Issues and promise. *American Journal of Education, 102,* 421–499.

Porter, A. C., Floden R., Freeman D., Schmidt, W., & Schwille, J. (1988). Content determinants in elementary school mathematics. In D. A. Grouws & T. J. Clooney (Eds.), *Perspectives on research on effective mathematics teaching* (pp. 96–113). Hillsdale, NJ: Erlbaum.

Rosenthal, R., & Jacobson, L. (1968). *Pygmalion in the classroom.* New York: Holt, Rinehart, and Winston.

Sarason, S. (1996). *Revisiting* The Culture of the School and the Problem of Change. New York: Teachers College Press.

Sergiovanni, T., & Moore, J. (1989). *Schooling for tomorrow: Directing reforms to issues that count.* Boston: Allyn & Bacon.

Sizer, T. R., & Sizer, N. F. (1999). *The students are watching: Schools and the moral contract.* Boston: Beacon Press.

Spillane, J. P. (1998). State policy and the non-monolithic nature of the local school district: Organizational and professional considerations. *American Educational Research Journal, 35*(1), 33–63.

Suárez-Orozco, C., & Suárez-Orozco, M. (1995). *Transformations: Immigration, family life, and achievement motivation among Latino adolescents.* Stanford, CA: Stanford University Press.

Tyack, D., & Cuban, L. (1995). *Tinkering toward utopia: A century of public school reform.* Cambridge, MA: Harvard University Press.

Zeichner, K. (1991). Contradictions and tensions in the professionalization of teaching and the democratization of schools. *Teachers College Record, 92,* 363–377.

Zeichner, K. (1996). Educating teachers for cultural diversity. In K. Zeichner, S. Melnick, & M. L. Gomez (Eds.), *Currents of reform in preservice teacher education* (pp. 133–175). New York: Teachers College Press.

PART ONE

▼▼▼▼▼

Race, Culture, Power, and Language

The Silenced Dialogue:
Power and Pedagogy in Educating
Other People's Children

LISA D. DELPIT

A Black male graduate student who is also a special education teacher in a predominantly Black community is talking about his experiences in predominantly White university classes:

> There comes a moment in every class where we have to discuss "The Black Issue" and what's appropriate education for Black children. I tell you, I'm tired of arguing with those White people, because they won't listen. Well, I don't know if they really don't listen or if they just don't believe you. It seems like if you can't quote Vygotsky or something, then you don't have any validity to speak about your *own* kids. Anyway, I'm not bothering with it anymore, now I'm just in it for a grade.

A Black woman teacher in a multicultural urban elementary school is talking about her experiences in discussions with her predominantly White fellow teachers about how they should organize reading instructions to best serve students of color:

> When you're talking to White people they still want it to be their way. You can try to talk to them and give them examples, but they're so headstrong, they think they know what's best for *everybody*, for *everybody's* children. They won't listen, White folks are going to do what they want to do *anyway*.
>
> It's really hard. They just don't listen well. No, they listen, but they don't *hear* — you know how your mama used to say you listen to the radio, but you *hear* your mother? Well they don't *hear* me.
>
> So I just try to shut them out so I can hold my temper. You can only beat your head against a brick wall for so long before you draw blood. If I try to stop arguing with them I can't help myself from getting angry. Then I end up walking around praying all day "Please Lord, remove the bile I feel for these people so I can sleep tonight." It's funny, but it can become a cancer, a sore.

Harvard Educational Review Vol. 58 No. 3 August 1988, 280–298

So, I shut them out. I go back to my own little cubby, my classroom, and I try to teach the way I know will work, no matter what those folk say. And when I get Black kids, I just try to undo the damage they did.

I'm not going to let any man, woman, or child drive me crazy — White folks will try to do that to you if you let them. You just have to stop talking to them, that's what I do. I just keep smiling, but I won't talk to them.

A soft-spoken Native Alaskan woman in her forties is a student in the Education Department of the University of Alaska. One day she storms into a Black professor's office and very uncharacteristically slams the door. She plops down in a chair and, still fuming, says, "Please tell people, just don't help us anymore! I give up. I won't talk to them again!"

And finally, a Black woman principal who is also a doctoral student at a well-known university on the West Coast is talking about her university experiences, particularly about when a professor lectures on issues concerning educating Black children:

If you try to suggest that that's not quite the way it is, they get defensive, then you get defensive, then they'll start reciting research.

I try to give them my experiences, to explain. They just look and nod. The more I try to explain, they just look and nod, just keep looking and nodding. They don't really hear me.

Then, when it's time for class to be over, the professor tells me to come to his office to talk more. So I go. He asks for more examples of what I'm talking about, and he looks and nods while I give them. Then he says that that's just my experiences. It doesn't really apply to most Black people.

It becomes futile because they think they know everything about everybody. What you have to say about your life, your children, doesn't mean anything. They don't really want to hear what you have to say. They wear blinders and earplugs. They only want to go on research they've read that other White people have written.

It just doesn't make any sense to keep talking to them.

Thus was the first half of the title of this text born — "The Silenced Dialogue." One of the tragedies in the field of education is that scenarios such as these are enacted daily around the country. The saddest element is that the individuals that the Black and Native American educators speak of in these statements are seldom aware that the dialogue *has* been silenced. Most likely the White educators believe that their colleagues of color did, in the end, agree with their logic. After all, they stopped disagreeing, didn't they?

I have collected these statements since completing a recently published article (Delpit, 1986). In this somewhat autobiographical account, entitled "Skills and Other Dilemmas of a Progressive Black Educator," I discussed my perspective as a product of a skills-oriented approach to writing and as a teacher of process-oriented approaches. I described the estrangement that I and many teachers of color feel from the progressive movement when writing-process advocates dismiss us as too "skills oriented." I ended the article suggesting that it was incumbent upon writing-process advocates — or indeed, advocates of any progressive movement — to enter into dialogue with teachers of color, who may not share their enthusiasm about so-called new, liberal, or progressive ideas.

In response to this article, which presented no research data and did not even cite a reference, I received numerous calls and letters from teachers, professors, and even state school personnel from around the country, both Black and White. All of the White respondents, except one, have wished to talk more about the question of skills versus process approaches — to support or reject what they perceive to be my position. On the other hand, *all* of the non-White respondents have spoken passionately on being left out of the dialogue about how best to educate children of color.

How can such complete communication blocks exist when both parties truly believe they have the same aims? How can the bitterness and resentment expressed by the educators of color be drained so that the sores can heal? What can be done?

I believe the answer to these questions lies in ethnographic analysis, that is, in identifying and giving voice to alternative world views. Thus, I will attempt to address the concerns raised by White and Black respondents to my article "Skills and Other Dilemmas" (Delpit, 1986). My charge here is not to determine the best instructional methodology; I believe that the actual practice of good teachers of all colors typically incorporates a range of pedagogical orientations. Rather, I suggest that the differing perspectives on the debate over "skills" versus "process" approaches can lead to an understanding of the alienation and miscommunication, and thereby to an understanding of the "silenced dialogue."

In thinking through these issues, I have found what I believe to be a connecting and complex theme: what I have come to call "the culture of power." There are five aspects of power I would like to propose as given for this presentation:

1. Issues of power are enacted in classrooms.
2. There are codes or rules for participating in power; that is, there is a "culture of power."
3. The rules of the culture of power are a reflection of the rules of the culture of those who have power.
4. If you are not already a participant in the culture of power, being told explicitly the rules of that culture makes acquiring power easier.
5. Those with power are frequently least aware of — or least willing to acknowledge — its existence. Those with less power are often most aware of its existence.

The first three are by now basic tenets in the literature of the sociology of education, but the last two have seldom been addressed. The following discussion will explicate these aspects of power and their relevance to the schism between liberal educational movements and that of non-White, non-middle-class teachers and communities.[1]

1. Issues of power are enacted in classrooms.

These issues include: the power of the teacher over the students; the power of the publishers of textbooks and of the developers of the curriculum to determine the view of the world presented; the power of the state in enforcing compulsory schooling; and the power of an individual or group to determine another's intelligence or "normalcy." Finally, if schooling prepares people for jobs, and the kind of job a person has determines her or his economic status and, therefore, power, then schooling is intimately related to that power.

2. There are codes or rules for participating in power; that is, there is a "culture of power."

The codes or rules I'm speaking of relate to linguistic forms, communicative strategies, and presentation of self; that is, ways of talking, ways of writing, ways of dressing, and ways of interacting.

3. The rules of the culture of power are a reflection of the rules of the culture of those who have power.

This means that success in institutions — schools, workplaces, and so on — is predicated upon acquisition of the culture of those who are in power. Children from middle-class homes tend to do better in school than those from non-middle-class homes because the culture of the school is based on the culture of the upper and middle classes — of those in power. The upper and middle classes send their children to school with all the accoutrements of the culture of power; children from other kinds of families operate within perfectly wonderful and viable cultures but not cultures that carry the codes or rules of power.

4. If you are not already a participant in the culture of power, being told explicitly the rules of that culture makes acquiring power easier.

In my work within and between diverse cultures, I have come to conclude that members of any culture transmit information implicitly to co-members. However, when implicit codes are attempted across cultures, communication frequently breaks down. Each cultural group is left saying, "Why don't those people say what they mean?" as well as, "What's wrong with them, why don't they understand?"

Anyone who has had to enter new cultures, especially to accomplish a specific task, will know of what I speak. When I lived in several Papua New Guinea villages for extended periods to collect data, and when I go to Alaskan villages for work with Alaskan Native communities, I have found it unquestionably easier — psychologically and pragmatically — when some kind soul has directly informed me about such matters as appropriate dress, interactional styles, embedded meanings, and taboo words or actions. I contend that it is much the same for anyone seeking to learn the rules of the culture of power. Unless one has the leisure of a lifetime of "immersion" to learn them, explicit presentation makes learning immeasurably easier.

And now, to the fifth and last premise:

5. Those with power are frequently least aware of — or least willing to acknowledge — its existence. Those with less power are often most aware of its existence.

For many who consider themselves members of liberal or radical camps, acknowledging personal power and admitting participation in the culture of power is distinctly uncomfortable. On the other hand, those who are less powerful in any situation are most likely to recognize the power variable most acutely. My guess is that the White colleagues and instructors of those previously quoted did not perceive themselves to have power over the non-White speakers. However, either by virtue of their position, their numbers, or their access to that particular code of power of calling upon research to validate one's position, the White educators had the authority to establish what was to be considered "truth" regardless of the opinions of the people of color, and the latter were well aware of that fact.

A related phenomenon is that liberals (and here I am using the term "liberal" to refer to those whose beliefs include striving for a society based upon maximum individual freedom and autonomy) seem to act under the assumption that to make any rules or expectations explicit is to act against liberal principles, to limit the freedom and autonomy of those subjected to the explicitness.

I thank Fred Erickson for a comment that led me to look again at a tape by John Gumperz[2] on cultural dissonance in cross-cultural interactions. One of the episodes showed an East Indian interviewing for a job with an all-White committee. The interview was a complete failure, even though several of the interviewers appeared to really want to help the applicant. As the interview rolled steadily downhill, these "helpers" became more and more indirect in their questioning, which exacerbated the problems the applicant had in performing appropriately. Operating from a different cultural perspective, he got fewer and fewer clear clues as to what was expected of him, which ultimately resulted in his failure to secure the position.

I contend that as the applicant showed less and less aptitude for handling the interview, the power differential became ever more evident to the interviewers. The "helpful" interviewers, unwilling to acknowledge themselves as having power over the applicant, became more and more uncomfortable. Their indirectness was an attempt to lessen the power differential and their discomfort by lessening the power-revealing explicitness of their questions and comments.

When acknowledging and expressing power, one tends toward explicitness (as in yelling to your ten-year-old, "Turn that radio down!"). When de-emphasizing power, there is a move toward indirect communication. Therefore, in the interview setting, those who sought to help, to express their egalitarianism with the East Indian applicant, became more and more indirect — and less and less helpful — in their questions and comments.

In literacy instruction, explicitness might be equated with direct instruction. Perhaps the ultimate expression of explicitness and direct instruction in the primary classroom is Distar. This reading program is based on a behaviorist model in which reading is taught through the direct instruction of phonics generalizations and blending. The teacher's role is to maintain the full attention of the group by continuous questioning, eye contact, finger snaps, hand claps, and other gestures, and by eliciting choral responses and initiating some sort of award system.

When the program was introduced, it arrived with a flurry of research data that "proved" that all children — even those who were "culturally deprived" — could learn to read using this method. Soon there was a strong response, first from academics and later from many classroom teachers, stating that the program was terrible. What I find particularly interesting, however, is that the primary issue of the conflict over Distar has not been over its instructional efficacy — usually the students did learn to read — but the expression of explicit power in the classroom. The liberal educators opposed the methods — the direct instruction, the explicit control exhibited by the teacher. As a matter of fact, it was not unusual (even now) to hear of the program spoken of as "fascist."

I am not an advocate of Distar, but I will return to some of the issues that the program — and direct instruction in general — raises in understanding the differences between progressive White educators and educators of color.

To explore those differences, I would like to present several statements typical of those made with the best of intentions by middle-class liberal educators. To the surprise of the speakers, it is not unusual for such content to be met by vocal opposition or stony silence from people of color. My attempt here is to examine the underlying assumptions of both camps.

"I want the same thing for everyone else's children as I want for mine."
To provide schooling for everyone's children that reflects liberal, middle-class values and aspirations is to ensure the maintenance of the status quo, to ensure that power, the culture of power, remains in the hands of those who already have it. Some children come to school with more accoutrements of the culture of power already in place — "cultural capital," as some critical theorists refer to it (for example, Apple, 1979) — some with less. Many liberal educators hold that the primary goal for education is for children to become autonomous, to develop fully who they are in the classroom setting without having arbitrary, outside standards forced upon them. This is a very reason-

able goal for people whose children are already participants in the culture of power and who have already internalized its codes.

But parents who don't function within that culture often want something else. It's not that they disagree with the former aim, it's just that they want something more. They want to ensure that the school provides their children with discourse patterns, interactional styles, and spoken and written language codes that will allow them success in the larger society.

It was the lack of attention to this concern that created such a negative outcry in the Black community when well-intentioned White liberal educators introduced "dialect readers." These were seen as a plot to prevent the schools from teaching the linguistic aspects of the culture of power, thus dooming Black children to a permanent outsider caste. As one parent demanded, "My kids know how to be Black — you all teach them how to be successful in the White man's world."

Several Black teachers have said to me recently that as much as they'd like to believe otherwise, they cannot help but conclude that many of the "progressive" educational strategies imposed by liberals upon Black and poor children could only be based on a desire to ensure that the liberals' children get sole access to the dwindling pool of American jobs. Some have added that the liberal educators believe themselves to be operating with good intentions, but that these good intentions are only conscious delusions about their unconscious true motives. One of Black anthropologist John Gwaltney's (1980) informants reflects this perspective with her tongue-in-cheek observation that the biggest difference between Black folks and White folks is that Black folks *know* when they're lying!

Let me try to clarify how this might work in literacy instruction. A few years ago I worked on an analysis of two popular reading programs, Distar and a progressive program that focused on higher-level critical thinking skills. In one of the first lessons of the progressive program, the children are introduced to the names of the letter *m* and *e*. In the same lesson they are then taught the sound made by each of the letters, how to write each of the letters, and that when the two are blended together they produce the word *me*.

As an experienced first-grade teacher, I am convinced that a child needs to be familiar with a significant number of these concepts to be able to assimilate so much new knowledge in one sitting. By contrast, Distar presents the same information in about forty lessons.

I would not argue for the pace of the Distar lessons; such a slow pace would only bore most kids — but what happened in the other lesson is that it merely provided an opportunity for those who already knew the content to exhibit that they knew it, or at most perhaps to build one new concept onto what was already known. This meant that the child who did not come to school already primed with what was to be presented would be labeled as needing "remedial" instruction from day one; indeed, this determination would be made before he or she was ever taught. In fact, Distar was "successful" because it actually *taught* new information to children who had not already acquired it at home. Although the more progressive system was ideal for some children, for others it was a disaster.

I do not advocate a simplistic "basic skills" approach for children outside of the culture of power. It would be (and has been) tragic to operate as if these children were incapable of critical and higher-order thinking and reasoning. Rather, I suggest that schools must provide these children the content that other families from a different cultural orientation provide at home. This does not mean separating children according to family background, but instead, ensuring that each classroom incorporate strategies appropriate for all the children in its confines.

And I do not advocate that it is the school's job to attempt to change the homes of poor and non-White children to match the homes of those in the culture of power. That may indeed be a form of cultural genocide. I have frequently heard schools call poor parents "uncaring" when parents respond to the school's urging, that they change their home life in order to facilitate their children's learning, by saying, "But that's the school's job." What the school personnel fail to understand is that if the parents were members of the culture of power and lived by its rules and codes, then they would transmit those codes to their children. In fact, they transmit another culture that children must learn at home in order to survive in their communities.

"Child-centered, whole language, and process approaches are needed in order to allow a democratic state of free, autonomous, empowered adults, and because research has shown that children learn best through these methods."

People of color are, in general, skeptical of research as a determiner of our fates. Academic research has, after all, found us genetically inferior, culturally deprived, and verbally deficient. But beyond that general caveat, and despite my or others' personal preferences, there is little research data supporting the major tenets of process approaches over other forms of literacy instruction, and virtually no evidence that such approaches are more efficacious for children of color (Siddle, 1986).

Although the problem is not necessarily inherent in the method, in some instances adherents of process approaches to writing create situations in which students ultimately find themselves held accountable for knowing a set of rules about which no one has ever directly informed them. Teachers do students no service to suggest, even implicitly, that "product" is not important. In this country, students will be judged on their product regardless of the process they utilized to achieve it. And that product, based as it is on the specific codes of a particular culture, is more readily produced when the directives of how to produce it are made explicit.

If such explicitness is not provided to students, what it feels like to people who are old enough to judge is that there are secrets being kept, that time is being wasted, that the teacher is abdicating his or her duty to teach. A doctoral student in my acquaintance was assigned to a writing class to hone his writing skills. The student was placed in the section led by a White professor who utilized a process approach, consisting primarily of having the students write essays and then assemble into groups to edit each others' papers. That procedure infuriated this particular student. He had many angry encounters with the teacher about what she was doing. In his words:

> I didn't feel she was teaching us anything. She wanted us to correct each others' papers and we were there to learn from her. She didn't teach anything, absolutely nothing.
>
> Maybe they're trying to learn what Black folks knew all the time. We understand how to improvise, how to express ourselves creatively. When I'm in a classroom, I'm not looking for that, I'm looking for structure, the more formal language.
>
> Now my buddy was in [a] Black teacher's class. And that lady was very good. She went through and explained and defined each part of the structure. This [White] teacher didn't get along with that Black teacher. She said that she didn't agree with her methods. But *I* don't think that White teacher *had* any methods.

When I told this gentleman that what the teacher was doing was called a process method of teaching writing, his response was, "Well, at least now I know that she *thought* she was doing *something*. I thought she was just a fool who couldn't teach and didn't want to try."

This sense of being cheated can be so strong that the student may be completely turned off to the educational system. Amanda Branscombe, an accomplished White teacher, recently wrote a letter discussing her work with working-class Black and White students at a community college in Alabama. She had given these students my "Skills and Other Dilemmas" article (Delpit, 1986) to read and discuss, and wrote that her students really understood and identified with what I was saying. To quote her letter:

> One young man said that he had dropped out of high school because he failed the exit exam. He noted that he had then passed the GED without a problem after three weeks of prep. He said that his high school English teacher claimed to use a process approach, but what she really did was hide behind fancy words to give herself permission to do nothing in the classroom.

The students I have spoken of seem to be saying that the teacher has denied them access to herself as the source of knowledge necessary to learn the forms they need to succeed. Again, I tentatively attribute the problem to teachers' resistance to exhibiting power in the classroom. Somehow, to exhibit one's personal power as expert source is viewed as disempowering one's students.

Two qualifiers are necessary, however. The teacher cannot be the only expert in the classroom. To deny students their own expert knowledge *is* to disempower them. Amanda Branscombe, when she was working with Black high school students classified as "slow learners," had the students analyze RAP songs to discover their underlying patterns. The students became the experts in explaining to the teacher the rules for creating a new RAP song. The teacher then used the patterns the students identified as a base to begin an explanation of the structure of grammar, and then of Shakespeare's plays. Both student and teacher are expert at what they know best.

The second qualifier is that merely adopting direct instruction is not the answer. Actual writing for real audiences and real purposes is a vital element in helping students to understand that they have an important voice in their own learning processes. Siddle (1988) examines the results of various kinds of interventions in a primarily process-oriented writing class for Black students. Based on readers' blind assessments, she found that the intervention that produced the most positive changes in the students' writing was a "mini-lesson" consisting of direct instruction about some standard writing convention. But what produced the *second* highest number of positive changes was a subsequent student-centered conference with the teacher. (Peer conferencing in this group of Black students who were not members of the culture of power produced the least number of changes in students' writing. However, the classroom teacher maintained — and I concur — that such activities are necessary to introduce the elements of "real audience" into the task, along with more teacher-directed strategies.)

"It's really a shame but she (that Black teacher upstairs) seems to be so authoritarian, so focused on skills and so teacher directed. Those poor kids never seem to be allowed to really express their creativity. (And she even yells at them.)"

This statement directly concerns the display of power and authority in the classroom. One way to understand the difference in perspective between Black teachers and their progressive colleagues on this issue is to explore culturally influenced oral interactions.

In *Ways With Words,* Shirley Brice Heath (1983) quotes the verbal directives given by the middle-class "townspeople" teachers (p. 280):

- "Is this where the scissors belong?"
- "You want to do your best work today."

By contrast, many Black teachers are more likely to say:

- "Put those scissors on that shelf."
- "Put your name on the papers and make sure to get the right answer for each question."

Is one oral style more authoritarian than another?

Other researchers have identified differences in middle-class and working-class speech to children. Snow et al. (1976), for example, report that working-class mothers use more directives to their children than do middle- and upper-class parents. Middle-class parents are likely to give the directive to a child to take his bath as, "Isn't it time for your bath?" Even though the utterance is couched as a question, both child and adult understand it as a directive. The child may respond with "Aw Mom, can't I wait until . . . ," but whether or not negotiation is attempted, both conversants understand the intent of the utterance.

By contrast, a Black mother, in whose house I was recently a guest, said to her eight-year-old son, "Boy, get your rusty behind in that bathtub." Now I happen to know that this woman loves her son as much as any mother, but she would never have posed the directive to her son to take a bath in the form of a question. Were she to ask, "Would you like to take your bath now?" she would not have been issuing a directive but offering a true alternative. Consequently, as Heath suggests, upon entering school the child from such a family may not understand the indirect statement of the teacher as a direct command. Both White and Black working-class children in the communities Heath studied "had difficulty interpreting these indirect requests for adherence to an unstated set of rules" (p. 280).

But those veiled commands are commands nonetheless, representing true power, and with true consequences for disobedience. If veiled commands are ignored, the child will be labeled a behavior problem and possibly officially classified as behavior disordered. In other words, the attempt by the teacher to reduce an exhibition of power by expressing herself in indirect terms may remove the very explicitness that the child needs to understand the rules of the new classroom culture.

A Black elementary school principal in Fairbanks, Alaska, reported to me that she has a lot of difficulty with Black children who are placed in some White teachers' classrooms. The teachers often send the children to the office for disobeying teacher directives. Their parents are frequently called in for conferences. The parents' response to the teacher is usually the same: "They do what I say; if you just *tell* them what to do, they'll do it. I tell them at home that they have to listen to what you say." And so, does not the power still exist? Its veiled nature only makes it more difficult for some children to respond appropriately, but that in no way mitigates its existence.

I don't mean to imply, however, that the only time the Black child disobeys the teacher is when he or she misunderstands the request for certain behavior. There are other factors that may produce such behavior. Black children expect an authority figure to act with authority. When the teacher instead acts as a "chum," the message sent is that this adult has no authority, and the children react accordingly. One reason this is so is that Black people often view issues of power and authority differently than people from mainstream middle-class backgrounds.[3] Many people of color expect authority to be earned by personal efforts and exhibited by personal characteristics. In other words, "the authoritative person gets to be a teacher because she is authoritative." Some members of middle-class cultures, by contrast, expect one to achieve authority by the acquisition of an authoritative role. That is, "the teacher is the authority because she is the teacher."

In the first instance, because authority is earned, the teacher must consistently prove the characteristics that give her authority. These characteristics may vary across cultures, but in the Black community they tend to cluster around several abilities. The authoritative teacher can control the class through exhibition of personal power; establishes meaningful interpersonal relationships that garner student respect; exhibits a strong belief that all students can learn; establishes a standard of achievement and "pushes" the students to achieve that standard; and holds the attention of the students by incorporating interactional features of Black communicative style in his or her teaching.

By contrast, the teacher whose authority is vested in the role has many more options of behavior at her disposal. For instance, she does not need to express any sense of personal power because her authority does not come from anything she herself does or says. Hence, the power she actually holds may be veiled in such questions/commands as "Would you like to sit down now?" If the children in her class understand authority as she does, it is mutually agreed upon that they are to obey her no matter how indirect, soft-spoken, or unassuming she may be. Her indirectness and soft-spokenness may indeed be, as I suggested earlier, an attempt to reduce the implication of overt power in order to establish a more egalitarian and non-authoritarian classroom atmosphere.

If the children operate under another notion of authority, however, then there is trouble. The Black child may perceive the middle-class teacher as weak, ineffectual, and incapable of taking on the role of being the teacher; therefore, there is no need to follow her directives. In her dissertation, Michelle Foster (1987) quotes one young Black man describing such a teacher:

> She is boring, bo::ing.* She could do something creative. Instead she just stands there. She can't control the class, doesn't know how to control the class. She asked me what she was doing wrong. I told her she just stands there like she's meditating. I told her she could be meditating for all I know. She says that we're supposed to know what to do. I told her I don't know nothin' unless she tells me. She just can't control the class. I hope we don't have her next semester. (pp. 67–68)

But of course the teacher may not view the problem as residing in herself but in the student, and the child may once again become the behavior-disordered Black boy in special education.

What characteristics do Black students attribute to the good teacher? Again, Foster's dissertation provides a quotation that supports my experience with Black students. A young Black man is discussing a former teacher with a group of friends:

* *Editor's note:* The colons [::] refer to elongated vowels.

We had fu::an in her class, but she was mean. I can remember she used to say, "Tell me what's in the story, Wayne." She pushed, she used to get on me and push me to know. She made us learn. We had to get in the books. There was this tall guy and he tried to take her on, but she was in charge of that class and she didn't let anyone run her. I still have this book we used in her class. It's a bunch of stories in it. I just read one on Coca-Cola again the other day. (p. 68)

To clarify, this student was *proud* of the teacher's "meanness," an attribute he seemed to describe as the ability to run the class and pushing and expecting students to learn. Now, does the liberal perspective of the negatively authoritarian Black teacher really hold up? I suggest that although all "explicit" Black teachers are not also good teachers, there are different attitudes in different cultural groups about which characteristics make for a good teacher. Thus, it is impossible to create a model for the good teacher without taking issues of culture and community context into account.

And now to the final comment I present for examination:

"Children have the right to their own language, their own culture. We must fight cultural hegemony and fight the system by insisting that children be allowed to express themselves in their own language style. It is not they, the children, who must change, but the schools. To push children to do anything else is repressive and reactionary."

A statement such as this originally inspired me to write the "Skills and Other Dilemmas" article. It was first written as a letter to a colleague in response to a situation that had developed in our department. I was teaching a senior-level teacher education course. Students were asked to prepare a written autobiographical document for the class that would also be shared with their placement school prior to their student teaching.

One student, a talented young Native American woman, submitted a paper in which the ideas were lost because of technical problems — from spelling to sentence structure to paragraph structure. Removing her name, I duplicated the paper for a discussion with some faculty members. I had hoped to initiate a discussion about what we could do to ensure that our students did not reach the senior level without getting assistance in technical writing skills when they needed them.

I was amazed at the response. Some faculty implied that the student should never have been allowed into the teacher education program. Others, some of the more progressive minded, suggested that I was attempting to function as gatekeeper by raising the issue and had internalized repressive and disempowering forces of the power elite to suggest that something was wrong with a Native American student just because she had another style of writing. With few exceptions, I found myself alone in arguing against both camps.

No, this student should not have been denied entry to the program. To deny her entry under the notion of upholding standards is to blame the victim for the crime. We cannot justifiably enlist exclusionary standards when the reason this student lacked the skills demanded was poor teaching at best and institutionalized racism at worst.

However, to bring this student into the program and pass her through without attending to obvious deficits in the codes needed for her to function effectively as a teacher is equally criminal — for though we may assuage our own consciences for not participating in victim blaming, she will surely be accused and convicted as soon as she leaves the university. As Native Alaskans were quick to tell me, and as I understood through my own experience in the Black community, not only would she not be hired as a teacher, but those who did not hire her would make the (false) assumption that the university was putting out only incompetent natives and that they should stop looking seriously at any Native applicants. A White applicant who exhibits problems is an individual with problems. A person of color who exhibits problems immediately becomes a representative of her cultural group.

No, either stance is criminal. The answer is to *accept* students but also to take responsibility to *teach* them. I decided to talk to the student and found out she had recognized that she needed some assistance in the technical aspects of writing soon after she entered the university as a freshman. She had gone to various members of the education faculty and received the same two kinds of responses I met with four years later: faculty members told her either that she should not even attempt to be a teacher, or that it didn't matter and that she shouldn't worry about such trivial issues. In her desperation, she had found a helpful professor in the English Department, but he left the university when she was in her sophomore year.

We sat down together, worked out a plan for attending to specific areas of writing competence, and set up regular meetings. I stressed to her the need to use her own learning process as insight into how best to teach her future students those "skills" that her own schooling had failed to teach her. I gave her some explicit rules to follow in some areas; for others, we devised various kinds of journals that, along with readings about the structure of the language, allowed her to find her own insights into how the language worked. All that happened two years ago, and the young woman is now successfully teaching. What the experience led me to understand is that pretending that gatekeeping points don't exist is to ensure that many students will not pass through them.

Now you may have inferred that I believe that because there is a culture of power, everyone should learn the codes to participate in it, and that is how the world should be. Actually, nothing could be further from the truth. I believe in a diversity of style, and I believe the world will be diminished if cultural diversity is ever obliterated. Further, I believe strongly, as do my liberal colleagues, that each cultural group should have the right to maintain its own language style. When I speak, therefore, of the culture of power, I don't speak of how I wish things to be but of how they are.

I further believe that to act as if power does not exist is to ensure that the power status quo remains the same. To imply to children or adults (but of course the adults won't believe you anyway) that it doesn't matter how you talk or how you write is to ensure their ultimate failure. I prefer to be honest with my students. Tell them that their language and cultural style is unique and wonderful but that there is a political power game that is also being played, and if they want to be in on that game there are certain games that they too must play.

But don't think that I let the onus of change rest entirely with the students. I am also involved in political work both inside and outside of the educational system, and that political work demands that I place myself to influence as many gatekeeping points as possible. And it is there that I agitate for change — pushing gatekeepers to open their doors to a variety of styles and codes. What I'm saying, however, is that I do not believe that political change toward diversity can be effected from the bottom up, as do some of my colleagues. They seem to believe that if we accept and encourage diversity within class-rooms of children, then diversity will automatically be accepted at gate-keeping points.

I believe that will never happen. What will happen is that the students who reach the gatekeeping points — like Amanda Branscombe's student who dropped out of high school because he failed his exit exam — will under-stand that they have been lied to and will react accordingly. No, I am certain that if we are truly to effect societal change, we cannot do so from the bottom up, but we must push and agitate from the top down. And in the meantime, we must take the responsibility to *teach*, to provide for students who do not al-ready possess them, the additional codes of power.[4]

But I also do not believe that we should teach students to passively adopt an alternate code. They must be encouraged to understand the value of the code they already possess as well as to understand the power realities in this country. Otherwise they will be unable to work to change these realities. And how does one do that?

Martha Demientieff, a masterly Native Alaskan teacher of Athabaskan In-dian students, tells me that her students, who live in a small, isolated, rural vil-lage of less than two hundred people, are not aware that there are different codes of English. She takes their writing and analyzes it for features of what has been referred to by Alaskan linguists as "Village English," and then covers half a bulletin board with words or phrases from the students' writing, which she labels "Our Heritage Language." On the other half of the bulletin board she puts the equivalent statements in "standard English," which she labels "Formal English."

She and the students spend a long time on the "Heritage English" section, savoring the words, discussing the nuances. She tells the students, "That's the way we say things. Doesn't it feel good? Isn't it the absolute best way of getting that idea across?" Then she turns to the other side of the board. She tells the students that there are people, not like those in their village, who judge others by the way they talk or write.

> We listen to the way people talk, not to judge them, but to tell what part of the river they come from. These other people are not like that. They think everybody needs to talk like them. Unlike us, they have a hard time hearing what people say if they don't talk exactly like them. Their way of talking and writing is called "Formal English."
>
> We have to feel a little sorry for them because they have only one way to talk. We're going to learn two ways to say things. Isn't that better? One way will be our Heritage way. The other will be Formal English. Then, when we go to get jobs, we'll be able to talk like those people who only know and can only really listen to one way. Maybe after we get the jobs we can help them to learn how it feels to have another language, like ours, that feels so good. We'll talk like them when we have to, but we'll always know our way is best.

Martha then does all sorts of activities with the notions of Formal and Heritage or informal English. She tells the students,

> In the village, everyone speaks informally most of the time unless there's a potlatch or something. You don't think about it, you don't worry about following any rules — it's sort of like how you eat food at a picnic — nobody pays attention to whether you use your fingers or a fork, and it feels *so* good. Now, Formal English is more like a formal dinner. There are rules to follow about where the knife and fork belong, about where people sit, about how you eat. That can be really nice, too, because it's nice to dress up sometimes.

The students then prepare a formal dinner in the class, for which they dress up and set a big table with fancy tablecloths, china, and silverware. They speak only Formal English at this meal. Then they prepare a picnic where only informal English is allowed.

She also contrasts the "wordy" academic way of saying things with the metaphoric style of Athabaskan. The students discuss how book language always uses more words, but in Heritage language, the shorter way of saying something is always better. Students then write papers in the academic way, discussing with Martha and with each other whether they believe they've said enough to sound like a book. Next, they take those papers and try to reduce the meaning to a few sentences. Finally, students further reduce the message to a "saying" brief enough to go on the front of a T-shirt, and the sayings are put on little paper T-shirts that the students cut out and hang throughout the room. Sometimes the students reduce other authors' wordy texts to their essential meanings as well.

The following transcript provides another example. It is from a conversation between a Black teacher and a Southern Black high school student named Joey, who is a speaker of Black English. The teacher believes it very important to discuss openly and honestly the issues of language diversity and power. She has begun the discussion by giving the student a children's book written in Black English to read.

Teacher: What do you think about that book?

Joey: I think it's nice.

Teacher: Why?

Joey: I don't know. It just told about a Black family, that's all.

Teacher: Was it difficult to read?

Joey: No.

Teacher: Was the text different from what you have seen in other books?

Joey: Yeah. The writing was.

Teacher: How?

Joey: It use more of a southern-like accent in this book.

Teacher: Uhm-hmm. Do you think that's good or bad?

Joey: Well, uh, I don't think it's good for people down this a way, cause that's the way they grow up talking anyway. They ought to get the right way to talk.

Teacher: Oh. So you think it's wrong to talk like that?

Joey: Well . . . [*Laughs.*]

Teacher: Hard question, huh?

Joey: Uhm-hmm, that's a hard question. But I think they shouldn't make books like that.

Teacher: Why?

Joey: Because they not using the right way to talk and in school they take off for that and li'l chirren grow up talking like that and reading like that so they might think that's right and all the time they getting bad grades in school, talking like that and writing like that.

Teacher: Do you think they should be getting bad grades for talking like that?

Joey: [*Pauses, answers very slowly.*] No . . . No.

Teacher: So you don't think that it matters whether you talk one way or another?

Joey: No, not long as you understood.

Teacher: Uhm-hmm. Well, that's a hard question for me to answer, too. It's ah, that's a question that's come up in a lot of schools now as to whether they should correct children who speak the way we speak all the time. Cause when we're talking to each other we talk like that even though we might not talk like that when we get into other situations, and who's to say whether it's —

Joey: [*Interrupting.*] Right or wrong.

Teacher: Yeah.

Joey: Maybe they ought to come up with another kind of . . . maybe Black English or something. A course in Black English. Maybe Black folks would be good in that cause people talk, I mean Black people talk like that, so . . . but I guess there's a right way and wrong way to talk, you know, not regarding what race. I don't know.

Teacher: But who decided what's right or wrong?

Joey: Well that's true . . . I guess White people did.

[*Laughter. End of tape.*]

Notice how throughout the conversation Joey's consciousness has been raised by thinking about codes of language. This teacher further advocates having students interview various personnel officers in actual workplaces about their attitudes toward divergent styles in oral and written language. Students begin to understand how arbitrary language standards are, but also how politically charged they are. They compare various pieces written in different styles, discuss the impact of different styles on the message by making translations and back translations across styles, and discuss the history, apparent purpose, and contextual appropriateness of each of the technical writing rules presented by their teacher. *And* they practice writing different forms to different audiences based on rules appropriate for each audience. Such a program not only "teaches" standard linguistic forms, but also explores aspects of power as exhibited through linguistic forms.

Tony Burgess, in a study of secondary writing in England by Britton, Burgess, Martin, McLeod, and Rosen (1975/1977), suggests that we should not teach "iron conventions . . . imposed without rationale or grounding in communicative intent, . . . [but] critical and ultimately cultural awareness" (p. 54). Courtney Cazden (1987) calls for a two-pronged approach:

1. Continuous opportunities for writers to participate in some authentic bit of the unending conversation . . . thereby becoming part of a vital community of talkers and writers in a particular domain, and
2. Periodic, temporary focus on conventions of form, taught as cultural conventions expected in a particular community. (p. 20)

Just so that there is no confusion about what Cazden means by a focus on conventions of form, or about what I mean by "skills," let me stress that neither of us is speaking of page after page of "skill sheets" creating compound words or identifying nouns and adverbs, but rather about helping students gain a useful knowledge of the conventions of print while engaging in real and useful communicative activities. Kay Rowe Grubis, a junior high school teacher in a multicultural school, makes lists of certain technical rules for her eighth graders' review and then gives them papers from a third grade to "correct." The students not only have to correct other students' work, but also tell them why they have changed or questioned aspects of the writing.

A village teacher, Howard Cloud, teaches his high school students the conventions of formal letter writing and the formulation of careful questions in the context of issues surrounding the amendment of the Alaska Land Claims Settlement Act. Native Alaskan leaders hold differing views on this issue, critical to the future of local sovereignty and land rights. The students compose letters to leaders who reside in different areas of the state seeking their perspectives, set up audioconference calls for interview/debate sessions, and, finally, develop a videotape to present the differing views.

To summarize, I suggest that students must be *taught* the codes needed to participate fully in the mainstream of American life, not by being forced to attend to hollow, inane, decontextualized subskills, but rather within the context of meaningful communicative endeavors; that they must be allowed the resource of the teacher's expert knowledge, while being helped to acknowledge their own "expertness" as well; and that even while students are assisted in learning the culture of power, they must also be helped to learn about the arbitrariness of those codes and about the power relationships they represent.

I am also suggesting that appropriate education for poor children and children of color can only be devised in consultation with adults who share their culture. Black parents, teachers of color, and members of poor communities must be allowed to participate fully in the discussion of what kind of instruction is in their children's best interest. Good liberal intentions are not enough. In an insightful study entitled "Racism without Racists: Institutional Racism in Urban Schools," Massey, Scott, and Dornbusch (1975) found that under the pressures of teaching, and with all intentions of "being nice," teachers had essentially stopped attempting to teach Black children. In their words: "We have shown that oppression can arise out of warmth, friendliness, and concern. Paternalism and a lack of challenging standards are creating a distorted system of evaluation in the schools" (p. 10). Educators must open themselves to, and allow themselves to be affected by, these alternative voices.

In conclusion, I am proposing a resolution for the skills/process debate. In short, the debate is fallacious; the dichotomy is false. The issue is really an illusion created initially not by teachers but by academics whose world view demands the creation of categorical divisions — not for the purpose of better teaching, but for the goal of easier analysis. As I have been reminded by many teachers since the publication of my article, those who are most skillful at educating Black and poor children do not allow themselves to be placed in "skills" or "process" boxes. They understand the need for both approaches, the need to help students to establish their own voices, but to coach those voices to produce notes that will be heard clearly in the larger society.

The dilemma is not really in the debate over instructional methodology, but rather in communicating across cultures and in addressing the more fundamental issue of power, of whose voice gets to be heard in determining what is best for poor children and children of color. Will Black teachers and parents continue to be silenced by the very forces that claim to "give voice" to our children? Such an outcome would be tragic, for both groups truly have something to say to one another. As a result of careful listening to alternative points of view, I have myself come to a viable synthesis of perspectives. But both sides do need to be able to listen, and I contend that it is those with the most power, those in the majority, who must take the greater responsibility for initiating the process.

To do so takes a very special kind of listening, listening that requires not only open eyes and ears, but open hearts and minds. We do not really see through our eyes or hear through our ears, but through our beliefs. To put our beliefs on hold is to cease to exist as ourselves for a moment — and that is not easy. It is painful as well, because it means turning yourself inside out, giving up your own sense of who you are, and being willing to see yourself in the unflattering light of another's angry gaze. It is not easy, but it is the only way to learn what it might feel like to be someone else and the only way to start the dialogue.

There are several guidelines. We must keep the perspective that people are experts on their own lives. There are certainly aspects of the outside world of which they may not be aware, but they can be the only authentic chroniclers of their own experience. We must not be too quick to deny their interpretations, or accuse them of "false consciousness." We must believe that people are rational beings, and therefore always act rationally. We may not understand their rationales, but that in no way militates against the existence of these rationales or reduces our responsibility to attempt to apprehend them. And finally, we must learn to be vulnerable enough to allow our world to turn upside down in order to allow the realities of others to edge themselves into our consciousness. In other words, we must become ethnographers in the true sense.

Teachers are in an ideal position to play this role, to attempt to get all of the issues on the table in order to initiate true dialogue. This can only be done, however, by seeking out those whose perspectives may differ most, by learning to give their words complete attention, by understanding one's own power, even if that power stems merely from being in the majority, by being unafraid to raise questions about discrimination and voicelessness with people of color, and to listen, no, to *hear* what they say. I suggest that the results of such interactions may be the most powerful and empowering coalescence yet seen in the educational realm — for *all* teachers and for *all* the students they teach.

NOTES

1. Such a discussion, limited as it is by space constraints, must treat the intersection of class and race somewhat simplistically. For the sake of clarity, however, let me define a few terms: "Black" is used herein to refer to those who share some or all aspects of "core Black culture" (Gwaltney, 1980, p. xxiii), that is, the mainstream of Black America — neither those who have entered the ranks of the bourgeoisie nor those who are

participants in the disenfranchised underworld. "Middle-class" is used broadly to refer to the predominantly. White American "mainstream." There are, of course, non-White people who also fit into this category; at issue is their cultural identification, not necessarily the color of their skin. (I must add that there are other non-White people, as well as poor White people, who have indicated to me that their perspectives are similar to those attributed herein to Black people.)

2. *Multicultural Britain: "Crosstalk,"* National Centre of Industrial Language Training, Commission for Racial Equality, London, England, John Twitchin, Producer.
3. I would like to thank Michelle Foster, who is presently planning a more in-depth treatment of the subject, for her astute clarification of the idea.
4. Bernstein (1975) makes a similar point when he proposes that different educational frames cannot be successfully institutionalized in the lower levels of education until there are fundamental changes at the postsecondary levels.

REFERENCES

Apple, M. W. (1979). *Ideology and curriculum.* Boston: Routledge & Kegan Paul.

Bernstein, B. (1975). Class and pedagogies: Visible and invisible. In B. Bernstein, *Class, codes, and control* (Vol. 3). Boston: Routledge & Kegan Paul.

Britton, J., Burgess, T., Martin, N., McLeod, A., & Rosen, H. (1975/1977). *The development of writing abilities.* London: Macmillan Education for the Schools Council, and Urbana, IL: National Council of Teachers of English.

Cazden, C. (1987, January). *The myth of autonomous text.* Paper presented at the Third International Conference on Thinking, Hawaii.

Delpit, L. D. (1986). Skills and other dilemmas of a progressive Black educator. *Harvard Educational Review, 56,* (4), 379–385.

Foster, M. (1987). *It's cookin' now: An ethnographic study of the teaching style of a successful Black teacher in an urban community college.* Unpublished doctoral dissertation, Harvard University.

Gwaltney, J. (1980). *Drylongso.* New York: Vintage Books.

Heath, S. B. (1983). *Ways with words.* Cambridge: Cambridge University Press.

Massey, G. C., Scott, M. V., & Dornbusch, S. M. (1975). Racism without racists: Institutional racism in urban schools. *Black Scholar, 7*(3), 2–11.

Siddle, E. V. (1986). *A critical assessment of the natural process approach to teaching writing.* Unpublished qualifying paper, Harvard University.

Siddle, E. V. (1988). *The effect of intervention strategies on the revisions ninth graders make in a narrative essay.* Unpublished doctoral dissertation, Harvard University.

Snow, C. E., Arlman-Rup, A., Hassing, Y., Josbe, J., Joosten, J., & Vorster, J. (1976). Mother's speech in three social classes. *Journal of Psycholinguistic Research, 5,* 1–20.

I take full responsibility for all that appears herein; however, aside from those mentioned by name in this text, I would like to thank all of the educators and students around the country who have been so willing to contribute their perspectives to the formulation of these ideas, especially Susan Jones, Catherine Blunt, Dee Stickman, Sandra Gamble, Willard Taylor, Mickey Monteiro, Denise Burden, Evelyn Higbee, Joseph Delpit Jr., Valerie Montoya, Richard Cohen, and Mary Denise Thompson.

Because You Like Us:
The Language of Control

▼▼▼▼▼

CYNTHIA BALLENGER

This article is the result of a year spent in conversations about teaching —
difficult conversations in which I, a seasoned teacher and fledgling
sociolinguist, was only rarely the informed party.[1] Mike Rose, in *Lives on
the Boundary* (1989), uses the metaphor of "entering the conversation" to describe the process of learning to participate in academic discourse. In my
case, there was a multitude of different conversations I was trying to enter,
and in each I had a different role to play.

During that same time I was teaching preschool, as I have done for most of
the past fifteen years. The school was in the Haitian community in Dor-
chester, Massachusetts, and primarily served the children of Haitian immigrants. I went there because in my previous work as an early childhood special
education teacher I had noticed that more and more Haitian children were
being referred to my class. These children were arriving attended by all kinds
of concerns from the educational professionals: they were "wild," they had
"no language," their mothers were "depressed." There were certainly some
children I saw who had genuine problems, and yet time and time again I
found that, after a period of adjustment, they were responsive, intelligent
children; their mothers were perhaps homesick and unhappy in a strange,
cold country, but generally not clinically depressed. During that period, however, we did make many mistakes, and I became interested in learning the
Haitian culture and language in order to see the children more clearly. After
a period at graduate school studying sociolinguistics, I took a position as a
preschool teacher in a bilingual school where both Haitian Creole and English were spoken and where, as I came to understand, Haitian culture was
quite central. I was the only teacher at this school who was not Haitian and, although by this time I spoke Creole, I was still getting to know the culture.

During that time I was one of two instructors of a course in child development that a local college offered for Haitian people who wished to work in
day-care centers. My Haitian co-instructor and I designed this course based
on the model of a conversation about child rearing — a dialogue between

Harvard Educational Review   Vol. 62   No. 2   Summer 1992, 199–208

Haitians and North Americans about their attitudes on the subject. I was also a new member of the Brookline Teacher-Researcher Seminar (BTRS), a group of public school teachers and academic researchers who are attempting to develop a common language and a shared set of values with which to approach classroom issues (Michaels & O'Connor, in press; Phillips, 1991). As a graduate student in sociolinguistics, I had done research; as a teacher, I had thought about teaching; I was now involved in trying to approach issues in ways that incorporated both of these perspectives. The work that I will report on here was part of these conversations. I will try to let the reader hear some of the different voices that I heard.

In this article, I will discuss the process I went through in learning to control a class of four-year-old Haitian children. Researchers who regard language as the principal vehicle by which children are socialized into their particular family and culture have consistently regarded control and discipline as central events — events where language patterns and cultural values intersect in visible ways (Boggs, 1985; Cook-Gumperz, 1973; Watson-Gegeo & Gegeo, 1990). When, as in my case, the adult does not share the same cultural background and the same experience of socialization as the children, one becomes very aware of learning how to enter and manage the relevant conversation. Although it can be argued that my participation in the events I relate here was in some ways informed by sociolinguistic theory, I present this more as a story than as a research report. This is my attempt to discuss this experience in a way that will not deny access to the conversation to those who helped form my understanding of it. I must stress, however, that all of these conversations would not have been possible if there hadn't been room in the preschool day for talk — the school was run jointly by the teachers and we spent considerable time each day together — and if there had not been some financial support for the Brookline Teacher-Researcher Seminar (Phillips, 1991). This support, in the form of small stipends, xeroxing, money for an occasional day off to reflect, and a sense of being valued, combined with the nature of the school where I was teaching, made my situation luxurious compared with that of many teachers faced with problems similar to mine.

THE PROBLEM

Having had many years of experience teaching in early childhood programs, I did not expect to have problems when I came to this Haitian preschool three years ago. However, I did. The children ran me ragged. In the friendliest, most cheerful, and affectionate manner imaginable, my class of four-year-olds followed their own inclinations rather than my directions in almost everything. Though I claim to be a person who does not need to have a great deal of control, in this case I had very little — and I did not like it.

My frustration increased when I looked at the other classrooms at my school. I had to notice that the other teachers, all Haitian women, had orderly classrooms of children who, in an equally affectionate and cheerful manner, *did* follow directions and kept the confusion to a level that I could have tolerated. The problem, evidently, did not reside in the children, since the Haitian teachers managed them well enough. Where then did it reside? What was it that the Haitian teachers did that I did not do?

The group of Haitian preschool teachers whom I was teaching in the child-development course recognized the problem in their own terms. As part of the course, they were all interning in various day-care centers, some with me at the Haitian school, the majority in other centers. Many of the teachers in the other centers were extremely concerned about behavior problems. What they told me and each other was that many of the children in their centers were behaving very poorly; many felt that this was particularly true of the Haitian children. They felt that the way in which they were being instructed as teachers to deal with the children's behavior was not effective. One woman explained to me that when she was hit by a four-year-old, she was instructed to acknowledge the anger he must be feeling, then to explain to him that he could not hit her. She told me that, from her point of view, this was the same as suggesting politely, "Why don't you hit me again?"

When I talked with Haitian parents at my school, I again heard similar complaints. From the point of view of many of the people I talked with, the behavior tolerated in their neighborhood schools was disrespectful; the children were allowed to misbehave. A common refrain in these conversations was, "We're losing a generation of children"; that is, the young children here now, who were not brought up first in Haiti, were not being brought up with the same values. However, when I asked for specific advice about things I might do to manage the children better, the teachers and I could never identify any behaviors of mine that I could try to change.

I took my problem to the Brookline Teacher-Researcher Seminar. The members of BTRS have come to share a focus on language — the language of instruction; children's language in a wide variety of situations; the language of science talk, of book talk, of conflict; and so on. Thus, in our conversations, the BTRS group encouraged me to approach my problem by discovering what it was that the Haitian teachers *said* to the children in situations where directions were being given. The Seminar members have also come to believe that an important part of a research project is examining where a particular research question comes from in one's own life — why it seems important, what its value is to the teacher-researcher. In many cases, this is a matter of investigating one's own socialization, a kind of self-reflection that became an important part of my investigation.

SITUATIONS AS TEXTS

I began to write down what the Haitian teachers said to the children in situations where the children's behavior was at issue. I then carried these texts to the various conversations of which I was a part: the Haitian teachers in the child development course, the North American teachers in the Brookline Seminar, and the parents and teachers at the school where I was teaching. I will present here some texts that I consider typical in their form and content, and then share some of the responses and the thinking engendered by these texts among the people with whom I had been conversing.

I present first Clothilde's account of an event at her day-care center. Clothilde is a middle-aged Haitian woman and a student in the child-development course. She has a great deal of experience with children — both from raising her own and from caring for other people's — and many of her class-mates turn to her for advice. The text below is from a conversation in which she had been complaining to me about the behavior of the Haitian children in the day-care center where she was student teaching. She felt that the North American teachers were not controlling the children adequately.

One day, as Clothilde arrived at her school, she watched a teacher telling a little Haitian child that the child needed to go into her classroom, that she could not stay alone in the hall. The child refused and eventually kicked the teacher. Clothilde had had enough. She asked the director to bring her all the Haitian kids right away. The director and Clothilde gathered the children into the large common room. The following is the text of what she told me she said to the children:

Clothilde: Does your mother let you bite?

Children: No.

Clothilde: Does your father let you punch kids?

Children: No.

Clothilde: Do you kick at home?

Children: No.

Clothilde: You don't respect anyone, not the teachers who play with you or the adults who work upstairs. You need to respect adults — even people you see on the streets. You are taking good ways you learn at home and not bringing them to school. You're taking the bad things you learn at school and taking them home. You're not going to do this anymore. Do you want your parents to be ashamed of you?

According to Clothilde, the Haitian children have been well-behaved ever since. Other Haitian teachers with whom I have shared this text have con-firmed that that was what the children needed to hear. However, they also said that Clothilde will have to repeat her speech because the children won't remain well-behaved indefinitely without a reminder.

The next text involves an incident at my school. Josiane, who has taught for many years both here and in Haiti, was reprimanding a group of children who had been making a lot of noise while their teacher was trying to give them directions:

Josiane: When your mother talks to you, don't you listen?

Children: Yes.

Josiane: When your mother says, go get something, don't you go get it?

Children: Yes.

Josiane: When your mother says, go to the bathroom, don't you go?

Children: Yes.

Josiane: You know why I'm telling you this. Because I want you to be good children. When an adult talks to you, you're supposed to listen so you will become a good person. The adults here like you, they want you to become good children.

Finally, we have Jérémie's father speaking to him. Jérémie is a very active four-year-old, and the staff had asked his father for help in controlling his behavior:

Father: Are you going to be good? (Jérémie nods at each pause)

Are you going to listen to Miss Cindy?

Are you going to listen to Miss Josiane?

Because they like you.

They love you.

Do it for me.

Do it for God.

Do you like God?

God loves you.

REFLECTING

The content and the form of these texts are different from what I, and many other North American teachers, would probably have said in the same circumstances. I shared these and other texts and observations with many parents and teachers, both Haitian and North American. I asked them to reflect with me on how these conversations were different and what underlay them. What follows is a blend of many people's observations and self-reflections, including my own. Here I want to note that I am assuming that the North American teachers, including myself, shared similar training and enculturation. Although we differed in many ways, I would characterize our culture — as Heath does in *Ways with Words* (1983) — as "mainstream culture." The Haitian teachers also shared some, although not all, values and assumptions. Although I am trying to distill these conversations in order to identify "typical" practices of Haitian or North American teachers, I do not mean to imply that all North American or all Haitian teachers are the same.

The Haitian preschool teachers had clear insights into behavior characteristic of North American teachers. Clothilde commented that the North American teachers she knows frequently refer to the children's internal states and interpret their feelings for them; for example, "you must be angry," "it's hard for you when your friend does that," and so on. Clothilde pointed out to me that in her speech she makes no reference to the children's emotions; other Haitian teachers I have observed also do not do this as a rule.

Rose, another Haitian teacher, also commented that North American teachers often make reference to particular factors in the child's situation that, in the teacher's opinion, may have influenced his or her behavior. For example, Michel, whose mother had left him, was often told that the teachers understood that he missed his mother, but that he nevertheless needed to share his toys. When a child pushes or pinches another child sitting next to him or her, many North American teachers will suggest that, if the child does not like people to sit so close, he or she should say so rather than pinch. Rose felt, and from my observation I concurred, that Haitian teachers rarely do this. Josiane suggested further that if she were concerned about an individual child and his or her particular problems, instead of articulating them for him or her, her goal would be "to make him or her feel comfortable with the group." If the child were misbehaving, she felt she would say, "You know I'm your friend," and then remind him or her that "we don't do that." In fact, I have seen her do exactly that many times, with excellent results.

These examples suggest to me a difference in focus between the North American and Haitian teachers. It seems that North American teachers characteristically are concerned with making a connection with the individual child, with articulating his or her feelings and problems. On the other hand, Clothilde, Josiane, and the many other Haitian people I spoke with and observed, emphasize the group in their control talk, articulating the values and responsibilities of group membership. For example, we have seen that both North American and Haitian teachers make reference to the family, but in different ways. North American teachers are likely to mention particular characteristics of a child's family, characteristics that are specific to that family and are seen as perhaps responsible for the child's individual actions. The Haitian teachers emphasize instead what the families have in common. The families do not differ in their desire that the children respect adults, that the children behave properly, and that their behavior not shame them. The children's answers, when they are given in unison as in Josiane's text above, present a vivid enactment of the sort of unity the Haitian teachers' approach may engender.

Another difference the Haitian teachers noted is the use of consequences. North American teachers typically present the particular consequences of an act of misbehavior. For example, I often say something like, "He's crying because you hit him," or, "If you don't listen to me, you don't know what to do." Haitian teachers are less likely to differentiate among particular kinds of misbehavior; they condemn them all, less in terms of their results than as examples of "bad" behavior. Clothilde is typical of the Haitian teachers in that the immediate consequences are not made explicit; she does not explain why she is against biting or punching. She instead refers to such behavior as "bad," and then explains to the children the consequences of bad behavior in general, such as shame for the family. Jérémie's father simply tells Jérémie to be good, to be good for those who love him. Josiane, too, tells the children to be good because the people who like them want them to be good. I have heard other Haitian teachers refer to the impression that bad behavior would create in a passer-by, or to the necessity of modeling good behavior for younger children. But Haitian teachers rarely mention the specific consequences of particular acts, a clear difference from North American teachers.

In the Haitian texts, one has the impression that the children share the adult's understanding of what bad behavior is. Clothilde's series of rhetorical questions, like "Do your parents let you kick?" is an example of the form that many Haitian teachers adopt when addressing children about their behavior. The children understand their role without difficulty; they repeat the expected answers in choral unison. The choice of this form — that is, questions to which the answer is assumed — emphasizes the fact that the children already know that their behavior is wrong.

In the North American control situation, on the other hand, the child often appears to be receiving new information. If there is a consensus about behavior — certain behavior is bad, certain other behavior is good — we don't present it this way. North Americans frequently explain the consequences of particular actions as if they were trying to convince the child that there was a problem with his or her behavior. As presented in school, misbehavior is considered wrong not because of anything inherent in it, but because of its particular consequences, or perhaps because the behavior stems from feelings that the child has failed to identify and control.

These differences, as I came to recognize them, seemed significant enough to account for some of the difficulties I had been experiencing in my classroom. But what to do about them?

PRACTICE

With the overwhelming evidence that these children were used to a kind of control talk other than what I had been providing, I have since begun to adopt some of the style of the Haitian teachers. I assume that I am not very good at it, that I have no idea of the nuances, and I continue to include many of the ways I have typically managed behavior in my teaching. Nevertheless, I have developed a more or less stable melange of styles, and my control in the classroom has improved significantly. In addition, I find that I love trying out this Haitian way. I was struck by an experience I had the other day, when I was reprimanding one boy for pinching another. I was focusing, in the Haitian manner, on his prior, indisputable knowledge that pinching was simply no good. I also used my best approximation of the facial expression and tone of voice that I see the Haitian teachers use in these encounters. I can tell when I have it more or less right, because of the way that the children pay attention. As I finished this particular time, the other children, who had been rapt, all solemnly thanked me. They were perhaps feeling in danger of being pinched and felt that I had at last been effective. This solemn sort of response, which has occurred a few other times, gives me the sense that these situations are very important to them.

The following anecdote may suggest more about the way in which these interactions are important to the children. Recently I was angrily reprimanding the children about their failure to wait for me while crossing the parking lot:

Cindy: Did I tell you to go?

Children: No.

Cindy: Can you cross this parking lot by yourselves?

Children: No.

Cindy: That's right. There are cars here. They're dangerous. I don't want you to go alone. Why do I want you to wait for me, do you know?

"Yes," says Claudette, "because you like us."

Although I was following the usual Haitian form — rhetorical questions with "no" answers — I had been expecting a final response based on the North American system of cause and effect, something like, "Because the cars are dangerous." Claudette, however, although she understands perfectly well the dangers of cars to small children, does not expect to use that information in this kind of an interaction. What, then, *is* she telling me? One thing that she is saying, which is perhaps what the solemn children also meant, is that, from her point of view, there is intimacy in this kind of talk. This is certainly the feeling I get from these experiences. I feel especially connected to the children in those instances in which I seem to have gotten it right.

THE LARGER CONTEXT

North American teachers generally think of reprimands — particularly of young children who are just learning to control their behavior — as put-downs, and are reluctant to give them. North American preschool teachers, in particular, will take great pains to avoid saying "no" or "don't." In contrast, I have learned from working with Haitian children and teachers that there are situations in which reprimands can be confirming, can strengthen relationships, and can, in a sense, define relationships for the child, as seems to have been the case for Claudette in the example given above.

Such an opportunity may be lost when we go to great lengths to avoid actually telling a child that he is wrong, that we disagree or disapprove. When we look at the difference between the ways in which things are done at home and at school, and the negative consequences that may result from these mismatches for children coming from minority cultural backgrounds, the area of misbehavior and the way it is responded to seem particularly important because it affects so directly the nature of the relationship between child and teacher.

I was not unaware when I began that this subject was a hotbed of disagreement: North Americans perceive Haitians as too severe, both verbally and in their use of physical punishment, while Haitians often perceive North American children as being extraordinarily fresh and out of control.[2] Haitian immigrant parents here are at once ashamed and defiantly supportive of their community's disciplinary standards and methods. In order to represent the views of Haitians I spoke with independent of my process of understanding, I asked them to reflect again on our two cultures after they had heard my interpretations.

People, of course, offered many varied points of view, yet everybody emphasized a sense of having grown up very "protected" in Haiti, of having been safe there both from getting into serious trouble and from harm. This sense of being protected was largely based on their understanding that their entire extended family, as well as many people in the community, were involved in their upbringing. Haitian families in the United States, some pointed out, are smaller and less extended. The community here, while tight in many ways, is more loosely connected than in Haiti. This change in social structure was bemoaned by the people I spoke with, especially with reference to bringing up children. They attributed to this change their sense that this generation of children, particularly those born here, is increasingly at risk. They are at risk not only of falling away from their parents' culture, but also, and consequently, of falling prey to the drugs, crime, and other problems of urban life that they see around them.

And yet everyone I spoke with also recalled some pain in their growing up, pain they relate to the respect and obedience they were required to exhibit to all adults, which at times conflicted with their own developing desire to state their opinions or make their own choices. This pain was nevertheless not to be discarded lightly. For many of the Haitian people with whom I spoke, religious values underlie these twin issues of respect and obedience; respect for parents and other adults is an analogue for respect and obedience to God and God's law.

Many people seemed to agree with the ambivalence expressed by one Haitian lawyer and mother who told me that, while she had suffered as a child because of the uncompromising obedience and respect demanded of her in her family, she continued to see respect as a value she needed to impart to her children. She said to me, "There must be many other ways to teach respect." She was one of many Haitians who told me of instances where a child from a poor family, a child with neither the clothes nor the supplies for school, had succeeded eventually in becoming a doctor or a lawyer. In these accounts, as in her own case, it is in large measure the strictness of the family that is regarded as the source of the child's accomplishment, rather than the talent or the power of the individual.

Presumably, there is some tension in all societies between individual and community. In these accounts is some suggestion of the form this tension sometimes takes within Haitian culture. For my part, I am struck and troubled by the powerful individualism underlying the approach I characterize as typical of me and many North American teachers. It appears that North Americans do speak as if something like the child's "enlightened self-interest" were the ultimate moral guidepost. In comparison to the language used by the Haitian teachers, North American teachers' language seems to place very little emphasis on shared values, on a moral community.

The process of gaining multicultural understanding in education must, in my opinion, be a dual one. On the one hand, cultural behavior that at first seems strange and inexplicable should become familiar; on the other hand, one's own familiar values and practices should become at least temporarily strange, subject to examination. In addition to the information I have gained that helps me to manage and form relationships with Haitian children in my classroom, I also value greatly the extent to which these conversations, by forcing me to attempt to empathize with and understand a view of the world that is in many ways very different from my customary one, have put me in a position to reexamine values and principles that had become inaccessible under layers of assumptions.

I am not teaching Haitian children this year, although I continue to visit them. Next year I expect to have a classroom with children from a wide range of backgrounds. It is difficult to say how my last experience will illuminate the next — or, analogously, how my experience can be of use to teachers in different kinds of classrooms. I do believe that teachers need to try to open up and to understand both our own assumptions and the cultural meaning that children from all backgrounds bring to school. It seems to me that accommodation must be made on all sides so that no group has to abandon the ways in which it is accustomed to passing on its values. I have been fortunate that the knowledge and collaboration of so many people, Haitian and North American, were available to help me begin to understand my own experience. All of these conversations have been their own rewards — I have made new friends and, I believe, become a better teacher.

NOTES

1. Earlier versions of this work have been presented at the Penn Ethnography in Educational Research Forum in February 1991 and the Brookline Teacher-Researcher Seminar in June 1990. My research was carried out as a member of that seminar with teachers and children at my school. In this article, all teachers' and children's names have been changed.

2. It must be stated that the consequences of this disagreement are, of course, vastly more painful for the powerless. Contact with schools, with social-service institutions, with the police, is in many cases highly problematic for Haitian families. The Haitian family, in these situations, is frequently met with a lack of understanding that leads easily to a lack of respect. Mainstream assumptions about "proper" ways of talking and dealing with children's behavior often stand in the way of distinguishing a functioning family, for example, from a dysfunctional one, in distinguishing a child whose parents are strict in order to help him or her succeed from one whose family simply does not want to deal with the child's problems. Such assumptions often stand in the path of appropriate help as well. The school where I taught was often called on to discuss cultural differences with social-service groups, hospitals, and other schools. Occasionally, we were asked to provide some assistance for particular cases. But, of course, there were countless instances in which Haitian families were involved with these various powerful institutions and the families were without such aid.

REFERENCES

Boggs, S. (1985). *Speaking, talking and relating: A study of Hawaiian children at home and at school.* Norwood, NJ: Ablex.

Cook-Gumperz, J. (1973). *Social control and socialization.* London: Routledge & Kegan Paul.

Heath, S. B. (1983). *Ways with words.* Cambridge, Eng.: Cambridge University Press.

Michaels, S., & O'Connor, M. C. (in press). *Literacy as reasoning within multiple discourses: Implications for policy and educational reform.* Newton, MA: Education Development Center.

Phillips, A. (1991, February). *Hearing children's stories: A report on the Brookline Teacher-Researcher Seminar.* Paper presented at the Penn Ethnography in Educational Research Forum, Philadelphia, PA.

Rose, M. (1989). *Lives on the boundary.* New York: Penguin.

Watson-Gegeo, K., & Gegeo, D. (1990). *Disentangling: The discourse of conflict and therapy in the Pacific Islands.* Norwood, NJ: Ablex.

Apprenticing Adolescent Readers
to Academic Literacy

▼▼▼▼▼

CYNTHIA L. GREENLEAF
RUTH SCHOENBACH
CHRISTINE CZIKO
FAYE L. MUELLER

INTO THE HEART OF READING

In a back room off the school library in an urban high school, a boisterous group of ten ninth-grade students talks about their Academic Literacy course. These young people — multiethnic, multilingual, multicultural — come to this high school from the poorest neighborhoods in San Francisco. Like many of the young people we meet in city schools, they are bright, optimistic, and articulate. They are willing to say what they think. It is early December, and these students are frank about their experiences in the course, telling the adult interviewer what they do and do not like. The interviewer asks the students what, if anything, has changed for them as readers since the beginning of the year.

A chorus of voices erupts, each one vying for conversational space. LaKeisha,[1] an African American student, shares her new vision of reading, which reflects the metacognitive inquiry into reading that she has been engaged in since September: "There should be a little voice in your head like the storyteller is saying it. And if it's not, then you just lookin' at the words." Other students agree, echoing one of the mantras of the course: "You read with your mind, not with your mouth."

Soon after, the students reveal with some degree of puzzlement that they had stopped reading in middle school. They describe, in painful detail, how they have faked "reading" during their silent-reading periods, even at the beginning of their Academic Literacy course this school year. They show the interviewer how long to wait before turning a page to fool the teacher into thinking you are reading. Anyone who has listened to young people brag about such exploits cannot help but be impressed by their strategic intelligence and worried about the colossal waste of energy expended.

Harvard Educational Review Vol. 71 No. 1 Spring 2001, 79–129

Yet, as these students begin to reveal, the Academic Literacy course has generated a profound shift in their relationship to reading. They are reading more than they used to, several students claim. Others say they have learned what they like to read and that this has opened up new worlds of reading for them. Some, like LaKeisha, think they are making better sense of the reading they do by using strategies they have learned while reading together in class. Only Michael leans back in his chair, arms crossed in a parody of disaffection. "Man, she's tryin' to be sneaky!" he complains, referring to his teacher, a codesigner of the course. The interviewer turns to this young African American man for elaboration. "Sneaky?" she asks. "Yeah. She wants you to pick a book that you are interested in so you could read it more," he charges. "That's like, what hooks you onto reading. She wants you to find a book that you like, but you don't want to read! She makes you find a book that you like so you *have* to read it. Because you like it!"

While other students tease Michael, amused at the weak complaint he has just made, Jason, a Filipino American student, turns the topic to something that has changed for him as a reader through the course. In an exchange with the interviewer, Jason shares how the strategic reading of difficult texts in Academic Literacy has affected his independent reading of his history textbook:

Jason: I understand the book more. I get more stuff out of it than I do [*sic*] so far because it didn't make sense to me.

Interviewer: Do you think it was because you were reading something too hard for you, or what?

Jason: No. It was kind of in the middle of easy and hard.

Interviewer: Why does it make sense to you now?

Jason: Because I have learned more stuff, like harder things, like in the RT groups.[2] So, like when you are reading and it doesn't make sense, like try to restate it in your own words. Make questions so you can understand better. Now I read differently. I read in between the lines. I basically get into the story, get into the heart of it. Like reading deeper into what it is saying.

These voices and those of the many other young people we have worked with in urban schools echo in our ears as we confront the growing concern among educators about how to define and address the problems faced by middle and high school students who struggle to read texts assigned in their courses. Increasingly, we see concerned and well-meaning educators advocate remedial reading courses focused on basic skills for struggling adolescent readers who are, more often than not, the kinds of linguistically, culturally, and socioeconomically diverse adolescents we know. These students are often underprepared for the academic tasks they face in high school and, as a result, are underrepresented in institutions of higher education. Too often they have gone through many years of schooling without being encouraged to pay attention to the "storytellers" inside their heads, as LaKeisha described her internal reading voice. These are students we would like to get "hooked onto reading," as Michael says, but we know that for the vast majority of adolescents who can decode but not comprehend a variety of texts, a return to basic-skills instruction will only further distance them from that goal. Rather, we believe the young people in our urban schools have lacked sufficient help in learning to make sense of texts, to find their way into the heart of reading, which is often hidden from view. We write this article to argue for a powerful alternative to remedial reading instruction for the majority of young people who struggle with the literacy demands of the secondary curriculum.

In this article, we give a brief overview of our program of work in urban public schools that focuses on addressing the literacy learning needs of young people who face increasingly challenging reading tasks as they advance through school. We outline the reasons we believe that remedial, basic-skills instruction is problematic and unnecessarily limiting for the majority of secondary students, and set forth a model that draws on the assets and expertise of both adolescents and subject-area teachers. We describe an instructional framework — Reading Apprenticeship — that foregrounds the role of social mediation in learning (Vygotsky, 1978) and is based on a socially and cognitively complex conception of literacy.

To support our argument for the power of this instructional framework as an alternative to basic skills remediation, we describe an Academic Literacy course for ninth-grade students as a specific example of Reading Apprenticeship and discuss the results of our study of students' reading development in the course. As part of this discussion, we carry out a detailed analysis of one student's reading of an academic text, demonstrating her appropriation of more powerful conceptions of reading, as well as specific mental tools, from her experiences in Academic Literacy. We conclude by stepping back from this detailed picture of student reading development to consider some of the broader implications of this work. The work described in these pages demonstrates a more powerful vision of the complexity of academic reading, the strategic resources and capabilities of young people, and the expertise of teachers than is prevalent in much of the current educational policy and legislation on the problem of low literacy achievement in the United States. We ask readers to consider the implications of this vision for secondary curriculum and instruction, as well as for the professional development of middle and high school subject-area teachers.

DEFINING THE PROBLEM OF ADOLESCENT LITERACY

For the past several years, a vitriolic ideological battle about how best to teach reading to our nation's children has been waged in the headlines of the national press, among school board members and in school districts across the country, in the halls of Congress, and around the dinner tables of concerned families. While much has been written about code-based versus meaning-based instruction for beginning reading, there is broad and substantial agreement among literacy researchers that young readers need instruction that skillfully integrates phonics and word-level instruction into meaningful reading activities (see Snow, Burns, & Griffin, 1998; Taylor, Anderson, Au, & Raphael, 1999). Nevertheless, a spate of federal and state legislative mandates have focused on systematic phonics instruction and allocated professional development dollars to this approach, with the aim of assuring that American children learn to read independently by grade three (see also Manzo, 1998).

While strengthening early literacy instruction is no doubt a worthy investment, many politicians, educators, and members of the public seem to believe that this investment will pay automatic dividends in accelerated literacy learning, enabling children to make the leap from learning to read to reading to learn and, ultimately, to reading to solve complex and specific problems with ease. When students arrive in middle or high school unable to access the complex texts they encounter there, the assumption is often that early literacy instruction failed. Assumed to be the products of a poor educational system, these students are increasingly pulled off the academic track and placed in remedial courses where they encounter isolated skills instruction focused on phonics, word attack, vocabulary, and spelling, as well as controlled readers, worksheets, and computer-based skill-building programs (see, for example, studies of secondary reading programs by Barry, 1997). Many of these programs were initially developed to give very structured support for discrete language skills to students with specific language-based learning disabilities and are now being adopted for use with a broader range of students.[3] These programs may serve the populations for whom they were designed quite well. However, our concern is with the over-application of such approaches to the diverse populations of students with whom we are working.

Recent National Assessment of Education Progress (NAEP) test results indicate that while the vast majority of American youth reach basic literacy levels, as measured by this test, few are gaining the literacy knowledge, skills, and dispositions that would enable them to successfully engage in higher level, problem-solving literacy of the kind required in an information generating and information transforming economy (Donahue, Voelkl, Campbell, & Mazzeo, 1999; Mullis et al., 1994). According to the most recent report, *The NAEP 1998 Reading Report Card for the Nation and the States* (Donahue et al., 1999), while 74 percent of the nation's eighth graders and 77 percent of twelfth graders perform at or above the *basic* level of reading achievement, only 33 percent of eighth graders and 40 percent of twelfth graders perform at or above the *proficient* level, and a mere three percent and six percent, respectively, perform at the *advanced* level. These reports suggest that attaining particular, higher level uses of literacy is and has been the greater problem facing American students (see, for example, Gee, 1999). In response to a "pervasive neglect of adolescent reading" (International Reading Association, 1999a, p. 1), a resolution on adolescent literacy by the International Reading Association addresses the rights of adolescent readers, calling for homes, communities, and a nation that will not only support their efforts to achieve advanced levels of literacy but also provide the resources necessary for them to succeed (International Reading Association, 1999b; Moore, Bean, Birdyshaw, & Rycik, 1999). The resolution cites the escalating literacy needs of adolescent readers in an increasingly complex communication age and describes a crisis in adolescent literacy of disturbing magnitude.

Alarm bells have sounded frequently in our country, announcing literacy crises and the grand failure of U.S. schools, the scope of which seemed poised to threaten our very ways of life (see also Gee, 1999; Hourigan, 1994; McQuillan, 1998). Yet, as scholars of literacy argue, definitions of what we mean by literacy, what counts as a demonstration of having attained it, and what groups of students we aim to cultivate as literate have undergone tremendous changes over our brief history, making comparisons between earlier "golden ages" of literacy learning and current levels of accomplishment difficult, if not impossible (e.g., Graff, 1979, 1987; Hull & Rose, 1989; Myers, 1998; Ohmann, 1987). While we do not adopt the alarmist and historically naive view that we are currently undergoing the latest in a series of "literacy crises," we remain dissatisfied with counter evidence demonstrating that more of our young people are being educated to higher levels of achievement than at any previous time in our history (Berliner & Biddle, 1995). In our view, the recent NAEP results, coupled with the persistent achievement gap between mainstream populations and those who are socioeconomically, ethnically, culturally, or linguistically outside of that mainstream (Gee, 1999; Jencks & Phillips, 1998; Snow et al., 1998), provide ample evidence that we are not now, nor have we ever been, doing a good enough job. Because reading habits and literacy achievement make important contributions to individuals' socioeconomic mobility, access to higher education, and civic participation (Guthrie & Greany, 1991; Guthrie, Schafer, & Hutchinson, 1991), educators bear a special responsibility to help all students achieve high levels of literacy.

However, once students move beyond elementary school and take separate courses with different instructors focused on particular subject areas, it is no one's job to "teach" reading. As children move up the grade levels, subject-area teachers increasingly view their role as getting across the content of their discipline, be it science, math, literature, or history/social studies, expecting that students will come equipped with the reading skills they need to learn from course materials. Often, teachers are frustrated to see how much difficulty their students encounter with these materials. The conception of reading that is therefore reflected in the organization of schooling and curriculum in the United States is that reading is a kind of technical and basic skill that one acquires once and for all early in the school career. Indeed, a "simple view of reading" (Gough, 1983; Gough & Hillinger, 1980; Gough & Tumner, 1986) is pervasive in current policy and legislative mandates on early reading instruction.

Many secondary teachers operate with this simple view of reading, assuming that reading comprehension proceeds quite automatically from skill in decoding, and that there is something straightforward and uncomplicated about the process. When students come to middle and high school unable to access the texts they encounter, the assumption teachers often make is that early literacy instruction failed, that these students have weak decoding and word-level skills, and that specialized help is needed from someone who "knows how to teach reading" in a way that helps build basic skills. Students who score poorly on standardized reading tests are identified for such skill-based programs and pulled out of the regular academic curriculum for remediation. When reading is seen as a basic skill and thereby as a prerequi-site to reading history or science or literature, it is not seen as in the purview of subject-area teachers. Yet, reading researchers have long recognized both the need to teach comprehension and reading to learn across the curriculum and its pervasive neglect in secondary classrooms (e.g., Pearson, 1996). These researchers lament that secondary subject-area teachers are resistant to teaching reading as part of their content, or, more generously, that these teachers face organizational and curriculum constraints that are powerful de-terrents to taking up this work (Alvermann & Moore, 1991; Konopak, Wilson, & Readence, 1994; Moje & Wade, 1997).

In addition, a great deal of research has documented persistent inequities in the limited and limiting types of learning opportunities afforded to stu-dents who are ethnically or socioeconomically outside of the mainstream. These students receive a higher proportion of isolated basic-skills instruction than their mainstream peers, who are more frequently engaged in higher or-der thinking processes (e.g., Allington, 1991; Darling-Hammond, 1995; Levin, 1997). The abundant documentation of these differential learning op-portunities for poor and minority students suggests that isolated skills-based instruction may perpetuate low literacy achievement rather than accelerate literacy growth (e.g., Allington & McGill-Franzen, 1989; Hiebert, 1991; Hull & Rose, 1989; Knapp & Turnbull, 1991).

Because of this history of differential instructional opportunity for poor and minority students, in a recent report, Taylor and colleagues (1999) warn against the potential misuse of research findings and test scores to narrow the curriculum for students from diverse backgrounds. Similarly, Moje, Young, Readance, and Moore (2000) caution against drawing conclusions for adoles-cent literacy based on research focused on early literacy. To us, these warn-ings seem timely: due to increased public scrutiny and real concern about the perceived crisis in literacy achievement, many secondary schools and districts are turning to discrete skills-focused commercial programs for reading in-struction. In these programs, phonics and word-level instruction figure prominently, despite little evidence that explicit phonics instruction serves students beyond the first and second grades (National Reading Panel, 2000). Even for beginning readers, an extended daily diet of discrete phonics skills has never been recommended by reading researchers (National Reading Panel, 2000; Snow et al., 1998; Stahl, 1998). Yet the diverse young people in our urban schools, historically underserved by the educational experiences they have had, seem destined once more to fill the lower ranks of the educational system in programs designed as remedial, skills-focused interventions for struggling readers.

In the urban subject-area classrooms of the San Francisco Bay Area where we have long worked as teachers, teacher educators, and classroom-based researchers, the vast majority of the students we meet are *inexperienced, but not beginning* readers. They understand the alphabetic principle (that letters can represent sounds) and they can decode the words on the page. However, they often cannot tell us what words on the page add up to, what sense they make. In these urban schools, many students come from socioeconomically, ethnically, and linguistically diverse backgrounds and do not often share the language or world experiences reflected in course curricula and texts (Banks, 1995). Perhaps it is no accident, then, that by the time young people reach middle school, their interest in both recreational and academic reading has waned (McKenna, Kear, & Ellsworth, 1995).

The majority of these inexperienced adolescent readers do *not* need further instruction in phonics or decoding skills. What many of them *do* need, however, is the opportunity and instructional support to read many and varied kinds of materials in order to build their experience, fluency, and range as readers (Kuhn & Stahl, 2000; Stahl, 1998). Many also need guidance and the opportunity to read books of their own choosing in order to develop as independent, lifelong readers. They may also profit from being engaged as pattern-*finders* in word and sentence study at various levels (rimes, roots and affixes, sentence construction), an approach to word-level skills that can engage their strategic thinking ability and increase their agency as learners (Templeton, Beer, Invernizzi, & Johnston, 1996). However, what virtually *all* middle and high school students need — those who struggle academically as well as those who have been more successful — is help acquiring and extending the complex comprehension processes that underlie skilled reading in the subject areas.

THE STRATEGIC LITERACY INITIATIVE[4]
IN URBAN SECONDARY SCHOOLS

In 1995, Cynthia Greenleaf and Ruth Schoenbach, building on their respective backgrounds and prior joint work in literacy research and teaching, curriculum design, and professional development, established a professional development organization and a multifaceted program of work to address what we and our teacher colleagues had begun to call the "literacy ceiling" limiting the academic performance and opportunities of secondary students.[5] Our first effort was to understand the sources of students' reading difficulties by conducting case studies of the reading histories and reading performances of thirty ninth-grade students.[6] As part of these case studies, we videotaped interviews with students as they read a variety of self-chosen and assigned texts as we inquired into their understandings of these texts, their reading processes, and their reflections on reading tasks. We read research on reading theory and practice and began to surface and articulate our own reading processes as we read a variety of difficult texts as a way to tap into our own tacit reading knowledge.

The understandings and insights gained from our collaborative work with teachers and these case studies of adolescent readers have resulted in a number of ongoing projects. We have designed inquiry materials and approaches for the professional development of secondary subject-area teachers. Using these inquiry approaches, we carry out a broad program of professional development with several ongoing teacher networks. We have developed an instructional framework designed to take advantage of the particular social and cognitive assets and interests of adolescents in order to help students move beyond their limiting conceptions of and approaches to reading. We have also designed, implemented, and assessed a ninth-grade course in Academic Literacy that embodies this framework in specific curriculum units and activities. Below we present the conception of literacy that underlies this program of work.

LITERACY APPRENTICESHIPS: LEARNING SPECIALIZED "WAYS WITH WORDS"

We understand reading and writing to be much more than a collection of basic skills. Rather, reading and writing are essentially social and communicative practices (see also Bruffee, 1984). Each act of reading or writing involves socially developed and culturally embedded ways of using text to serve particular social or cultural purposes (Moje, Dillon, & O'Brien, 2000; Gee, 1999; Hourigan, 1994; Lee, 1995; Scribner & Cole, 1981; Street, 1984). All texts are shaped by specific conventions and structures of language, and proficient reading of all texts therefore demands the use of these conventions to navigate layers of meaning (e.g., Cope & Kalantzis, 1993; New London Group, 1996; Scott, 1993). Additionally, the resources and processes used by proficient readers are influenced by the specific contexts and situations in which reading occurs and the social functions that it serves (e.g., Courts, 1997; Gee, 1996; Heath, 1983; Scribner & Cole, 1981).

The implications of this view for the literacy learning of diverse populations of students are profound. Increasingly, students in U.S. schools come from a variety of economic, linguistic, cultural, and ethnic backgrounds, bringing significantly different experiences and expectations about how to initiate and sustain conversations, how to interact with teachers and peers, how to identify and solve different types of problems, and how to go about particular reading and writing tasks (e.g., Greenleaf, Hull, & Reilly, 1994; Lee, 1995; Moje, Dillon, & O'Brien, 2000). In addition, literacy practices become increasingly specialized throughout the school career, reflecting the broader literate, scientific, or historical conversations that characterize the academic disciplines (e.g., Applebee, 1996; Eeds & Wells, 1989; Grossman, 1990; Grossman & Shulman, 1994; Harste, 1994; Langer, 1995; Langer, Confer, & Sawyer, 1993; Lemke, 1990; Rabinowitz & Smith, 1998; Wilson & Wineburg, 1988; Wineburg, 1991; Wineburg & Wilson, 1990). Academic literacy at higher grade levels therefore requires particular interpretive and communicative competencies, or specialized "ways with words" (Heath, 1983) for skilled participation as a reader or writer (Bartholomae, 1985; Gee, 1996; Hull, 1989; Rose, 1985).

For these reasons, learning to read at early grade levels will not automatically translate into higher level academic literacy. Instead, literacy researchers have argued that for all students to learn to perform high-level, academically linked literacy tasks, teachers will need to make explicit the tacit reasoning processes, strategies, and discourse rules that shape successful readers' and writers' work (e.g., Delpit, 1988, 1995; Fielding & Pearson, 1994; Freedman, Flower, Hull, & Hayes, 1995; Gee, 1996, 1999; Hillocks, 1995; Pressley, 1998). Our own work with students from richly different backgrounds has underscored the necessity of not only *telling* students what to do and providing engaging and authentic opportunities for them to do it, but also painstakingly and explicitly *showing them how*, building bridges from their cultural knowledge and language experiences to the language and literacy practices valued and measured in school and society.

Helping students master academic literacy practices, however, does not mean a return to isolated skills-based instruction. Rather, ample studies over the past few decades have demonstrated that integrating the explicit teaching of comprehension strategies, text structures, and word-level strategies into compelling sense-making activities with texts increases student reading achievement (Baumann & Duffy, 1997; Beck, McKeown, Hamilton, & Kucan, 1997; Borkowski, Carr, Rellinger, & Pressley, 1990; Dowhower, 1999; Duffy et al., 1994; Fitzgerald, 1995; Goatley, Brock, & Raphael, 1995; Guthrie, McGough, Bennett, & Rice, 1996; Hillocks, 1995; Keene & Zimmerman, 1997; Pearson, 1996; Pressley et al., 1992; Pressley, 1998; Roehler & Duffy, 1991; Rosenshine & Meister, 1994). These researchers argue that for the reading and reasoning processes of the academic disciplines to become part of the repertoires of a broader population of students, teachers need to engage all students in complex academic literacy tasks while at the same time providing the explicit teaching and support necessary for students to perform these tasks successfully (see Pearson, 1996, for a review of this research).

Drawing from both sociocultural studies of learning and cognitive studies of expert and novice performance on a variety of complex mental tasks, some researchers have adopted the metaphor of "cognitive apprenticeship" to describe a type of teaching designed to assist students in acquiring more expert, or proficient, cognitive processes for particular valued tasks, such as reading comprehension, composing, and mathematical problem-solving (e.g., Bayer, 1990; Brown, Collins, & Newman, 1989; Lave & Wenger, 1991; Lee, 1995; Rogoff, 1990). In an apprenticeship, an expert practitioner or mentor draws on his or her expertise to model, direct, support, and shape the apprentice's growing repertoire of practice. Apprenticeship also generally involves learning while doing. It is hard to imagine learning to paint without actually working with canvas and brush, or learning to jump hurdles without getting out on the track.

When the desired proficiency is a cognitive practice such as composing or comprehending a text, the invisible mental processes involved in the task must be made visible and available to apprentices as they actually engage in meaningful literacy activities (Freedman et al., 1995; Pearson, 1996). To help students develop as readers and writers, then, teachers must begin to create "literacy apprenticeships," engaging students in meaningful and complex literacy practices while *demystifying* these literacy practices (Brown et al., 1989; Lee, 1995; Schoenbach, Greenleaf, Cziko, & Hurwitz, 1999).

This conception of literacy apprenticeship also suggests that the best teachers of specific discipline-based literacy practices are those who themselves have mastered these practices. These include the subject-area teachers and academicians who have acquired scientific, historical, mathematical, or literary discourses during their own educational careers. We argue, therefore, that for all students to attain high-level literacy, apprenticeships that demystify the literacy practices and discourses of the academic disciplines must be embedded in subject-area instruction across the curriculum, rather than becoming the sole purview of the English department. For subject-area teachers to embrace this work, they must reconceptualize subject-area teaching as an apprenticeship into discipline-based practices of thinking, talking, reading, and writing (see Applebee, 1996). To assist teachers in constructing this new conception of teaching and, specifically, of reading in the content areas, we have developed an instructional framework, Reading Apprenticeship, derived from the socially and cognitively complex view of literacy and drawing on the core metaphor of cognitive apprenticeship described above.

READING APPRENTICESHIP: AN INSTRUCTIONAL FRAMEWORK

In a Reading Apprenticeship, the teacher serves as a "master" reader of subject-area texts to his or her student apprentices, paralleling the role of more proficient "expert" in descriptions of socially mediated cognitive apprenticeships (e.g., Bayer, 1990; Brown et al., 1989; Lee, 1995). This instruction takes place in the process of teaching subject-area content, rather than as an instructional add-on or additional curriculum. Briefly summarized, Reading Apprenticeship involves teachers and their students as partners in a collaborative inquiry into reading and reading processes as they engage with subject-area texts (see Schoenbach et. al., 1999, ch. 2, for a more complete description of the model). This instructional framework explicitly draws on students' strengths and abilities to provide crucial resources for the inquiry partnership.

The aim of Reading Apprenticeship is to help students become better readers of a variety of texts by making the teacher's discipline-based reading processes and knowledge visible to students; by making the students' reading processes and the social contexts, strategies, knowledge, and understandings they bring to the task of making sense of subject-matter texts visible to the teacher and to one another; by helping students gain insight into their own reading processes; and by helping them acquire a repertoire of problem-solving strategies with the varied texts of the academic discipline. In other words, *how* we read and *why* we read in the ways we do become part of the curriculum, accompanying *what* we read in subject-matter classes.

As depicted in Figure 1, Reading Apprenticeship involves teachers in orchestrating and integrating four interacting dimensions of classroom life in order to draw on adolescents' particular strengths and help them develop the knowledge, strategies, and dispositions they need to become more powerful readers:

Social: This dimension of community-building in the classroom includes developing a safe environment for students to share their confusion and difficulties with texts and recognizing the diverse perspectives and resources brought by each member (see, e.g., Alvermann & Moore, 1991; Moje, Dillon, & O'Brien, 2000). Together, teacher and students build interest in books and reading, a community of readers, and a culture of reading (e.g., Allen, 1995; Atwell, 1998; Burke, 2000; Wilhelm, 1997). Work in this dimension draws on adolescents' interests in larger social, political, economic, and cultural issues through explorations of the relationships between literacy and different types of power in society.

Personal: This dimension includes developing and extending students' identities and self-awareness as readers; their purposes for reading; and their own goals for reading improvement, including increasing reading fluency and comfort with a variety of texts (e.g., Beers & Samuels, 1998; Stahl, 1998). It also includes developing students' sense of agency in a variety of ways: students are given frequent choices about the books they will read, invited to connect personal experiences to texts, asked to bring in examples of out-of-school texts that matter to them, supported in setting and working toward fluency and other reading goals, given assistance to develop and express preferences for reading materials, and asked to assess how well their reading strategies are serving their own needs as readers. Work in this dimension draws on students' strategic skills used in out-of-school settings, as well as their interest in exploring new aspects of their own identities (see Davidson & Koppenhaver, 1993).

Cognitive: The cognitive dimension, frequently the entire focus of reading-comprehension instruction, is only one aspect of life in a Reading Apprenticeship classroom. Work in this dimension includes developing readers' mental processes, including their repertoire of specific comprehension and problem-solving strategies such as rereading, questioning, paraphrasing or summarizing, and the like (e.g., Beers & Samuels, 1998; Brown, Palincsar, &

FIGURE 1 *Dimensions of Classroom Life Supporting Reading Apprenticeship*

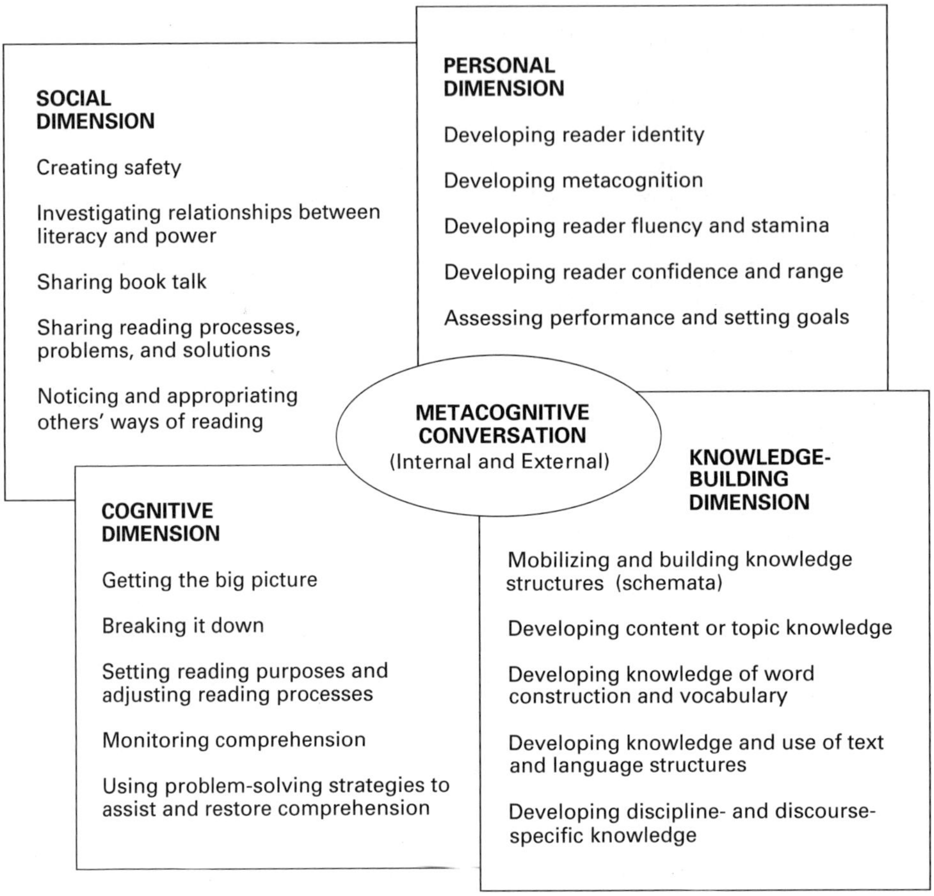

SOCIAL DIMENSION

Creating safety

Investigating relationships between literacy and power

Sharing book talk

Sharing reading processes, problems, and solutions

Noticing and appropriating others' ways of reading

PERSONAL DIMENSION

Developing reader identity

Developing metacognition

Developing reader fluency and stamina

Developing reader confidence and range

Assessing performance and setting goals

METACOGNITIVE CONVERSATION (Internal and External)

COGNITIVE DIMENSION

Getting the big picture

Breaking it down

Setting reading purposes and adjusting reading processes

Monitoring comprehension

Using problem-solving strategies to assist and restore comprehension

KNOWLEDGE-BUILDING DIMENSION

Mobilizing and building knowledge structures (schemata)

Developing content or topic knowledge

Developing knowledge of word construction and vocabulary

Developing knowledge and use of text and language structures

Developing discipline- and discourse-specific knowledge

Armbruster, 1994; Fitzgerald, 1995; Keene & Zimmerman, 1997; Kucan & Beck, 1997). Importantly, the work of unveiling cognitive strategies that can support reading comprehension is carried out through classroom inquiry (see Wells & Chang-Wells, 1992).

Knowledge-Building: This dimension includes identifying and expanding the kinds of knowledge readers bring to a text and then further develop through personal and social interaction with that text, including knowledge about word construction, vocabulary, text structure, genre, and language (e.g., Beck et al., 1997; Berkowitz, 1986; Taylor, 1992; Templeton et al., 1996); knowledge about the topics and content embedded in the text (e.g., Anderson, 1994; Bransford, 1994); and knowledge about the disciplinary conversation or social discourse in which the text is situated (e.g., Gee, 1992; Rabinowitz & Smith, 1998).

DEMYSTIFYING SUBJECT-AREA READING THROUGH
METACOGNITIVE CONVERSATION

These four interacting areas of classroom life are woven into subject-area teaching through a metacognitive conversation, a conversation about the thinking processes teachers and students are engaged in as they read (see Flavell, 1976, and Garner, 1994, for a description of metacognition). Teachers and students work collaboratively to make sense of texts, while simultaneously engaging in a conversation about *what constitutes reading* in specific academic disciplines and *how* they are going about it. New knowledge, strategies, and dispositions to reading develop in an ongoing conversation in which teacher and students think about and discuss their personal relationships to reading, larger issues of literacy and power, the social environment and resources of the classroom, their cognitive activity, the structure and language of particular types of texts, and the kinds of knowledge required to make sense of reading materials. This metacognitive conversation is carried on both internally, as teacher and students reflect on their own mental processes, and externally, as they share their reading processes, strategies, knowledge resources, motivations, and interactions with and affective responses to texts.

The metacognitive conversation occurs through many means — class discussions between teachers and students, small-group conversations, written private reflections and logs, letters to the teacher or even to characters in books. Such conversations and reflections, if they become routine, offer students ongoing opportunities to consider what they are doing as they read — how they are trying to make sense of texts and how well their strategies and approaches are working for them (Borkowski et al., 1990; Kucan & Beck, 1997). These conversations about reading and reading processes *demystify* the invisible ways we read and make sense of texts. Through the metacognitive conversation, readers' knowledge, strategies, and ways of reading particular kinds of texts become an explicit part of the secondary curriculum.

Reading Apprenticeship is at heart a partnership of expertise, drawing both on what subject-area teachers know and do as discipline-based readers and on adolescents' unique and often underestimated strengths as learners. We have come to see secondary students as young adults with powerful resources that can be tapped in a learning environment that is safe, respectful, and collaborative. Adolescents are frequently strategic and resourceful problem-solvers in their lives outside of the classroom. They are also at a point in their lives when their social identity matters most to them. Precisely at this time in their lives, they can be encouraged to try on new reader identities, to explore and expand their visions of who they are and can become (Davidson & Koppenhaver, 1993; Gee, 1996). Despite their veneer of cynicism, the majority of young people we have worked with desire to be part of something larger than themselves and to make the world a better place; this can motivate them to master the "power codes" of our society (Delpit, 1995). Adolescents thus carry with them into the classroom a wealth of proficiencies and dispositions that can be drawn upon to support their reading development. Teachers can work with, rather than against, some of these developmental characteristics by inviting students' self-awareness, strategic problem-solving, idealism, knowledge, and experience, and even their confusion, to serve instructional ends.

DESIGNING AND IMPLEMENTING AN ACADEMIC LITERACY COURSE

Our work with subject-area teachers has demonstrated that these teachers are key resources in supporting adolescents to develop high-level subject-area literacies and that this work can be powerfully and successfully integrated into ongoing subject-area instruction (Greenleaf, Schoenbach, Cziko, & Mueller, 1999; Schoenbach & Greenleaf, 2000). In the process of carrying out this professional development work, we were offered the opportunity to develop a course that would provide students with an intensive experience of Reading Apprenticeship. Working collaboratively as teacher/implementers and researcher/support providers, we designed this course for all ninth-grade students in a local urban high school, naming it "Academic Literacy".[7]

Thurgood Marshall Academic High School, a school serving some of the poorest neighborhoods of San Francisco, was established by court decree to provide a college preparatory education for the Latino, African American, and immigrant students who had been historically deprived of such educational opportunities. The school opened in 1994 with many recent high school reforms in place, including block scheduling, family groupings of students with academic core faculty, and project-based, interdisciplinary teaching and learning. However, by the fall of 1995, Marshall's faculty was expressing increasing concern that students coming into academically rigorous classes were unprepared to read the texts necessary to be successful in these courses. In response to this need, the Academic Literacy course began in the fall of 1996 as a mandatory course for all incoming ninth-graders.

According to school reports, in 1996–1997 the demographic composition of the ninth grade at Thurgood Marshall was roughly 30 percent African American, 25 percent Latino, 24 percent Chinese American, 7 percent Filipino American, 8 percent other non-White students, and 3 percent White students. Approximately 7 percent of the ninth-grade students were classified as special education students eligible for support services, and 14 percent were identified as English-language learners. This entire freshman class was enrolled in twelve sections of Academic Literacy, which met for two 90-minute block periods and one 50-minute period per week. Christine Cziko, the lead teacher of the course, recruited three other teachers to teach Academic Literacy, among them a first-year English teacher and two history teachers.

For Academic Literacy, we designed three units to focus on the role and use of reading in one's personal, public, and academic worlds: *Reading Self and Society, Reading Media,* and *Reading History.* The course had three goals: to increase students' engagement, fluency, and competency in reading (see Baumann & Duffy, 1997; Guthrie & Alvermann, 1991; Guthrie & Wigfield, 1997; Stahl, 1998). The course aimed to increase adolescent students' sense of agency and control of their own reading practices (Davidson & Koppenhaver, 1993). Throughout the three units, students in the course were invited into an inquiry through a set of essential questions the course was designed to explore: What is reading? and What do successful readers do when they read? Students were to gain a greater metacognitive awareness of their reading and to come to understand their own reading practices and habits by asking themselves questions such as, What kind of reader am I? and What strategies do I use as I read? The course was also designed to increase student motivation for reading by revealing, within the students' frame of reference, the power of literacy to shape lives. The students explored such questions as, What role does reading serve in people's personal and public lives? which lead students to a clearer understanding of the role reading will play in their future educational and career goals and help them set goals they can work toward to help themselves develop as readers. Finally, the course had a meta-discourse focus, exploring how texts are designed and conventionally structured through such questions as, What kinds of vocabulary can I expect from different texts? What kinds of sentences are found in different kinds of texts? and What do I need to know to be able to understand these different kinds of texts? Students encountered and revisited these questions through a series of units and activities designed to engage them in ideas, strategies, and practices to demystify discipline-based reading and apprentice them as academic readers.

Within the three units, specific subject-area content provided what we hoped would be compelling learning opportunities as well as sites for integration of reading strategies and practices. In *Reading Self and Society*, students focused on inquiry into the personal and public worlds of reading through guided reflection into their own and others' reading histories and experiences. While conducting personal inquiries into their own reading, they read narratives from authors such as Malcolm X, Claude Brown, Frederick Douglass, Maxine Hong Kingston, Richard Rodriguez, Emily Dickinson, and others, taking the perspectives of these authors in addressing the question, Why read? They interviewed family and community members about the role reading played in their lives as adults. Simultaneously, they started sustained silent reading (SSR) of self-chosen books, reading in class for twenty minutes of each block period for the school year.

The second unit, *Reading Media*, introduced students to commercials as visual texts similar to the kinds of printed texts they had studied previously. Students explored ideas such as: these and all texts are devised and constructed in particular times and places, and with specific purposes and agendas; all texts selectively include (address) and exclude particular readers or audiences; audiences (readers) negotiate meaning using the design and messages of the text as well as their own knowledge, experience, and responses to these design properties and content; and, texts are fallible sources of information.

Students analyzed television commercials and formed advertising production teams to create their own commercials, working with visual metaphors, visual icons and symbolism, and techniques of persuasion; identifying and constructing key messages; casting; sketching storyboards; composing and interpreting production notes, and targeting specific audiences. During this unit, they also watched a documentary film about how and for what purposes media are created and they read a challenging theoretical essay from a college course on media about the role of the media in our understanding of experiences in which we cannot participate directly. In order to make sense of both of these expository pieces, one visual and the other text based, they began to use their growing understanding of their own reading processes and the reading strategies that they had learned in the previous units.

The third unit, *Reading History*, was designed to help students put their personal experiences in a historical context by understanding the historical roots of modern issues of totalitarianism and intergroup hatred and aggression. In addition, it was designed to help students reconceptualize the discipline of history as an interpretive and contentious enterprise rather than a burdensome exercise in memorization. Students were assisted in developing a set of strategies to enable them to learn from a set of subject-area textbooks and from primary source documents. They built background knowledge through extensive reading across a variety of topic-relevant texts, including modern films about historical events. They read analyses of the social, historical, and psychological precursors and explanations for intergroup hostility and violence. They viewed historical documentaries about the Armenian genocide, as well as segments of *The Wave* and *Swing Kids* — the former a film depicting the unintended and horrific outcome of an experiment in in-group and out-group identity formation among teenagers, and the latter a film set in Nazi Germany as a group of jazz-loving teenagers comes of age, is forced to make choices, and begins to take on or resist roles in Germany's increasingly totalitarian and genocidal society. As a culminating unit, students assumed the role of historian in an investigative project centered on the Holocaust. Working in groups and with primary- and secondary-source documents related to a specific event such as the Warsaw Ghetto Uprising or the evolution of anti-Semitic laws in Germany, students interpreted and analyzed and finally presented their historical analyses of the event they had investigated.

To help students gain more powerful conceptions of literacy, as well as an expanded repertoire of problem-solving strategies they could draw on when facing academic texts, explicit strategy and text instruction was integrated into these units of study as students worked with texts and engaged in an ongoing inquiry into the essential questions. Key instructional strategies included Reciprocal Teaching (RT) and explicit, integrated instruction in self-monitoring, cognitive strategies, and text analysis that would facilitate reading a variety of materials. Teacher "think-alouds" modeling reading and problem-solving with texts, as well as student writing and discussion about their own reading processes and confusion, were daily features of the learning environment. Because adolescents are often keenly aware of their confusion but also reluctant to expose it, teachers worked to create a safe environment where "it's cool to be confused" (Cziko, 1998). It quickly became clear that being able to identify comprehension problems and to stimulate collaborative problem-solving and inquiry using a variety of strategic approaches, rather than having the right answers about texts, was valued in this class.

Academic Literacy teachers engaged students in practicing the component strategies of RT — questioning, summarizing, clarifying, and predicting — as they read a variety of texts and conducted inquiries into reading. Students were also given specific instruction, as well as modeling and thinking aloud opportunities, as they examined the features of different text genres. They learned and practiced techniques for note-taking; paraphrasing; using graphic organizers and mapping to identify text structure and support processing of information in texts; identifying root words, prefixes, and suffixes; and developing semantic networks to increase their command of vocabulary learning strategies. As the need arose with difficult expository texts, students also learned to "chunk" or break down complex sentences, and even words, into understandable bites. The overarching goal of putting students in control of their own engagement in and assessment of these strategies for themselves as readers ran through these instructional routines.

To give students opportunities to develop both fluency and knowledge about themselves as readers, as well as increased motivation for reading, students read books of their choice for sustained silent reading (SSR), drawing from extensive classroom libraries and from community and school book collections. They kept a "metacognitive log" during SSR, in which they wrote about their reading processes using a variety of sentence starters such as, "I was confused by . . .", "I got stuck when . . .", "I lost track of time because . . .", and the like. In addition, students wrote reflective letters to their teachers monthly, describing what they were learning about themselves as readers through SSR. To create a social context for self-chosen reading, students shared their metacognitive log entries with one another, made book recommendations through posters and book talks, and discussed ways of picking good books to read. Through the shared inquiry into reading, students were encouraged to reappraise their current conceptions of literacy, set and accomplish personal goals for reading development, and draw on the social resources of the classroom community in developing new and more powerful reading repertoires.

A STUDY OF THE IMPACT OF ACADEMIC LITERACY ON STUDENT READING

To evaluate the impact of the course on student learning, we collected a variety of data, including both standardized test scores and qualitative data, to gauge student thinking and learning. Standardized measures included pre- and post-tests of reading proficiency using the Degrees of Reading Power test.[8] Qualitative measures included pre- and postcourse reading surveys adapted from Atwell (1998, Appendix E; see Figure 2)[9]; students' written reflections, self-assessments, and course evaluations; focus group interviews; classroom observations; and samples of course work for thirty students selected randomly from the class rosters of two of the Academic Literacy teachers. In addition, we carried out intensive case studies of eight of these thirty students, videotaping interviews with them three times during the year as they carried out their reading assignments for the course.

The eight case-study students were volunteers recruited by their teachers as typical ninth graders who represented the cultural and gender diversity of students in their classes. These students understood that they were not only helping to evaluate the impact of the course on student learning but also assisting in a larger inquiry into adolescent reading, with the goal of helping secondary teachers meet the needs of students like themselves. During each of the three units of the course, we interviewed the case-study students as they read from self-chosen or assigned texts, responded to interview questions, and discussed their reading processes. These interviews were audio- and videotaped. Students read on from where they had left off in class or at home with these texts, reading a copy of the text that had been segmented into four sections. The students read the segmented text in four ways during the interview: reading aloud, reading silently, being read to, and thinking aloud while reading. After each section of text, the interviewer probed not only into what sense the students were making of the texts, but also how they were doing so.

These reading interviews were designed to provide valuable information as we implemented the course. Interviews with Academic Literacy students could show us the degree to which students were appropriating the reading practices available to them in the instructional setting (Vygotsky, 1978, 1986). The interviews were conducted as a kind of dynamic assessment of students' problem-solving during reading in which it would become apparent what the student was able and unable to understand independently, as well as what type and degree of support the adult in the interview situation provided to assist the case-study student with the reading task.[10] The interviews could thus point to aspects of academic reading tasks and texts, as well as class resources, that helped or hindered students as they engaged in reading, helping us to improve the course even as we taught it.

In addition to these data, we have continued to follow the progress of the original cohort of Academic Literacy students as they have moved up through the grades. During 1997–1998, their tenth-grade year, we interviewed twenty students who had been in Academic Literacy about the impact of the course on their learning and preparation for other courses, about its utility in their lives, and about their lives as readers. We also collected reading surveys and administered the DRP test to the tenth-grade students at the end of the year. These students continued to inform us about the impact of the course through surveys, standardized tests, and interviews as they moved through the school toward their graduation in June 2000.

1   If you had to guess, how many books would you say you owned?
2   How many books would you say are in your house?
3   How many books would you say you've read in the last twelve months?
4   How did you learn to read?
5   Why do people read?
6   What does someone have to do in order to be a good reader?
7   Do you consider yourself a good reader? Why or why not?
8   What kinds of books do you like to read?
9   How do you decide which books you'll read?
10   Have you ever reread a book? If so, can you name it/them here?
11   Do you ever read novels at home for pleasure? If so, how often do you read at home for pleasure?
12   Who are your favorite authors?
13   Do you like to have your teacher read to you? If so, is there anything special you'd like to hear?
14   In general, how do you feel about reading?

A CASE STUDY

Rosa was a Latina student in one of Christine Cziko's Academic Literacy classes. Her first language was Spanish, but she was a fluent English speaker by the time she entered Thurgood Marshall in the ninth grade. Rosa's parents often attended school functions, asking that meetings be translated into Spanish for themselves and other Spanish-speaking parents. Rosa's father was actively involved in community work in the Mission District, the largely Latino neighborhood in which they lived. Rosa was typical of the students in the class, in that she was inexperienced as an academic reader and unprepared for the demands of a college preparatory high school program. Reflecting recently on why she had chosen Rosa for case study, as typical of students in her classes, Christine Cziko recalled:

> Rosa was interesting to me because she was articulate, sociable, active in the life of the school, but academically a B- or C student. She was also aware of social injustice in the world, perhaps because of her father's community activism, so she had a broad picture of the world outside of the classroom. When it came to work with text, though, her ability to negotiate the world in her everyday life was not apparent. She didn't bring the strategic thinking and competence and engagement that I knew she had in other aspects of her life — her social and community lives in the school and her neighborhood — to academic tasks. She was never hostile; it wasn't as though she was making a political statement like "I won't learn from you." She was cooperative, friendly to teachers, and responded positively to her teachers and to what she thought she was being asked to do. But it was as though she brought only

a shadow of herself to the academic aspect of her school life. The real Rosa was much more vibrant, confident, articulate.

In this regard, Rosa was typical of many students at Thurgood Marshall, including the ninth graders Cziko described teaching:

> You see this with so many kids. In the hall, in the cafeteria, in their communities, in all these places there are these active, engaged, bright, funny kids. They come into the classroom and they turn into a ghost of themselves, like a shroud just drops over them. Their academic identities are these fragile, ghostly things, not robust in the way their whole person identities are because of so many things — repeated failures, being told what they can and cannot do, being mystified by what is asked of them in school. Then there are the kids who don't become ghosts — they're demons. They're acting out, they're bringing their most angry selves into the classroom. The source of these seemingly opposite classroom identities may be very much the same.

ROSA'S READING OF HISTORY

The reading interview excerpted below was done in March of 1997, after Rosa had been in the Academic Literacy class for six months. The interview we will analyze was the second in a series of reading interviews with Rosa and seven other case-study students, and focused on her reading of a chapter on totalitarianism from a tenth-grade modern world history textbook. The interview questions were designed to assess Rosa's ability to use the predicting, summarizing, questioning, and clarifying strategies that are components of Reciprocal Teaching (RT); to probe her thinking and reasoning about the text; and to stimulate reflection on her reading experience, on other reading experiences with history texts, and on her development as a reader in Academic Literacy. (See Appendix A for the interview protocol.)

In our analysis of the reading interview, we focus on key literacy practices that Rosa participated in as part of her Academic Literacy class: strategic control of the reading process; metacognition, or knowledge of self as a reader; and metadiscourse, or knowledge of texts and textual practices. In the following transcribed segments of the interview, the interviewer prompts Rosa to carry out particular reading processes and reflect on her reading. In our analysis, we are interested not only in whether Rosa carries out these practices when asked to do so by the interviewer but also whether Rosa carries out these practices without the interviewer's prompt when her reading suggests the need to do so. Through this analysis of the reading interview, we consider whether Rosa has appropriated for her own use as a reader the key literacy practices she participated in during the Academic Literacy course. We are also able to trace the impact of these literacy practices on Rosa's development as a reader of, and participant in, the academic discourse of history.

Metadiscourse: Knowledge about Texts and Reading Practices

The interviewer begins by inviting Rosa to share what she thinks about the history textbook and the kinds of reading she is doing with it in Academic Literacy. Rosa tells the interviewer that her experience reading this particular textbook seems different from her usual textbook experience. When asked to explain, she voices a common student opinion about studying history in school:[11]

8   *Rosa:* A textbook just really, much more, just throws the facts at you, and you're just
9   like, here are all these facts. And it's kinda boring. You read all these facts about
10 dead people and what happened and sometimes you wonder, like, "Why am I
11 studying this thing?" You know? Why? But in these books it seems more realistic. I
12 don't know why.
13 *Interviewer:* Why is that? What's the difference?
14 *Rosa:* I don't know . . . It's like, for the um — we're like talking about hate groups right
15 now. And we watched the movie, *The Wave.* And it like, it tied in with the book and
16 it kind of made us realize that it can happen again. If you don't know what happened
17 back then, y'know, it can repeat itself. So this book is more, I don't know, realistic to
18 me. I understand it more.

The interviewer steps in to clarify what Rosa thinks is different: the text, the reading practices that accompany the text in her Academic Literacy class, or her own interest in the topic:

20 *Int.:* Well, let me just ask you about that. Is it that the book is different or is it that your
21 talking in class around the book is different? Like, the topic — is it the topic that's
22 more realistic? Is it the connection you can make to your own life? Or is it
23 something about the way the book is written?

Rosa considers:

24 *Rosa:* It's sort of like the way the book is written. It's not really, I mean, I don't know.
25 Here they give you examples and you know, you're thinking, "okay.". And the
26 way we talk in class is different. And it's just like the talking in class and the way
27 the book is written and the way you read it, and all of that ties in and it gives you
28 like this whole different atmosphere. And it's not really all that boring to read
29 anymore.

Rosa goes on to offer a fairly serious and specific indictment of a common type of textbook and attendant classroom reading practice:

31 Um, usually in like a regular history class, like the one I had last year? Which
32 was just pretty much all writing? Okay, "read from page so-n-so to so-n-so,
33 answer the red square questions and the unit questions and turn them in." And he
34 corrects them and says, "You did this wrong, you did this right. Okay, here you

35   go." And that was pretty much the basic way every single day was gone. So,
36   from day one to the end of the year, that's pretty much all we did. Answer the red
37   square questions. And pretty much it's been like that since I got to middle school.
38   In fifth grade it was a little more different because we actually discussed the
39   books. But before that it was like, we didn't have books, like pretty much for
40   history. You know before fifth grade, it was pretty much kids don't really
41   understand so they don't have those books. And in fifth grade was when we
42   started with books. And it was pretty much, answer the red square questions,
43   explain a little, red square questions, explain a little. And the questions just pretty
44   much had to do with what you were reading. And it wasn't like it was spread all
45   over the place, like you had to read it. It was just like, if the red square question
46   was here, you knew it was somewhere around that area right there. And you
47   could just look for the answer and copy it down and you got full credit for it. So
48   you didn't have to read. It was something that you could like slide by without
49   them knowing. I don't know if they cared or not, but that's the way everybody
50   did it. You see the red square question and you sort of calculate where it's
51   around, you find the answer, and you write it down and that's it.

Comparing this familiar textbook reading practice to reading in the Academic Literacy unit, Rosa explains:

52   *Rosa:* Now it's like, you have to talk about it. You have to explain what you read.
53   You have to make a tree about it, okay? And figure out those details. You have to get
54   more into the book than you realize. So, this book is kind of different. Also the way
55   we're talking in class.

In these exchanges, Rosa demonstrates how she is thinking about history and reading history in a new way. She is considering how historical events connect to her life and her responsibilities as a person who knows that "it can happen again." The "whole different atmosphere" of her historical reading practice in Academic Literacy has helped her to understand and value types of reading and thinking that were unavailable to her when all she was asked to do was to "answer the red square questions" in her history reading. Rosa's interview also demonstrates one of the more powerful results of Reading Apprenticeship: the development of students' abilities to critically evaluate and appraise texts and textual practices themselves.

Strategic Control of the Reading Process

The interviewer then refers to the text itself, asking Rosa how she would go about reading it if her teacher assigned it for class. Demonstrating that she has appropriated routines from her Academic Literacy classroom into her own repertoire of reading behaviors, Rosa answers:

80   *Rosa:* I guess I'd have to start by the title. And then, um, just try to relate the first
81   paragraph, second paragraph. And just sort of, kind of, read through it and see
82   what it's about. Because it usually explains it in the first paragraph and it just

83   goes on from there. So if I understand like the first paragraph, then I would see
84   what like the subheadings are about, like what it has to deal with. Then I would
85   start reading, and, um, just keep on going, I guess. Just keep reading and if I have
86   any questions just try to answer them within the reading. Pretty much do what we
87   do with RT.

In this brief description of how Rosa would approach her reading, she displays an awareness and analysis of text structure and organization (the functions of headings, subheadings, and first paragraphs), the importance of identifying central ideas ("what it has to deal with"), and the need to link parts of the text to one another and construct a coherent meaning ("to relate the first paragraph, second paragraph"). Rosa also demonstrates here her awareness of her own active role in reading, describing this activity as "seeing what it's about," "trying to relate" parts of the text, moving on if she "understands" the first paragraph, and, if she has any questions, "just trying to answer them within the reading."

The interview continues with a review of the section of the chapter on totalitarianism that Rosa has already read and analyzed with her class. Rosa tells the interviewer what she remembers about this section and describes the importance of this topic, relating the analysis of the historical roots of intolerance contained in the chapter to her own experience of interracial hatred and hate crimes in her community. After this discussion the interviewer turns to the next section of the text that Rosa has not yet read, inviting her to share how she would use RT strategies in her reading. The section of the text is excerpted below:

Propaganda and indoctrination orchestrated feelings.

Perhaps the most important tools of the new totalitarian states were propaganda and indoctrination. By repeatedly playing on the peoples' hopes and fears, propaganda could whip people into a fever pitch of hatred for an external enemy — or for a group of people at home who were "different" or did not conform. People who supported the leader were portrayed as self-sacrificing heroes. The enemy or domestic opponents of the regime were pictured as devils or beasts who were corrupt and depraved. Once fully in power, totalitarian states quickly turned to indoctrination, or the systematic use of propaganda to form habits and attitudes. It is no coincidence that totalitarian states such as Nazi Germany, the Soviet Union, and Communist China took over complete control of children's education. Young people were often enrolled in special camps or movements such as the Hitler Youth. Children were even turned against their own parents, told to spy on them, and given rewards for turning them in to the authorities. (Krieger & Neill, 1994, p. 89)*

* From *Issues of the Modern Era* by Larry S. Krieger and Kenneth Neill. Copyright © 1994 by D. C. Heath and Company. All rights reserved. Reprinted by permission of McDougal Littell Inc.

140   *Int.:* Okay, let's go on to the next section, the propaganda section.
141   And what I'd like you to do is just take a look at the heading and predict
142   what you're going to read about in this section. The heading is
143   *"Propaganda and indoctrination orchestrated feelings."*
144   *Rosa:* Well usually if like I don't understand a part of the heading, it usually explains it
145   later on. Like indoctrination? It's in bold right here, so, um, that would pretty much
146   define that one. And so, now I have to read it [okay] and make sure I understand the
147   heading.
148   *Int.:* Okay, fine. [Rosa looks briefly at the text, then continues.]
149   *Rosa:* Okay, I guess we're gonna find out about like, more about I guess the media
150   and propaganda and how it affects hate crimes, I guess.
151   *Int.:* Um-hmm. Okay, great.[12]

In this sequence, Rosa is asked to predict and does so, displaying her understanding that prediction means what "we're gonna find out about" in the text (lines 149 and 150). Specifically, she predicts that she will learn more about how the media and propaganda affect hate crimes. (Note, too, that Rosa has made the connection between media and propaganda independently, using media as a synonym for propaganda. Media is not specifically mentioned in this section of the text.) This brief interchange is evidence that Rosa can and does use the predicting strategy when prompted by the interviewer. But before she can attempt to make a prediction, she first interrupts herself, without being prompted, and carries out the strategy of clarifying (lines 144–147), one of the key comprehension practices taught in Academic Literacy. In this interruption, she demonstrates important self- and text-knowledge. She knows that usually when she doesn't understand a part of the heading, she will benefit from reading the text to clarify the word meaning. She also knows that she can count on the text explaining the term "later on." She demonstrates her knowledge that words often are defined in the text and, furthermore, that key vocabulary is often typed in boldface in textbooks. Using these cues, Rosa locates some text that helps her define the word *indoctrination.* This unprompted clarification sequence is evidence that Rosa has appropriated strategies for clarifying as she reads and is able to recognize when they may assist her reading.

Rosa then reads the paragraph of text aloud, stopping at the end of a sentence containing the word *regime* to ask the interviewer what it means, again clarifying using available resources (including the interviewer) without prompting. When she finishes reading, she is prompted for a summary. However, before she provides a summary, she initiates a long clarification sequence in which she reads the text closely, with the assistance of the interviewer, to work out the word meaning and to monitor the reliability of the meaning she has made so far. We analyze this sequence below:

175   *Int.:* Okay, great. So why don't you tell me in your own words what that was about, what
176   you just read?

177 *Rosa:* Um, I guess it was about . . . I'm not sure because I did not understand that word
178 *totalitarian?*
179 *Int.:* Uh-huh, good.[13] So if you were doing RT you would say . . .
180 *Rosa:* I didn't understand the word. And then I guess I would describe the word and
181 since I didn't understand it someone would have to like describe it and if we
182 didn't know we would ask Ms. Cziko and Ms. Cziko would tell us the definition.
183 Or if it was home, I would pretty much use the dictionary.
184 *Int.:* Okay, so what have you talked about in class so far about totalitarianism?
185 About totalitarian states?
186 *Rosa:* I don't think we have talked about that because we used um *totalitarianism* for
187 our test and it wasn't in the reading until this next paragraph. So, I don't
188 remember if we were defining the word. I don't remember that. But I guess we
189 did. But I don't remember the definition of it.
190 *Int.:* Do you have anything in mind? Kind of a guess or a hunch about what it
191 might mean?
192 *Rosa:* I don't know why, when I think of that word I think of tolerance.
193 *Int.:* You do?
194 *Rosa:* I think of tolerance. I don't know why, but that's what I think of. And um I
195 know genocide is trying to kill a group of people for a reason, whatever it might
196 be. So I know genocide is bad so totalitarianism has to be good, I guess in a way.
197 *Int.:* You think it's the opposite of genocide?
198 *Rosa:* I guess it has to be because it says "turned hate into genocide." Oh, actually no,
199 it has to be bad. No, it has to be bad. Um, I don't know what it means. I'm kind of
200 stuck.

In this sequence, Rosa postpones giving a summary for the paragraph she has read, instead focusing on what, for her, is a key stumbling block to her comprehension, the term *totalitarianism.* At the suggestion of the interviewer, she first struggles to recall what has been said about this concept in class, but since she can't remember this information, she turns to the word itself and her own word knowledge as a source of information, again at the suggestion of the interviewer (lines 184–185). Attempting to find a similar, known word, Rosa associates totalitarianism with the word *tolerance,* an association that misdirects her search for the meaning of totalitarianism (line 192). Yet she does not stop with this association. She continues to draw a mental web of related ideas and concepts, looking back in the text and bringing in the word *genocide* from the title of this section of the chapter she is reading, which is "Totalitarianism turned hate into genocide." She attempts to contrast genocide with totalitarianism (lines 194–196). At this point, her understanding of the word *totalitarianism* is still colored in the positive hues of tolerance: "I know genocide is bad so totalitarianism has to be good." Yet, she does not express confidence ("I guess in a way"). Instead, she turns back to the text to test her growing definition: "I guess it has to be because it says 'turned hate into genocide.'"

Even as she reads this title aloud, Rosa realizes her error, that something turning hate into a worse crime, genocide, must be bad (lines 198–199). Though she has so far failed to clarify the meaning of totalitarianism, Rosa demonstrates, in this sequence, her ability to wrestle with the text and use context, semantic associations, text structures, and syntactical constructions to shape the meaning she constructs with the text. Throughout this sequence, the interviewer follows Rosa's lead, asking questions to clarify the state of Rosa's ongoing problem-solving (lines 193 and 197). Following this exchange, the interviewer summarizes Rosa's search for meaning and encourages her to continue it (lines 201 and 202, below):

201 *Int.:* Okay, so you're thinking about this word and you're using some hints that you have
202 here. What could you do next to try and clarify this?
203 *Rosa:* Well, I guess try to read where that word is and try to define it by that.
204 *Int.:* Um-hmm. So why don't you try that and see what happens?
205 *Rosa:* Um, it says that "tools of the new totalitarian states were propaganda and
206 indoctrination." So, so they were propaganda and indoctrination? I'm not sure if
207 that's right.
208 *Int.:* Those are some tools that um, totalitarian states use.
209 *Rosa:* Okay, um . . . Um . . . Then, could that mean, taken over by a certain person or
210 something?
211 *Int.:* Like um, you mean like dictatorships where somebody takes over?
212 *Rosa:* Yeah, like that.

In line 203, Rosa describes a strategy she could use to help her define totalitarianism. When the interviewer encourages Rosa to "try that and see what happens" (line 204), Rosa finds a sentence where propaganda and indoctrination, the concepts that she has just wrestled with, are connected with totalitarianism. Trying to establish the nature of the connection, she asks the interviewer for help (lines 205–207). Responding to this request in a limited way to give Rosa an opportunity to solve as much of the comprehension problem she is experiencing on her own, the interviewer focuses Rosa on the word *tools* in the text — "Those are some tools that um, totalitarian states use" (line 208) — and Rosa connects these tools to her previous reading to hypothesize, "Then, could that mean taken over by a certain person or something?" (lines 209–210), a conjecture that draws her closer to the meaning of totalitarianism. The interviewer's clarifying question, "You mean like dictatorships . . . ?" (line 211) gives Rosa yet another semantic clue and confidence, as she recognizes the connection (line 212), that she is on the right track.

At this point, the interviewer, still responding to Rosa's request for help, affirms the direction of Rosa's search and asks Rosa to describe what she is doing to investigate the word *totalitarianism* in more detail (lines 213–214 below). Rosa's description (lines 217–220) makes clear that she is scanning back in the paragraph she has read for instances of this word and reading the sentences in which it is contained to see if these new contexts shed light on the concept. Although she starts by rereading a prior section, she also makes it clear that if she did not get enough help there, she would go on to scan ahead in the text. She summarizes her strategy, saying, "I'm trying to find the definition of it through what I read" (lines 218–219):

213 *Int.:* There are some real similarities with that concept, with that idea. Where are
214 you looking as you're looking? I'm just curious.
215 *Rosa:* I'm trying to look for the word.
216 *Int.:* In this paragraph that you just read?
217 *Rosa:* I just try to look for that word as much as I can. And when I find it I try to
218 read around it. If I don't find it after it, I find it before it. I'm trying to find
219   the definition of it through what I read. I'm not sure if it defines it later on.
220 *Int.:* I sure don't think so.

The interviewer then tests whether Rosa has enough of a sense of the word to continue her reading of the passage (lines 221– 224, below), whether she can live with her tentative understanding as she reads on. But Rosa is not finished clarifying: "It's pretty much not enough" (line 225). We see Rosa's persistence here as evidence that she is able to assess not only her own understanding, but how important the meaning of this word will be to the meaning of the text (lines 225–226). Finally, in lines 226–231, she "puts the heading to chapter two [Totalitarianism turned hate into genocide.] and what I just read" together to formulate an idea about totalitarianism: "There has to be some kind of person dictating what you think, and then . . . making you believe that what you're feeling is because of somebody else." While not a conventional definition, the key ideas of dictatorship and manipulation or control of thought help her feel like she "can understand it a little more" (line 233).

221 *Int.:* So you've gotten a few ideas. That there's propaganda and indoctrination. That, you
222 have this hunch that it has something to do with um, with somebody taking over like a
223 dictator. What might you do next? Or is that enough? Do you feel like you have enough
224 of an idea to go on?
225 *Rosa:* It's pretty much not enough. I mean, I'm really not defining it so I really can't
226 understand it until I kind of get that defined. And putting the heading to I guess
227 you'd say chapter two and what I just read, I mean there has to be some kind of
228 person sort of dictating what you think, and then using your hate against, and
229 turning it into like something else, like making you believe that what you're feeling
230 is because of somebody else. I guess it would have something to do with that. I'm
231 not totally sure about that, though.
232 *Int.:* Um-hmm. So, do you feel settled then with that enough to go on?
233 *Rosa:* It makes me feel like I can understand it a little more . . .
234 *Int.:* Okay, so when I asked you before what was this paragraph about, you said you were
235 stuck because you didn't understand totalitarianism. What if I asked you now? What do
236 you think this paragraph is about? What would you say you just read in your own words?

When prompted again (lines 234–236), Rosa returns to the task of summarizing this paragraph (lines 238–244, below). In this summary, Rosa indicates her understanding that totalitarianism is something that became possible once it was possible to use technologies of communication to that end: "Somebody . . . can easily now confuse people and make them believe things." She is also working with the concept of "tool" that was introduced in the passage and underscored by the interviewer: ". . . turn their hatred into something else, use it as a tool . . . against people . . . used the children against their parents . . . they used something to get something else."

238 *Rosa:* I guess in my own words what I would say was somebody or, what this thing
239 was about is um, people are, I mean can easily now confuse people and make them
240 believe things and turn their hatred into something else, use it as a tool, I guess,
241 against people? [*Int.:* Um-hmm] And some examples of that being Nazi Germany,
242 the Soviet Union, and Communist China. Which are, like, places that used the
243 children against their parents. So, I mean, they used something to get something
244 else. I'm not sure I explained it very well. But that's what I got.
245 *Int.:* Okay, great. So let's um, those are the main points. Like if you were summarizing
246 that's what you would say.

The work of clarifying the term *totalitarianism* has brought relationships among agents (dictators), tools of oppression (propaganda), and ends that serve the totalitarian regime (using children against their parents, turning hatred into something else) into greater focus for Rosa. Rosa is able to summarize her reading only after asserting her need to clarify the passage, and carrying out this clarification using a wide array of textual and cognitive resources, including signals within the text, grammatical and semantic relationships among words and sentences, and her own repertoire of problem-solving strategies. In this interview, Rosa demonstrates not only the struggle to construct meaning that she is now capable of carrying out with difficult academic text, but also the various tools and resources she is able to employ to serve that struggle. Moreover, she knows what she needs as a reader to move on in the work of reading and is able to assert the priority of these needs, even before a video camera and a waiting interviewer who is prompting her for a prediction or a summary before she is ready to give one. In an inspiring way, Rosa remains in control of her reading throughout the interview, helping to shape this reading event — a videotaped reading performance — as an enterprise of making sense rather than one of merely running through a protocol or answering the questions that are put to her.

Metacognition: Monitoring Comprehension and Drawing on Knowledge about Self as Reader

The next segment of the textbook chapter on totalitarianism includes a narrative excerpt from the *Gulag Archipelago*. The text shifts from exposition to this reflective narrative written in a literary style, and the connection between the narrative and the exposition is implied rather than stated explicitly. After reading this segment of the *Gulag* silently, Rosa stumbles a bit when asked to summarize it and finally says, "I'm not sure, I'm kind of confused right now." She talks about being sleepy, complains that the text seems beyond her ninth-grade level, and says, "It's just kind of all a big blur right now." As she did earlier in her reading, Rosa then marshals a set of tools for constructing meaning with this text, including skimming back over the text looking for key words, rereading, and connecting the text to what she already knows and has been learning in her Reading History unit. She refers repeatedly to "the excerpt," "the book part," and "his reflection," displaying both her ability to recognize text markers that delineate borrowings from other text sources, as well as her adoption of a language for talking about text. Later in the interview, after Rosa has successfully comprehended this segment of the text, the interviewer recalls Rosa's "confusion":

551 *Int.:* When I asked you to read this section silently, do you remember, and we've
552 been through a lot since you first started this, do you remember when you
553 were reading it, what was going through your mind? What were you trying to
554 do?
555 *Rosa:* Um, when I was reading this, I was trying to like stay focused on the, focused on
556 the reading. Because I knew that, 'cause when I got half way through that
557 excerpt from the book, I started losing the beginning and I started turning fuzzy.
558 And I knew that I was going to lose it by the end of the reading. So I was like,
559 "Okay, I have to go back." So I went sort of back, skimmed through it, got the
560 main idea, went, kept on reading, skimmed through that a little bit more, and went
561 all the way down, and skimmed through that a little bit more, and just kept
562 skimming back. So it kind of took me longer than it would usually. I was just
563 trying to stay focused on what I was reading to make sure I didn't lose it but I did.
564 *Int.:* Uh-huh. [Interviewer and Rosa laugh.]
565 *Rosa:* It didn't work.
566 *Int.:* But you knew that you were losing it. That's interesting.
567 *Rosa:* I knew that I was losing it because the minute that I got to like this word [points in
568 text], I had forgotten the first word. And I mean, it was just like I got from the
569 beginning of the paragraph to the end and I had dropped what I had read at the
570 beginning. And it was like, too soon to lose it. I mean it was like, you read it and you
571 forget what it is so it's just going word by word. So I knew I was losing it, somehow I
572 knew that I was going to lose it. It was just kind of something that I couldn't avoid
573 very well.

In this exchange, we see that the practices of metacognition — especially being aware of reading processes, setting goals for purposeful engagement with reading, and deliberately controlling attention — are well within Rosa's grasp. She is aware of her mental "blur" and takes deliberate steps to avoid "losing it." She knows that she can generally retain meaning for a certain length of text, and recognizes that it is "too soon to lose it" after such a short passage.

In this reading interview with Rosa, we are able to see clear reflections of the instructional practices that the Academic Literacy course constructed to support her reading development. What she has accomplished in the socially mediated setting of the classroom is now visible in her interaction with the interviewer, in her reflective talk about herself as a reader, in her comprehension monitoring, in her deliberate control of attention, and in her unprompted use of repair strategies when her comprehension fails. In essence, the Reading Apprenticeship practices of the class have created a zone of proximal development (Vygotsky, 1978, 1986) in which Rosa is able to appropriate powerful knowledge, strategies, and dispositions to guide her reading. We can also see how Rosa assesses these practices, how she is able to externalize and characterize ways of reading and their usefulness to her. In Academic Literacy, Rosa, her classmates, and their teacher have been sharing what and how they read, "thinking aloud" in a metacognitive conversation. From this practice, Rosa has gained not only strategies for intentionally constructing meaning with print and monitoring her own comprehension, but also a vocabulary for talking about her reading performance.

We believe the metacognitive, metadiscursive, and strategic reading practices of the Academic Literacy course will assist Rosa and other adolescent readers in not only grappling with academic texts to construct meaning, but also in participating in the ways of thinking that characterize the academic disciplines. We see evidence of this in Rosa's shifting understanding of what it means to read history, moving from answering red square questions to struggling to clarify meanings and connect them to one's own life experiences. During the interview, Rosa also shows how she has apprenticed herself to particular ways of thinking historically. When asked what question she would ask an RT group based on her reading of this text, she voices a question that has animated much historical scholarship, as well as moral inquiry, in the past half century. We hear the Reverend Niemoller's now famous litany in Rosa's question for her RT group:[14]

532 *Rosa:* Why didn't people fight back? Why didn't they do anything? Why did they just
533 sit there and say, "Okay, well I'm glad it's not me who's in trouble, it's them"?

Rosa's reading of this history text calls to mind the skillful problem-solving, negotiation of meaning, and connection to others that is captured in Rexford Brown's eloquent phrase, "a literacy of thoughtfulness" (Brown, 1991). Imagine, for a moment, that Rosa had been in a reading course focused on building basic reading skills. While such a course may have strengthened her word analysis and vocabulary skills, we doubt that Rosa would have developed the kind of intellectual and ethical engagement and personal agency she demonstrates here. When we imagine such a limited outcome, we are struck with a keen sense of loss and unfulfilled potential, not only for Rosa, but for the many young people with whom we work.

Interviews with Rosa and the other case-study students mirrored the metacognitive conversation these students had participated in as members of the Academic Literacy course. Like metacognitive conversations in the classroom, these interviews traced students' reading processes and meaning-making and asked students to reflect on and articulate how they were approaching reading tasks. The interviews demonstrated that ninth-grade students can self-consciously appraise their own strengths and weaknesses as readers, set goals and work to accomplish them, and develop metacognitive monitoring and strategic control of reading processes. The interviews also affirmed that when students participate as apprentices in an inquiry into academic reading practices, they can and do appropriate the comprehension activities and dispositions toward texts available to them in the context of instruction. Further, through these interviews we were able to witness students' emerging academic identities as students engaged, as Rosa did here, in literacies of thoughtfulness.

OTHER ASSESSMENTS OF STUDENT READING DEVELOPMENT

Standardized Reading Comprehension Tests

While reading interviews gave us impressive evidence of students' appropriation of the reading practices of the course, we had many other indicators of the positive impact of the course on student reading development. As we have reported elsewhere (Greenleaf & Schoenbach, 2000; Greenleaf et al., 1999; Schoenbach et al., 1999), the ninth-grade Academic Literacy students improved their performance on standardized tests of reading comprehension. Table 1 shows that Academic Literacy students improved their performance significantly on the Degree of Reading Power (DRP) test, gaining an average of four points in raw score and moving from the 47th to nearly the 49th percentile in national ranking in the seven months of instructional time between October and May of their ninth-grade year. When special education students were omitted from the Academic Literacy sample, as they were from the national norming population, the mean scores of the Academic Literacy students increased further, moving these students above the 50th percentile ranking.

The DRP test is both norm and criterion referenced. In comparison with the national norm, the ninth graders in Academic Literacy classes started the year reading on average at a late seventh-grade level, moving to a late ninth-grade level (catching up to the national norm for ninth graders) by May. In terms of familiar texts, by the test-makers' estimates, students were able independently to read and comprehend texts similar in difficulty to *Charlotte's Web, Old Yeller,* or children's magazines at the start of the year. By May, the test-makers estimate they were able to independently read and comprehend texts similar in difficulty to *To Kill a Mockingbird, The Adventures of Tom Sawyer,* and teen reading materials. The increase of nearly four units on the Degree of Reading Power criterion-referenced scale from fall to spring is significantly greater than the norm, based on samples of large, national populations of same-grade students, in which "growth from Fall to Spring is smaller — about 1–2 DRP units" (Touchstone Applied Science Associates, 1995, p. 48). Students' increased average reading levels in May, as estimated by the DRP, suggested that they should be able to handle all but the most difficult high school textbooks with instructional support, and that with instructional support, these students should be able to tackle difficult literature like *The Prince* or *The Scarlet Letter.*

These results gain in significance when one considers that the norming sample against which the performance of Academic Literacy students was compared was developed to approximate a national population. In this norming population, only 13.5 percent were eligible for free or reduced school lunch programs, compared to 33.2 percent of the Thurgood Marshall students. In addition, the demographics of the norming sample were 12 percent African American, 4.6 percent Spanish surname, 1.4 percent Asian, and 63 percent White students, a sample that is clearly not representative of the diverse population of students at Thurgood Marshall. Yet the kinds of socio-economically, linguistically, and ethnically diverse students served by the Academic Literacy course are those for whom a persistent achievement gap has been regularly documented (see Jencks & Phillips, 1998; Means, Chelemer, & Knapp, 1991; Williams, 1996).

Even though the course was taught by teachers with different levels of experience and from different disciplinary backgrounds, students in all of the teachers' classes made significant progress. A multivariate test of the interaction of teacher placement with change in mean DRP scores showed no statistical difference between students assigned to the different teachers in performance on these tests (F = .594, df = 3, NS). Moreover, the course was successful for all groups of students, regardless of ethnic or language background. The performance of different ethnic groups of students did not differ significantly from one another on the DRP tests, nor did their mean gain in score differ significantly from fall to spring (F = .654, df = 6, NS). The two lowest scoring groups in the fall, Latino and other non-White students, many of them Southeast Asian second-language learners, made the largest gains from fall to spring, suggesting that the course may have been especially valuable to these students.

Thus, as measured by a well-known standardized test, the Academic Literacy course had a significant impact on the reading performance of this highly diverse population of students, who developed what is normally two years of reading proficiency in only seven months of instructional time *while engaging in rigorous, academic work*. Follow-up studies show that Academic Literacy students retained their reading improvement, as measured by the DRP, continuing to grow as readers at an accelerated rate into and through their tenth-grade year.[15]

STUDENT RESPONSES TO READING SURVEYS

Additional evidence for the positive impact of Academic Literacy came from student surveys and reflective letters. We summarize their responses here, giving samples of typical student reflections and survey responses as illustrations.

After reading his pre- and post-surveys, one student wrote in a reflective letter to his teacher, "Before I didn't consider myself a good reader but now I do. I think that my attitude about reading has changed a lot 'cause since we started reading I got used to it. Now I feel more confident as a reader."

TABLE 1   *Mean DRP Scores and Mean Score Gains (delta) from Fall (F) to Spring (S) for Academic Literacy Students (n = 216)*

Paired Scores	Mean Scores	Std. Dev.	Mean delta	T-Test	Degrees of Freedom	Signifi- cance
Raw Scores	S = 47.4352 F = 43.5139	13.4270 14.1678	3.9213	7.558	215	**
Percentiles	S = 49.0741 F = 47.1389	23.9263 23.5698	1.9352	2.107	215	*
NCE Scores	S = 49.7731 F = 48.5602	15.0503 16.0773	1.2130	1.833	215	*

* $p < .05$ ** $p < .01$,

Making a similar testimony to this changed relationship to reading, a ninth-grade girl wrote, "I've learned this month that I've really started reading very good [*sic*]. I've done it so much that it's become a custom. I took both of my books everywhere I went. I even took them to Great America with me and read in the lines to get on rides." These students recognized for themselves what became clear to us in comparing the October and June survey responses of the Academic Literacy students: that students' reading ease, reading habits, and reading preferences changed profoundly as they began to read for SSR and share books with one another through official classroom projects as well as through social talk.

For example, the number of books students reported reading almost doubled from the fall to the spring, according to their pre- and post-course surveys (from 5.58 in fall to 10.99 in spring). At the same time, students gained knowledge about particular kinds of books available to them, identified favorite authors, and learned ways to select books they might find engaging. In the classroom community of readers, particular books changed hands from reader to reader, gaining popularity through reputation. By June, 80 percent of the students wrote that they actually read parts of books to inform their choices. A testimony to the sustained focus on reading and sharing books, the percentage of students who were unable to list a favorite author dropped from 42 percent in October to 20 percent by June. Importantly, author R. L. Stine and several writers of color, notably Terry McMillan, were high on the list of favorites for this diverse audience, suggesting not only that classroom libraries should reflect the cultural diversity of the students, but also that books that are attractive to teenagers while still being easy enough for independent reading (R. L. Stine is often considered to be more suitable for younger readers) should be included for the benefit of less fluent readers.

Students' survey responses revealed important "reasons to read" (Guthrie et al., 1996) that Academic Literacy students gained from their inquiries into reading: "I love to read because reading can take you to a time you did not know," "I love it because you get to go through what that character's going through," "That way you can think more and expand your mind," "I like to read, it keeps me busy," "It feels good when you finish reading a book and have memories of a life or experience that you did not have to live through," "I love to read. It helps me to understand life." In addition to these testimonies to student immersion in reading, students reconsidered the role reading will play in their futures: "I'm cool with it because the more you read, the more you become a better reader. And as time passes by, you'll probably have a successful career, and if you take the SAT proficiency test, CTBS [California Test of Basic Skills], etc., you'll do great."

By June, a full 94 percent of the Academic Literacy students said they liked or loved reading or thought reading was "okay" when asked to summarize their general feelings about this activity. Only six percent said they did not enjoy reading at the end of the school year. At the same time, there was little change in the proportion of students actually reading novels for pleasure at home. We view these responses as evidence that continuing efforts are needed to make these potential habits more robust, and to help reading compete with other attractive options for student attention, such as sports, socializing, and TV and movie viewing. Moreover, we suspect that for busy teenagers, teachers must make room for self-chosen reading in the curriculum if reading is to get done at all, and if it is to become a sustained practice for young people. Further underscoring this point, many tenth-grade students told us in follow-up interviews that even though they'd like to be reading recreationally, once they began their courses in the fall they lost any discretionary time for pleasure reading.

While Academic Literacy students described their changing motivations and attitudes toward reading, they also recognized their changing reading processes in their self-reflections and survey responses. One student explained, "What I can really do that I didn't do before is think about what the book is saying and try to reflect and give some thought to what is going on in the book instead of closing it and not thinking anything when I read it." In the beginning of the year, most students responded that to be a good reader, a person must know a lot of words, pronounce them correctly, and read fast and fluently aloud. By year's end, they increasingly saw that good readers also are mentally active, making sense of what they read and using strategies to monitor and control their reading.

As these examples suggest, overall the Academic Literacy students recognized that they were now reading more, reengaging as readers after a hiatus of several years, or engaging in reading for the first time in this year. Increasingly, they saw reading as sense-making rather than oral performance. They were more keenly aware of their own preferences, and had come to see reading as an activity they could control by using strategies and choosing books they are drawn to, rather than as a set of skills one either does or does not possess. Student responses revealed reasons to read as well as internal and external catalytic factors pushing students to pick up books. They came to value reading in new ways, and they acquired a greater sense of their own agency, responsibility, and control of how they read over the course of the school year, as well as a much more elaborate set of ideas, strategies, and resources for tackling texts of various kinds. Students' engagement in self-chosen reading, embedded as it was in a collaborative, metacognitive conversation about reading, readers, authors, and texts, made key contributions to the students' growth in Academic Literacy.

BROADER CONSIDERATIONS: TOWARD DEFINING ANDADDRESSING THE NEEDS OF ADOLESCENT READERS

In these pages, we have shared some of the ways a diverse group of urban ninth graders developed as readers in an Academic Literacy course designed to build their reading proficiency while engaging them in academically challenging coursework. Through its impact on student reading, the course demonstrates the power and promise of a framework for adolescent reading instruction — Reading Apprenticeship. Through inquiry, social mediation, and ongoing practice, Reading Apprenticeship engages students in building more complex conceptions of high-level literacy practices, increased fluency and range as readers, and broader repertoires of problem-solving strategies and approaches.

There are clear instructional implications based on the changes in student reading that we document here. Most clearly, the kinds of reading practices we ask students to engage in, as part of subject-area learning, matter because they make a difference in the resulting reading proficiencies that students develop. In Rosa's descriptions of her early experiences of reading in history classes, we see that the reading tasks assigned to her conveyed not only distinct conceptions of reading, but also specific conceptions of history itself. Rosa's "red square question" version of reading in history impoverished not only her interest in and engagement with history texts, but also her very idea of the practice of history as a discipline. History, in this view, was an exercise in retaining and reporting facts. In contrast, Rosa's reading of the totalitarianism text engaged her in a strategic and purposeful inquiry, an inquiry in which she not only had the right, but felt the responsibility, to ask why historical events occurred and why human beings acted as they did in these events. Throughout her inquiry-focused reading of this text, she was engaged in making sense of history as well as the text, carrying out a new reading practice through which she demonstrated her growing understanding of history as an interpretive discipline (e.g., Wineburg, 1991). Rosa's reading of this history text demonstrates that what we ask students to read, how we ask them to read, and to what ends, shapes not only their conceptions of reading, but also their conceptions of the disciplines.

The tools we give students to assist them in engaging successfully in these reading practices also matter. In Rosa's reading of the history textbook, her growing strategic control of the reading process is evident. Questioning, paraphrasing, and clarifying her understanding of the text, Rosa displayed key strategic moves she had been explicitly taught to make in the context of purposeful, often self-chosen, and authentic reading experiences in her Academic Literacy class. Further, in Rosa's reflections on her own reading needs, in her redirection of the reading interview, and in her descriptions of previous history reading experiences, she exhibited self-assurance and self-knowledge as a reader that grew out of her engagement in an ongoing, collaborative classroom inquiry into reading and texts.

Students' reading skills and capabilities thus matter for what students can accomplish when faced with the complex demands of academic reading. As we hope our descriptions of Reading Apprenticeship and the Academic Literacy course have made evident, we are deeply committed to helping adolescents become skillful readers. However, our conception of reading, our definition of reading skills, and our appraisal of what students need to be successful academic readers differ profoundly from the more prevalent basic-skills conceptions often found in remedial reading courses. How the problem of low literacy achievement among our nation's secondary students is defined matters a great deal because it prescribes, and often circumscribes, the ways we begin to address the problem. Skillful comprehension of various texts requires mastery of a complex set of interpretive mental activities associated with academic disciplines (e.g., Harste, 1994; Lee, 1995). These are communicative competencies that can, and must, be taught. Yet, Rosa's appraisal that "you didn't have to read" in the "red square question" version of history reading seems to illustrate the paucity of attention paid to discipline-based reading in U.S. middle and high schools.

In our view, all students need to be taught how to participate in specific reading practices and given the tools they will need to do so if they are to enter into and succeed in multiple and varied social worlds, including the worlds of the academic disciplines. The default, for children from poor, urban, minority neighborhoods, too often is a kind of basic-skills approach, resulting in a literacy ceiling that limits their academic and other opportunities. We are convinced by scholars like Lisa Delpit, (1986, 1988, 1995) and by our own experiences in nurturing and creating Reading Apprenticeships in secondary classrooms, that "if you are not already a participant in the culture of power, being told explicitly the rules of that culture makes acquiring power easier" (Delpit, 1988, p. 238). Yet all around us we see that without first offering middle and high school students a program of subject-area instruction that provides them with ongoing, skillful, teacher mediation of academic reading, educators and policymakers are prescribing skill-based remedial programs for under-achieving adolescent students. We believe this approach mislocates the problem as a failure to learn, rather than a failure to teach reading as the complex mental activity it is.

In our program of professional development with middle and high school subject-area teachers to integrate Reading Apprenticeship into ongoing subject-area instruction, we see teachers embrace new and complex conceptions of reading as well as ways to develop their students' skill as academic readers. When these teachers have opportunities to explore their own reading processes, to discover and articulate the resources and strategic mental habits they bring to reading, to share their reading processes with colleagues, and to discover patterns and contrasts among the disciplines, they build richer, more complex conceptions of reading. When they have opportunities to explore the reading performances of students like Rosa, they gain insight into what makes reading particular kinds of texts challenging for students, as well as the resources and strategies students bring to academic reading tasks. They begin to see more clearly the promise of these often underprepared students (Hull, Rose, Greenleaf, & Reilly, 1991), locating the problem of student reading in the complexity of reading itself and beginning to see texts as sites for common inquiry in their classrooms (Greenleaf, Schoenbach, Morehouse, Katz, & Mueller, 1999).

Armed with new conceptions of reading, new awareness of their own expertise as discipline-based readers, and new perceptions of students as strategic and resourceful, subject-area teachers begin to embrace, rather than resist, the teaching of reading in their subject areas. They challenge instead the constraints of curriculum coverage and the impositions of standards and exams that value student "absorption of knowledge" over student "construction of meaning" (Newmann, King, & Rigdon, 1997). They struggle to make time for reading in the curriculum-pressed subject-area classroom, where they can apprentice their students into reading in their disciplines.

Our collaborative work with subject-area teachers of diverse urban middle and high school students, as well as our evidence that students can and do develop as readers in a rigorous, meaningful curriculum, prompt us to question the necessity of basic skills approaches for the majority of secondary students who struggle with the literacy demands of the secondary curriculum. We are mindful of the history of remediation in U.S. education and its costs to the very students now purported to require remedial programs (e.g., Brown, 1991; Hull & Rose, 1989; Knapp, 1995a) and aware that such instruction has been a well-documented feature of the impoverished curriculum offered to the linguistically, culturally, and socioeconomically diverse students with whom we work (e.g., Oakes, 1985; Sizer, 1992). For the past few decades, educators concerned about inequities in educational opportunities for poor and minority students have championed important reforms aimed at detracking the curriculum to include all students in richer, more academically rigorous learning (e.g., Brown, 1991; Knapp, 1995b; Oakes, 1985). We hope our work to apprentice adolescent readers to academic literacy, and thereby help students through the literacy ceiling that limits their participation in such rigorous academic work, can help to fulfill the promise of this democratic vision.

If we as a nation care deeply about the achievement of students like Rosa, LaKeisa, Michael, and Jason, as well as the many middle and high school students like them, we must be alert to the learning opportunities they will miss as a consequence of their placement in skills-focused reading courses. These students have barely begun to benefit from a prolonged battle to reform and detrack our nation's schools in order to guarantee all students access to a rigorous academic curriculum (e.g., Brown, 1991; Hull & Rose, 1989). As we have demonstrated in these pages, investing resources and effort into demystifying academic reading through ongoing, collaborative inquiry into reading and texts can move students through and beyond the "literacy ceiling" to increased understanding, motivation, opportunity, and agency as readers and learners.

A wholesale return to remedial programs for academically underperforming students heralds the retracking of the secondary curriculum and provides unwarranted support for the enduring perception that only some students are academically capable. The costs of such proscribed instructional approaches outweigh any possible benefits when there are demonstrated alternatives. We can make significant progress in narrowing the reading achievement gap for diverse urban students, not only through courses like Academic Literacy, but also in the context of regular subject-area classes. To achieve this outcome, we must build on the strengths of our young people by inviting them to be active participants in their own learning, by demystifying the hidden processes of reading for understanding, by putting their confusion and difficulties to classroom use, and by helping them make connections between their strategic thinking and behavior outside of school and their academic performance and reading achievement inside school. Doing so will require that we invest, not in skills-based remedial programs, but in the professional development of secondary teachers, helping them to draw on their own subject-area reading expertise to nurture and sustain Reading Apprenticeships in their classrooms.

NOTES

1. Throughout this manuscript, students are given pseudonyms to protect their identities.
2. Jason refers here to Reciprocal Teaching (Palincsar & Brown, 1989), one of the instructional routines embedded in his Academic Literacy course. In Reciprocal Teaching, individual students take turns being the instructional leader — the one who either attempts or calls for questions, summaries, clarifications, and predictions about a text — hence the name, Reciprocal Teaching. Its purpose is to give students frequent and supported opportunities to practice these key comprehension processes while reading, in order to internalize these powerful strategies for making sense of texts.
3. In California middle and high schools, for instance, frequently adopted programs include Language! published by Sopris West and Corrective Reading by Science Research Associates.
4. The Strategic Literacy Initiative was formerly known as the Humanities Education, Research and Language Development (HERALD) Project in the San Francisco Unified School District, one of the Collaboratives in Humanities and Arts Teaching funded by the Rockefeller Foundation. The HERALD Project began work in 1988 to increase the

oral and written language proficiencies of the highly diverse student populations in San Francisco public high schools through a program of professional development for teachers across the high school curriculum. As we worked with high school teachers to design and implement language-rich, interdisciplinary curriculum projects to engage students in reading, writing, and constructing knowledge in various ways, teachers repeatedly expressed their concerns about student reading proficiency. In response to these concerns, we organized the Strategic Literacy Initiative, now housed at WestEd, one of the national regional laboratories. Beginning in 1995 as a teacher-researcher collaborative at the high school level involving teachers of English and history for both English-speaking students and English-language learners, the Strategic Literacy Initiative now provides inquiry-focused professional development programs for several networks of middle and high school teachers across the core curriculum of English/language arts, math, science, and history (see www. wested.org/stratlit for more information about this initiative). This article thus reflects our learning from a long history of collaborative work with teachers in urban public secondary schools.

5. We struck on the metaphor of the "literacy ceiling" not only because it calls to mind the various "job ceiling" and "glass ceiling" metaphors in common usage, but also because student competence in reading a variety of types of texts and engaging in a variety of activities with texts places a ceiling on what students can learn and do, as well as on what their teachers can hope to accomplish in the classroom.

6. Case studies were conducted collaboratively, with classroom teachers selecting a student or students for each case study and collecting data, including notes based on their review of students' cumulative records, observations of student participation in class activities, and student work samples throughout the school year. The Strategic Literacy Initiative research staff, primarily Greenleaf but also Schoenbach and Mueller, conducted audiotaped literacy history interviews and a series of videotaped reading interviews with case-study students. The teachers and researchers then worked together to identify some common patterns from this large body of case data and to create professional development materials for other teachers from the case studies.

7. See Schoenbach et al. (1999, ch. 3–6) for a more detailed description of the Academic Literacy course.

8. As part of our study of the impact of the Academic Literacy course on student reading development, we wanted to measure changes in student reading comprehension *processes*. Given the intense focus on curriculum and instruction demanded when teachers are first implementing a new curriculum, we also wanted the assessment to demand little from the teachers in the way of time and interpretation, while yielding information useful in instructional decisionmaking. Because we were not planning to conduct a controlled study and wanted to be able to speak to a broad constituency including administrators and policymakers, we sought a norm-referenced test that would measure ninth-grade student performance and progress against that of a larger population of age- and grade-matched students. The Degrees of Reading Power (DRP) test by Touchstone Applied Science Associates came closest to meeting these various criteria. The DRP test measures students' ability to "process and understand increasingly more difficult prose material" (Touchstone Applied Science Associates, 1995, p. 11), focusing on student comprehension of the surface meaning of texts in order to measure "the process of reading rather than products of reading such as main idea and author purpose" (p. 1). The test consists of nonfiction paragraphs on a variety of topics. Within these paragraphs, words have been deleted and the student is asked to select the correct word for each deletion in text from a set of multiple-choice options (a modified form of cloze passage). The items assess students' ability to use the information in the text to figure out the meaning of the text and thereby select the correct word from the multiple-choice options given. The items require that students read and understand the entire passage in order to answer correctly. Omitted words are all common words, even if

the passage is difficult; thus, failure to respond correctly should indicate failure to comprehend the passage rather than failure to understand the response options. The test is constructed to eliminate the likelihood that guessing or other nonreading activities can be used to generate correct responses.

9. These surveys are most appropriately viewed as elicitation devices, presenting students with a variety of questions, all of which required a written response by the students. Thus, they are open-ended questions, asking students to clothe their thoughts about reading in their own words. A few questions ask for quantitative responses, but the majority focus on student preferences, experiences, and beliefs about reading that may assist a teacher with instructional planning and individual recommendations.

10. Vygotsky (1978) argued that it is possible to distinguish between a child's actual or completed developmental level as demonstrated by the child's independent problem-solving on tasks, and his level of potential development when problem-solving with adult guidance or in collaboration with more capable peers. Vygotsky called the distance in performance between what a child is capable of doing independently and with guidance the "zone of proximal development" (p. 86). He argued that this zone was a concept of great utility in developmental research, permitting researchers to "delineate the child's immediate future and his dynamic developmental state, allowing not only for what already has been achieved developmentally but also for what is in the course of maturing" (p. 87). We designed the role of the interviewer in our dynamic reading assessments to provide limited support to students, giving them comprehension questions, prompting them to carry out particular comprehension strategies, and asking them to reflect on their reading processes. The interviewer was to give support on word meanings and pronunciations only as requested by the students themselves. The prompting of the interviewer thus would support the ongoing reading comprehension processes engaged in by the students, but in a limited way.

11. The numbers throughout this interview refer to line numbers in the interview transcript. They are included here for ease of reference in guiding the reader to specific parts of the interview.

12. Throughout the interview, expressions like "um-hmm" and "great" function as conversational turn-taking mechanisms (see Sacks, Schegloff, & Jefferson, 1978), giving Rosa social feedback that she is receiving the sustained attention of the interviewer (Goffman, 1964, as cited in Sacks, Schegloff, & Jefferson, 1978). Space does not permit an analysis demonstrating the function of these expressions in the interview. While these expressions may appear to be evaluative and therefore to steer Rosa's responses to the interviewer in a pre-ordained direction, they are not intended, nor are they taken by Rosa, as evaluations of her performance. Rather, they work to establish the interviewer's right to speak next. Readers familiar with conversational analysis will be familiar with these functions of speech.

13. Again, the interviewer's response here does not evaluate Rosa's reading. It certainly was not meant as a celebration of the fact that Rosa does not understand the word *totalitarianism*. Again, it is best understood as functioning to keep the interview going. At the same time, the interviewer's role is not neutral. She is guiding the interview to probe into Rosa's ability to carry out particular meaning-making strategies, giving as little help as she can while maintaining Rosa's forward movement through the text. This calibrated support is precisely what is meant by dynamic assessment. If Rosa was not able to carry out much of the meaning-making on her own, the interviewer would have to be doing much more explanation of the textual references, vocabulary, and concepts than she is doing throughout this interview. As it is, the interviewer provides a kind of procedural facilitation (Bereiter & Scardamalia, 1982), following Rosa's lead as she carries out prompted and unprompted reading strategies.

14. Reverend Niemoller, who spent seven years in concentration camps after protesting the Nazi mistreatment of Jews, wrote the following: "First they came for the Jews and I

did not speak out because I was not a Jew. Then they came for the Communists and I did not speak out because I was not a Communist. Then they came for the trade union-ists and I did not speak out because I was not a trade unionist. Then they came for me and there was no one left to speak out for me" (quoted in McGhee & Munzenmaier, 2000, p. 4).

15. In the spring of their tenth-grade year, Academic Literacy students from the 1996–1997 pilot year were asked to take another DRP test to measure whether they had re-tained the gains from the prior year. The tenth graders were enrolled in regular aca-demic and elective courses and were not given any special course in reading. Unfortu-nately, the state of California had mandated a new battery of tests, the SAT-9, and the district mandated several other standardized tests. The teachers and students alike were naturally loathe to participate in yet another test, and for this reason we were able to test a smaller population of students than we would have liked. However, for the 114 students whom we were able to retest, the results suggest that the students were given a jump start in ninth grade that continued to accelerate their reading growth into and through their tenth-grade year. The mean independent reading scores for these stu-dents increased to fifty-eight DRP units in the spring of 1998, an increase of another two years' scaled growth in reading, according to the test-makers. In addition, NCE scores from spring 1997 to spring 1998 showed significant gains (t = -3.143, df = 113, p < .05). These students continued to rise in percentile ranking to the 53rd percentile by the spring of 1998.

REFERENCES

Allen, J. (1995). *It's never too late: Leading adolescents to lifelong literacy.* Portsmouth, NH: Heinemann.

Allington, R. L. (1991). Children who find learning to read difficult: School responses to di-versity. In E. H. Hiebert (Ed.), *Literacy for a diverse society: Perspectives, practices, and policies* (pp. 237–252). New York: Teachers College Press.

Allington, R. L., & McGill-Franzen, A. (1989). School response to reading failure: Chapter 1 and special education students in grades 2, 4, and 8. *Elementary School Journal, 89,* 529–542.

Alvermann, D., & Moore, D. (1991). Secondary school reading. In R. Barr, M. L. Kamil, P. Mosenthal, & P. D. Pearson (Eds.), *Handbook of reading research* (vol. 2, pp. 951–983). New York: Longman.

Anderson, R. (1994). Role of the reader's schema in comprehension, learning, and mem-ory. In R. B. Ruddell, M. R. Ruddell, & H. Singer (Eds.), *Theoretical models and processes of reading* (4th ed., pp. 469–482). Newark, DE: International Reading Association.

Applebee, A. (1996). *Curriculum as conversation: Transforming traditions of teaching and learn-ing.* Chicago: University of Chicago Press.

Atwell, N. (1998). *In the middle: New understandings about writing, reading, and learning* (2nd ed., p. 495). Portsmouth, NH: Heinemann.

Banks, J. A. (1995). Multicultural education: Historical development, dimensions, and practice. In J. A. Banks & C. A. M. Banks (Eds.), *Handbook of research on multicultural edu-cation* (pp. 3–24). New York: Macmillan.

Barry, A. L. (1997). High school reading programs revisited. *Journal of Adolescent and Adult Literacy, 40,* 524–531.

Bartholomae, D. (1985). Inventing the university. In M. Rose (Ed.), *When a writer can't write: Studies in writer's block and other composing process problems* (pp. 134–165). New York: Guilford Press.

Baumann, J. F., & Duffy, A. M. (1997). *Engaged reading for pleasure and learning: A report from the National Reading Research Center.* Athens, GA: National Reading Research Center.

Bayer, A. S. (1990). *Collaborative apprenticeship learning: Language and thinking across the curriculum, K–12*. Mountain View, CA: Mayfield.

Beck, I. L., McKeown, M. G., Hamilton, R. L., & Kucan, L. (1997). *Questioning the author: An approach for enhancing student engagement with text*. Newark, DE: International Reading Association.

Beers, K., & Samuels, B. (1998). *Into focus: Understanding and creating middle school readers*. Norwood, MA: Christopher Gordon.

Bereiter, C., & Scardamalia, M. (1982). From conversation to composition: The role of instruction in a developmental process. In R. Glaser (Ed.), *Advances in instructional psychology* (vol. 2, pp. 1–64). Hillsdale, NJ: Lawrence Erlbaum Associates.

Berliner, D., & Biddle, B. (1995). *The manufactured crisis: Myths, fraud, and the attack on America's public schools*. Reading, MA: Addison-Wesley.

Berkowitz, S. (1986). Effects of instruction in text organization on sixth-grade students' memory for expository reading. *Reading Research Quarterly, 21*, 161–178.

Borkowski, J. G., Carr, M., Rellinger, E., & Pressley, M. (1990). Self-regulated strategy use: Interdependence of metacognition, attributions, and self-esteem. In B. F. Jones & L. Idol (Eds.), *Dimensions of thinking: Review of research* (pp. 2–60). Hillsdale, NJ: Erlbaum.

Bransford, J. (1994). Schema activation and schema acquisition. In R. B. Ruddell, M. R. Ruddell, & H. Singer (Eds.), *Theoretical models and processes of reading* (4th ed., pp. 483–495) Newark, DE: International Reading Association.

Brown, A., Palincsar, A. M., & Armbruster, B. (1994). Instructing comprehension-fostering activities in interactive learning situations. In R. B. Ruddell, M. R. Ruddell, & H. Singer (Eds.), *Theoretical models and processes of reading* (4th ed., pp. 757–787). Newark, DE: International Reading Association.

Brown, J. S., Collins, A., & Newman, S. (1989). The new cognitive apprenticeship: Teaching the craft of reading, writing, and mathematics. In L. B. Resnick (Ed.), *Knowing, learning and instruction: Essays in honor of Robert Glaser* (pp. 453–494). Hillsdale, NJ: Erlbaum.

Brown, R. G. (1991). *Schools of thought: How the politics of literacy shape thinking in the classroom*. San Francisco: Jossey-Bass.

Bruffee, K. (1984). Peer tutoring and the "conversation of mankind." *College English, 46*, 635–652.

Burke, J. (2000). *Reading reminders: Tools, tips, and techniques*. Portsmouth, NH: Heinemann.

Courts, P. L. (1997). *Multicultural literacies: Dialect, discourse, and diversity*. New York: Peter Lang.

Cope, B., & Kalantzis, M. (1993). *The powers of literacy*. Pittsburgh: University of Pittsburgh Press.

Cziko, C. (1998). Reading happens in your mind, not in your mouth: Teaching and learning "academic literacy" in an urban high school. *California English, 3*(4), 6–7.

Darling-Hammond, L. (1995). Inequality and access to knowledge. In J. A. Banks & C. A. M. Banks (Eds.), *Handbook of research on multicultural education* (pp. 465–483). New York: Macmillan.

Davidson, J., & Koppenhaver, D. (1993). *Adolescent literacy: What works and why* (2nd ed.). New York: Garland.

Delpit, L. D. (1986). Skills and other dilemmas of a progressive Black educator. *Harvard Educational Review, 56*, 379–385.

Delpit, L. D. (1988). The silenced dialogue: Power and pedagogy in educating other people's children. *Harvard Educational Review, 58*, 280–298.

Delpit, L. D. (1995). *Other people's children: Cultural conflict in the classroom*. New York: New Press.

Donahue, P. L., Voelkl, K. E., Campbell, J. R., & Mazzeo, J. (1999). *The NAEP 1998 reading report card for the nation and the states*. Washington, DC: National Center for Education Statistics.

Dowhower, S. L. (1999). Supporting a strategic stance in the classroom: A comprehension framework for helping teachers help students to be strategic. *Reading Teacher, 52,* 672–688.

Duffy, G., Roehler, L., Sivan, E., Rackliffe, G., Book, C., Meloth, M., Vavrus, L., Wesselman, R., Putnam, J., & Bassiri, D. (1994). Effects of explaining the reasoning associated with using reading strategies. *Reading Research Quarterly, 22,* 347–368.

Eeds, M., & Wells, D. (1989). Grand conversations: An exploration of meaning construction in literature study groups. *Research in the Teaching of English, 23*(10), 4–29.

Fielding, L. G., & Pearson, D. P. (1994). Reading comprehension: What works. *Educational Leadership, 51,* 62–68.

Fitzgerald, J. (1995). English-as-a-second-language learners' cognitive reading processes: A review of research in the United States. *Review of Educational Research, 65,* 145–190.

Flavell, J. H. (1976). Metacognitive dimensions of problem-solving. In L. B. Resnick (Ed.), *The nature of intelligence* (pp. 231–236). Hillsdale, NJ: Erlbaum.

Freedman, S. W., Flower, L., Hull, G., & Hayes, J. R. (1995). *Ten years of research: Achievements of the National Center for the Study of Writing and Literacy* (Technical Report No. 1-C). Berkeley, CA: National Center for the Study of Writing.

Garner, R. (1994). Metacognition and executive control. In R. B. Ruddell, M. R. Ruddell, & H. Singer (Eds.), *Theoretical models and processes of reading* (4th ed., pp. 715–732). Newark, DE: International Reading Association.

Gee, J. (1992). *The social mind: Language, ideology, and social practice.* New York: Bergin & Garvey.

Gee, J. (1996). *Social linguistics and literacies: Ideology in discourses* (2nd ed.). London: Falmer Press.

Gee, J. (1999). Critical issues: Reading and the new literacy studies. Reframing the National Academy of Science Report on Reading. *Journal of Literacy Research, 31,* 355–374.

Goatley, V. J., Brock, D. H., & Raphael, T. E. (1995). Diverse learners participating in regular education "book clubs." *Reading Research Quarterly, 30,* 352–380.

Gough, P. (1983). The beginning of decoding. *Reading and writing: An Interdisciplinary Journal, 5,* 181–192.

Gough, P., & Hillinger, M. (1980). Learning to read: An unnatural act. *Bulletin of the Orton Society, 30,* 179–196.

Gough, P., & Tumner, W. (1986). Decoding, reading, and reading disability. *Remedial and Special Education, 7,* 6–10.

Graff, H. J. (1979). *The literacy myth: Literature and social structure in the nineteenth century city.* New York: Academic Press.

Graff, H. J. (1987). *The legacies of literacy: Continuities and contradictions in Western culture and society.* Bloomington: University of Indiana Press.

Greenleaf, C., Hull, G., & Reilly, B. (1994). Learning from our diverse students: Helping teachers rethink problematic teaching and learning situations. *Teaching and Teacher Education, 10,* 521–541.

Greenleaf, C., & Schoenbach, R. (2000, March). Tapping the developmental strengths of adolescence: A reading apprenticeship approach to academic literacy. In *Proceedings from the Secondary Reading Symposium.* Washington, DC: Office of Educational Research and Innovation.

Greenleaf, C., Schoenbach, R., Cziko, C., & Mueller, F. (1999, April). *Apprenticing adolescents to academic literacy.* Paper presented at the annual meeting of the American Educational Research Association, Montreal.

Greenleaf, C., Schoenbach, R., Morehouse, L., Katz, M., & Mueller, F. (1999, April). *Close readings: Developing inquiry tools and practices for generative professional development.* Paper presented at the annual meeting of the American Educational Research Association, Montreal.

Grossman, P. (1990). What are we talking about anyway? Subject matter knowledge of secondary English teachers. In J. Brophy (Ed.), *Advances in research on teaching: Teacher's subject matter knowledge and classroom instruction* (vol. 2, pp. 245–264). Greenwich, CT: JAI Press.

Grossman, P. L., & Shulman, L. S. (1994). Knowing, believing, and the teaching of English. In T. Shanahan (Ed.), *Teachers thinking, teachers knowing: Reflections on literacy and language education* (pp. 3–22). Urbana, IL: National Council of Teachers of English.

Guthrie, J. T., & Alvermann, D. E. (1991). *Engaged reading: Processes, practices, and policy implications.* New York: Teachers College Press.

Guthrie, J., & Greaney, V. (1991). Literacy acts. In R. Barr, M. L. Kamil, P. Mosenthal, & P. D. Pearson (Eds.), *Handbook of reading research* (vol. 2, pp. 68–96). New York: Longman.

Guthrie, J. T., McGough, K., Bennett, L., & Rice, M. E. (1996). Concept-oriented reading instruction: An integrated curriculum to develop motivations and strategies for reading. In L. Baker, P. Afflerbach, & D. Reinking (Eds.), *Developing engaged readers in school and home communities* (pp. 165–190). Mahwah, NJ: Lawrence Erlbaum Associates.

Guthrie, J., Schafer, W., & Hutchinson, S. (1991). Relations of document literacy and prose literacy to occupational and societal characteristics of young Black and White adults. *Reading Research Quarterly, 26,* 30–48.

Guthrie, J. T., & Wigfield, A. (Eds.). (1997). *Reading engagement: Motivating readers through integrated instruction.* Newark, DE: International Reading Association.

Harste, J. C. (1994). Literacy as curricular conversations about knowledge, inquiry, and morality. In R. B. Ruddell, M. R. Ruddell, & H. Singer (Eds.), *Theoretical models and processes of reading* (4th ed., pp. 1220–1242) Newark, DE: International Reading Association.

Heath, S. B. (1983). *Ways with words: Language, life, and work in communities and classrooms.* Cambridge, Eng.: Cambridge University Press.

Hiebert, E. (1991). *Literacy for a diverse society: Perspectives, policies, and practices.* New York: Teachers College Press.

Hillocks, G., Jr. (1995). *Teaching writing as reflective practice.* New York: Teachers College Press.

Hourigan, M. (1994). *Literacy as social exchange: Intersections of class, gender, and culture.* New York: State University of New York.

Hull, G. A. (1989). Research on writing: Building a cognitive and social understanding of composing. In L. B. Resnick & L. E. Klopfer (Eds.), *Toward the thinking curriculum: Current cognitive research, 1989 ASCD yearbook* (pp. 104–128). Alexandria, VA: Association for Supervision and Curriculum Development.

Hull, G. A., & Rose, M. (1989). Rethinking remediation: Toward a social-cognitive understanding of problematic reading and writing. *Written Communication, 8,* 139–154.

Hull, G. A., Rose, M., Greenleaf, C., & Reilly, B. (1991). Seeing the promise of the underprepared. *Quarterly of the National Writing Project and the Center for the Study of Writing and Literacy, 13,* 6–13, 25.

International Reading Association. (1999a). Adolescent literacy comes of age. *Reading Today, 17*(1), 1, 22.

International Reading Association. (1999b). *Summary of "Adolescent literacy, a position statement for the Commission on Adolescent Literacy of the International Reading Association."* Available: http://www.ira.org/advocacy/policies/adol_lit.html

Jencks, C., & Phillips, M. (Eds.). (1998). *The Black-White test score gap.* Washington, DC: Brookings Institution.

Keene, E. O., & Zimmermann, S. (1997). *Mosaic of thought: Teaching comprehension in a reader's workshop.* Portsmouth, NH: Heinemann.

Knapp, M. S. (1995). *Teaching for meaning in high-poverty classrooms.* New York: Teachers College Press.

Knapp, M. S., Shields, P. S. & Turnbull, B. J. (1995). Academic challenge in high poverty classrooms. *Phi Delta Kappan, 76,* 770–776.

Knapp, M. S., & Turnbull, B. (1991). *Better schools for the children in poverty: Alternatives to conventional wisdom.* Berkeley, CA: McCutchan.

Konopak, B. C., Wilson, E. K., & Readence, J. E. (1994). Examining teachers' beliefs, decisions, and practices about content-area reading in secondary social studies. In C. K. Kinzer & D. J. Leu (Eds.), *Multidimensional aspects of literacy research, theory, and practice.* (pp. 127–136). Chicago: National Reading Conference.

Krieger, L. S., & Neill, K. (1994). *Issues of the modern age.* Lexington, MA: D. C. Heath.

Kucan, L., & Beck, I. L. (1997). Thinking aloud and reading comprehension research: Inquiry, instruction, and social interaction. *Review of Educational Research, 67,* 271–299.

Kuhn, M. R., & Stahl, S. A. (2000). *Fluency: A review of developmental and remedial practices* (Report No. 2-008). Ann Arbor, MI: Center for the Improvement of Early Reading Achievement.

Langer, J. (1995). *Envisioning literature.* New York: Teachers College Press.

Langer, J. A., Confer, C., & Sawyer, M. (1993). *Teaching disciplinary thinking in academic coursework* (Report Series 2.19). Albany, NY: National Research Center on English Learning and Achievement.

Lave, J., & Wenger, E. (1991). *Situated learning: Legitimate peripheral participation.* Cambridge, Eng.: Cambridge University Press.

Lee, C. (1995). A culturally based cognitive apprenticeship: Teaching African American high school students skills in literary interpretation. *Reading Research Quarterly, 30,* 608–630.

Lemke, J. L. (1990). *Talking science: Language, learning, and values.* Norwood, NJ: Ablex.

Levin, H. (1997). *Powerful learning: Conceptual foundations.* Stanford, CA: Stanford University, National Center for the Accelerated Schools Project.

Manzo, K. K. (1998, April 29). More states moving to make phonics the law. *Education Week,* pp. 24, 27.

McGee, M., & Munzenmaier, C. (Eds.) (2000). *Voices of the Holocaust* (p. 4). Logan, IA: Perfection Learning Corporation.

McKenna, M. C., Kear, D. J., & Ellsworth, R. A. (1995). Children's attitudes toward reading: A national survey. *Reading Research Quarterly, 30,* 934–956.

McQuillan, J. (1998). *The literacy crisis: False claims, real solutions.* Portsmouth, NH: Heinemann.

Means, B., Chelemer, C., & Knapp, M. (1991). *Teaching advanced skills to at-risk students: Views from research and practice.* San Francisco: Jossey-Bass.

Moje, E. B., Dillon, D. R., & O'Brien, D. G. (2000). Re-examining the roles of the learner, the text, and the context in secondary literacy. *Journal of Educational Research, 93,* 165–180.

Moje, E. B., & Wade, S. E. (1997). What case discussions reveal about teacher thinking. *Teaching and Teacher Education, 13,* 691–712.

Moje, E. B., Young, J. P., Readence, J. E., & Moore, D. W. (2000). Reinventing adolescent literacy for new times: Perennial and millennial issues. *Journal of Adolescent and Adult Literacy, 43,* 400–410.

Moore, D. W., Bean, T. W., Birdyshaw, D., & Rycik, J. A. (1999). *Adolescent literacy: A position statement for the Commission on Adolescent Literacy of the International Reading Association.* Newark, DE: International Reading Association.

Mullis, I. V., Dossey, A., Campbell, J. R., Gentile, C. A., O'Sullivan, C., & Latham, A. S. (1994). *NAEP 1992 trends in academic progress* (Report No. 23-TR01). Washington, DC: U.S. Government Printing Office.

Myers, M. (1998). *Changing our minds: Negotiating English and literacy.* Urbana, IL: National Council of Teachers of English.

National Reading Panel. (2000). *Teaching children to read: An evidence-based assessment of the scientific research literature on reading and its implications for reading instruction.* Washington, DC: National Institute on Child Health and Human Development.

New London Group. (1996). A pedagogy of multiliteracies: Designing social futures. *Harvard Educational Review, 66,* 60–92.

Newmann, F., King, B., & Rigdon, M. (1997). Accountability and school performance: Implications from restructuring schools. *Harvard Educational Review, 67,* 41–74.

Oakes, J. (1985) *Keeping track: How schools structure inequality.* New Haven, CT: Yale University Press.

Ohmann, R. (1987). *The politics of letters.* Middletown, CT: Wesleyan University Press.

Palincsar, A. S., & Brown, A. L. (1989). Instruction for self-regulated reading. In L. B. Resnick & L. E. Klopfer (Eds.), *Toward the thinking curriculum: Current cognitive research* (pp. 19–39). Alexandria, VA: Association for Supervision and Curriculum Development.

Pearson, P. D. (1996). Reclaiming the center. In M. Graves, P. van den Broek, & B. M. Taylor (Eds.), *The first R: Every child's right to read* (pp. 259–274). New York: Teacher's College Press.

Pressley, M. (1998). *Reading instruction that works: The case for balanced teaching.* New York: Guilford Press.

Pressley, M., El-Dinary, P. B., Gaskins, I., Schuder, T., Berman, J. L., Almasi, J. L., & Brown, R. (1992). Beyond direct explanation: Transactional instruction of reading comprehension strategies. *Elementary School Journal, 92,* 513–555.

Rabinowitz, P. J., & Smith, M. (1998). *Authorizing readers: Resistance and respect in the teaching of literature.* New York: Teachers College Press.

Roehler, L., & Duffy, G. (1991). Teachers' instructional actions. In R. Barr, M. L. Kamil, P. Mosenthal, & P. D. Pearson (Eds.), *Handbook of reading research* (vol. 2, pp. 861–883). New York: Longman.

Rogoff, B. (1990). *Apprenticeship in thinking: Cognitive development in social context.* New York: Oxford University Press.

Rose, M. (1985). *When a writer can't write: Studies in writer's block and other composing process problems.* New York: Guilford Press.

Rosenshine, B., & Meister, C. (1994). Reciprocal reaching: A review of the research. *Review of Educational Research, 64,* 479–530.

Sacks, H., Schegloff, E., & Jefferson, G. (1978). A simplest systematics for the organization of turn taking for conversation. In J. Schenkein (Ed.), *Studies in the organization of conversational interaction* (pp. 7–55). New York: Academic Press.

Schoenbach, R., & Greenleaf, C. (2000, March). Tapping teachers' reading expertise: Generative professional development with middle and high school content-area teachers. In *Proceedings from the Secondary Reading Symposium.* Washington, DC: Office of Educational Research and Innovation (Report No. ED-99-CO-0154, B-5).

Schoenbach, R., Greenleaf, C., Cziko, C., & Hurwitz, L. (1999). *Reading for understanding: A guide to improving reading in middle and high school classrooms.* San Francisco: Jossey-Bass.

Scott, J. (1993). *Science and language links: Classroom implications.* Portsmouth, NH: Heinemann.

Scriber, S., & Cole, M. (1981). *The psychology of literacy.* Cambridge, MA: Harvard University Press.

Stahl, S. A., Duffy-Hester, A., & Stahl, K. (1998). Everything you wanted to know about phonics (but were afraid to ask). *Reading Research Quarterly, 33,* 338–355.

Sizer, T. (1992). *Horace's compromise: The dilemma of the American high school.* Boston: Houghton Mifflin.

Snow, C., Burns, S., & Griffin, P. (1998). *Preventing reading difficulties in young children.* Washington, DC: National Academy Press.

Street, B. (1984). *Literacy in theory and practice.* London: Cambridge University Press.

Taylor, B. M. (1992). Text structure, comprehension, and recall. In S. J. Samuels & A. E. Farstrup (Eds.), *What research has to say about reading instruction* (2nd ed., pp. 220–228). Newark, DE: International Reading Association.

Taylor, B. M., Anderson, R. C., Au, K. H., & Raphael, T. E. (1999). *Discretion in the translation of reading research to policy* (Report No. 3-006). Ann Arbor, MI: Center for the Improvement of Early Reading Achievement

Templeton, S., Beer, D., Invernizzi, M., & Johnston, F. (1996). *Words their way: Word study for phonics, vocabulary, and spelling instruction*. Englewood Cliffs, NJ: Prentice-Hall.

Touchstone Applied Science Associates. (1995). *DRP handbook: G & H test forms*. Brewster, NY: Touchstone Applied Science Associates.

Vygotsky, L. S. (1978). *Mind in society*. Cambridge, MA: Harvard University Press.

Vygotsky, L. S. (1986). *Thought and language* (rev. ed.). Cambridge, MA: MIT Press.

Wells, G., & Chang-Wells, G. L. (1992). *Constructing knowledge together: Classrooms as centers of inquiry and literacy*. Portsmouth, NH: Heinemann.

Wilhelm, J. D. (1997). *You gotta be the book: Teaching engaged and reflective reading with adolescents*. New York: Teachers College Press.

Williams, B. (1996). *Closing the achievement gap: A vision for changing beliefs and practices*. Alexandria, VA: Association for Supervision and Curriculum Development.

Wilson, S. M., & Wineburg, S. S. (1988). Peering at history through different lenses: The role of disciplinary perspectives in teaching history. *Teachers College Record, 89,* 525–539.

Wineburg, S. S. (1991). On the reading of historical texts: Notes on the breach between school and academy. *American Educational Research Journal, 28,* 495–519.

Wineburg, S. S., & Wilson, S. M. (1990). Subject matter knowledge in the teaching of history. In J. Brophy (Ed.), *Advances in research on teaching: Vol 2. Teacher's subject matter knowledge and classroom instruction*. Greenwich, CT: JAI Press.

The work described in these pages has received the invaluable support of the Spencer/MacArthur Program in Professional Development Research and Documentation, the Stuart Foundations, the William and Flora Hewlett Foundation, the San Francisco Foundation, the Gabilan Foundation, and WestEd, a nonprofit educational research and development agency serving communities and schools. We are wealthy indeed in our colleagues Jane Braunger, Peg Griffin, Marean Jordan, and Mira Katz, whose careful readings of numerous drafts of this article have helped us bring our ideas into clearer focus. We are also grateful to Sarah Burns for encouraging us to write this article. Finally, we thank the anonymous reviewers and the editorial staff of the *Harvard Educational Review* for their assistance in making this article a more powerful representation of our work.

Appendix A

INTERVIEW PROTOCOL FOR READING EXPOSITION

ISSUES OF THE MODERN AGE

Chapter 5: Totalitarianism in the Modern World, p. 88

Section 2. Totalitarianism turned hate into genocide.

Ms. Cziko said you read this section individually and wrote questions, summaries, clarifications, and predictions for each paragraph. Is that right? Did you get a chance to do that?

What do you remember about this part? [allow time to look back over it if needed] If you had to say what the main ideas of this passage were, what would you say?

There are some descriptions in here of violent action against different groups of people. What do you think about when you read these descriptions? Do you have any personal experiences, family stories, or other connections to this kind of anti-group violence?

Were there any words or parts that were confusing for you?

Do you know what the Inquisition was? Do you have any idea what that refers to?

What do you think a totalitarian state is?

Okay, let's go on to the next section.

Propaganda and indoctrination orchestrated feelings.

Take a look at the heading and tell me what you predict you will read about in this section.

Do you have any idea what propaganda is? Indoctrination? What do you think the phrase, "Propaganda and indoctrination orchestrated feelings" might mean?

Okay, please read this section aloud.

1. Retelling: In your own words, tell me what you just read.
2. Clarifying: Was there anything that didn't make sense to you in what you just read? Any words that you weren't sure of?
3. Summarizing: What do you think were the major points the author wanted to get across in this section? Why do you think these are the major points?
4. Making connections: Can you think of any examples of propaganda? How about indoctrination? What do you think is the difference between these two things?

5. Text awareness: This section talks about the effects of propaganda and indoctrination. Who is it that carries out the propaganda? Who indoctrinates the people? Who is it that gets indoctrinated? Who are the victims of propaganda?

6. Recalling facts, drawing inferences: According to this section, which totalitarian states took over complete control of children's education? Is that important? Why?

Fear and isolation paralyzed resistance.

Take a look at the heading and tell me what you predict you will read about in this section.

Do you know what that phrase might mean? "Fear and isolation paralyzed resistance?" How can fear and isolation paralyze? Who is it that is afraid? Isolated? What is resistance? Who is it that resists?

Okay, read this section silently.

1. Retelling: Okay, what was that section about?

2. Clarifying: Were there any words or phrases or ideas that didn't make sense to you or that you weren't sure of?

3. Background knowledge: What is the Stalinist terror? The Gulag Archipelago? Do you have any idea? Have you ever heard of Alexander Solzhenitsyn? Who would you guess he was?

4. Summarizing: What do you think were the major points the author wanted to get across in this section? How did you pick these out as the major points?

5. Recalling facts: According to Solzhenitsyn, what could have stopped the Stalinist security operatives from arresting citizens?

6. Interpreting language: What does this phrase mean: "The cursed machine would have ground to a halt!"?

7. Interpreting language: How about the phrase, "The dictators used terror to demoralize the people and made an example of any individual who protested"?

8. Interpreting language: What does it mean, "As each group in turn bore the brunt of persecution, other groups comforted themselves"?

9. Text awareness: Why does that paragraph look different from the rest of the text? Why did the author put this in the book? What do you think is its purpose in this section? What makes you think that?

10. Strategies: When I asked you to read this section silently, what was the first thing you did? How did you go about reading? What did you think about? Did you look for particular ideas? Did you skip around? Did you read some parts first and then read the whole thing? Did you ask yourself questions? Test your understanding in any way? Put things into your own words? Form any mental pictures? Try to remember anything in particular?

Blind Vision: Unlearning Racism
in Teacher Education

▼▼▼▼▼

MARILYN COCHRAN-SMITH

Literary theorist Barbara Hardy (1978) once asserted that narrative ought not be regarded as an "aesthetic invention used by artists to control, manipulate, and order experience, but as a primary act of mind transferred to art from life" (p. 12). Elaborating on the primacy of narrative in both our interior and exterior lives, Hardy suggests that

> storytelling plays a major role in our sleeping and waking lives. We dream in narrative, daydream in narrative, remember, anticipate, hope, despair, believe, doubt, plan, revise, criticize, construct, gossip, learn, hate and love by narrative. (p. 13)

From this perspective, narrative can be regarded as locally illuminating, a central way we organize and understand experience (Mishler, 1986; Van Manen, 1990). It is also a primary way we construct our multiple identities as human beings for whom race, gender, class, culture, ethnicity, language, ability, sexual orientation, role, and position make a profound difference in the nature and interpretation of experience (Tatum, 1997; Thompson & Tyagi, 1996).

In this article, I explore and write about *un*learning racism in teaching and teacher education. I do not begin in the scholarly tradition of crisply framing an educational problem by connecting it to current policy and practice and/or to the relevant research literature. Instead, I begin with a lengthy narrative based on my experiences as a teacher educator at a moment in time when issues of race and racism were brought into unexpectedly sharp relief. I do so with the assumption that narrative is not only locally illuminating, as Hardy's work suggests, but also that it has the capacity to contain and entertain within it contradictions, nuances, tensions, and complexities that traditional academic discourse with its expository stance and more distanced impersonal voice cannot (Fine, 1994; Gitlin, 1994; Metzger, 1986).

The idea that racism is something that all of us have inevitably learned simply by living in a racist society is profoundly provocative (King, Hollins, & Hayman, 1997; McIntosh, 1989; Tatum, 1992). For many of us, it challenges

Harvard Educational Review Vol. 70 No. 2 Summer 2000, 157–190

not only our most precious democratic ideals about equitable access to opportunity, but also our most persistent beliefs in the possibilities of school and social change through enlightened human agency (Apple, 1996; Giroux, 1988; Leistyna, Woodrum, & Sherblom, 1996; Noffke, 1997). Perhaps even more provocative is the position that part of our responsibility as teachers and teacher educators is to struggle along with others in order to *un*learn racism (Britzman, 1991; Cochran-Smith, 1995a; Sleeter, 1992), or to interrogate the racist assumptions that may be deeply embedded in our own courses and curricula, to own our own complicity in maintaining existing systems of privilege and oppression, and to grapple with our own failures to produce the kinds of changes we advocate. Attempting to make the unending process of *un*learning racism explicit and public is challenging and somewhat risky. Easily susceptible to misinterpretation and misrepresentation, going public involves complex nuances of interpretation, multiple layers of contradiction, competing perspectives, and personal exposure (Cochran-Smith, 1995b; Cole & Knowles, 1998; Rosenberg, 1997). I go public with the stories in this article not because they offer explicit directions for unlearning racism, but because they pointedly suggest some of the most complex questions we need to wrestle with in teacher education: In our everyday lives as teachers and teacher educators, how are we complicit — intentionally or otherwise — in maintaining the cycles of oppression (Lawrence & Tatum, 1997) that operate daily in our courses, our universities, our schools, and our society? Under what conditions is it possible to examine, expand, and alter long-standing (and often implicit) assumptions, attitudes, beliefs, and practices about schools, teaching, students, and communities? What roles do collaboration, inquiry, self-examination, and story play in learning of this kind? As teacher educators, what should we say about race and racism, what should we have our students read and write? What should we tell them about who can teach whom, who can speak for whom, and who has the right to speak at all about racism and teaching?

BLIND VISION: A STORY FROM A TEACHER EDUCATOR

A White European American woman, I taught for many years at the University of Pennsylvania, a large research university in urban Philadelphia whose population was predominantly White, but whose next-door neighbors in west Philadelphia were schools and communities populated by African Americans and Asian immigrants. Seventy-five to 80 percent of the students I taught were White European Americans, but they worked as student teachers primarily in the public schools of Philadelphia where the population was often mostly African American or — in parts of north and northeast Philadelphia — mostly Latino. In those schools that appeared on the surface to be more ideally integrated, the racial tension was sometimes intense, with individual groups insulated from or even hostile toward one another.

The teacher education program I directed had for years included in the curriculum an examination of race, class, and culture and the ways these structure both the U.S. educational system and the experiences of individuals in that system.[1] For years my students read Comer (1989), Delpit (1986, 1988), Giroux (1984), Heath (1982 a, 1982b), Ogbu (1978), as well as Asante (1991), McIntosh (1989), Moll, Amanti, Neff, and Gonzalez (1992), Rose (1989), Sleeter and Grant (1987), Tatum (1992), and others who explore issues of race, class, culture, and language from critical and other perspectives. I thought that the commitment of my program to urban student-teaching placements and to devoting a significant portion of the curriculum to issues of race and racism gave me a certain right to speak about these issues as a teacher educator. I thought this with some degree of confidence until an event occurred that was to change forever the way I thought about racism and teacher education. This event was to influence the work I did with colleagues in the Penn program over the next six years, as well as the work in which I am presently engaged as a teacher educator at Boston College, where I collaborate with other teacher educators, teachers, and student teachers in the Boston area.

The event that is described in the following narrative occurred at the end of a two-hour student teaching seminar that was held biweekly for the thirty-some students in the Penn program at the time.[2]

*   *   *   *   *

We had come to the end of a powerful presentation about the speaker's personal experiences with racism, both as a young Native boy in an all-White class and later as the single minority teacher in a small rural school. The presentation had visibly moved many of us. The guest speaker — a Native American who worked in a teacher education program at another university — asked my student teachers about their program at Penn. I had no qualms. Our program was well known and well received. Students often raved about it to visitors from outside. Knowing and sharing the commitment of my program to exploring issues of race, my guest asked in the last few minutes of our two-hour seminar, "And what does this program do to help you examine questions about race and racism in teaching and schooling?" Without hesitation, one student teacher, a Puerto Rican woman, raised her hand and said with passion and an anger that bordered on rage, "Nothing! This program does *nothing* to address issues of race!" After a few seconds of silence that felt to me like hours, two other students — one African American and one Black South African — agreed with her, adding their frustration and criticism to the first comment and indicating that we read nothing and said nothing that addressed these questions. I was stunned. With another class waiting to enter the room, students — and I — quickly exited the room.

My first responses to this event included every personally defensive strategy I could muster. In the same way that my students sometimes did, I identified and equated myself with "the program." And in certain important ways, I suppose I *was* the program in that I had been the major architect of its social and organizational structures, and I was ultimately responsible for its decisions. I relived the final moments of the seminar, turning the same thoughts over and over in my head: How could she say that? How could others agree? After all, the compelling presentation we had all just heard was in and of itself evidence that we addressed issues of race in our program. And besides, just a few days earlier, she and a group of five other women students had presented a paper at a teacher research conference at Penn. They had chosen to be part of an inquiry group that was to write a paper about race and their student-teaching experiences because I had invited them to, I had suggested the topic. They had used the data of their writing and teacher research projects from my class to examine the impact of race and racism on their student-teaching experiences. How could she say that?

I counted up the ongoing efforts I had made to increase the diversity in our supervisory staff and in our pool of cooperating teachers. I had insisted that we send student teachers to schools where the population was nearly 100 percent African American and Latino, schools that some colleagues cautioned me were too tough for student teachers, that some student teachers complained were too dangerous, and one had once threatened to sue me if I made her go there even for a brief field visit. I talked about issues of race openly and, I thought, authentically in my classes — all of them, no matter what the course title or the topic. I thought about the individual and personal efforts I had made on behalf of some of those students — helping them get scholarships, intervening with cooperating teachers or supervisors, working for hours with them on papers, lending books and articles. I constructed a long and convincing mental argument that I was one of the people on the right side of this issue. Nobody can do everything, and I was sure that I already paid more attention to questions of racism and teaching than did many teacher educators. How could she say that? I was stunned by what had happened, and deeply hurt — surprised as much as angry.

During the first few days after that seminar session, many students — most of them White — stopped by my office to tell me that they thought we were indeed doing a great deal to address issues of race and racism in the program, but they had clearly heard the outrage and dissatisfaction of their fellow students and they wanted to learn more, to figure out what we should do differently. Some students — both White students and students of color — stopped by or wrote notes saying that they thought we were currently doing exactly what we should be doing to address issues of race in the program. And a few students — all White — stopped by to say that all we ever talked about in the program and in my classes was race and racism and what they really wanted to know was when we were going to learn how to teach reading.

I knew that the next meeting of the seminar group would be a turning point for me and for the program. I struggled with what to say, how to proceed, what kind of stance I needed to take and would be able to take. I knew that I needed to open (not foreclose) the discussion, to acknowledge the frustration and anger (even the rage) that had been expressed, and, above all, I knew that I needed not to be defensive. I felt very heavy — it was clear to me that I was about to teach my student teachers one of the most important lessons I would ever teach them. I was about to teach them how a White teacher, who — notwithstanding the rhetoric in my classes about collaboration, shared learning, and co-construction of knowledge — had a great deal of power over their futures in the program and in the job market, how that White teacher, who fancied herself pretty liberal and enlightened, responded when confronted directly and angrily about some of the issues of race that were right in front of her in her own teaching and her own work as a teacher educator.

The very different responses of my students and my own shock and hurt at some of those responses pointed out to me on a visceral level the truth that many of the articles we were reading in class argued on a more intellectual level: how we are positioned in terms of race and power vis-à-vis others has a great deal to do with how we see, what we see or want to see, and what we are able not to see. I thought of Clifford Geertz's discussion of the difficulties involved in representing insider knowledge and meaning perspectives. He suggests that, ultimately, anthropologists cannot really represent "local knowledge" — what native inhabitants see — but only what they see through; that is, their interpretive perspectives on their own experiences. This situation laid bare the enormous differences between what I — and people differently situated from me — saw and saw through as we constructed our lives as teachers and students.

I didn't decide until right before the seminar exactly what I would say. I had thought of little else during the week. I felt exposed, failed, trapped, and completely inadequate to the task. In the end, I commented briefly then opened up the two hours for students to say whatever they wished. I tried to sort out and say back as clearly as I could both what I had heard people say at the seminar and the quite disparate responses I had heard in the ensuing week. It was clear from these, I said, that nobody speaks for anybody or everybody else. As I spoke, I tried not to gloss over the scathing critique or make the discrepancies appear to be less discrepant than they were. Especially for many of the students of color in the program, I said that I had clearly heard that there was a feeling of isolation, of being silenced, a feeling that we had not dealt with issues of race and racism in a "real" way — briefly perhaps, but in ways that were too intellectualized and theoretical rather than personal and honest. Notwithstanding the view expressed by some students that all we ever talked about was race, I reported a strong consensus that an important conversation had been opened up and needed to continue, although I also noted that it was clear some conversations about race and racism, maybe the most important ones, could not be led by me, a White teacher.

I concluded by saying that despite my deep commitments to an antiracist curriculum for all students, whether children or adults, and despite my inten-

tions to promote constructive discourse about the issues in teacher education, I realized I didn't "get it" some (or much) of the time. This seemed to be
one of those times. I admitted that these things were hard, uncomfortable,
and sometimes even devastating to hear, but we needed to hear, to listen
hard, and to stay with it.

What I remember most vividly about that seminar are the tension and the
long silence that followed my comments and my open invitation to others to
speak. My seminar co-leader (and friend) told me later that she was sure we
all sat in silence for at least twenty minutes (my watch indicated that about
three minutes had passed). The same woman who had responded so angrily
the week before spoke first, thanking us for hearing and for providing time
for people to name the issues. Others followed. All of the women of color in
the program spoke, most of them many times. A small portion of the White
students participated actively. Students critiqued their inner-city school
placements, describing the inability or unwillingness of some of the experienced teachers at their schools to talk about issues of race and racism, to be
mentors to them about these issues. They said we needed more cooperating
teachers and more student teachers of color. They spoke of middle-class,
mostly White teachers treating poor children, mostly children of color, in
ways that were abrupt and disrespectful at best, reprehensible and racist at
worst. Some spoke passionately about the disparities they had observed between their home schools and the schools they had cross-visited — disparities
in resources and facilities, but even more in the fundamental ways teachers
treated children in poor urban schools on the one hand, and in middle-class
urban or suburban schools on the other. They complained that our Penn faculty and administrators were all White, naming and counting up each of us
and assuming I had the power and authority, but not the will, to change
things. They said that the lack of faculty of color and the small number of students of color in the program gave little validation to the issues they wished to
raise as women and prospective teachers of color. Many of them were angry,
bitter. They spoke with a certain sense of unity as if their scattered, restrained
voices had been conjoined, unleashed.

The coleader and I avoided eye contact with one another, our faces serious
and intense but carefully trying not to signal approval or disapproval, agreement or disagreement. Many White students were silent, some almost ashen.
Some seemed afraid to speak. One said people were at different levels with issues of race and racism, implying that others in the room might not understand but that she herself was beyond that. Another commented that she too
had experienced racism, especially because her boyfriend was African American. One said that when she looked around her student-teaching classroom,
she saw only children, not color. Another complained that she didn't see why
somebody couldn't just tell her what she didn't get so she could just get it and
get on with teaching. I cringed inside at some of these comments, while several of the women of color rolled their eyes, whispered among themselves.
One who was older than most of the students in the program eventually

stopped making any attempt to hide her hostility and exasperation. She was openly disdainful in her side comments. Finally, a young White woman, with clear eyes and steady voice, turned to the older woman and said she was willing to hear any criticism, any truth about herself, but she wanted it said in front of her, to her face. The only man of color in the program, who sat apart from the other students, said all he wanted to do was to be an effective teacher. He did not want to be seen as a Black male teacher and a role model for Black children, but as a good teacher. Others immediately challenged him on the impossibility and irresponsibility of that stance.

For nearly two hours, the tension in the room was palpable, raw. As leaders we said little, partly because we had little idea what to say, partly because we had agreed to open up the time to the students. We nodded, listened, took notes. Toward the end, we asked for suggestions — how the group wanted to spend the two or three seminar sessions remaining in the year that had any flexibility in terms of topic, schedule, or speakers. We asked for recommendations. There were many suggestions but only a few that we could actually do something about in the six weeks or so that remained before the students graduated, given the already full schedule and the final press of certification and graduation details. (Many of the suggestions that we took up in the following year are described in the remainder of this article. For the current year, we opened up discussion time and included student teachers in planning and evaluation groups.)

Two students wrote me letters shortly after this seminar. One was appreciative, one was disgusted. Both, I believe, were heartfelt. A White woman wrote: "When you began to speak at the last seminar, I held my breath. The atmosphere in the room was so loaded, so brooding. It felt very unsafe. What would you say? What could you say? It would have been so very easy at this point to retreat into academe — to play The Professor, The Program Director, and not respond or address the fact that there were painful unresolved issues to be acknowledged, if not confronted. . . . Instead you responded honestly and openly, telling us how you were thinking about things, how you felt and the dilemmas you encountered as you too struggled to 'get it.' . . . Your words were carefully considered . . . and seemed spoken not without some cost to you." In contrast, a White man wrote:

> After this evening's seminar, I thought I would drop you this note to let you know how I react to the issues that were (and were not) confronted. . . . To be honest, I feel that the critical issues of race and racism have been made apparent and important in my studies . . . since I began [the program]. That they should have been made the fulcrum point of the curriculum and each course is problematic. I would say no; others (more vehemently) would insist on it. . . . I really have no idea how to most effectively proceed. I do know one thing. I am committed to bringing issues of race into my classroom, wherever I may teach. However, being nonconfrontational by nature, and with sincere respect for the opinions of my fellow students, I will probably not attend another session about this. Frankly, I, my students, and my career in education

will benefit a lot more by staying at home and spending a few hours trying to integrate multicultural issues into my lesson plans than they will by talking one more time about race.

* * * * *

It would be an understatement to say that these events were galvanizing as well as destabilizing for me, for the people I worked closely with, and for the students who graduated just six weeks later. Everything was called into question — what we thought we were about as a program, who we were as a community, what learning opportunities were available in our curriculum, whose interests were served, whose needs were met, and whose were not. But it would be inaccurate to say that these events *caused* changes in the program over the next six years or that we proceeded from this point in a linear way, learning from our "mistakes" and then correcting them. Although the story of "so then what happened?" is of course chronological in one sense, it is decidedly *not* a story of year-by-year, closer and closer approximations of "the right way" to open and sustain a discourse about race and racism in teacher education programs aimed at preparing both students of color and White students to be teachers in both urban and other schools. Rather, the story is an evolving, recursive, and current one about what it means to grapple with the issues of racism and teaching in deeper and more uncertain ways.

It is also important to say, I think, that the above account of what happened is a fiction, not reality or truth, but my interpretation of my own and other people's experience in a way that makes sense to me and speaks for me. Although part of my intention in telling this story is to uncover my failure and unravel my complicity in maintaining the existing system of privilege and oppression, it is impossible for me to do so without sympathy for my own predicament. My experience as a first-generation-to-college, working-class girl who pushed into a middle-class, highly educated male profession has helped give me some vision about the personal and institutional impact of class and gender differences on work, status, and ways of knowing. But my lifelong membership in the privileged racial group has helped keep me blind about much of the impact of race. In fact, I have come to think of the story related above as a story of "blind vision" — a White female teacher educator with a vision about the importance of making issues of race and diversity explicit parts of the preservice curriculum and, in the process, grappling (sometimes blindly) with the tension, contradiction, difficulty, pain, and failure inherent in unlearning racism.

Of course, it is what we do after we tell stories like this one that matters most, or, more correctly, it is what we do afterwards that makes these stories matter at all. In the remainder of this article, I examine what I tried to do as a teacher educator and what we tried to do in our teacher education community after this story was told. We wanted to do nothing short of total transformation, nothing short of inventing a curriculum that was once and for all free of racism. What we *did* do over time was much more modest. Over time we struggled to unlearn racism by learning to read teacher education as racial text,[3] a process that involved analyzing and altering the learning opportunities available in our program along the lines of their implicit and explicit messages about race, racism, and teaching, as well as — and as important as — acknowledging to each other and to our students that this process would never be finished, would never be "once and for all." In the pages that follow, I analyze and illustrate this process, drawing on the following experiences and data sources: the evolution of three courses I regularly taught during the years that followed these events; the changes we made over time in the intellectual, social, and organizational contexts of the program; and the persistent doubts, questions, and failures we experienced as recorded in notes, reflections, conversations, and other correspondence.[4] In the final section of the article, I consider lessons learned and unlearned. I address the implications of reading teacher education as racial text for my own continuing efforts as a teacher educator now working with student teachers and teacher educators in a different urban context (Cochran-Smith et al., 1999; Cochran-Smith & Lytle, 1998).

READING TEACHER EDUCATION AS RACIAL TEXT

Reading teacher education as racial text is an analytical approach that draws from three interrelated and somewhat overlapping ideas. First is the idea that teaching and teacher education — in terms of both curriculum and pedagogy — can be regarded and read as "text." Second is the idea that preservice teacher education has both an explicit text (a sequence of required courses and fieldwork experiences, as well as the public documents that advertise or represent the goals of a given program) and a subtext (implicit messages, subtle aspects of formal and informal program arrangements, and the underlying perspectives conveyed in discourse, materials, and consistency/inconsistency between ideals and realities). Third is the notion that any curriculum, teacher education or otherwise, can and — given the racialized society in which we live — ought to be read not simply as text but as racial text.

Teaching as Text

A number of recent writers have advanced the idea that the work of teaching can be regarded as "text" that can — like any other text — be read, reread, analyzed, critiqued, revised, and made public by the teacher and his or her local community. This assumes that teaching, like all human experience, is constructed primarily out of the social and language interactions of participants. To make teaching into readable "text," it is necessary to establish space between teachers and their everyday work in order to find what McDonald (1992) calls "apartness." He suggests:

> This is the gist of reading teaching, its minimal core: to step outside the room, figuratively speaking, and to search for perspective on the events inside. It is simple work on its face, private and comparatively safe, the conse-

quence perhaps of deliberately noticing one's own practice in the eyes of a student teacher, of undertaking some classroom research, even — as in my case — of keeping a simple journal and doing a little theoretical browsing. By such means, teachers may spot the uncertainty in their own practice. They may spot it, as I did, in unexpected tangles of conflicting values, in stubborn ambivalence, in a surprising prevalence of half-steps. (p. 11)

McDonald suggests that reading teaching collaboratively is difficult and complex, requiring group members to set aside the pretensions and fears born of isolation, but also allowing, eventually, for the discovery of voice and a certain sense of unity.

Along related but different lines, I have been suggesting in work with Susan Lytle (Cochran-Smith & Lytle, 1992, 1993, 1999) that communities of teachers use multiple forms of inquiry to help make visible and accessible everyday events and practices and the ways they are differently understood by different stakeholders in the educational process. Oral and written inquiry that is systematic and intentional, we have argued, "transforms what is ordinarily regarded as 'just teaching' . . . into multi-layered portraits of school life" (Cochran-Smith & Lytle, 1992, p. 310). These portraits and the ways teachers shape and interpret them draw on, but also make problematic, the knowledge about teaching and learning that has been generated by others. At the same time, they help to build bodies of evidence, provide analytic frameworks, and suggest cross-references for comparison. Part of the point in McDonald's work, and in ours, is that "reading teaching as text" means representing teaching through oral and written language as well as other means of documentation that can be revisited, "REsearched" — to use Ann Berthoff's language (Berthoff, 1987) — connected to other "texts" of teaching, and made accessible and public beyond the immediate local context. Using the metaphor "teaching as text" makes it possible to see that connecting the various texts of teaching in the context of local inquiry communities (Cochran-Smith & Lytle, 1999) can be understood as a kind of social and collective construction of intertextuality or dialogue among texts. This leads to the second aspect of conceptualizing teacher education as text — examining not only what is explicit (the major text), but also what is not easily visible or openly public (the subtext).

Texts and Subtexts in Teacher Education

As text, teacher education is dynamic and complex — much more than a sequence of courses, a set of fieldwork experiences, or the readings and written assignments that are required for certification or credentialing purposes. Although these are part of what it means to take teacher education as text, they are not all of it. This also means examining its subtexts, hidden texts, and intertexts — reading between the lines as well as reading under, behind, through, and beyond them. This includes scrutinizing what is absent from the main texts and what themes are central to them, what happens to the formal texts, how differently positioned people read and write these texts differently, what they do and do not do with them, and what happens that is not planned or public. Ginsburg and Clift's (1990) concept of the hidden curriculum in teacher education is illuminating here, as is Rosenberg's (1997) discussion of the underground discourses of teacher education. Both of these call attention to the missing, obscured, or subverted texts — what is left out, implied, veiled, or subtly signaled as the norm by virtue of being unmarked or marked with modifying language. Ginsburg and Clift suggest that

> [the] sources of hidden curricular messages include the institutional and broader social contexts in which teacher education operates and the structure and processes of the teacher education program, including pedagogical techniques and texts and materials within the program. Messages are also sent by the . . . interpersonal relationships that exist between the numerous groups who might be considered to be educators of teachers. (p. 451)

Along more specific lines, Rosenberg (1997) describes the underground discourse about race in a small teacher education program in a rural area of New England. Rosenberg refers to "the presence of an absence," or the figurative presence of racism even in the actual absence of people of color at an overwhelmingly White institution. Rosenberg's characterization of an underground discourse about race connects to the third idea I have drawn upon in this discussion: the necessity of reading teacher education not just as complicated and dynamic text, but as racial text.

Teacher Education as Racial Text

Castenell and Pinar (1993) argue that curriculum can and ought to be regarded as racial text. Their introduction to a collection of essays by that name, *Understanding Curriculum as Racial Text*, develops this argument by locating current curriculum issues within the context of public debates about the canon and about the racial issues that are embedded within curriculum controversies. To understand curriculum as racial text, they suggest, is to understand that

> all Americans are racialized beings; knowledge of who we have been, who we are, and who we will become is a story or text we construct. In this sense curriculum — our construction and reconstruction of this knowledge for dissemination to the young — is racial text. (p. 8)

In forwarding this view of curriculum, Castenell and Pinar imply that it is critical to analyze any curriculum to see what kind of message or story about race and racism is being told, what assumptions are being made, what identity perspectives and points of view are implicit, and what is valued or devalued. They acknowledge, of course, that curriculum is not only racial text, but is also a text that is political, aesthetic, and gendered. They argue, however, that it is, "to a degree that European Americans have been unlikely to acknowledge, racial text" (p. 4). In conceptualizing curriculum as racial text, then, they link knowledge and identity, focusing particularly on issues of representation and difference. They argue that, although it is true that "We are what we know. We are, however, also what we do not know" (p. 4).

Taken together, the three ideas just outlined — that all teaching (including teacher education) can be regarded as text, that teacher education has both public and implicit or hidden texts, and that the text of teacher education is (in large part) racial text — lay the groundwork for the two sections that follow. In these sections I suggest that my colleagues and I — as participants in one teacher education community — struggled to unlearn racism by learning to read teacher education as racial text. In the first section I discuss both the possibilities and the pitfalls of making race and racism central to the curriculum by using "up close and personal" narratives, as well as distanced and more intellectualized theories and accounts. Next I show that it is necessary to "read between the lines," or to scrutinize closely the implicit messages about perspective, identity, and difference in a curriculum even after race and racism have been made central. Finally I turn to more general issues in teacher education offering brief lessons learned and unlearned when teacher education is regarded as racial text and when narrative is used to interrogate race and racism.

GETTING PERSONAL: USING STORIES ABOUT RACE AND RACISM IN THE CURRICULUM

For the teacher education community referred to in the opening narrative of this article, reading teacher education as racial text came to mean making issues of diversity (particularly of race and racism) central and integral, rather than marginal and piecemeal, to what we as student teachers, cooperating teachers, and teacher educators read, wrote, and talked about. Consciously deciding to privilege these issues meant rewriting course syllabi and program materials, reinventing the ways we evaluated student teachers, changing the composition of faculty and staff, drawing on the expertise and experience of people beyond ourselves, and altering the content of teacher research groups, student seminars, and whole-community sessions. For example, in response to the events described above, we worked the following year with a group of outside consultants to plan and participate in a series of "cultural diversity workshops" jointly attended by students, cooperating teachers, supervisors, and program directors. In the next year, we focused monthly seminars for the same groups on race and culture through the medium of story, led by Charlotte Blake Alston, a nationally known African American storyteller and staff-development leader. In the years to follow, we participated in sessions on Afrocentric curriculum led by Molefi Asante; on Black family socialization patterns and school culture led by Michele Foster; on multicultural teaching and Asian American issues in urban schools led by Deborah Wei; on constructing curriculum based on Hispanic children's literature, particularly using books with Puerto Rican themes and characters, led by Sonia Nieto; and on learning to talk about racial identity and racism led by Beverly Tatum. In addition, we offered sessions on using children's cultural and linguistic resources in the classroom and on constructing antiracist pedagogy led by our program's most experienced cooperating teachers — both teachers of color and White teachers — from urban and suburban, public and private, poor and privileged schools in the Philadelphia area.

Telling Stories

A central part of these activities was "getting personal" about race and racism — putting more emphasis on reading, writing, and sharing personal experiences of racism and digging at the roots of our own attitudes at the same time that we continued to read the more intellectualized, and thus somewhat safer, discourse of the academy. This meant making individual insider accounts (even though not as well known as the writing of the academy) a larger part of the required reading. Along with the usual reading of Comer, Delpit, Ogbu, Heath, and Tatum we began to read more of Parham, Foreman, Eastman, Cohen, and Creighton — all of whom were student teachers, cooperating teachers, and supervisors in our program.[5]

All of us in the community wrote and read personal accounts about race and class that were published in-house in an annual collection we called, "A Sense of Who We Are." These were used as the starting point for many class discussions, school-site meetings, and monthly seminars. For example, Daryl Foreman, an experienced cooperating teacher, wrote about her experiences as a child whose mother took her north to Pennsylvania for a summer visit. She wrote about the sights and scenes of 1960s Harrisburg and then turned to one unforgettable experience:

> It had been four days since my mother left Harrisburg. . . . She left us in the warm and capable hands of my aunt. We'd been behaving as tourists. But now, my younger sister and I had to accompany my aunt to work. For years, she'd been employed by a well-to-do White family whom I'd never met. . . .
>
> At four o'clock, I was starving and my aunt informed me that it was "normal" for us to eat in the kitchen while [the family] dined elsewhere.
>
> Before dinner, the woman of the house entered the kitchen offering to set the tables — one in the kitchen and the other in the dining room. She grabbed two sets of dishes from the cupboard. She delivered a pretty set of yellow plastic plates to the kitchen dining area and a set of blue china to the dining room. After dinner she came back and thanked my aunt for the delicious meal, then prepared to feed the dog. She walked toward the cupboard and opened it. Her eyes and hands traveled past the pretty set of plastic dishes and landed on the blue china plates. After she pulled a blue china plate from the cupboard, she filled it with moist dog food and placed it on the floor. He ran for the plate. I shrieked! . . .
>
> To this day, I'm not sure if I shrieked at the shock of [people] sharing dinnerware with a dog or because the dog got a piece of blue china while I ate from yellow plastic.

David Creighton, a student teacher, wrote about working in an Italian restaurant in South Philadelphia in the 1990s:

"Yo, Dave, what *are* you anyway?" said Tony Meoli, a waiter in LaTrattoria in South Philadelphia.

"Whaddaya mean?" I, the new busboy, said.

"Like, uh, what's your nationality? You know, where are you from? I mean, you're obviously not Italian."

"Oh. Well, I'm Russian with some German mixed in," I said.

"Well, just as long as you're not Jewish," said Tony. "We don't like Jews around here."

"Actually, I am Jewish," I said.

"Oh, sorry, I was just kiddin' you know."

"Don't worry about it," I said . . .

Creighton went on to describe the culture of South Philadelphia, pointing out the racial and ethnic insulation and the considerable hostility between and among various groups. Then he continued:

I had only worked there about four months when at the end of my Sunday night shift I was told with no warning, "We won't be needing you anymore."

"What?" I said. I felt I had done a good job. No one ever complained about my work. I was always on time, and I was developing a good rapport with the waiters who often commended me on my efforts. Also, I really needed the money. "Why?" I said.

"I don't know," said the bartender.

"You know, Dave, Hitler had the right idea for you people, with the gas chambers and all," said Joe Piselli only half jokingly. "One day I'm gonna gas you down there in the kitchen."

"You know, Joe, Hitler wasn't all that crazy about Catholics either. You woulda been next," I said.

"Yeah, well at least I ain't no Jew," he said.

"Thank God," I said.

Reading and writing first-person accounts like these as starting points for interrogating unexamined assumptions and practices can evoke a shared vulnerability that helps a group of loosely connected individuals gel into a community committed to dealing with issues of race more openly. Accounts like these can move a preservice curriculum beyond the level of celebrating diversity, enhancing human relations, or incorporating ethnic studies into the curriculum, positions that are rightly criticized for their focus on ethnicity as individual choice and their limited goal of attitudinal change (McCarthy, 1990, 1993; Nieto, 1999; Sleeter & Grant, 1987) rather than analysis of systemic and institutional structures and practices that perpetuate racism and oppression. As I pointed out above, narratives also have the capacity to contain many of the contradictions, nuances, and complexities that are necessary for understanding the roots and twists of racism and the many ways these interact with the social life of schools and classrooms. But the considerable power of accounts that "get personal" about race is also their pitfall. They can use some people's pain in the service of others' understanding, as I suggest below, and they can also imply that we all share similar experiences with racism, experiences that beneath the surface of their details and contexts are the same. Over the years, I have come to realize that this lesson in unlearning racism, which is an especially difficult one to hold onto, helps to explain some of the depth of anger expressed by the student teachers in the story with which this article began.

Stories about Whom? Stories for Whom?

Several of the students of color in the blind vision story related above claimed we had done nothing in the program to help students understand issues of race, that we did not talk about it in "real" ways. Factually, this was not the case. We had read a large number of articles by both White scholars and scholars of color, and we had shared some personal incidents in class and had intellectualized discussions. It is clear to me now, though, that these discussions were framed primarily for the benefit of White students who were invited to learn more about racism through stories of other people's oppression. The stories were not sufficiently linked to larger issues or framed in ways that pushed everybody to learn not *regardless of* but *with full regard for* differences in race, culture, and ethnicity.

I should have learned this lesson a long time ago. I had known it in certain ways even at the time of the incident described in my narrative — my detailed notes indicate that it was one of the points I tried to make to the students after the incident occurred. But for me, as a White teacher educator, it is a lesson that needs to be learned over and over again. Although I thought I had learned this lesson then, I learned it again several years later from Tuesday Vanstory, an African American woman who was a supervisor in the program that year but had been a student in the program years before. We had had a difficult discussion about race in our supervisors' inquiry group where we had considered ways to respond to a particularly troubling journal entry written by a White student teacher. In it she had complained about the students of color in the program sometimes separating themselves from the others, sitting together on the perimeter of the classroom and/or not participating in certain discussions. The journal writer used the phrase "reverse discrimination" and questioned how we could ever move forward if everybody would not even talk to each other. Several White members of the supervisors' group voiced somewhat similar concerns. They were genuinely distressed, wanting open conversations and resentful of the figurative as well as literal separation along racial lines of some members from the larger group when certain topics arose.

Vanstory had sat silent for a long time during this discussion, then finally burst out and demanded, "But *who* are those discussions *for*? *Who* do they really serve?" There was silence for a while and then confusion. She wrote to me that same day about the discussion:

I must say that I was very upset after today's supervisors' meeting. There's nothing like a discussion on race, class, and culture to get my blood boiling, especially when I am one of a few who is in the "minority." Believe me, it is not at all comfortable. I really wanted to say nothing. I didn't want to blow my cool. I wanted to remain silent, tranquil. Instead I spouted off in what felt like a very emotional and, at times, a nonsensical response. . . .

I ran across a sociological term a few years ago: "master status." It is the thing you can never get away from, the label that others give you that they won't ever release and they won't let you forget. Can you imagine the constant confrontation of the issue of race permeating every day of your life for one reason or another? (Over representation or under representation of people who look like you do in whatever arena, the blatant inequities in quality of life for the masses — educational opportunities, housing, ability to pass down wealth or privilege, the stinging humiliations that come from the mouths or pens of others who may or may not be well-intentioned, IQ scores being thrown in your face, etc.). It is reality for us. It is not a discussion, not a theory. It is flesh and blood. . . .

And to come to school and have to play "educator" to the others who want to discuss race or understand, or release some guilt, or even in a very few cases, people who want to see a real change . . . It gets tired . . .

Marilyn, I think that you are very brave and genuine to ask the tough questions that you ask yourself and your White students. But the truth is, your perspective, your reality does not necessarily reflect ours.

In *Teaching to Transgress* (1994), bell hooks makes a point remarkably similar to Vanstory's. Although hooks is discussing White feminist writers rather than teachers or teacher educators as Vanstory was, her comments contribute to a larger argument about the necessity of rethinking pedagogy in the current age of multiculturalism:

Now Black women are placed in the position of serving White female desire to know more about race and racism, to "master" the subject. Drawing on the work of Black women, work that they once dismissed as irrelevant, they now reproduce the servant-served paradigms in their scholarship. Armed with new knowledge of race, their willingness to say that their work is coming from a White perspective (usually without explaining what that means), they forget that the very focus on racism emerged from the concrete political effort to forge meaningful ties between women of different race and class groups. This struggle is often completely ignored. (pp. 103–104)

I am convinced that reading and writing accounts about race and racism that get personal, as well as reading more intellectualized arguments about these issues, is vital to preservice teacher education. As I have tried to suggest, however, reading teacher education as racial text reveals that this is also a complex activity that is fraught with problems. Compelling personal stories often evoke a strong sense of empathy for others (Rosenberg, 1997), a false sense that all of us have experienced hurt and frustration varying in degree but not in kind, that all of us underneath have the same issues, that all of us can understand racism as personal struggle, as individual instance of cruelty, discrete moment of shame, outrage, or fear. In addition to using some people's experience in the service of others' education, then, personal narratives can also obscure more direct confrontation of the ways that individual instances of prejudice are *not* all the same — that some are deeply embedded in and entangled with institutional and historical systems of racism based on power and privilege, and some are not. Reading teacher education as racial text means trying to make issues of racism central, not marginal, and close and personal, not distant and academic. But it also means helping all of the readers and writers of such stories understand that schools and other organizational contexts are always sites for institutional and collective struggles of power and oppression (Villegas, 1991), not neutral backdrops for individual achievement and failure (McCarthy, 1993). And it means being very careful about what is said after stories are told and considering carefully whose stories are used in whose interest.

The foregoing discussion is not meant to suggest that racism was or should be the only topic in the teacher education curriculum or that everything else is secondary. I am not suggesting here that student teachers and their more experienced mentors should talk only about racism or that if we learn to talk about race and racism constructively, we do not need to learn anything else in the teacher education curriculum. It is a problem, for example, if there is no time in courses on language and literacy in the elementary school to explore and critique process writing, basal reading programs, whole language, phonics instruction, and standardized and nonstandardized means of assessing verbal aptitude and achievement. But issues of language, race, and cultural diversity are implicated in and by all of these topics, as I discuss in the next section of this article, and it is a fallacy to assume that there is a forced and mutually exclusive choice in preservice education — emphasizing *either* pedagogical and subject matter knowledge *or* knowledge about culture, racism, and schools as reflections of societal conflicts and sites for power struggle.

READING BETWEEN THE LINES: PERSPECTIVES, IDENTITY, AND DIFFERENCE

Understanding curriculum as racial text requires thorough scrutiny of implicit perspectives about race and careful attention to issues of identity and difference (Castenell & Pinar, 1993). In teacher education this means not looking simply at a synopsis of the "plot" of a preservice program (to carry the text metaphor further). It also means examining the roles of starring and supporting characters and analyzing the plot line by line, as well as between the lines, for underlying themes and for the twists and turns of the stories told or implied about race, racism, and teaching.

Following the events recounted in the "blind vision" story, our teacher education community attempted not only to make issues of race up close and personal, but also to "read between the lines" of the curriculum. As director of the program and instructor of core courses on language, learning, and literacy, I had earlier examined class discussions that explicitly dealt with racism and teaching, as well as the essays and projects my students completed (see Cochran-Smith, 1995a, 1995b). In these analyses, I had tried to understand how student teachers constructed issues related to race and racism and how they linked these to their roles as prospective teachers. I had also looked at how I constructed the issues and how I linked them to my role as teacher educator and mentor. But at this point, as part of our group's larger, more intensive efforts, I wanted to look further — between and underneath the explicit lines that narrated my courses. I wanted to get at the implicit, more subtle perspectives by scrutinizing what was included and omitted from readings and discussions, how issues were sequenced and juxtaposed with one another, which messages were consistent and fundamental, and — inevitably — which were not. To do so, I used as data the evolution of course syllabi, assignments, and activities, as well as students' responses, class discussions, and my own detailed notes and reflections on three required courses I taught (a two-course sequence on reading and language arts in the elementary school and a course on children's literature). All three were designed to explore the relationships of literacy, learning, and culture and their implications for the teaching of reading, writing, literature, and oral language development.

What I found was in one sense exactly what I expected to find. Over the years we had increased the amount of time and attention we gave to questions of culture, race, and racism. In fact, these issues had become a central theme of my courses and of the program in general. But what I found when I read between and under the lines of the curriculum as racial text was a contradiction. On the one hand, the first part of the course presented heavy critique of the inequities embedded in the status quo and of the ways these were perpetuated by the current arrangements of schooling. On the other hand, the latter part of the course privileged pedagogical perspectives drawn from theories and practices developed primarily by White teachers and scholars of child development, language learning, and progressive education. There was as well an underlying White European American construction of self-identity and other, of "we" and "they."

White Theory, White Practice

My courses were intended to help students think through the relationships of theory and practice, learn how to learn from children, and construct principled perspectives about teaching and assessing language and literacy learning. Two themes ran throughout that were not about literacy and literature per se but were intended to be fundamental to these courses and to the entire program: 1) understanding teaching as an intellectual and political activity and the teacher as active constructor (not simply receiver) of meaning, knowledge, and curriculum; and 2) developing critical perspectives about the relationships of race, class, culture, and schooling.

A between-the-lines analysis revealed a sharp contrast in the subtle messages my courses projected about these two themes. The notion of teacher as a constructor of meaning and active decisionmaker was consistent. Readings and class discussions conceptualized the teacher as knowledge generator, as well as critical consumer of others' knowledge, as active constructor of interpretive frameworks as well as poser and ponderer of questions, and as agent for school and social change within local communities and larger social movements. Student teachers were required to construct (rather than simply implement) literature and literacy curriculum, critique teachers' manuals and reading textbooks according to their assumptions about teacher and student agency, and function as researchers by treating their ongoing work with children as sites for inquiry about language learning access and opportunity. Research and writing by experienced teachers from the local and larger inquiry communities were part of the required reading for every topic on the syllabi.

In addition, the knowledge and interpretive frameworks generated by teachers were regarded as part of the knowledge base for language and literacy teaching. They were *not* mentioned only when the topic was teacher research itself or when the point was to provide examples of classroom practice or of the application of others' ideas. Guest speakers included teachers as often as university-based experts. Teachers' ways of analyzing and interpreting data, creating theories, assessing children's progress, and constructing and critiquing practice (Lytle & Cochran-Smith, 1992) were foregrounded and valued as much as those generated by researchers based outside classrooms and schools. In addition, in multiple assignments in my courses, students were required to alter and analyze conventional curriculum and pedagogy based on systematic data collection about teaching and learning. They were prompted to challenge conventional labeling and grouping practices, and they were invited to be part of teacher-initiated alternative professional development groups struggling to "teach against the grain" (Cochran-Smith, 1991). Reading between and under the lines exposed little discrepancy, with regard to teachers' roles as knowledge generators and change agents, between the texts and subtexts of the curriculum.

By contrast, the same kind of close reading with regard to critical perspectives on race and racism led to different and more troubling insights. In my two-semester language and literacy course, a major segment early in the syllabus had to do with race, class, and culture. For this segment students read selections by the well-known scholars mentioned earlier, as well as personal narratives written by members of the local and larger teacher education communities. Spread over three to four weeks, this portion of the course emphasized the following: both schooling systems and individuals' school experiences are deeply embedded within social, cultural, and historical contexts, including institutional and historical racism; European perspectives are not universal standards of the evolution of higher order thought, but culturally and historically constructed habits of mind; and the standard "neutral" U.S.

school and its curriculum have been generated out of, and help to sustain, unearned advantages and disadvantages for particular groups of students based on race, class, culture, gender, linguistic background, and ability/disability. Described in detail elsewhere (Cochran-Smith, 1995b), this part of the course gave students the opportunity to "rewrite their autobiographies" or reinterpret some of their own life stories and experiences based on new insights about power, privilege, and oppression. This part of the course also prompted students to "construct uncertainty" — that is, to pose and investigate questions of curriculum and instructional strategies informed by their experiences as raced, classed, and gendered beings and contingent upon the varying school contexts and student populations with whom they worked.

The remainder of the course was organized around major topics in elementary school language and literacy: controversies about learning to read and write (including child language acquisition, whole language as a theory of practice, basal reading approaches, reading groups, and phonics instruction); teaching reading and writing in elementary classrooms (including emergent literacy and extending literacy through reading aloud, language experience, literature study, process writing, journals, and other activities and strategies); and interpretation and use of assessments in language and literacy (including standardized tests and alternative assessments such as portfolios, informal reading inventories, and holistic assessments). For each topic, underlying assumptions about the nature of language, children as learners, teaching and learning as constructive processes, and classrooms/schools as social and cultural contexts were identified and critiqued.

The pedagogy that was advocated was more or less "progressive," "whole language," "developmental," and "meaning-centered," with emphasis on children as readers and writers of authentic texts and the classroom as a social context within which children and teachers together construct knowledge. There was a distinct bias against skills-centered approaches that taught reading and writing in isolated bits and pieces using texts and exercises constructed specifically for that purpose. Instead it was emphasized that language skills emerged from authentic language use and from instruction within the context of language use.

Reading between the lines forced other realizations. The pedagogy I advocated was drawn from theories and practices developed primarily by White teachers and scholars. The prominent names on this part of the syllabus were revealing — Dewey (1916), Britton (1987), Berthoff (1987), Graves (1983), Calkins (1991, 1994), Edelsky, Altwerger, and Flores (1991), Dyson (1987), Paley (1979), Rosenblatt (1976), and Goodman (1988), as well as teachers and teacher groups at the North Dakota Study Group (Strieb, 1985), the Prospect School (Carini, 1986), the National Writing Project (Pincus, 1993; Waff, 1994), the Breadloaf School of English (Goswami & Stillman, 1987), the Philadelphia Teachers Learning Cooperative (1984), and other local teacher and practitioner groups.[6] Absent from these segments of the syllabus and from our discussions were contrasting cultural perspectives on child language and learning and child socialization. Also absent were rich accounts of successful pedagogies, particularly with poor children and children of color, that were not necessarily "progressive" or "whole language" oriented.

Notwithstanding the fact that students read Lisa Delpit, Shirley Brice Heath, and others earlier in the course, it became clear to me by reading between the lines that there was a powerful contradictory subtext in the course about pedagogy for language and literacy. The subtle message was that pedagogy developed primarily from research and writing by and about White mainstream persons was the pedagogy that was best for everybody — Dewey's argument, more or less, that what the "wisest and best" parent wants for his or her child is what we should want for all children, or what we should want for "other people's children" (Delpit, 1988, 1995; Kozol, 1991). This subtle message implied that "progressive" language pedagogy was culture neutral, although just weeks earlier the course had emphasized that all aspects of schooling were socially and culturally constructed and needed to be understood within particular historical and cultural contexts. Because progressive language pedagogy was unmarked as cultural theory, culturally embedded practice, and/or cultural perspective, however, the subtle message was that it was an a-cultural position about how best to teach language and literacy that applied across contexts, historical moments, and school populations.

Part of what this meant was that my courses offered student teachers no theoretical framework for understanding the successful teachers they observed in their fieldwork schools who used traditional, skills-based reading and writing pedagogies with their students, particularly in urban schools where there were large numbers of poor children and children of color. Although my courses explicitly emphasized the importance of teachers' knowledge, there was a contradictory and perhaps more powerful implicit message: the knowledge of some teachers was more valuable than others, the knowledge of teachers who worked (successfully) from a more or less skills-based, direct-instruction perspective was perhaps not so important, and the pedagogy of these teachers was somewhat misguided and out of date. Reading between the lines of my students' discussions and writings revealed that they were confused about what to make of the successes they observed in urban classrooms when the pedagogy we read about and valued in class was not apparent. On the other hand, my student teachers knew precisely what to make of the unsuccessful teachers they observed in those same contexts. My students had a powerful framework for critique and could easily conclude that many urban teachers were unsuccessful because they were too traditional, too focused on skills, not progressive enough.

What was missing from the sections of my courses that dealt specifically with reading and language pedagogy were theories of practice developed by and about people of color, as well as rich and detailed analyses of successful teachers of urban children, particularly poor children of color, who used a variety of pedagogies including, but not necessarily limited to, those pedagogies that could be called "progressive." Gloria Ladson-Billings's work

(1994, 1995) had just been published at the time I was struggling to read deeply between the lines of my courses and our larger curriculum. Hers and related analyses of culturally appropriate, culturally relevant, and/or culturally sensitive pedagogies (Au & Kawakami, 1994; Ballenger, 1992; Foster, 1993, 1994; Hollins, King, & Hayman, 1994; Irvine, 1990; Irvine & York, 1995; King, 1994) were extremely useful in my efforts to rethink the ways I taught my courses and structured the program. In fact, Ladson-Billings's book, *The Dreamkeepers: Successful Teachers of African American Children* (1994), speaks directly to the issue of skills- and whole language–based approaches to language instruction by contrasting two very different but highly successful teachers of reading to African American children. One of these taught from a (more or less) whole language perspective, focusing on student-teacher interactions, skills in the context of meaning, and use of literature and other authentic texts, while the other taught from a (more or less) traditional skills perspective, focusing on direct instruction, phonics and word identification skills, and basal texts written for the explicit purpose of instruction. Ladson-Billings points out what is wrong with framing the debate about how to teach African American children in terms of whole language versus a purely skill-based approach:

> In some ways their differences represent the larger debate about literacy teaching, that of whole-language versus basal-text techniques. However, beneath the surface, at the personal ideological level, the differences between these instructional strategies lose meaning. Both teachers want their students to become literate. Both believe that their students are capable of high levels of literacy. (p. 116)

Ladson-Billings's commentary lifts the debates about literacy instruction out of the realm of language theory and practice *only* and into the realm of ideology and politics as well — that is, into the realm of teachers' commitments to communities, to parents, and to activism.[7] Her analysis of successful and culturally relevant pedagogy for African American children repeatedly emphasizes teachers' ties to the school community, teachers' belief in the learning ability of all children (not just an exceptional few who, through education, can make their way "out" of the lives common to their parents and community members), and teachers' strategies for establishing personal connections with students and helping them connect new knowledge to previous experiences and ideas.

When I revised my language and reading courses, Ladson-Billings's *The Dreamkeepers* was one of the central texts, and I included in discussions about reading/writing pedagogy many other readings about culturally relevant language pedagogy (e.g., Au & Kawakami, 1994; Ballenger, 1992; Foster, 1993). In addition to readings about language and literacy theory, debates about pedagogy, and so on, new additions were intended in part to alter the curriculum as racial text. Particularly, they were intended to provide frameworks for understanding successful and unsuccessful teaching of poor and privileged White children and children of color — frameworks that were not dichotomous and that included but were more complex than whole language versus basals. These were also intended to prompt more attention to issues of community, as well as richer and more diverse perspectives on pedagogy, skills, and explicit versus implicit instruction (Delpit, 1988). I also wanted to diminish the implicit subtext of criticism of teachers who worked successfully, particularly with children of color, using methods other than those that might be termed "progressive" or "whole." Including these new readings also made the course more complicated and made its underlying conception of teaching as an uncertain activity (Dudley-Marling, 1997; McDonald, 1992) even more pronounced than it had been. Always eschewing the possibility of "best practices" that cut across the contexts and conditions of local settings, I had for years told students that the answer to most questions about "the best" ways to teach something was "it depends" (Cochran-Smith, 1995b). Having uncovered unintended contradictions in the lessons I taught my students made me realize that pedagogical decisions "depend" on an even wider, richer, and more nuanced array of variables and conditions than I had implied.[8]

Identity and Difference: We and They

Understanding the racial narrative that underlies a curriculum is a process that requires intense self-critical reflection and analysis, as Castenell and Pinar (1993) have made clear:

> Debates over what we teach the young are also — in addition to being debates over what knowledge is of most worth — debates over who we perceive ourselves to be, and how we will represent that identity, including what remains as "left over," as "difference." (p. 2)

Reading between the lines of my own courses and of the larger teacher education curriculum revealed a White European American construction of self-identity and "other." "We," I came to realize, often referred not to "we who are committed to teaching elementary school differently and improving the life chances of all children," but to "we White people (especially we White women) who are trying to learn how to teach people who are different from us." On the one hand, it could be argued that this perspective is exactly what is needed, given the demographic disparities, now well documented (National Education Goals Panel, 1997; Quality Education for Minorities Project, 1990), between the racial composition of the group entering the nation's teaching force (more than 90% White European American) and the nation's schoolchildren (increasingly a wide array of racial, cultural, and language groups). In elementary education, in addition to being White and European American, the group entering the teaching force is also overwhelmingly female. In a certain sense, then, one could make a persuasive case that a White European American and female construction of self and other is just what the preservice teacher education curriculum ought to have. On the other hand, the program I directed had 20–25 percent students of color and 15–20 percent male students. A curriculum for "White girls" was surely not the answer. Rather, we were committed to constructing a curriculum that helped all student teachers — with full acknowledgement of differences in race, culture, and gender — interrogate their experiences, understand schools and schooling as sites for struggles over power, and become prepared to teach in an increasingly multiracial and multicultural society. To do so, we had to revise the story the curriculum told about identity and rewrite the characters who were central in that story, particularly who "we and they," "self and other," "regular and left over" were.

One incident from my course on literature for children, which I have taught in various iterations for more than twenty years, provides an example of the ways I tried consciously to alter the assumed definition of self and other, we and they, in my courses. What I wanted to do was to construct discussions where "we and they" shifted *away from* "we White people who are trying to learn to teach those other people — those people of color" *and toward* "we educators who are trying to be sensitive to, and learn to teach, all students — both those who are different from us and those who are like us in race, class, and culture." I began to use Lynne Reid Banks's *The Indian in the Cupboard* (1981) as one of the six or eight novels my students read in common for the literature course.[9] My course had for years included many children's books that were highly regarded for their portrayals of the perspectives of African American, Asian, and Hispanic family and childhood experiences (Harris, 1993), and the course had for years focused on the politics of children's literature (Taxel, 1993). The point of adding *The Indian in the Cupboard* was *not* to add "the Native American experience" to the list of cultures represented in the course. Rather, the point was to create an opportunity to prompt an altered conception of self and other, an altered sense of who "we" were as teachers.

Published in 1981, when the *New York Times* called it "the best novel of the year," *The Indian in the Cupboard* continues to be highly acclaimed and widely used as a whole-class text in upper elementary and middle schools, and its popularity has increased since it was made into a Disney motion picture. A fantasy about Omri, a British boy who receives as a present a collector's cupboard, the book revolves around a plastic Indian figure who comes to life (but remains three inches high) when the boy casually places him inside the cupboard and closes the door. A toy cowboy and soldier eventually come to life too and interact with the Indian and the boy. The book is charming in many ways, well written and pivoting on premises that are extremely appealing to children — being bigger than adults, having toys come to life, and keeping a powerful secret. But in addition to positive reviews about the popularity of the book and the high quality of its writing, the book has also been criticized as racist, perpetuating stereotypes about Native Americans at the same time that it charms and appeals. The first year I used the book, all of my students were prospective teachers, many of whom were just completing a year of student teaching in urban schools where the population was primarily African American, Asian, and/or Puerto Rican. I asked the class to read the novel and jot down their responses and then read the critical commentary I had assigned.

In an excoriating critique of images of Native Americans in children's books, MacCann (1993) argues that the vast majority of children's books with Native American characters or themes are written from a non-Native perspective. With few exceptions, they portray Native American cultures as futile and obsolete and turn on the "persistent generalization" that American society has been "shaped by the pull of a vacant continent drawing population westward" and available to any enterprising European (p. 139). About *The Indian in the Cupboard* specifically, MacCann writes:

> Even in the fantasy genre the displacement of American Indian societies can be an underlying theme, as in *The Indian in the Cupboard* [Banks, 1981] and its sequel *The Return of the Indian* [Banks, 1986]. These narratives are set in modern times . . . but the cultural content is rooted in the image of the Indian as presented in Hollywood westerns and dime novels. Little Bear is a plastic toy Indian who comes to life in the boy's magical cupboard, but remains just three inches in height. He grunts and snarls his way through the story, attacking the child, Omri, with a hunting knife, and later attacking a traditional enemy, a three-inch cowboy. At every turn of plot, Little Bear is either violent or childishly petulant until he finally tramples upon his ceremonial headdress as a sign of remorse. The historical culpability of the cowboy and others who invaded [Native American] territory is ignored. Native Americans are seen as the primary perpetrators of havoc, even as they defend their own borders. (p. 145)

In *Through Indian Eyes* (Slapin & Seale, 1992), a collection of articles written primarily by Native Americans, the review of *The Indian in the Cupboard* and its sequel is also wholly negative. It concludes:

> My heart aches for the Native child unfortunate enough to stumble across, and read, these books. How could she, reading this, fail to be damaged? How could a White child fail to believe that he is far superior to the bloodthirsty, sub-human monsters portrayed here? (p. 122)

My students read these critiques after they had read and responded to the novel and came to class prepared to discuss both.

Most of my students reported that they were completely engrossed in the unfolding story, and some were shocked by the negative critiques and even embarrassed that they had not noticed the racist overtones (and undertones) until after they finished the book. Many were uncertain about what to think. The discussion was intense and animated:[10]

The book is full of stereotypes. If a book has stereotypes, does that mean you just shouldn't use it in your classroom?

There are lots of stereotypes about Indians, but there are also stereotypes about cowboys and soldiers — doesn't this make the book sort of balanced?

The very idea of an American Indian adult as the possession (and a miniature possession at that) of a White English child is totally offensive and off-putting — does it really matter what else the book does or doesn't do?

Since the boy's wrong assumptions about Indians are for the most part pointed out and corrected by the narrator as the story goes along, doesn't it actually sort of "teach" some correct facts?

In the final analysis, isn't what really matters how engaging the story is for kids and what the quality of the writing is?

How can we evaluate the realism of the characters in a story that is obviously fantasy rather than history or biography?

Since none of us had any Native American children in the classes we student taught this year, does that make the issue of potentially hurting a Native child reader irrelevant?

Students were divided about what they thought of the book. Many saw it as more or less harmless, assuming that those who considered the book racist were self-interested extremists, interested only in what was "politically correct," or manufacturing problems where there were none. Others strongly disagreed, assessing the book as promoting shallow stereotypes with little redeeming social value. At some point in this very intense discussion, I inserted, "What if it were *The Jew in the Cupboard* or *The Black in the Cupboard?* Would that be all right?" For a few minutes there was dead silence. The looks on the faces of my students, many of whom were Jewish, African American, or Hispanic, indicated that it would decidedly *not* be all right to have a children's book with those titles or those story lines. Why then, I asked, was it all right for elementary and middle school teachers each year to teach to the whole class a children's book that had an Indian in the cupboard?

This was a turning point in the course, one that prompted some of the best discussion of the semester. Several students, African American and Hispanic, talked about how this opened their eyes to racism in a different way. They admitted that they had never worried too much about "Redskins" and tomahawks as symbols for sports teams, or grotesque caricatures and cigar-store Indians as icons for margarine, sports utility vehicles, and blue jeans. The discussion about race and racism changed that day. For a while everybody seemed to have new questions, and nobody seemed as sure as they had been about the answers. I believe this was because in this discussion there was a different underlying construction of identity and difference, an altered perspective on what was assumed to be the standard from which we defined "regular and different," "self and other." When "other" was Native American and "self" everyone else in the room, there were new opportunities for students to interrogate their assumptions, new opportunities to struggle with the issue of what it means to teach those who are different from and the same as our multiple selves.

Telling the story of what happened when I added *The Indian in the Cupboard* to my course is in no way intended to suggest that all we have to do in teacher education is figure out who is "not in the room" and then construct that person as the "other," that all we have to do is be certain to include in the curriculum fictional or research literature about racial or cultural groups that are not actually represented in a given teacher education program. That is not at all the point here. Nor is the point to claim that this kind of "inclusion" would be desirable or even possible. The point I do wish to make is that it is critically important to scrutinize the often very subtle messages about identity and difference that float between the lines of the curriculum and consciously work to construct opportunities in which all the members of the community are able to interrogate their constructions of self and other. As I have argued already, however, these opportunities must always be connected to larger understandings of the histories of oppression and privilege and must always be couched in understandings of institutional and organizational racism.

CONCLUSION: LESSONS LEARNED AND UNLEARNED

What are the lessons learned here about unlearning racism? One has to do with the power of narrative *in* teacher education and, as importantly, the power of teacher education *as* narrative. As I have tried to show throughout this article, both the personal and the fictional stories about race and racism that we invite participants to read and write can break down the barriers of distanced, academic discourse and make possible revelations about participants' positions, identity, and standpoint. Stories can serve as touchstones for shared experience and commitment. As one primary way we understand and construct our professional lives and our multiple identities, stories can help us scrutinize our own work and theorize our own experience. But stories can also be extremely negative, particularly when the stories of some groups are used — unintentionally or not — in the service of others' desire to learn and/or when powerful emotions are unleashed and participants are then left to fend for themselves in the aftermath. Stories can be negative if they prompt a false sense of sameness and personal empathy that is unconnected to historical and institutional racism, to schools as sites for power struggles, or to ownership of the roles privilege and oppression play in everyday life. It may also be the case that there are some stories that individuals should not be coaxed to share in mixed racial groups and some that group leaders should not attempt to solicit. Finally, it must be understood that the narratives we use as tools and texts in the teacher education curriculum confound and are confounded by larger and more deeply embedded messages, messages that are revealed only when the curriculum is interrogated, or consciously read as racial text.

The second lesson is connected to the title of this article, which implies two contradictions: blind vision, a phrase that suggests simultaneous seeing and not seeing; and "*un*learning," a word that signifies both growth and the undoing or reversing of that growth. These contradictions are intentional, chosen not only to signal the enormous complexities inherent in the ways race and culture are implicated in teaching and teacher education, but also to caution that blindness is an inevitable aspect of trying to act on a vision about including racism in the teacher education curriculum, that failing is an inherent aspect of unlearning racism. I am completely convinced that "reading the curriculum as racial text," in the sense that I have described it in this article, is critical to a vision for preservice education. But I am also convinced that this is a slow and stumbling journey and that along the way difficulty, pain, self-exposure, and disappointment are inevitable. To teach lessons about race and racism in teacher education is to struggle to unlearn racism itself — to interrogate the assumptions that are deeply embedded in the curriculum, to own our own complicity in maintaining existing systems of privilege and oppression, and to grapple with our own failure.

Nikki Giovanni's "A Journey" (1983, p. 47) eloquently conjures up the image of blind vision that I wish to connect to the idea of unlearning racism. I conclude this article with her poem:

A Journey*

It's a journey . . . that I propose . . . I am not the guide . . . nor
technical assistant . . . I will be your fellow passenger . . .

Though the rail has been ridden . . . winter clouds cover . . .
autumn's exuberant guilt . . . we must provide our own guideposts . .
.

I have heard . . . from previous visitors . . . the road washes out
sometimes . . . and passengers are compelled . . . to continue
groping . . . or turn back . . . I am not afraid . . .

I am not afraid of rough spots . . . or lonely times . . . I don't
fear . . . the success of this endeavor . . .
I promise you nothing . . . I accept your promise . . . of the
same we are simply riding . . . a wave . . . that may carry or crash . . .
It's a journey . . . and I want . . . to go . . .

* "A Journey" from *Those Who Ride the Night Winds* by Nikki Giovanni. Copyright © 1983 by Nikki Giovanni. Reprinted by permission of HarperCollins Publishers, Inc.

NOTES

1. I have outlined the ways this program addressed issues of race, class, and culture in a number of articles, particularly an earlier *Harvard Educational Review* piece (Cochran-Smith, 1995b).

2. This narrative was constructed based on my own and a colleague's notes about the seminar sessions, my own written reflections shortly following the event, notes on conversations with students and with other teacher educators prior to and following the sessions, written communications from students, and other program documents that described the structure and context of the program. Excerpts from written communications and students' comments and papers are used with permission of the authors.

3. The idea of "reading teacher education as racial text" emerges from a number of sources, as described in the following section. The term itself draws from Castenell and Pinar's (1993) concept of "understanding curriculum as racial text," which is also the title of their edited collection of articles about identity and difference in education, particularly how these are represented in curriculum.

4. The analysis I offer here is based on multiple curriculum and teaching documents, as well as experiences captured in my own reflections over a six-year period at the University of Pennsylvania. These include syllabi and assignments for courses that I taught each year during that time period; program handbooks and advertising literature; my own and others' writing about the program (both formal papers and more personal reflections), detailed notes from meetings of student teachers, university-based supervisors, and whole-community meetings that included school-based cooperating teachers; letters and personal notes sent to me by program participants; two student group papers about racism and teaching that were written and presented in public forums during this time; and analytic descriptions of several key events and critical incidents that occurred.

5. These members of the teacher education community shared their personal accounts with the larger group by presenting orally, including their pieces in the course reading packet and in-house booklets, and facilitating small-group discussions.

6. These were some of the readings regularly used.

7. This is in no way intended to suggest that whole language proponents are unaware of the political and ideological aspects of language instruction, nor is it intended to suggest that they do not address issues of culture. Many whole language theorists locate their work and the debates about whole language perspectives squarely within a cultural and political context (Dudley-Marling, 1997; Edelsky, 1986, 1990; Edelsky, Altwerger, & Flores, 1991; Goodman, 1988; Shannon, 1988). Indeed, Carol Edelsky, arguably one of the best known and most articulate spokespersons and theorists for the whole language movement, gives explicit attention to the politics of pedagogy and to whole language as a theory of practice aimed at social justice and democracy (Edelsky, 1990; Edelsky et al., 1991). Edelsky's work on bilingual education is also explicitly connected to cultural contexts. The popular media debates about whole language and phonics, however, rarely frame these issues as cultural and political questions, and some of those who advocate whole language ignore cultural and political issues altogether and speak as if teaching from a whole language perspective were merely a matter of using certain materials and approaches to teaching.

8. The questions my students posed, the interpretations they constructed, and the pedagogies they developed when their readings and discussions included these new additions are part of a larger analysis I am currently completing.

9. I have used this example in a different way in a discussion about the politics of children's literature and the responsibility of teachers as agents for social change (see Cochran-Smith, 1999).

10. These excerpts represent a range of comments made by students in class discussions and/or in brief written responses to the book. This is not a direct transcription of the actual discussion that unfolded, but is rather a set of excerpts from written and oral comments.

REFERENCES

Apple, M. (1996). *Cultural politics in education.* New York: Teachers College Press.
Asante, M. (1991). The Afro-centric idea in education. *Journal of Negro Education, 62,* 170–180.
Au, K., & Kawakami, A. (1994). Cultural congruence in instruction. In E. Hollins, J. King, & W. Hayman (Eds.), *Teaching diverse population: Formulating a knowledge base* (pp. 5–23). Albany: State University of New York Press.
Ballenger, C. (1992). Because you like us: The language of control. *Harvard Educational Review, 62,* 199–208.
Banks, L. (1981). *The Indian in the cupboard.* Garden City, NY: Doubleday.
Banks, L. (1986). *The return of the Indian.* Garden City, NY: Doubleday.
Berthoff, A. (1987). The teacher as researcher. In D. Goswami & P. R. Stillman (Eds.), *Reclaiming the classroom: Teacher research as an agency for change* (pp. 28–48). Upper Montclair, NJ: Boynton/Cook.
Britton, J. (1987). A quiet form of research. In D. Goswami & P. Stillman (Eds.), *Reclaiming the classroom: Teacher research as an agency for change* (pp. 13–19). Upper Montclair, NJ: Boynton/Cook.
Britzman, D. (1991). *Practice makes practice: A critical study of learning to teach.* Albany: State University of New York Press.
Calkins, L. (1991). *Living between the lines.* Portsmouth, NH: Heinemann.
Calkins, L. (1994). *The art of teaching writing.* Portsmouth, NH: Heinemann.
Carini, P. (1986). *Prospect's documentary process.* Bennington, VT: Prospect School Center.
Castenell, L., & Pinar, W. (Eds.). (1993). *Understanding curriculum as racial text: Representations of identity and difference in education.* Albany: State University of New York Press.
Cochran-Smith, M. (1991). Learning to teach against the grain. *Harvard Educational Review, 51,* 279–310.
Cochran-Smith, M. (1995a). Color blindness and basket making are not the answers: Confronting the dilemmas of race, culture, and language diversity in teacher education. *American Educational Research Journal, 32,* 493–522.
Cochran-Smith, M. (1995b). Uncertain allies: Understanding the boundaries of race and teaching. *Harvard Educational Review, 65,* 541–570.
Cochran-Smith, M. (1999). Learning to teach for social justice. In G. Griffin (Ed.), *98th yearbook of NSSE: Teacher education for a new century: Emerging perspectives, promising practices, and future possibilities.* Chicago: University of Chicago Press.
Cochran-Smith, M., Dimattia, P., Dudley-Marling, C., Freedman, S., Friedman, A., Jackson, J., Jackson, R., Loftus, F., Mooney, J., Neisler, O., Peck, A., Pelletier, C., Pine, G., Scanlon, D., & Zollers, N. (1999, April). *Seeking social justice: A teacher education faculty's self study, year III.* Paper presented at the Annual Meeting of the American Educational Research Association, Montreal.
Cochran-Smith, M., & Lytle, S. (1992). Communities for teacher research: Fringe or forefront. *American Journal of Education, 100,* 298–323.
Cochran-Smith, M., & Lytle, S. (1993). *Inside/outside: Teacher research and knowledge.* New York: Teachers College Press.
Cochran-Smith, M., & Lytle, S. (1998). Teacher research: The question that persists. *International Journal of Leadership in Education, 1*(1), 19–36.

Cochran-Smith, M., & Lytle, S. (1999). Relationships of knowledge and practice: Teacher learning in communities. In A. Iran-Nejad & C. D. Pearson (Eds.), *Review of research in education* (vol. 24, pp. 251–307). Washington, DC: American Educational Research Association.

Cole, A., & Knowles, J. (1998). The self-study of teacher education practices and the reform of teacher education. In M. L. Hamilton (Ed.), *Reconceptualizing teaching practice: Self-study in teacher education* (pp. 224–234). London: Falmer Press.

Comer, J. (1989). Racism and the education of young children. *Teachers College Record, 90,* 352–361.

Delpit, L. (1986). Skills and other dilemmas of a progressive Black educator. *Harvard Educational Review, 56,* 379–385.

Delpit, L. (1988). The silenced dialogue: Power and pedagogy in educating other people's children. *Harvard Educational Review, 58,* 280–298.

Delpit, L. (1995). *Other people's children: Cultural conflict in the classroom.* New York: New Press.

Dewey, J. (1916). *Democracy and education: An introduction to the philosophy of education.* New York: Free Press.

Dudley-Marling, C. (1997). *Living with uncertainty: The messy reality of classroom practice.* Portsmouth, NH: Heinemann.

Dyson, A. (1987). The value of "time off-task": Young children's spontaneous talk and deliberate text. *Harvard Educational Review, 57,* 396–420.

Edelsky, C. (1986). *Writing in a bilingual program.* Norwood, NJ: Ablex.

Edelsky, C. (1990). Whose agenda is this anyway? A response to McKenna, Robinson, and Miller. *Educational Researcher, 19* (8), 3–6.

Edelsky, C., Altwerger, B., & Flores, B. (1991). *Whole language: What's the difference?* Portsmouth, NH: Heinemann.

Fine, M. (Ed.). (1994). *Chartering urban school reform: Reflections on pubic high schools in the midst of change.* New York: Teachers College Press.

Foster, M. (1993). Educating for competence in community and culture: Exploring views of exemplary African-American teachers. *Urban Education, 27,* 370–394.

Foster, M. (1994). Effective Black teachers: A literature review. In E. Hollins, J. King, & W. Hayman (Eds.), *Teaching diverse populations: Formulating a knowledge base* (pp. 225–241). Albany: State University of New York Press.

Ginsberg, M., & Clift, R. (1990). The hidden curriculum of preservice teacher education. In R. W. Houston (Ed.), *Handbook of research on teacher education* (pp. 450–468). New York: MacWilliams.

Giovanni, N. (1983). A journey. In *Those who ride the night winds* (p. 47) New York: William Morrow.

Giroux, H. (1984). Rethinking the language of schooling. *Language Arts, 61,* 33–40.

Giroux, H. (1988). *Teachers as intellectuals: Toward a pedagogy of learning.* Westport, CT: Bergin & Garvey.

Gitlin, A. (Ed.). (1994). *Power and method: Political activism and educational research.* New York: Routledge.

Goodman, K. (1988). *Report card on basal readers.* New York: Richard C. Owen.

Goswami, P., & Stillman, P. (1987). *Reclaiming the classroom: Teacher research as an agency for change.* Upper Montclair, NJ: Boynton/Cook.

Graves, D. (1983). *Writing: Teachers and children at work.* Portsmouth, NH: Heinemann.

Hardy, B. (1978). Towards a poetics of fiction: An approach through narrative. In M. Meek & G. Barton (Eds.), *The cool web* (pp. 12–23). New York: Antheneum.

Harris, V. (Ed.). (1993). *Teaching multicultural literature in grades K–8.* Norwood, MA: Christopher-Gordon.

Heath, S. (1982a). Questioning at home and at school: A comparative study. In G. Spindler (Ed.), *Doing an ethnography of schooling* (pp. 103–131). New York: Holt, Rinehart & Winston.

Heath, S. (1982b). What no bedtime story means: Narrative skills at home and school. *Language in Society, 11,* 49–76.

Hollins, E., King, J., & Hayman, W. (Eds.). (1994). *Teaching diverse populations: Formulating a knowledge base.* Albany: State University of New York Press.

hooks, b. (1994). *Teaching to transgress: Education as the practice of freedom.* New York: Routledge.

Irvine, J. (1990). *Black students and school failure: Policies, practice and prescriptions.* New York: Greenwood Press.

Irvine, J., & York, D. (1995). Learning styles and culturally diverse students: A literature review. In J. A. Banks & C. A. M. Banks (Eds.), *Handbook of research on multicultural education.* (pp. 494–497). New York: Macmillan.

King, J. (1994). The purpose of schooling for African American children: Including cultural knowledge. In E. R. Hollins, J. E. King, & W. C. Hayman (Eds.), *Teaching diverse populations: Formulating a knowledge base* (pp. 25–56). Albany: State University of New York Press.

King, J., Hollins, E., & Hayman, W. (Eds.). (1997). *Preparing teachers for cultural diversity.* New York: Teachers College Press.

Kozol, J. (1991). *Savage inequalities: Children in America's schools.* New York: Crown.

Ladson-Billings, G. (1994). *The dreamkeepers: Successful teachers of African-American children.* San Francisco: Jossey Bass.

Ladson-Billings, G. (1995). Toward a theory of culturally relevant pedagogy. *American Educational Research Journal, 32,* 465–491.

Lawrence, S., & Tatum, B. (1997). Teachers in transition: The impact of antiracist professional development on classroom practice. *Teachers College Record, 99,* 162–178.

Leistyna, P., Woodrum, A., & Sherblom, S. A. (Eds.). (1996). *Breaking free: The transformative power of critical pedagogy.* Cambridge, MA: Harvard Educational Review.

Lytle, S., & Cochran-Smith, M. (1992). Teacher research as a way of knowing. *Harvard Educational Review, 62,* 447–474.

MacCann, D. (1993). Native Americans in books for the young. In V. Harris (Ed.), *Teaching multicultural literature in grades K–8* (pp. 137–170). Norwood, MA: Christopher-Gordon.

McCarthy, C. (1990). Multicultural education, minorities, identities, textbooks, and the challenge of curriculum reform. *Journal of Education, 172,* 118–129.

McCarthy, C. (1993). Multicultural approaches to racial inequality in the United States. In L. A. Castenell & W. F. Pinar (Eds.), *Understanding curriculum as racial text,* (pp. 245–246). Albany: State University of New York Press.

McDonald, J. (1992). *Teaching: Making sense of an uncertain craft.* New York: Teachers College Press.

McIntosh, P. (1989). White privilege: Unpacking the invisible knapsack. *Peace and Freedom, 49*(4), 10–12.

Metzger, D. (1986). Circles of stories. *Parabola, 4*(4), 1–4.

Mishler, E. (1986). *Research interviewing: Context and marriage.* Cambridge, MA: Harvard University Press.

Moll, L., Amanti, C., Neff, D., Gonzalez, N. (1992). Funds of knowledge for teaching: Using a qualitative approach to connect homes and classrooms. *Theory Into Practice, 31,* 32–41.

National Education Goals Panel. (1997). *National education goals report.* Washington, DC: Author.

Nieto, S. (1999). *The light in their eyes: Creating multicultural learning communities.* New York: Teachers College Press.

Noffke, S. (1997). Professional, personal, and political dimensions of action research. In M. Apple (Ed.), *Review of research in education* (pp. 305–343). Washington, DC: American Educational Research Association.

Ogbu, J. (1978). *Minority education and caste.* New York: Academic Press.

Paley, V. (1979). *White teacher.* Cambridge, MA: Harvard University Press.

Philadelphia Teachers Learning Cooperative. (1984). On becoming teacher experts: Buying time. *Language Arts, 6,* 731–735.

Pincus, M. (1993). Following the paper trail. In M. Cochran-Smith & S. Lytle, *Inside/outside: Teacher research and knowledge* (pp. 249–255). New York: Teachers College Press.

Quality Education for Minorities Project. (1990). *Education that works: An action plan for the education of minorities.* Cambridge, MA: Author.

Rodriguez, A. (1998). What is (should be) the researcher's role in terms of agency? A question for the 21st century. *Journal of Research in Science Teaching, 35,* 963–965.

Rose, M. (1989). *Lives on the boundary.* New York: Penguin.

Rosenberg, P. (1997). Underground discourses: Exploring Whiteness in teacher education. In M. Fine, L. Weis, L. Powell, & L. Wong (Eds.), *Off-white: readings on race and power in society* (pp. 79–86). New York: Routledge.

Rosenblatt, L. (1976). *Literature as exploration.* New York: Noble & Noble.

Shannon, P. (1988). *Merging literacy: Reading instruction in 20th century America.* South Hadley, MA: Bergin & Garvey.

Sleeter, C. (1992). Restructuring schools for multicultural education. *Journal of Teacher Education, 43,* 141–148.

Sleeter, C., & Grant, C. (1987). An analysis of multicultural education in the United States. *Harvard Educational Review, 57,* 421–444.

Slapin, B., & Seale, B. (1992). *Through Indian eyes: The native experience in books for children.* Philadelphia: New Society.

Strieb, L. (1985). *A (Philadelphia) teacher's journal.* Grand Forks: North Dakota Study Group Center for Teaching and Learning.

Tatum, B. (1992). Talking about race, learning about racism: The applications of racial identity development theory. *Harvard Educational Review, 62,* 1–24.

Tatum, B. (1994). Teaching White students about racism: The search for White allies and the restoration of hope. *Teachers College Record, 95,* 462–476.

Tatum, B. (1997). *"Why are all the Black kids sitting together in the cafeteria?" and other conversations about the development of racial identity.* New York: Basic Books.

Taxel, J. (1993) The politics of children's literature: Reflections on multiculturalism and Christopher Columbus. In V. Harris (Ed.), *Teaching multicultural literature in grades K–8* (pp. 1–36). Norwood, MA: Christopher-Gordon.

Thompson, B., & Tyagi, S. (Eds.). (1996). *Names we call home: Autobiography on racial identity.* New York: Routledge.

Van Manen, M. (1990). *Researching lived experience: Human science for an action sensitive pedagogy.* Albany: State University of New York Press.

Villegas, A. (1991). *Culturally responsive pedagogy for the 1990s and beyond.* Princeton, NJ: Educational Testing Service.

Waff, D. (1994). Romance in the classroom: Inviting discourse on gender and power. *The Voice, 3*(1), 7–14.

PART TWO

▼▼▼▼▼

Teacher Expectations and School Effectiveness

Student Social Class and Teacher Expectations: The Self-Fulfilling Prophecy in Ghetto Education

▼▼▼▼▼

RAY C. RIST

Thirty years after Ray Rist's classic article "Student Social Class and Teacher Expectations" first appeared in the Harvard Educational Review, *the Editorial Board reprinted it with a new introduction by Rist, which is reprinted here along with the original work.*

Author's Introduction:
The Enduring Dilemmas of Class and Color
in American Education

When asked by the editors of the *Harvard Educational Review* to prepare this short note as the introduction to the reprint of my 1970 article, my first reaction was that it cannot already be thirty years since the publication of "Student Social Class and Teacher Expectations." But it is, and thus I offer these brief observations on three areas germane to this piece: the state of urban education then and now; the qualitative research methods used then and now, especially the "insider-outsider" issue of myself as a White person doing research in the African American community; and, finally, several personal reflections.

THE STATE OF URBAN EDUCATION

Raising this issue with a thirty-year retrospective is almost to enter a time warp. So much of what was the reality of the education of Black youth thirty years ago is no different today. Urban schools so often did not do well by their charges then, and in many ways, they still do not do so. Schools are still facing

Harvard Educational Review Vol. 70 No. 3 Fall 2000, 257–301

many of the same issues now as they did then. It would not be misleading, to paraphrase an old cliché, to say that the more time passes, the more things stay the same.

Intersecting with the highly visible and flammable issues in urban education of violence, drugs, academic failure, and collapsing infrastructures are the twin pivots of class and color. When I titled the original article, I emphasized the matter of student social class. I did so because the classrooms, the school, and its neighborhood community in St. Louis at that time were of one ethnic/racial group — African American. What I had observed was that as color was held constant, the realities of the social-class differences became not only apparent but pivotal in the construction of reality. Indeed, there was such a strong fit between the social class of the students and their academic tracking that it was striking how powerful this variable was for understanding their present and future treatment within that school setting. And when I expanded the analysis into a book, I again emphasized the class dimension by entitling the book, *The Urban School: A Factory for Failure* (1973).

Let me be clear. I was not then arguing that class superceded color, but that they together created a powerful interaction. I had colleagues at the time who were adamant in their arguments that one or the other was preeminent. Any number of them posited that color overrode any considerations of class. Stated differently, racism was so pervasive and so powerful in defining the situation in the United States that it had to be recognized as the dominant reality in any study of African Americans. Conversely, any number of my sociological colleagues at the time believed that the most appropriate analysis was through a framework of social class. In their opinion, Karl Marx was correct, and the best understanding of the situation of Black Americans was to view them as an exploited internal colony.

In contrast to this either-or approach, I found in the school a reality where class interacted with color. Of course, racism was powerful and ever present — otherwise why would the city schools of St. Louis be so entirely segregated that all-Black and all-White schools were the norm? And how could it be that I was the only White person to ever enter into that school building week after week after week? But social-class differentiation was equally a reality. Poor students in that school received neither the rewards nor the attention that was granted to the few middle-class students. Why is it that one might expect African Americans, including the teachers studied, not to respond to many of the same social-class forces that influence the behaviors and values of other groups in the society, whether majority or minority? In a school world of segregation, racism, and isolation, the power of social class was still evident. As an analyst, I could not avoid addressing the presence of both and how each played off against or in concert with the other.

The geographical compression of the broader social-class structure of the Black community into a restricted set of residential areas meant that the opportunities back in the 1960s to create geographically dispersed communities based on social class were few to nonexistent. (Indeed, the level of residential segregation in St. Louis was among the highest in the country.) Whereas White communities could differentiate among themselves on matters of social class with all the space they needed in the suburbs (where communities calibrated themselves at $10,000 intervals), the Black communities had no such opportunities. Thus, like an accordion squeezed shut, the Black community found its social classes compressed in on one another. And while I have no comparative data on urban White schools, my suspicion would be that the social-class diversity within each White school was less than in Black schools; that is, that poor White students were going to school predominately or exclusively with other poor White students.

There is an ironic twist to one aspect of the improvement in race relations in the United States over these past three decades. As the Black middle class has grown and suburban housing has opened up, the Black children remaining in the urban schools are now overwhelmingly poor. Thus, a kind of perverse equality has emerged between poor urban Whites, poor urban Blacks, and poor urban Hispanics — they are now each in schools populated by other poor students.

Parenthetically, I see this reality as having played for years into the issue of school integration, as it also does now with vouchers. The bottom line is that non-poor folks do not like to see their children going to school with poor children. One of the realities that cut deep into the issue of school integration was that it meant poor Black children were being brought into schools of non-poor Whites. Color and class then collided. This I documented in another of my ethnographic studies, where I studied how thirty Black children came each day on a bus to integrate a school of more than seven hundred White children (Rist, 1978). The voucher issue also has the underlying issues of color and class front and center, regardless of the rhetoric of market tests, choice, and breaking up monopolies. Vouchers imply mobility for poor children, most of whom are minorities. Why this concept continues to stall on the American political scene is not just a matter of costs or teacher and school board opposition, but because of the intruding realities of color and class.

The issue thirty years after my article is that there is scant evidence that the urban schools are now any better prepared or positioned to address issues of color and class. Poor children in general have a hard time making it through school. Poor children who are also minority children have an even tougher time making it through. These children are just not likely to ever find a seat at the American Feast. At this time in American society when wealth absolutely abounds and money sloshes around in staggering amounts, between 18 and 20 percent of all children are living in poverty. (The numbers for Black children and Hispanic children are 36 percent and 34 percent, respectively.) Indeed, on several key statistics of the well-being of American children, for example, infant mortality and the percentage of children living in households below 50 percent of the national median, to name but two, American children now lag behind children in many developing countries (Federal Interagency Forum on Child and Family Statistics, 2000). The sobering reality is that when it comes to both color and class, U.S. schools tend to conform much more to the contours of American society than they transform it. And this appears to be a lesson that we are not wanting to learn.

THE METHODOLOGY OF STUDYING IN A PUBLIC SCHOOL

There was, in the 1960s, something of an upstart movement of social scientists who thought that if one wanted to know the realities of the social problems in the United States, they had to be experienced and observed first hand. This was in contrast, at the time, to the predominant emphasis on large survey research projects, on quantitative analysis, and on deductive theory building. The quantitative/qualitative debate in the social sciences was just coming on the scene. Thus, Elliot Liebow studied homeless men in Washington, DC, Joyce Ladner studied large public housing projects in St. Louis, Carol Stack studied women struggling to subsist on welfare in Boston, Gerald Suttles studied the social order of a Chicago slum, and James Spradley studied skid row alcoholics in Seattle, to name but five classical studies. In all of these and many more, researchers used field-based methods derived from anthropology and sociology. The conventional and mainline funding organizations seldom supported such work, be they the National Science Foundation, the National Institutes of Health, or the foundations. Three federal agencies that did nurture such studies were the National Institute of Mental Health (NIMH), the Office of Economic Opportunity (OEO), which was to coordinate the "War on Poverty" under both presidents Kennedy and Johnson, and the Department of Health, Education, and Welfare (HEW).

The study of U.S. education was not overlooked by those wanting in-depth, qualitative assessments of the conditions of American children. There were a number of studies that addressed the intersection of poverty and education (both urban and rural), early childhood learning (linked to the creation and early years of Head Start), the education of minority groups, and the treatment of children in schools. Popular books like *Death at an Early Age* and *Up the Down Staircase* fueled an interest in learning more about the dynamics of what was happening to students, particularly those in urban schools. School systems were being portrayed as killers of the spirits of students, as completely succumbing to bureaucratic rules and regimens, and using teachers as agents of social control over the poor.

There was in all this qualitative work a slant toward an "underdog" approach. There was clearly sympathy with those whom the American system treated as marginal. Indeed, there was a not too subtle political agenda in all this as well, for it was to the benefit of the OEO, HEW, and the NIMH, for example, to fund studies that would document and portray American citizens as being locked out of economic opportunity, denied a fair chance for a decent life, and crushed under a burden of poverty. If the necessary political will was to be mobilized to address these issues, American society needed to know just how desperate the straits were for so many of their fellow citizens. It was, of course, also in the best political survival instincts of these federal agencies to document the breadth and depth of the problems they were mandated to address.

The research project that generated "Student Social Class and Teacher Expectations" was supported for three years with a grant from the HEW to Washington University in St. Louis. Jules Henry, a cultural anthropologist, was the study director. Three graduate students (myself being one) received funding to spend up to three years documenting the socialization of Black youth into the St. Louis public schools. All three of us were to begin with a group of children from their first day of kindergarten and follow them through the second grade. Each of us was to be in a different public elementary school, and given the emphasis on the study of minority youth, it turned out that each school had only Black children enrolled. (Again, this was not surprising, given the residential segregation patterns in St. Louis.) The other two graduate students were both women, one White and one Black.

From the beginning, Jules Henry directed the study according to an intensive field-based and observational/ethnographic methodology. The expectation was that there would be up to fifteen hours per week of field work, either in the school and classrooms or in the students' homes. We were to prepare elaborate and detailed field notes on each site visit and then subsequently code according to an evolving coding scheme that the team developed. No testing, no psychometric assessments, no formal surveys, and no quantitative classroom observation instruments were ever used. The study was entirely based on the systematic gathering of qualitative data via the observation of behavior in natural settings — classrooms, playgrounds, living rooms, a city park, etc.

What strikes me about this approach thirty years later is that it is still entirely appropriate, though there may now be a greater preference for multi-method strategies for the study design and the subsequent data collection and analysis. The methodological approach embedded in qualitative research has lost none of its appeal — and indeed is now more prevalent and legitimated than in the 1960s. Field-based work in applied social science areas such as evaluation, monitoring, and action research all now use qualitative approaches as basic tools of the trade.

But there is a question to ask and for which there is no real clear answer — could this same study be done today as it was then? There are a number of factors that leave me thinking it could not be done as it was. First, the gatekeeping function (within the public school system and within the university) was much more rudimentary then than it is now. There were no human subjects committees in the university at the time and there were no review committees in the school system for either the research protocol itself or for community acceptance. It is my recollection that Jules Henry needed only the permission of one assistant superintendent and the study was up and running. There was also, so far as I remember, no permission ever garnered from the students, their parents, the teachers, or any of the administrators in the school. We simply showed up the first day of school and were shown to a kindergarten classroom where we could begin our observations. This is not to say that the design of this project was flawed or that it abused those studied, but only that without any oversight or serious review, we did our study.

Second, there was the matter of the race of the graduate students doing the data collection and that of the principal investigator himself. Two of the three graduate students and Jules Henry were White. I will say only for myself that I never felt unwelcome in the school, at the PTA meetings, or when I joined the faculty volleyball team. (Indeed, during my third year at the school, I was asked if I would join the board of the PTA. I think it was because I had had perfect attendance for the past two years!) These types of activities (plus bringing donuts on Friday mornings for the faculty lounge) were part of building trust and rapport with the faculty over the three years of the study. It is quite simply one of the strengths of qualitative research that comes with time and effort. I am not sure what a White graduate student might find today in an all-Black elementary school. To say it simply, race relations today in the United States are more subtle and the overlay of social-class distinctions have blurred the codes of interaction. The result has been a real tenuousness in figuring out how to behave. How the question of being a racial "outsider" might play itself out at present is not clear to me. And related to the point above, I am not sure how a university review panel or a school district review panel might respond to this kind of racial mix on the study — that is, only one of the four researchers was African American. And I am hard pressed now to identify in the past few years ethnographic studies undertaken by Whites in Black urban schools that would help answer this question. But maybe the absence of such studies is itself the answer.

Finally, there is the matter of the political rhetoric and ideology now linked to such work. Regardless of the methodological strategy, the issue is one of the political lens through which such an urban school would be described by the author. Is there a political correctness to how one approaches the study of minority urban education? Does an "underdog" bias still exist? Would those who argue that only an "insider's" perspective is valid in the study of minority communities and institutions ever accept analysis done by an "outsider"? The questions can go on and on, but the point of the political lens is the core issue. The study thirty years ago took a rather straightforward, if somewhat optimistic, approach that urban schools were shortchanging their minority students and needed to do better. The question now is what message would (or could be allowed to) come from an ethnographic study of an inner-city school in a blighted neighborhood with a 100 percent minority student enrollment.

SOME FINAL OBSERVATIONS

To return to the theme at the beginning of this note, the issues of color and class inequality in American society are at the heart of the future of U.S. education. The basic challenge is that there is a profound disconnect between the rhetoric and the reality of American society for those on the bottom rung of the economic ladder. While the rhetoric is that of opportunity (be it through education, training, trickle-down economic growth, urban revitalization, etc.), the reality for those in the lowest 20 percent quintile of economic resources is quite different. Indeed, those in this bottom 20 percent have in the past thirty years actually lost ground to the rest of the society. The schism is real. The stratification of the American underclass is now more permanent and pervasive than thirty years ago. Add to this the isolation from the centers of economic growth of those who are both poor and minority and the picture is not a pretty one. That the present presidential campaign is silent on the matter is to be expected. But the fact remains, this condition is being ignored to the peril of the country.

The implications for urban schools are not upbeat. Into the foreseeable future, these schools now face the challenge of educating literally hundreds of thousands of children who are in both real and relative terms extremely poor. These children come into the schools each morning from poor surroundings and go back to them each afternoon. The ability of these schools to generate social and economic opportunities for this massive group of children when the rest of the social structure works to block their way onto the mobility escalator is simply quite limited. And never mind the growing digital divide (and is not this divide along color and class lines?) separating those with the access to and knowledge of these new ways of accumulating and managing information from those without.

Another issue facing urban schools that was emphasized in the original article, but not yet mentioned here, is that of the teachers — their quality, their longevity, and their intentions toward the poor. The question is straightforward: Who now wants to teach in urban schools and why? If it is now difficult to fill the teaching vacancies in the strong and wealthy suburban schools, how greater are the difficulties for the urban schools? Thirty years ago, teaching jobs in city schools were a sure means of middle-class stability and mobility for thousands of Black people. Indeed, the teachers college in St. Louis, Harris Teachers College, supplied Black professionals for the school system for decades. But now, those in the African American community who desire to be teachers are no longer restricted to looking only for positions in the city schools. The urban schools therefore no longer have a guaranteed work force of minority professionals. Thus the question of who comes to teach in urban classrooms.

The policy implications for the country in general and for urban districts in particular are multiple. Presuming that the United States can treat the present situation in urban schools with a business-as-usual mentality only leads to a continual downward spiral. Our strategies for urban schools and the teachers within them seem caught in a cul de sac. We go round and round with the same remedies and the situation does not improve. Defining schooling to involve entire families and their learning needs, continual training of the teachers, breaking the barriers on certification of teachers, opening facilities on an 18-hour-a-day, year-round basis, school/private sector partnerships that mean more than the private sector donating used computers, and true performance standards with real accountability are but a few propositions to consider that might start to send urban education in a new direction. Even these might be insufficient to the task at hand.

Finally, two personal comments: First, thirty years after publishing this article based on a qualitative design and methodology, I find myself more than ever convinced that the information that comes from this approach is vital to understanding the inner workings of American society, be it in board rooms or in classrooms. But while those with power and resources have access to the media and can shape perceptions to their own benefit, the same is not available to the poor. Thus, giving voice to those who are not often heard or seen is a distinct contribution of qualitative research. Their voice comes through unmuted by the aggregation of survey results and the unexplained variance in regression equations. Having a window into the actual lives and views of others, especially those who are not like one's self, can be a powerful means of conveying information and creating new awareness.

Second, and to some degree the other side of the coin, is my view that policymakers truly need this kind of information and analysis. I have spent more than fifteen years in the U.S. government (both executive and legislative branches), and now almost four years in an international development bank. I have been taken aback time and again about how those in positions of authority think they "know" what poor and marginalized peoples believe/ want/need. In reality, these decisionmakers so often did not have a clue. Without a means of giving voice to the poor and marginalized, decisions will be made that reflect nothing more than the perceptions and values of those making the decisions. Bringing the views and beliefs of those on the outside to those on the inside is no small feat. But to not hear the voices of the poor, to not legitimate the stake they have in their own future, and to incorrectly assume commonly shared realities is to ensure their peripheral status in American society.

REFERENCES

Federal Interagency Forum on Child and Family Statistics. (2000). *America's children: Key national indicators of well-being, 2000.* Washington, DC: Author.

Rist, R. C. (1973). *The urban school: A factory for failure.* Cambridge, MA: MIT Press.

Rist, R. C. (1978). *The invisible children: School integration in American society.* Cambridge, MA: Harvard University Press.

The views expressed here are those of the author and no endorsement by the World Bank Group is intended or should be inferred.

Student Social Class and Teacher Expectations: The Self-Fulfilling Prophecy in Ghetto Education

A dominant aspect of the American ethos is that education is both a necessary and a desirable experience for all children. To that end, compulsory attendance at some type of educational institution is required of all youth until somewhere in the middle teens. Thus on any weekday during the school year, one can expect slightly over 35,000,000 young persons to be distributed among nearly 1,100,000 classrooms throughout the nation (Jackson, 1968).

There is nothing either new or startling in the statement that there exist gross variations in the educational experience of the children involved. The scope of analysis one utilizes in examining these educational variations will reveal different variables of importance. There appear to be at least three levels at which analysis is warranted. The first is a macro-analysis of structural relationships where governmental regulations, federal, state, and local tax support, and the presence or absence of organized political and religious pressure all affect the classroom experience. At this level, study of the policies and politics of the Board of Education within the community is also relevant. The milieu of a particular school appears to be the second area of analysis in which one may examine facilities, pupil-teacher ratios, racial and cultural composition of the faculty and students, community and parental involvement, faculty relationships, the role of the principal, supportive services such as medical care, speech therapy, and library facilities — all of which may have a direct impact on the quality as well as the quantity of education a child receives.

Analysis of an individual classroom and the activities and interactions of a specific group of children with a single teacher is the third level at which there may be profitable analysis of the variations in the educational experience. Such micro-analysis could seek to examine the social organization of the class, the development of norms governing interpersonal behavior, and the variety of roles that both the teacher and students assume. It is on this third level — that of the individual classroom — that this study will focus. Teacher-student relationships and the dynamics of interaction between the teacher and students are far from uniform. For any child within the classroom, variations in the experience of success or failure, praise or ridicule, freedom or control, creativity or docility, comprehension or mystification may ultimately have significance far beyond the boundaries of the classroom situation (Henry, 1955, 1959, 1963).

It is the purpose of this paper to explore what is generally regarded as a crucial aspect of the classroom experience for the children involved — the

Reprinted from *Harvard Educational Review* Vol. 40 No. 3 August 1970, 411–451 process whereby expectations and social interactions give rise to the social organization of the class. There occurs within the classroom a social process whereby, out of a large group of children and an adult unknown to one another prior to the beginning of the school year, there emerge patterns of behavior, expectations of performance, and a mutually accepted stratification system delineating those doing well from those doing poorly. Of particular concern will be the relation of the teacher's expectations of potential academic performance to the social status of the student. Emphasis will be placed on the initial presuppositions of the teacher regarding the intellectual ability of certain groups of children and their consequences for the children's socialization into the school system. A major goal of this analysis is to ascertain the importance of the initial expectations of the teacher in relation to the child's chances for success or failure within the public school system. (For previous studies of the significance of student social status to variations in educational experience, see also Becker, 1953; Hollingshead, 1949; Lynd, 1937; Warner et al., 1944).

Increasingly, with the concern over intellectual growth of children and the long and close association that children experience with a series of teachers, attention is centering on the role of the teacher within the classroom (Sigel, 1969). A long series of studies have been conducted to determine what effects on children a teacher's values, beliefs, attitudes, and, most crucial to this analysis, a teacher's expectations may have. Asbell (1963), Becker (1952), Clark (1963), Gibson (1965), Harlem Youth Opportunities Unlimited (1964), Katz (1964), Kvaraceus (1965), MacKinnon (1962), Riessman (1962, 1965), Rose (1956), Rosenthal and Jacobson (1968), and Wilson (1963) have all noted that the teacher's expectations of a pupil's academic performance may, in fact, have a strong influence on the actual performance of that pupil. These authors have sought to validate a type of educational selffulfilling prophecy: if the teacher expects high performance, she receives it, and vice versa. A major criticism that can be directed at much of the research is that although the studies may establish that a teacher has differential expectations and that these influence performance for various pupils, they have not elucidated either the basis upon which such differential expectations are formed or how they are directly manifested within the classroom milieu. It is a goal of this paper to provide an analysis both of the factors that are critical in the teacher's development of expectations for various groups of her pupils and of the process by which such expectations influence the classroom experience for the teacher and the students.

The basic position to be presented in this paper is that the development of expectations by the kindergarten teacher as to the differential academic potential and capability of any student was significantly determined by a series of subjectively interpreted attributes and characteristics of that student. The argument may be succinctly stated in five propositions. First, the kindergarten teacher possessed a roughly constructed "ideal type" as to what characteristics were necessary for any given student to achieve "success" both in the public school and in the larger society. These characteristics appeared to be, in significant part, related to social class criteria. Second, upon first meeting her students at the beginning of the school year, subjective evaluations were made of the students as to possession or absence of the desired traits necessary for anticipated "success." On the basis of the evaluation, the class was divided into groups expected to succeed (termed by the teacher "fast learners") and those anticipated to fail (termed "slow learners"). Third, differential treatment was accorded to the two groups in the classroom, with the group designated as "fast learners" receiving the majority of the teaching time, reward-directed behavior, and attention from the teacher. Those designated as "slow learners" were taught infrequently, subjected to more frequent control-oriented behavior, and received little if any supportive behavior from the teacher. Fourth, the interactional patterns between the teacher and the various groups in her class became rigidified, taking on caste-like characteristics, during the course of the school year, with the gap in completion of academic material between the two groups widening as the school year progressed. Fifth, a similar process occurred in later years of schooling, but the teachers no longer relied on subjectively interpreted data as the basis for ascertaining differences in students. Rather, they were able to utilize a variety of informational sources related to past performance as the basis for classroom grouping.

Though the position to be argued in this paper is based on a longitudinal study spanning two and one-half years with a single group of Black children, additional studies suggest that the grouping of children both between and within classrooms is a rather prevalent situation within American elementary classrooms. In a report released in 1961 by the National Education Association related to data collected during the 1958–1959 school year, an estimated 77.6 percent of urban school districts (cities with a population above 2500) indicated that they practiced between-classroom ability grouping in the elementary grades. In a national survey of elementary schools, Austin and Morrison (1963) found that "more than 80% reported that they 'always' or 'often' use readiness tests for pre-reading evaluation [in first grade]." These findings would suggest that within-classroom grouping may be an even more prevalent condition than between-classroom grouping. In evaluating data related to grouping within American elementary classrooms, Smith (1971, in press) concludes, "Thus group assignment on the basis of measured 'ability' or 'readiness' is an accepted and widespread practice."

Two grouping studies which bear particular mention are those by Borg (1964) and Goldberg, Passow, and Justman (1966). Lawrence (1969) summarizes the import of these two studies as "the two most carefully designed and controlled studies done concerning ability grouping during the elementary years." Two school districts in Utah, adjacent to one another and closely comparable in size, served as the setting for the study conducted by Borg. One of the two districts employed random grouping of students, providing all students with "enrichment," while the second school district adopted a group system with acceleration mechanisms present which sought to adapt curricular materials to ability level and also to enable varying rates of presentation of materials. In summarizing Borg's findings, Lawrence states:

> In general, Borg concluded that the grouping patterns had no consistent, general effects on achievement at any level. . . . Ability grouping may have motivated bright pupils to realize their achievement potential more fully, but it seemed to have little effect on the slow or average pupils. (p. 1)

The second study by Goldberg, Passow, and Justman was conducted in the New York City Public Schools and represents the most comprehensive study to date on elementary school grouping. The findings in general show results similar to those of Borg indicating that narrowing the ability range within a classroom on some basis of academic potential will in itself do little to produce positive academic change. The most significant finding of the study is that "variability in achievement from classroom to classroom was generally greater than the variability resulting from grouping pattern or pupil ability" (Lawrence, 1969). Thus one may tentatively conclude that teacher differences were at least as crucial to academic performance as were the effects of pupil ability or methods of classroom grouping. The study, however, fails to investigate within-class grouping.

Related to the issue of within-class variability are the findings of the Coleman Report (1966) which have shown achievement highly correlated with individual social class. The strong correlation present in the first grade does not decrease during the elementary years, demonstrating, in a sense, that the schools are not able effectively to close the achievement gap initially resulting from student social class (pp. 290–325). What variation the Coleman Report does find in achievement in the elementary years results largely from within- rather than between-school variations. Given that the report demonstrates that important differences in achievement do not arise from variations in facilities, curriculum, or staff, it concludes:

> One implication stands out above all: That schools bring little influence to bear on a child's achievement that is independent of his background and general social context; and that this very lack of independent effect means that the inequalities imposed on children by their home, neighborhood, and peer environment are carried along to become the inequalities with which they confront adult life at the end of school. For equality of educational opportunity through the schools must imply a strong effect of schools that is independent of the child's immediate social environment, and that strong independent effect is not present in American Schools. (p. 325)

It is the goal of this study to describe the manner in which such "inequalities imposed on children" become manifest within an urban ghetto school and the resultant differential educational experience for children from dissimilar social class backgrounds.

METHODOLOGY

Data for this study were collected by means of twice weekly one and one-half hour observations of a single group of Black children in an urban ghetto school who began kindergarten in September of 1967. Formal observations were conducted throughout the year while the children were in kindergarten and again in 1969 when these same children were in the first half of their second-grade year. The children were also visited informally four times in the classroom during their first-grade year.[1] The difference between the formal and informal observations consisted in the fact that during formal visits, a continuous handwritten account was taken of classroom interaction and activity as it occurred. Smith and Geoffrey (1968) have labeled this method of classroom observation "microethnography." The informal observations did not include the taking of notes during the classroom visit, but comments were written after the visit. Additionally, a series of interviews were conducted with both the kindergarten and the second-grade teachers. No mechanical devices were utilized to record classroom activities or interviews.

I believe it is methodologically necessary, at this point, to clarify what benefits can be derived from the detailed analysis of a single group of children. The single most apparent weakness of the vast majority of studies of urban education is that they lack any longitudinal perspective. The complexities of the interactional processes which evolve over time within classrooms cannot be discerned with a single two- or three-hour observational period. Second, education is a social process that cannot be reduced to variations in IQ scores over a period of time. At best, IQ scores merely give indications of potential, not of process. Third, I do not believe that this school and the classrooms within it are atypical from others in urban Black neighborhoods (see also both the popular literature [Kohl, 1967; Kozol, 1967] and the academic literature [Eddy, 1967; Fuchs, 1969; Leacock, 1969; Moore, 1967] on urban schools. The school in which this study occurred was selected by the District Superintendent as one of five available to the research team. All five schools were visited during the course of the study and detailed observations were conducted in four of them. The principal at the school reported upon in this study commented that I was very fortunate in coming to his school since his staff (and kindergarten teacher in particular) were equal to "any in the city." Finally, the utilization of longitudinal study as a research method in a ghetto school will enhance the possibilities of gaining further insight into mechanisms of adaptation utilized by Black youth to what appears to be a basically White, middle-class value-oriented institution.

THE SCHOOL

The particular school which the children attend was built in the early part of the 1960s. It has classes from kindergarten through the eighth grade and a single special educational class. The enrollment fluctuates near the 900 level while the teaching staff consists of twenty-six teachers, in addition to a librarian, two physical education instructors, the principal, and an assistant principal. There are also at the school, on a part-time basis, a speech therapist, social worker, nurse, and doctor, all employed by the Board of Education. All administrators, teachers, staff, and pupils are Black. (The author is Caucasian.) The school is located in a blighted urban area that has 98 percent Black population within its census district. Within the school itself, nearly 500 of the 900 pupils (55%) come from families supported by funds from Aid to Dependent Children, a form of public welfare.

THE KINDERGARTEN CLASS

Prior to the beginning of the school year, the teacher possessed several different kinds of information regarding the children that she would have in her class. The first was the pre-registration form completed by thirteen mothers of children who would be in the kindergarten class. On this form, the teacher was supplied with the name of the child, his age, the name of his parents, his home address, his phone number, and whether he had had any pre-school experience. The second source of information for the teacher was supplied two days before the beginning of school by the school social worker who provided a tentative list of all children enrolled in the kindergarten class who lived in homes that received public welfare funds.

The third source of information on the child was gained as a result of the initial interview with the mother and child during the registration period, either in the few days prior to the beginning of school or else during the first days of school. In this interview, a major concern was the gathering of medical information about the child as well as the ascertaining of any specific parental concern related to the child. This latter information was noted on the "Behavioral Questionnaire" where the mother was to indicate her concern, if any, on twenty-eight different items. Such items as thumb-sucking, bedwetting, loss of bowel control, lying, stealing, fighting, and laziness were included on this questionnaire.

The fourth source of information available to the teacher concerning the children in her class was both her own experiences with older siblings, and those of other teachers in the building related to behavior and academic performance of children in the same family. A rather strong informal norm had developed among teachers in the school such that pertinent information, especially that related to discipline matters, was to be passed on to the next teacher of the student. The teachers' lounge became the location in which they would discuss the performance of individual children as well as make comments concerning the parents and their interests in the student and the school. Frequently, during the first days of the school year, there were admonitions to a specific teacher to "watch out" for a child believed by a teacher to be a "trouble-maker." Teachers would also relate techniques of controlling the behavior of a student who had been disruptive in the class. Thus, a variety of information concerning students in the school was shared, whether that information regarded academic performance, behavior in class, or the relation of the home to the school.

It should be noted that not one of these four sources of information to the teacher was related directly to the academic potential of the incoming kindergarten child. Rather, they concerned various types of social information revealing such facts as the financial status of certain families, medical care of the child, presence or absence of a telephone in the home, as well as the structure of the family in which the child lived, that is, number of siblings, whether the child lived with both, one, or neither of his natural parents.

THE TEACHER'S STIMULUS

When the kindergarten teacher made the permanent seating assignments on the eighth day of school, not only had she the above four sources of information concerning the children, but she had also had time to observe them within the classroom setting. Thus the behavior, degree and type of verbalization, dress, mannerisms, physical appearance, and performance on the early tasks assigned during class were available to her as she began to form opinions concerning the capabilities and potential of the various children. That such evaluation of the children by the teacher was beginning, I believe, there is little doubt. Within a few days, only a certain group of children were continually being called on to lead the class in the Pledge of Allegiance, read the weather calendar each day, come to the front for "show and tell" periods, take messages to the office, count the number of children present in the class, pass out materials for class projects, be in charge of equipment on playground, and lead the class to the bathroom, library, or on a school tour. This one group of children, that continually were physically close to the teacher and had a high degree of verbal interaction with her, she placed at Table 1.

As one progressed from Table 1 to Table 2 and Table 3, there was an increasing dissimilarity between each group of children at the different tables on at least four major criteria. The first criterion appeared to be the physical appearance of the child. While the children at Table 1 were all dressed in clean clothes that were relatively new and pressed, most of the children at Table 2, and with only one exception at Table 3, were all quite poorly dressed. The clothes were old and often quite dirty. The children at Tables 2 and 3 also had a noticeably different quality and quantity of clothes to wear, especially during the winter months. Whereas the children at Table 1 would come on cold days with heavy coats and sweaters, the children at the other two tables often wore very thin spring coats and summer clothes. The single child at Table 3 who came to school quite nicely dressed came from a home in which the mother was receiving welfare funds, but was supplied with clothing for the children by the families of her brother and sister.

An additional aspect of the physical appearance of the children related to their body odor. While none of the children at Table 1 came to class with an

TABLE I *Distribution of Socioeconomic Status Factors by Seating Arrangement at the Three Tables in the Kindergarten Classroom*

	Seating Arrangement*		
Factors	*Table 1*	*Table 2*	*Table 3*
Income			
1) Families on welfare	0	2	4
2) Families with father employed	6	3	2
3) Families with mother employed	5	5	5
4) Families with both parents employed	5	3	2
5) Total family income below $3,000/yr**	0	4	7
6) Total family income above $12,000/yr**	4	0	0
Education			
1) Father ever grade school	6	3	2
2) Father ever high school	5	2	1
3) Father ever college	1	0	0
4) Mother ever grade school	9	10	8
5) Mother ever high school	7	6	5
6) Mother ever college	4	0	0
7) Children with preschool experience	1	1	0
Family Size			
1) Families with one child	3	1	0
2) Families with six or more children	2	6	7
3) Average number of siblings in family	3–4	5–6	6–7
4) Families with both parents present	6	3	2

* There are nine children at Table 1, eleven at Table 2, and ten at Table 3.
** Estimated from stated occupation.

odor of urine on them, there were two children at Table 2 and five children at Table 3 who frequently had such an odor. There was not a clear distinction among the children at the various tables as to the degree of "Blackness" of their skin, but there were more children at the third table with very dark skin (five in all) than there were at the first table (three). There was also a noticeable distinction among the various groups of children as to the condition of their hair. While the three boys at Table 1 all had short hair cuts and the six girls at the same table had their hair "processed" and combed, the number of children with either matted or unprocessed hair increased at Table 2 (two boys and three girls) and eight of the children at Table 3 (four boys and four

TABLE 2   *Distribution of Socioeconomic Status Factors by Seating Arrangement in the Three Reading Groups in the Second-Grade Classroom*

	Seating Arrangement*		
Factors	*Tigers*	*Cardinals*	*Clowns*
Income			
1) Families on welfare	2	4	7
2) Families with father employed	8	5	1
3) Families with mother employed	7	11	6
4) Families with both parents employed	7	5	1
5) Total family income below $3,000/yr**	1	5	8
6) Total family income above $12,000/yr**	4	0	0
Education			
1) Father ever grade school	8	6	1
2) Father ever high school	7	4	0
3) Father ever college	0	0	0
4) Mother ever grade school	12	13	9
5) Mother ever high school	9	7	4
6) Mother ever college	3	0	0
7) Children with preschool experience	1	0	0
Family Size			
1) Families with one child	2	0	1
2) Families with six or more children	3	8	5
3) Average number of siblings in family	3–4	6–7	7–8
4) Families with both parents present	8	6	1

* There are twelve children in the Tiger group, fourteen in the Cardinal group, and nine in the Clown group.
** Estimated from stated occupation.

girls). None of the children in the kindergarten class wore their hair in the style of a "natural."

A second major criteria which appeared to differentiate the children at the various tables was their interactional behavior, both among themselves and with the teacher. The several children who began to develop as leaders within the class by giving directions to other members, initiating the division of the class into teams on the playground, and seeking to speak for the class to the teacher ("We want to color now"), all were placed by the teacher at Table 1. This same group of children displayed considerable ease in their interaction with her. Whereas the children at Tables 2 and 3 would often linger on the periphery of groups surrounding the teacher, the children at Table 1 most often crowded close to her.

The use of language within the classroom appeared to be the third major differentiation among the children. While the children placed at the first table were quite verbal with the teacher, the children placed at the remaining two tables spoke much less frequently with her. The children placed at the first table also displayed a greater use of Standard American English within the classroom. Whereas the children placed at the last two tables most often responded to the teacher in Black dialect, the children at the first table did so very infrequently. In other words, the children at the first table were much more adept at the use of "school language" than were those at the other tables. The teacher utilized Standard American English in the classroom and one group of children were able to respond in a like manner. The frequency of a "no response" to a question from the teacher was recorded at a ratio of nearly three to one for the children at the last two tables as opposed to Table 1. When questions were asked, the children who were placed at the first table most often gave a response.

The final apparent criterion by which the children at the first table were quite noticeably different from those at the other tables consisted of a series of social factors which were known to the teacher prior to her seating the children. Though it is not known to what degree she utilized this particular criterion when she assigned seats, it does contribute to developing a clear profile of the children at the various tables. Table 1 gives a summary of the distribution of the children at the three tables on a series of variables related to social and family conditions. Such variables may be considered to give indication of the relative status of the children within the room, based on the income, education, and size of the family. (For a discussion of why these three variables of income, education, and family size may be considered as significant indicators of social status, see also Frazier, 1962; Freeman et al., 1959; Gebhard et al., 1958; Kahl, 1957; Notestein, 1953; Reissman, 1959; Rose, 1956; Simpson & Yinger, 1958.)

Believing, as I do, that the teacher did not randomly assign the children to the various tables, it is then necessary to indicate the basis for the seating arrangement. I would contend that the teacher developed, utilizing some combination of the four criteria outlined above, a series of expectations about the potential performance of each child and then grouped the children according to perceived similarities in expected performance. The teacher herself informed me that the first table consisted of her "fast learners" while those at the last two tables "had no idea of what was going on in the classroom." What becomes crucial in this discussion is to ascertain the basis upon which the teacher developed her criteria of "fast learner" since there had been no formal testing of the children as to their academic potential or capacity for cognitive development. She made evaluative judgments of the expected capacities of the children to perform academic tasks after eight days of school.

TABLE 3   *Variations in Teacher-Directed Behavior for Three Second-Grade Reading Groups during Three Observational Periods within a Single Classroom*

| | Variations in Teacher-Directed Behavior | | |
Item	Control	Supportive	Neutral
*Observational Period #1**			
Tigers	5% (6)**	7% (8)	87% (95)
Cardinals	10% (7)	8% (5)	82% (58)
Clowns	27% (27)	6% (6)	67% (67)
Observational Period #2			
Tigers	7% (14)	8% (16)	85% (170)
Cardinals	7% (13)	8% (16)	85% (170)
Clowns	14% (44)	6% (15)	80% (180)
Observational Period #3			
Tigers	7% (15)	6% (13)	86% (171)
Cardinals	14% (20)	10% (14)	75% (108)
Clowns	15% (36)	7% (16)	78% (188)

* Forty-eight (48) minutes of unequal teacher access (due to one group's being out of the room) was eliminated from the analysis.
** Value within the parentheses indicates total number of units of behavior within that category.

Certain criteria became indicative of expected success and others became indicative of expected failure. Those children who closely fit the teacher's "ideal type" of the successful child were chosen for seats at Table 1. Those children that had the least "goodness of fit" with her ideal type were placed at the third table. The criteria upon which a teacher would construct her ideal type of the successful student would rest in her perception of certain attributes in the child that she believed would make for success. To understand what the teacher considered as "success," one would have to examine her perception of the larger society and whom in that larger society she perceived as successful. Thus, in the terms of Merton (1957), one may ask which was the "normative reference group" for Mrs. Caplow that she perceived as being successful.[2] I believe that the reference group utilized by Mrs. Caplow to determine what constituted success was a mixed Black-White, well-educated middle class. Those attributes most desired by educated members of the middle class became the basis for her evaluation of the children. Those who possessed these particular characteristics were expected to succeed while those who did not could be expected not to succeed. Highly prized middle-class status for the child in the classroom was attained by demonstrating ease of interaction among adults; high degree of verbalization in Standard American English; the ability to become a leader; a neat and clean appearance; coming from a family that is educated, employed, living together, and interested in the child; and the ability to participate well as a member of a group.

The kindergarten teacher appeared to have been raised in a home where the above values were emphasized as important. Her mother was a college graduate, as were her brother and sisters. The family lived in the same neighborhood for many years, and the father held a responsible position with a public utility company in the city. The family was devoutly religious and those of the family still in the city attend the same church. She and other members of her family were active in a number of civil rights organizations in the city. Thus, it appears that the kindergarten teacher's "normative reference group" coincided quite closely with those groups in which she did participate and belong. There was little discrepancy between the normative values of the mixed Black-White educated middle class and the values of the groups in which she held membership. The attributes indicative of "success" among those of the educated middle class had been attained by the teacher. She was a college graduate, held positions of respect and responsibility in the Black community, lived in a comfortable middle-class section of the city in a well-furnished and spacious home, together with her husband earned over $20,000 per year, was active in a number of community organizations, and had parents, brother, and sisters similar in education, income, and occupational positions.

The teacher ascribed high status to a certain group of children within the class who fit her perception of the criteria necessary to be among the "fast learners" at Table 1. With her reference group orientation as to what constitute the qualities essential for "success," she responded favorably to those children who possessed such necessary attributes. Her resultant preferential treatment of a select group of children appeared to be derived from her belief that certain behavioral and cultural characteristics are more crucial to learning in school than are others. In a similar manner, those children who appeared not to possess the criteria essential for success were ascribed low status and described as "failures" by the teacher. They were relegated to positions at Table 2 and 3. The placement of the children then appeared to result from their possessing or lacking the certain desired cultural characteristics perceived as important by the teacher.

The organization of the kindergarten classroom according to the expectation of success or failure after the eighth day of school became the basis for the differential treatment of the children for the remainder of the school year. From the day that the class was assigned permanent seats, the activities in the classroom were perceivably different from previously. The fundamental division of the class into those expected to learn and those expected not to permeated the teacher's orientation to the class.

The teacher's rationalization for narrowing her attention to selected students was that the majority of the remainder of the class (in her words) "just had no idea of what was going on in the classroom." Her reliance on the few students of ascribed high social status reached such proportions that on occasion, the teacher would use one of these students as an exemplar that the remainder of the class would do well to emulate:

> (It is Fire Prevention Week and the teacher is trying to have the children say so. The children make a number of incorrect responses, a few of which follow:) Jim, who had raised his hand, in answer to the question, "Do you know what week it is?" says, "October." The teacher says "No, that's the name of the month. Jane, do you know what special week this is?" and Jane responds, "It cold outside." Teacher says, "No, that is not it either. I guess I will have to call on Pamela. Pamela, come here and stand by me and tell the rest of the boys and girls what special week this is." Pamela leaves her chair, comes and stands by the teacher, turns and faces the rest of the class. The teacher puts her arm around Pamela, and Pamela says, "It fire week." The teacher responds, "Well Pamela, that is close. Actually it is Fire Prevention Week."

On another occasion, the Friday after Halloween, the teacher informed the class that she would allow time for all the students to come to the front of the class and tell of their experiences. She, in reality, called on six students, five of whom sat at Table 1 and the sixth at Table 2. Not only on this occasion, but on others, the teacher focused her attention on the experiences of the higher status students:[3]

> (The students are involved in acting out a skit arranged by the teacher on how a family should come together to eat the evening meal.) The students acting the roles of mother, father, and daughter are all from Table 1. The boy playing the son is from Table 2. At the small dinner table set up in the center of the classroom, the four children are supposed to be sharing with each other what they had done during the day — the father at work, the mother at home, and the two children at school. The Table 2 boy makes few comments. (In real life he has no father and his mother is supported by ADC funds.) The teacher comments, "I think that we are going to have to let Milt (Table 1) be the new son. Sam, why don't you go and sit down. Milt, you seem to be one who would know what a son is supposed to do at the dinner table. You come and take Sam's place."

In this instance, the lower-status student was penalized, not only for failing to have verbalized middle-class table talk, but more fundamentally, for lacking middle-class experiences. He had no actual father to whom he could speak at the dinner table, yet he was expected to speak fluently with an imaginary one.

Though the blackboard was long enough to extend parallel to all three tables, the teacher wrote such assignments as arithmetic problems and drew all illustrations on the board in front of the students at Table 1. A rather poignant example of the penalty the children at Table 3 had to pay was that they often could not see the board material:

Lilly stands up out of her seat. Mrs. Caplow asks Lilly what she wants. Lilly makes no verbal response to the question. Mrs. Caplow then says rather firmly to Lilly, "Sit down." Lilly does. However, Lilly sits down sideways in the chair (so she is still facing the teacher). Mrs. Caplow instructs Lilly to put her feet under the table. This Lilly does. Now she is facing directly away from the teacher and the blackboard where the teacher is demonstrating to the students how to print the letter, "O."

The realization of the self-fulfilling prophecy within the classroom was in its final stages by late May of the kindergarten year. Lack of communication with the teacher, lack of involvement in the class activities and infrequent instruction all characterized the situation of the children at Tables 2 and 3. During one observational period of an hour in May, not a single act of communication was directed towards any child at either Table 2 or 3 by the teacher except for twice commanding "sit down." The teacher devoted her attention to teaching those children at Table 1. Attempts by the children at Table 2 and 3 to elicit the attention of the teacher were much fewer than earlier in the school year.

In June, after school had ended for the year, the teacher was asked to comment on the children in her class. Of the children at the first table, she noted:

> I guess the best way to describe it is that very few children in my class are exceptional. I guess you could notice this just from the way the children were seated this year. Those at Table 1 gave consistently the most responses throughout the year and seemed most interested and aware of what was going on in the classroom.

Of those children at the remaining two tables, the teacher commented:

> It seems to me that some of the children at Table 2 and most all the children at Table 3 at times seem to have no idea of what is going on in the classroom and were off in another world all by themselves. It just appears that some can do it and some cannot. I don't think that it is the teaching that affects those that cannot do it, but some are just basically low achievers.

THE STUDENTS' RESPONSE

The students in the kindergarten classroom did not sit passively, internalizing the behavior the teacher directed towards them. Rather, they responded to the stimuli of the teacher, both in internal differentiations within the class itself and also in their response to the teacher. The type of response a student made was highly dependent upon whether he sat at Table 1 or at one of the two other tables. The single classroom of Black students did not respond as a homogenous unit to the teacher-inspired social organization of the room.

For the high-status students at Table 1, the response to the track system of the teacher appeared to be at least three-fold. One such response was the directing of ridicule and belittlement towards those children at Tables 2 and 3.

At no point during the entire school year was a child from Table 2 or 3 ever observed directing such remarks at the children at Table 1:

Mrs. Caplow says, "Raise your hand if you want me to call on you. I won't call on anyone who calls out." She then says, "All right, now who knows that numeral? What is it, Tony?" Tony makes no verbal response but rather walks to the front of the classroom and stands by Mrs. Caplow. Gregory calls out, "He don't know. He scared." Then Ann calls out, "It sixteen, stupid." (Tony sits at Table 3, Gregory and Ann sit at Table 1.)

Jim starts to say out loud that he is smarter than Tom. He repeats it over and over again, "I smarter than you. I smarter than you." (Jim sits at Table 1, Tom at Table 3.)

Milt came over to the observer and told him to look at Lilly's shoes. I asked him why I should and he replied, "Because they so ragged and dirty." (Milt is at Table 1, Lilly at Table 3.)

When I asked Lilly what it was that she was drawing, she replied, "A parachute." Gregory interrupted and said, "She can't draw nothin'."

The problems of those children who were of lower status were compounded, for not only had the teacher indicated her low esteem of them, but their peers had also turned against them. The implications for the future schooling of a child who lacks the desired status credentials in a classroom where the teacher places high value on middle-class "success" values and mannerisms are tragic.

It must not be assumed, however, that though the children at Tables 2 and 3 did not participate in classroom activities and were systematically ignored by the teacher, they did not learn. I contend that in fact they did learn, but in a fundamentally different way from the way in which the high-status children at Table 1 learned. The children at Table 2 and 3 who were unable to interact with the teacher began to develop patterns of interaction among themselves whereby they would discuss the material that the teacher was presenting to the children at Table 1. Thus I have termed their method of grasping the material "secondary learning" to imply that knowledge was not gained in direct interaction with the teacher, but through the mediation of peers and also through listening to the teacher though she was not speaking to them. That the children were grasping, in part, the material presented in the classroom, was indicated to me in home visits when the children who sat at Table 3 would relate material specifically taught by the teacher to the children at Table 1. It is not as though the children at Table 2 and 3 were ignorant of what was being taught in the class, but rather that the patterns of classroom interaction established by the teacher inhibited the low-status children from verbalizing what knowledge they had accumulated. Thus, from the teacher's terms of reference, those who could not discuss must not know. Her expectations continued to be fulfilled, for though the low-status children had accumulated knowledge, they did not have the opportunity to verbalize it and, consequently, the teacher could not know what they had learned. Children at Table

2 and 3 had learned material presented in the kindergarten class, but would continue to be defined by the teacher as children who could not or would not learn.

A second response of the higher status students to the differential behavior of the teacher towards them was to seek solidarity and closeness with the teacher and urge Table 2 and 3 children to comply with her wishes:

> The teacher is out of the room. Pamela says to the class, "We all should clean up before the teacher comes." Shortly thereafter the teacher has still not returned and Pamela begins to supervise other children in the class. She says to one girl from Table 3, "Girl, leave that piano alone." The child plays only a short time longer and then leaves.
>
> The teacher has instructed the students to go and take off their coats since they have come in from the playground. Milt says, "Ok y'al, let's go take off our clothes."
>
> At this time Jim says to the teacher, "Mrs. Caplow, they pretty flowers on your desk." Mrs. Caplow responded, "Yes, Jim, those flowers are roses, but we will not have roses much longer. The roses will die and rest until spring because it is getting so cold outside."
>
> When the teacher tells the students to come from their desks and form a semi-circle around her, Gregory scoots up very close to Mrs. Caplow and is practically sitting in her lap.
>
> Gregory has come into the room late. He takes off his coat and goes to the coat room to hang it up. He comes back and sits down in the very front of the group and is now closest to the teacher.

The higher-status students in the class perceived the lower status and esteem the teacher ascribed to those children at Tables 2 and 3. Not only would the Table 1 students attempt to control and ridicule the Table 2 and 3 students, but they also perceived and verbalized that they, the Table 1 students, were better students and were receiving differential treatment from the teacher:

> The children are rehearsing a play, Little Red Riding Hood. Pamela tells the observer, "The teacher gave me the best part." The teacher overheard this comment, smiled, and made no verbal response.
>
> The children are preparing to go on a field trip to a local dairy. The teacher has designated Gregory as the "sheriff" for the trip. Mrs. Caplow stated that for the field trip today Gregory would be the sheriff. Mrs. Caplow simply watched as Gregory would walk up to a student and push him back into line saying, "Boy, stand where you suppose to." Several times he went up to students from Table 3 and showed them the badge that the teacher had given to him and said, "Teacher made me sheriff."

The children seated at the first table were internalizing the attitudes and behavior of the teacher towards those at the remaining two tables. That is, as the teacher responded from her reference group orientation as to which type of children were most likely to succeed and which type most likely to fail, she behaved towards the two groups of children in a significantly different manner. The children from Table 1 were also learning through emulating the teacher how to behave towards other Black children who came from low-income and poorly educated homes. The teacher, who came from a well-educated and middle-income family, and the children from Table 1 who came from a background similar to the teacher's, came to respond to the children from poor and uneducated homes in a strikingly similar manner.

The lower-status students in the classroom from Tables 2 and 3 responded in significantly different ways to the stimuli of the teacher. The two major responses of the Table 2 and 3 students were withdrawal and verbal and physical in-group hostility.

The withdrawal of some of the lower-status students as a response to the ridicule of their peers and the isolation from the teacher occasionally took the form of physical withdrawal, but most often it was psychological:

Betty, a very poorly dressed child, had gone outside and hidden behind the door. . . . Mrs. Caplow sees Betty leave and goes outside to bring her back, says in an authoritative and irritated voice, "Betty, come here right now." When the child returns, Mrs. Caplow seizes her by the right arm, brings her over to the group, and pushes her down to the floor. Betty begins to cry. . . . The teacher now shows the group a large posterboard with a picture of a White child going to school.

The teacher is demonstrating how to mount leaves between two pieces of wax paper. Betty leaves the group and goes back to her seat and begins to color.

The teacher is instructing the children in how they can make a "spooky thing" for Halloween. James turns away from the teacher and puts his head on his desk. Mrs. Caplow looks at James and says, "James sit up and look here."

The children are supposed to make United Nations flags. They have been told that they do not have to make exact replicas of the teacher's flag. They have before them the materials to make the flags. Lilly and James are the only children who have not yet started to work on their flags. Presently, James has his head under his desk and Lilly simply sits and watches the other children. Now they are both staring into space. . . . (5 minutes later) Lilly and James have not yet started, while several other children have already finished. . . . A minute later, with the teacher telling the children to begin to clean up their scraps, Lilly is still staring into space.

The teacher has the children seated on the floor in front of her asking them questions about a story that she had read to them. The teacher says, "June, your back is turned. I want to see your face." (The child had turned completely around and was facing away from the group.)

The teacher told the students to come from their seats and form a semi-circle on the floor in front of her. The girls all sit very close to the piano where the teacher is seated. The boys sit a good distance back away from the girls and away from the teacher. Lilly finishes her work at her desk and comes and sits at the rear of the group of girls, but she is actually in the middle of the open space separating the boys and the girls. She speaks to no one and simply sits staring off.

The verbal and physical hostility that the children at Tables 2 and 3 began to act out among themselves in many ways mirrored what the Table 1 students and the teacher were also saying about them. There are numerous instances in the observations of the children at Tables 2 and 3 calling one another "stupid," "dummy," or "dumb dumb." Racial overtones were noted on two occasions when one boy called another a "nigger," and on another occasion when a girl called a boy an "almond head." Threats of beatings, "whoppins," and even spitting on a child were also recorded among those at Tables 2 and 3. Also at Table 2, two instances were observed in which a single child hoarded all the supplies for the whole table. Similar manifestations of hostility were not observed among those children at the first table. The single incident of strong anger or hostility by one child at Table 1 against another child at the same table occurred when one accused the other of copying from his paper. The second denied it and an argument ensued.

In the organization of hostility within the classroom, there may be at least the tentative basis for the rejection of a popular "folk myth" of American society, which is that children are inherently cruel to one another and that this tendency towards cruelty must be socialized into socially acceptable channels. The evidence from this classroom would indicate that much of the cruelty displayed was a result of the social organization of the class. Those children at Tables 2 and 3 who displayed cruelty appeared to have learned from the teacher that it was acceptable to act in an aggressive manner towards those from low-income and poorly educated backgrounds. Their cruelty was not diffuse, but rather focused on a specific group — the other poor children. Likewise, the incidence of such behavior increased over time. The children at Tables 2 and 3 did not begin the school year ridiculing and belittling each other. This social process began to emerge with the outline of the social organization the teacher imposed upon the class. The children from the first table were also apparently socialized into a pattern of behavior in which they perceived that they could direct hostility and aggression towards those at Table 2 and 3, but not towards one another. The children in the class learned who was vulnerable to hostility and who was not through the actions of the teacher. She established the patterns of differential behavior which the class adopted.

FIRST GRADE

Though Mrs. Caplow had anticipated that only twelve of the children from the kindergarten class would attend the first grade in the same school, eighteen of the children were assigned during the summer to the first-grade class-room in the main building. The remaining children either were assigned to a new school a few blocks north, or were assigned to a branch school designed to handle the overflow from the main building, or had moved away. Mrs. Logan, the first-grade teacher, had had more than twenty years of teaching experience in the city public school system, and every school in which she had taught was more than 90 percent Black. During the 1968–1969 school year, four informal visits were made to the classroom of Mrs. Logan. No visits were made to either the branch school or the new school to visit children from the kindergarten class who had left their original school. During my visits to the first-grade room, I kept only brief notes of the short conversations that I had with Mrs. Logan; I did not conduct formal observations of the activities of the children in the class.

During the first-grade school year, there were thirty-three children in the classroom. In addition to the eighteen from the kindergarten class, there were nine children repeating the first grade and also six children new to the school. Of the eighteen children who came from the kindergarten class to the first grade in the main building, seven were from the previous year's Table 1, six from Table 2, and five from Table 3.

In the first-grade classroom, Mrs. Logan also divided the children into three groups. Those children whom she placed at "Table A" had all been Table 1 students in kindergarten. No student who had sat at Table 2 or 3 in kindergarten was placed at Table A in the first grade. Instead, all the students from Table 2 and 3 — with one exception — were placed together at "Table B." At the third table which Mrs. Logan called "Table C," she placed the nine children repeating the grade plus Betty who had sat at Table 3 in the kindergarten class. Of the six new students, two were placed at Table A and four at Table C. Thus the totals for the three tables were nine students at Table A, ten at Table B, and fourteen at Table C.

The seating arrangement that began in the kindergarten as a result of the teacher's definition of which children possessed or lacked the perceived necessary characteristics for success in the public school system emerged in the first grade as a caste phenomenon in which there was absolutely no mobility upward. That is, of those children whom Mrs. Caplow had perceived as potential "failures" and thus seated at either Table 2 or 3 in the kindergarten, not one was assigned to the table of the "fast learners" in the first grade.

The initial label given to the children by the kindergarten teacher had been reinforced in her interaction with those students throughout the school year. When the children were ready to pass into the first grade, their ascribed labels from the teacher as either successes or failures assumed objective dimensions. The first-grade teacher no longer had to rely on merely the presence or absence of certain behavioral and attitudinal characteristics to ascertain who would do well and who would do poorly in the class. Objective records of the "readiness" material completed by the children during the kindergarten year were available to her. Thus, upon the basis of what material the various tables in kindergarten had completed, Mrs. Logan could form her first-grade tables for reading and arithmetic.

The kindergarten teacher's disproportionate allocation of her teaching time resulted in the Table 1 students' having completed more material at the end of the school year than the remainder of the class. As a result, the Table 1 group from kindergarten remained intact in the first grade, as they were the only students prepared for the first-grade reading material. Those children from Tables 2 and 3 had not yet completed all the material from kindergarten and had to spend the first weeks of the first-grade school year finishing kindergarten level lessons. The criteria established by the school system as to what constituted the completion of the necessary readiness material to begin first-grade lessons insured that the Table 2 and 3 students could not be placed at Table A. The only children who had completed the material were those from Table 1, defined by the kindergarten teacher as successful students and whom she then taught most often because the remainder of the class "had no idea what was going on."

It would be somewhat misleading, however, to indicate that there was absolutely no mobility for any of the students between the seating assignments in kindergarten and those in the first grade. All of the students save one who had been seated at Table 3 during the kindergarten year were moved "up" to Table B in the first grade. The majority of Table C students were those having to repeat the grade level. As a tentative explanation of Mrs. Logan's rationale for the development of the Table C seating assignments, she may have assumed that within her class there existed one group of students who possessed so very little of the perceived behavioral patterns and attitudes necessary for success that they had to be kept separate from the remainder of the class. (Table C was placed by itself on the opposite side of the room from Tables A and B.) The Table C students were spoken of by the first-grade teacher in a manner reminiscent of the way in which Mrs. Caplow spoke of the Table 3 students the previous year.

Students who were placed at Table A appeared to be perceived by Mrs. Logan as students who not only possessed the criteria necessary for future success, both in the public school system and in the larger society, but who also had proven themselves capable in academic work. These students appeared to possess the characteristics considered most essential for "middle-class" success by the teacher. Though students at Table B lacked many of the "qualities" and characteristics of the Table A students, they were not perceived as lacking them to the same extent as those placed at Table C.

A basic tenet in explaining Mrs. Logan's seating arrangement is, of course, that she shared a similar reference group and set of values as to what constituted "success" with Mrs. Caplow in the kindergarten class. Both women were well educated, were employed in a professional occupation, lived in middle-income neighborhoods, were active in a number of charitable and civil rights organizations, and expressed strong religious convictions and moral standards. Both were educated in the city teacher's college and had also attained graduate degrees. Their backgrounds as well as the manner in which they described the various groups of students in their classes would indicate that they shared a similar reference group and set of expectations as to what constituted the indices of the "successful" student.

SECOND GRADE

Of the original thirty students in kindergarten and eighteen in first grade, ten students were assigned to the only second-grade class in the main building. Of the eight original kindergarten students who did not come to the second grade from the first, three were repeating first grade while the remainder had moved. The teacher in the second grade also divided the class into three groups, though she did not give them number or letter designations. Rather, she called the first group the "Tigers." The middle group she labeled the "Cardinals," while the second-grade repeaters plus several new children assigned to the third table were designated by the teacher as "Clowns."[4]

In the second-grade seating scheme, no student from the first grade who had not sat at Table A was moved "up" to the Tigers at the beginning of second grade. All those students who in first grade had been at Table B or Table C and returned to the second grade were placed in the Cardinal group. The Clowns consisted of six second-grade repeaters plus three students who were new to the class. Of the ten original kindergarten students who came from the first grade, six were Tigers and four Cardinals. Table 2 illustrates that the distribution of social economic factors from the kindergarten year remained essentially unchanged in the second grade.

By the time the children came to the second grade, their seating arrangement appeared to be based not on the teacher's expectations of how the child might perform, but rather on the basis of past performance of the child. Available to the teacher when she formulated the seating groups were grade sheets from both kindergarten and first grade, IQ scores from kindergarten, listing of parental occupations for approximately half of the class, reading scores from a test given to all students at the end of the first grade, evaluations from the speech teacher and also the informal evaluations from both the kindergarten and first-grade teachers.

The single most important data utilized by the teacher in devising seating groups were the reading scores indicating the performance of the students at the end of the first grade. The second-grade teacher indicated that she attempted to divide the groups primarily on the basis of these scores. The Tigers were designated as the highest reading group and the Cardinals the middle. The Clowns were assigned a first-grade reading level, though they were, for the most part, repeaters from the previous year in second grade. The caste character of the reading groups became clear as the year progressed, in that all three groups were reading in different books and it was school policy that no child could go on to a new book until the previous one had been completed. Thus there was no way for the child, should he have demonstrated competence at a higher reading level, to advance, since he had to continue at the pace of the rest of his reading group. The teacher never allowed individual reading in order that a child might finish a book on his own and move ahead. *No matter how well a child in the lower reading groups might have read, he was destined to remain in the same reading group. This is, in a sense, another manifestation of the self-fulfilling prophecy in that a "slow learner" had no option but to continue to be a slow learner, regardless of performance or potential.* Initial expectations of the kindergarten teacher two years earlier as to the ability of the child resulted in placement in a reading group, whether high or low, from which there appeared to be no escape. The child's journey through the early grades of school at one reading level and in one social grouping appeared to be preordained from the eighth day of kindergarten.

The expectations of the kindergarten teacher appeared to be fulfilled by late spring. Her description of the academic performance of the children in June had a strong "goodness of fit" with her stated expectations from the previous September. For the first- and second-grade teachers alike, there was no need to rely on intuitive expectations as to what the performance of the child would be. They were in the position of being able to base future expectations upon past performance. At this point, the relevance of the self-fulfilling prophecy again is evident, for the very criteria by which the first- and second-grade teachers established their three reading groups were those manifestations of performance most affected by the previous experience of the child. That is, which reading books were completed, the amount of arithmetic and reading readiness material that had been completed, and the mastery of basic printing skills all became the significant criteria established by the Board of Education to determine the level at which the child would begin the first grade. A similar process of standard evaluation by past performance on criteria established by the board appears to have been the basis for the arrangement of reading groups within the second grade. Thus, again, the initial patterns of expectations and her acting upon them appeared to place the kindergarten teacher in the position of establishing the parameters of the educational experience for the various children in her class. The parameters, most clearly defined by the seating arrangement at the various tables, remained intact through both the first and second grades.

The phenomenon of teacher expectation based upon a variety of social status criteria did not appear to be limited to the kindergarten teacher alone. When the second-grade teacher was asked to evaluate the children in her class by reading group, she responded in terms reminiscent of the kindergarten teacher. Though such a proposition would be tenuous at best, the high degree of similarity in the responses of both the kindergarten and second-grade teachers suggests that there may be among the teachers in the school a common set of criteria as to what constitutes the successful and promising student. If such is the case, then the particular individual who happens to occupy the role of kindergarten teacher is less crucial. For if the expectations of all staff within the school are highly similar, then with little difficulty there could be an interchange of teachers among the grades with little or no notice-able effect upon the performance of the various groups of students. If all teachers have similar expectations as to which types of students perform well and which types perform poorly, the categories established by the kindergarten teacher could be expected to reflect rather closely the manner in which other teachers would also have grouped the class.

As the indication of the high degree of similarity between the manner in which the kindergarten teacher described the three tables and the manner in which the second-grade teacher described the "Tigers, Cardinals, and Clowns," excerpts of an interview with the second-grade teacher are presented, where she stated her opinions of the three groups.

Concerning the Tigers:

Q: Mrs. Benson, how would you describe the Tigers in terms of their learning ability and academic performance?

R: Well, they are my fastest group. They are very smart.

Q: Mrs. Benson, how would you describe the Tigers in terms of discipline matters?

R: Well, the Tigers are very talkative. Susan, Pamela, and Ruth, they are always running their mouths constantly, but they get their work done first. I don't have much trouble with them.

Q: Mrs. Benson, what value do you think the Tigers hold for an education?

R: They all feel an education is important and most of them have goals in life as to what they want to be. They mostly want to go to college.

The same questions were asked of the teacher concerning the Cardinals.

Q: Mrs. Benson, how would you describe the Cardinals in terms of learning ability and academic performance?

R: They are slow to finish their work . . . but they get finished. You know, a lot of them, though, don't care to come to school too much. Rema, Gary, and Toby are absent quite a bit. The Tigers are never absent.

Q: Mrs. Benson, how would you describe the Cardinals in terms of discipline matters?

R: Not too bad. Since they work so slow they don't have time to talk. They are not like the Tigers who finish in a hurry and then just sit and talk with each other.

Q: Mrs. Benson, what value do you think the Cardinals hold for an education?

R: Well, I don't think they have as much interest in education as do the Tigers, but you know it is hard to say. Most will like to come to school, but the parents will keep them from coming. They either have to baby sit, or the clothes are dirty. These are the excuses the parents often give. But I guess most of the Cardinals want to go on and finish and go on to college. A lot of them have ambitions when they grow up. It's mostly the parents' fault that they are not at the school more often.

In the kindergarten class, the teacher appeared to perceive the major ability gap to lie between the students at Table 1 and those at Table 2. That is, those at Tables 2 and 3 were perceived as more similar in potential than were those at Tables 1 and 2. This was not the case in the second-grade classroom. The teacher appeared to perceive the major distinction in ability as lying between the Cardinals and the Clowns. Thus she saw the Tigers and the Cardinals as much closer in performance and potential than the Cardinals and the Clowns. The teacher's responses to the questions concerning the Clowns lends credence to this interpretation:

Q: Mrs. Benson, how would you describe the Clowns in terms of learning ability and academic performance?

R: Well, they are really slow. You know most of them are still doing first-grade work.

Q: Mrs. Benson, how would you describe the Clowns in terms of discipline matters?

R: They are very playful. They like to play a lot. They are not very neat. They like to talk a lot and play a lot. When I read to them, boy, do they have a good time. You know, the Tigers and the Cardinals will sit quietly and listen when I read to them, but the Clowns, they are always so restless. They always want to stand up. When we read, it is really something else. You know — Diane and Pat especially like to stand up. All these children, too, are very aggressive.

Q: Mrs. Benson, what value do you think the Clowns hold for an education?

R: I don't think very much. I don't think education means much to them at this stage. I know it doesn't mean anything to Randy and George. To most of the kids, I don't think it really matters at this stage.

FURTHER NOTES ON THE SECOND GRADE:
REWARD AND PUNISHMENT

Throughout the length of the study in the school, it was evident that both the kindergarten and second-grade teachers were teaching the groups within their classes in a dissimilar manner. Variations were evident, for example, in the amount of time the teachers spent teaching the different groups, in the manner in which certain groups were granted privileges which were denied to others, and in the teacher's proximity to the different groups. Two additional considerations related to the teacher's use of reward and punishment.

Though variations were evident from naturalistic observations in the kindergarten, a systematic evaluation was not attempted of the degree to which such differential behavior was a significant aspect of the classroom interactional patterns. When observations were being conducted in the second grade, it appeared that there was on the part of Mrs. Benson a differentiation of reward and punishment similar to that displayed by Mrs. Caplow. In order to examine more closely the degree to which variations were present over time, three observational periods were totally devoted to the tabulation of each of the individual behavioral units directed by the teacher towards the children. Each observational period was three and one-half hours in length, lasting from 8:35 a.m. to 12:00 noon. The dates of the observations were the Fridays at the end of eight, twelve, and sixteen weeks of school — October 24, November 21, and December 19, 1969, respectively.

A mechanism for evaluating the varieties of teacher behavior was developed. Behavior on the part of the teacher was tabulated as a "behavioral unit" when there was clearly directed towards an individual child some manner of communication, whether it be verbal, nonverbal or physical contact. When, within the interaction of the teacher and the student, there occurred more than one type of behavior, that is, the teacher spoke to the child and touched him, a count was made of both variations. The following is a list of the nine variations in teacher behavior that were tabulated within the second-grade classroom. Several examples are also included with each of the alternatives displayed by the teacher within the class.

1. Verbal Supportive — "That's a very good job." "You are such a lovely girl." "My, but your work is so neat."

2. Verbal Neutral — "Laura and Tom, let's open our books to page 34." "May, your pencil is on the floor." "Hal, do you have milk money today?"

3. Verbal Control — "Lou, sit on that chair and shut up." "Curt, get up off that floor." "Mary and Laura, quit your talking."

4. Nonverbal Supportive — Teacher nods her head at Rose. Teacher smiles at Liza. Teacher claps when Laura completes her problem at the board.

5. Nonverbal Neutral — Teacher indicates with her arms that she wants Lilly and Shirley to move farther apart in the circle. Teacher motions to Joe and Tom that they should try to snap their fingers to stay in beat with the music.

6. Nonverbal Control — Teacher frowns at Lena. Teacher shakes finger at Amy to quit tapping her pencil. Teacher motions with hand for Rose not to come to her desk.

7. Physical Contact Supportive — Teacher hugs Laura. Teacher places her arm around Mary as she talks to her. Teacher holds Trish's hand as she takes out a splinter.

8. Physical Contact Neutral — Teacher touches head of Nick as she walks past. Teacher leads Rema to new place on the circle.

9. Physical Contact Control — Teacher strikes Lou with stick. Teacher pushes Curt down in his chair. Teacher pushes Hal and Doug to the floor.

Table 3 which follows is presented with all forms of control, supportive, and neutral behavior grouped together within each of the three observational periods. As a methodological precaution, since the categorization of the various types of behavior was decided as the interaction occurred and

163

there was no cross-validation check by another observer, all behavior was placed in the appropriate neutral category which could not be clearly distinguished as belonging to one of the established supportive or control categories. This may explain the large percentage of neutral behavior tabulated in each of the three observational periods.

The picture of the second-grade teacher, Mrs. Benson, that emerges from analysis of these data is of one who distributes rewards quite sparingly and equally, but who utilizes somewhere between two and five times as much control-oriented behavior with the Clowns as with the Tigers. Alternatively, whereas with the Tigers the combination of neutral and supportive behavior never dropped below 93 percent of the total behavior directed towards them by the teacher in the three periods, the lowest figure for the Cardinals was 86 percent and for the Clowns was 73 percent. It may be assumed that neutral and supportive behavior would be conducive to learning while punishment or control-oriented behavior would not. Thus for the Tigers, the learning situation was one with only infrequent units of control, while for the Clowns, control behavior constituted one-fourth of all behavior directed towards them on at least one occasion.

Research related to leadership structure and task performance in voluntary organizations has given strong indications that within an authoritarian setting there occurs a significant decrease in performance on assigned tasks that does not occur with those in a non-authoritative setting (Kelly & Thibaut, 1954; Lewin, Lippitt, & White, 1939). Further investigations have generally confirmed these findings.

Of particular interest within the classroom are the findings of Adams (1945), Anderson (1946), Anderson et al. (1946), Preston and Heintz (1949), and Robbins (1952). Their findings may be generalized to state that children within an authoritarian classroom display a decrease in both learning retention and performance, while those within the democratic classroom do not. In extrapolating these findings to the second-grade classroom of Mrs. Benson, one cannot say that she was continually "authoritarian" as opposed to "democratic" with her students, but that with one group of students there occurred more control-oriented behavior than with other groups. The group which was the recipient of this control-oriented behavior was that group which she had defined as "slow and disinterested." On at least one occasion Mrs. Benson utilized nearly five times the amount of control-oriented behavior with the Clowns as with her perceived high-interest and high-ability group, the Tigers. For the Clowns, who were most isolated from the teacher and received the least amount of her teaching time, the results noted above would indicate that the substantial control-oriented behavior directed towards them would compound their difficulty in experiencing significant learning and cognitive growth.

Here discussion of the self-fulfilling prophecy is relevant: given the extent to which the teacher utilized control-oriented behavior with the Clowns, data from the leadership and performance studies would indicate that it would be more difficult for that group to experience a positive learning situation. The question remains unanswered, though, as to whether the behavior of uninterested students necessitated the teacher's resorting to extensive use of control-oriented behavior, or whether that to the extent to which the teacher utilized control-oriented behavior, the students responded with uninterest. If the prior experience of the Clowns was in any way similar to that of the students in kindergarten at Table 3 and Table C in the first grade, I am inclined to opt for the latter proposition.

A very serious and, I believe, justifiable consequence of this assumption of student uninterest related to the frequency of the teacher's control-oriented behavior is that the teachers themselves contribute significantly to the creation of the "slow learners" within their classrooms. Over time, this may help to account for the phenomenon noted in the Coleman Report (1966) that the gap between the academic performance of the disadvantaged students and the national norms increased the longer the students remained in the school system. During one of the three and one-half hour observational periods in the second grade, the percentage of control-oriented behavior oriented toward the entire class was about 8 percent. Of the behavior directed toward the Clowns, however, 27 percent was control-oriented behavior — more than three times the amount of control-oriented behavior directed to the class as a whole. Deutsch (1968), in a random sampling of New York City public school classrooms of the fifth through eighth grades, noted that the teachers utilized between 50 and 80 percent of class time in discipline and organization. Unfortunately, he fails to specify the two individual percentages and thus it is unknown whether the classrooms were dominated by either discipline or organization as opposed to their combination. If it is the case, and Deutsch's findings appear to lend indirect support, that the higher the grade level, the greater the discipline and control-oriented behavior by the teacher, some of the unexplained aspects of the "regress phenomenon" may be unlocked.

On another level of analysis, the teacher's use of control-oriented behavior is directly related to the expectations of the ability and willingness of "slow learners" to learn the material she teaches. That is, if the student is uninterested in what goes on in the classroom, he is more apt to engage in activities that the teacher perceives as disruptive. Activities such as talking out loud, coloring when the teacher has not said it to be permissible, attempting to leave the room, calling other students' attention to activities occurring on the street, making comments to the teacher not pertinent to the lesson, dropping books, falling out of the chair, and commenting on how the student cannot wait for recess, all prompt the teacher to employ control-oriented behavior toward that student. The interactional pattern between the uninterested student and the teacher literally becomes a "vicious circle" in which control-oriented behavior is followed by further manifestations of uninterest, followed by further control behavior and so on. The stronger the reciprocity of this pattern of interaction, the greater one may anticipate the strengthening of the teacher's expectation of the "slow learner" as being either unable or unwilling to learn.

THE CASTE SYSTEM FALTERS

A major objective of this study has been to document the manner in which there emerges within the early grades a stratification system, based both on teacher expectations related to behavioral and attitudinal characteristics of the child and also on a variety of socioeconomic status factors related to the background of the child. As noted, when the child begins to move through the grades, the variable of past performance becomes a crucial index of the position of the child within the different classes. The formulation of the system of stratification of the children into various reading groups appears to gain a caste-like character over time in that there was no observed movement into the highest reading group once it had been initially established at the beginning of the kindergarten school year. Likewise, there was no movement out of the highest reading group. There was movement between the second and third reading groups, in that those at the lowest reading table one year are combined with the middle group for a following year, due to the presence of a group of students repeating the grade.

Though formal observations in the second-grade class of Mrs. Benson ended in December of 1969, periodic informal visits to the class continued throughout the remainder of the school year. The organization of the class remained stable save for one notable exception. For the first time during observations in either kindergarten, first or second grade, there had been a reassignment of two students from the highest reading group to the middle reading group. Two students from the Tiger group were moved during the third week of January, 1970 from the Tiger group to the Cardinal group. Two Cardinal group students were assigned to replace those in the Tiger group. Mrs. Benson was asked the reason for the move and she explained that neither of the two former Tiger group students "could keep a clean desk." She noted that both of the students constantly had paper and crayons on the floor beside their desks. She stated that the Tigers "are a very clean group" and the two could no longer remain with the highest reading group because they were "not neat." The two Cardinals who were moved into the Tiger reading group were both described as "extremely neat with their desk and floor."

POOR KIDS AND PUBLIC SCHOOLS

It has been a major goal of this paper to demonstrate the impact of teacher expectations, based upon a series of subjectively interpreted social criteria, on both the anticipated academic potential and subsequent differential treatment accorded to those students perceived as having dissimilar social status. For the kindergarten teacher, expectations as to what type of child may be anticipated as a "fast learner" appear to be grounded in her reference group of a mixed White-Black educated middle class. That is, students within her classroom who displayed those attributes which a number of studies have indicated are highly desired in children by middle-class educated adults as being necessary for future success were selected by her as possessing the potential to be a "fast learner." On the other hand, those children who did not possess the desired qualities were defined by the teacher as "slow learners." None of the criteria upon which the teacher appeared to base her evaluation of the children were directly related to measurable aspects of academic potential. Given that the IQ test was administered to the children in the last week of their kindergarten year, the results could not have been of any benefit to the teacher as she established patterns of organization within the class.[5] The IQ scores may have been significant factors for the first- and second-grade teachers, but I assume that consideration of past performance was the major determinant for the seating arrangements which they established.[6]

For the first-grade teacher, Mrs. Logan, and the second-grade teacher, Mrs. Benson, the process of dividing the class into various reading groups, apparently on the basis of past performance, maintained the original patterns of differential treatment and expectations established in the kindergarten class. Those initially defined as "fast learners" by the kindergarten teacher in subsequent years continued to have that position in the first group, regardless of the label or name given to it.

It was evident throughout the length of the study that the teachers made clear the distinctions they perceived between the children who were defined as fast learners and those defined as slow learners. It would not appear incorrect to state that within the classroom there was established by the various teachers a clear system of segregation between the two established groups of children. In the one group were all the children who appeared clean and interested, sought interactions with adults, displayed leadership within the class, and came from homes which displayed various status criteria valued in the middle class. In the other were children who were dirty, smelled of urine, did not actively participate in class, spoke a linguistic dialect other than that spoken by the teacher and students at Table 1, did not display leadership behavior, and came from poor homes often supported by public welfare. I would contend that within the system of segregation established by the teachers, the group perceived as slow learners were ascribed a caste position that sought to keep them apart from the other students.

The placement of the children within the various classrooms into different reading groups was ostensibly done on the promise of future performance in the kindergarten and on differentials of past performance in later grades. However, the placement may rather have been done from purely irrational reasons that had nothing to do with academic performance. The utilization of academic criteria may have served as the rationalization for a more fundamental process occurring with the class whereby the teacher served as the agent of the larger society to ensure that proper "social distance" was maintained between the various strata of the society as represented by the children.

Within the context of this analysis there appear to be at least two inter-actional processes that may be identified as having occurred simultaneously within the kindergarten classroom. The first was the relation of the teacher to the students placed at Table 1. The process appeared to occur in at least four stages. The initial stage involved the kindergarten teacher's developing ex-pectations regarding certain students as possessing a series of characteristics that she considered essential for future academic "success." Second, the teacher reinforced through her mechanisms of "positive" differential behav-ior those characteristics of the children that she considered important and desirable.

Third, the children responded with more of the behavior that initially gained them the attention and support of the teacher. Perceiving that verbal-ization, for example, was a quality that the teacher appeared to admire, the Table 1 children increased their level of verbalization throughout the school year. Fourth, the cycle was complete as the teacher focused even more specifi-cally on the children at Table 1 who continued to manifest the behavior she desired. A positive interactional scheme arose whereby initial behavioral pat-terns of the student were reinforced into apparent permanent behavioral pat-terns, once he had received support and differential treatment from the teacher.

Within this framework, the actual academic potential of the students was not objectively measured prior to the kindergarten teacher's evaluation of ex-pected performance. The students may be assumed to have had mixed poten-tial. However, the common positive treatment accorded to all within the group by the teacher may have served as the necessary catalyst for the self-fulfilling prophecy whereby those expected to do well did so.

A concurrent behavioral process appeared to occur between the teacher and those students placed at Tables 2 and 3. The student came into the class possessing a series of behavioral and attitudinal characteristics that within the frame of reference of the teacher were perceived as indicative of "failure." Second, through mechanisms of reinforcement of her initial expectations as to the future performance of the student, it was made evident that he was not perceived as similar or equal to those at the table of fast learners. In the third stage, the student responded to both the definition and actual treatment given to him by the teacher which emphasized his characteristics of being an educational "failure." Given the high degree of control-oriented behavior di-rected toward the "slower" learner, the lack of verbal interaction and encour-agement, the disproportionally small amount of teaching time given to him, and the ridicule and hostility, the child withdrew from class participation. The fourth stage was the cyclical repetition of behavioral and attitudinal char-acteristics that led to the initial labeling as an educational failure.

As with those perceived as having high probability of future success, the ac-ademic potential of the failure group was not objectively determined prior to evaluation by the kindergarten teacher. This group also may be assumed to have come into the class with mixed potential. Some within the group may have had the capacity to perform academic tasks quite well, while others perhaps did not. Yet the reinforcement by the teacher of the characteristics in the children that she had perceived as leading to academic failure may, in fact, have created the very conditions of student failure. With the "negative" treatment accorded to the perceived failure group, the teacher's definition of the situation may have ensured its emergence. What the teacher perceived in the children may have served as the catalyst for a series of interactions, with the result that the child came to act out within the class the very expectations defined for him by the teacher.

As an alternative explanation, however, the teacher may have developed the system of caste segregation within the classroom, not because the groups of children were so similar they had to be handled in an entirely different manner, but because they were, in fact, so very close to one another. The teacher may have believed quite strongly that the ghetto community inhibited the development of middle-class success models. Thus, it was her duty to "save" at least one group of children from the "streets." Those children had to be kept separate who could have had a "bad" influence on the children who appeared to have a chance to "make it" in the middle class of the larger society. Within this framework, the teacher's actions may be understood not only as an attempt to keep the slow learners away from those fast learners, but to ensure that the fast learners would not so be influenced that they themselves become enticed with the "streets" and lose their apparent opportunity for future middle-class status.

In addition to the formal separation of the groups within the classroom, there was also the persistence of mechanisms utilized by the teacher to socialize the children in the high reading group with feelings of aversion, revulsion, and rejection towards those of the lower reading groups. Through ridicule, belittlement, physical punishment, and merely ignoring them, the teacher was continually giving clues to those in the high reading group as to how one with high status and a high probability of future success treats those of low status and low probability of future success. To maintain within the larger society the caste aspects of the position of the poor vis à vis the remainder of the society, there has to occur the transmission from one generation to another the attitudes and values necessary to legitimate and continue such a form of social organization.

Given the extreme intercomplexity of the organizational structure of this society, the institutions that both create and sustain social organization can neither be held singularly responsible for perpetuating the inequalities nor for eradicating them (see also Leacock, 1969). The public school system, I believe, is justifiably responsible for contributing to the present structure of the society, but the responsibility is not its alone. The picture that emerges from this study is that the school strongly shares in the complicity of maintaining the organizational perpetuation of poverty and unequal opportunity. This, of course, is in contrast to the formal doctrine of education in this country to ameliorate rather than aggravate the conditions of the poor.

The teachers' reliance on a mixed Black-White educated middle class for their normative reference group appeared to contain assumptions of superiority over those of lower-class and status positions. For they and those members of their reference group, comfortable affluence, education, community participation, and possession of professional status may have afforded a rather stable view of the social order. The treatment of those from lower socioeconomic backgrounds within the classrooms by the teachers may have indicated that the values highly esteemed by them were not open to members of the lower groups. Thus the lower groups were in numerous ways informed of their lower status and were socialized for a role of lower self expectations and also for respect and deference towards those of higher status. The social distance between the groups within the classrooms were manifested in its extreme form by the maintenance of patterns of caste segregation whereby those of lower positions were not allowed to become a part of the peer group at the highest level. The value system of the teachers appeared to necessitate that a certain group be ostracized due to "unworthiness" or inherent inferiority. The very beliefs which legitimated exclusion were maintained among those of the higher social group which then contributed to the continuation of the pattern of social organization itself.

It has not been a contention of this study that the teachers observed could not or would not teach their students. They did, I believe, teach quite well. But the high quality teaching was not made equally accessible to all students in the class. For the students of high socioeconomic background who were perceived by the teachers as possessing desirable behavioral and attitudinal characteristics, the classroom experience was one where the teachers displayed interest in them, spent a large proportion of teaching time with them, directed little control-oriented behavior toward them, held them as models for the remainder of the class and continually reinforced statements that they were "special" students. Hypothetically, if the classrooms observed had contained only those students perceived by the teachers as having a desirable social status and a high probability of future success outside the confines of the ghetto community, the teachers could be assumed to have continued to teach well, and under these circumstances, to the entire class.

Though the analysis has focused on the early years of schooling for a single group of Black children attending a ghetto school, the implications are far-reaching for those situations where there are children from different status backgrounds within the same classroom. When a teacher bases her expectations of performance on the social status of the student and assumes that the higher the social status, the higher the potential of the child, those children of low social status suffer a stigmatization outside of their own choice or will. Yet there is a greater tragedy than being labeled as a slow learner, and that is being treated as one. The differential amounts of control-oriented behavior, the lack of interaction with the teacher, the ridicule from one's peers, and the caste aspects of being placed in lower reading groups all have implications for the future life style and value of education for the child.

Though it may be argued from the above that the solution to the existence of differential treatment for students is the establishment of schools catering to only a single segment of the population, I regard this as being antithetical to the goals of education — if one views the ultimate value of an education as providing insights and experience with thoughts and persons different from oneself. The thrust of the educational experience should be towards diversity, not homogeneity. It may be utopian to suggest that education should seek to encompass as wide a variety of individuals as possible within the same setting, but it is no mean goal to pursue.

The success of an educational institution and any individual teacher should not be measured by the treatment of the high-achieving students, but rather by the treatment of those not achieving. As is the case with a chain, ultimate value is based on the weakest member. So long as the lower-status students are treated differently in both quality and quantity of education, there will exist an imperative for change.

It should be apparent, of course, that if one desires this society to retain its present social class configuration and the disproportional access to wealth, power, social and economic mobility, medical care, and choice of life styles, one should not disturb the methods of education as presented in this study. This contention is made because what develops a "caste" within the classrooms appears to emerge in the larger society as "class." The low-income children segregated as a caste of "unclean and intellectually inferior" persons may very well be those who in their adult years become the car washers, dishwashers, welfare recipients, and participants in numerous other un- or underemployed roles within this society. The question may quite honestly be asked, "Given the treatment of low-income children from the beginning of their kindergarten experience, for what class strata are they being prepared other than that of the lower class?" It appears that the public school system not only mirrors the configurations of the larger society, but also significantly contributes to maintaining them. Thus the system of public education in reality perpetuates what it is ideologically committed to eradicate — class barriers which result in inequality in the social and economic life of the citizenry.

NOTES

1. The author, due to a teaching appointment out of the city, was unable to conduct formal observations of the children during their first-grade year.
2. The names of all staff and students are pseudonyms. Names are provided to indicate that the discussion relates to living persons, and not to fictional characters by the author.
3. Through the remainder of the paper, reference to "high" or "low" status students refers to status ascribed to the student by the teacher. Her ascription appeared to be based on perceptions of valued behavioral and cultural characteristics present or absent in any individual student.
4. The names were not given to the groups until the third week of school, though the seating arrangement was established on the third day.

5. The results of the IQ Test for the kindergarten class indicated that, though there were no statistically significant differences among the children at the three tables, the scores were skewed slightly higher for the children at Table 1. There were, however, children at Tables 2 and 3 who did score higher than several students at Table 1. The highest score came from a student at Table 1 (124) while the lowest came from a student at Table 3 (78). There appear to be at least three alternative explanations for the slightly higher scores by students at Table 1. First, the scores may represent the result of differential treatment in the classroom by Mrs. Caplow, thus contributing to the validation of the self-fulfilling prophecy. That is, the teacher by the predominance of teaching time spent with the Table 1 students, better prepared the students to do well on the examination than was the case for those students who received less teaching time. Second, the tests themselves may have reflected strong biases towards the knowledge and experience of middle-class children. Thus, students from higher-status families at Table 1 could be expected to perform better than did the low-status students from Table 3. The test resulted not in a "value free" measure of cognitive capacity, but in an index of family background. Third, of course, would be the fact that the children at the first table did possess a higher degree of academic potential than those at the other tables, and the teacher was intuitively able to discern these differences. This third alternative, however, is least susceptible to empirical verification.
6. When the second-grade teacher was questioned as to what significance she placed in the results of IQ tests, she replied, "They merely confirm what I already know about the student."

REFERENCES

Adams, R. G. (1945). *The behavior of pupils in democratic and autocratic social climates.* Abstracts of dissertations, Stanford University.

Anderson, H. (1946). *Studies in teachers' classroom personalities.* Stanford, CA: Stanford University Press.

Anderson, H., Brewer, J., & Reed, M. (1946). *Studies of teachers' classroom personalities, III: Follow-up studies of the effects of dominative and integrative contacts on children's behavior* (Applied Psychology Monograph). Stanford, CA: Stanford University Press.

Asbell, B. (1963, October). Not like other children. *Redbook,* pp. 114–118.

Austin, M. C., & Morrison, C. (1963). *The first r: The Harvard report on reading in elementary schools.* New York: Macmillan.

Becker, H. S. (1952). Social class variation in teacher-pupil relationship. *Journal of Educational Sociology, 25,* 451–465.

Borg, W. (1964). *Ability grouping in the public schools* (Cooperative Research Project No. 557). Salt Lake City: Utah State University.

Clark, K. B. (1963). Educational stimulation of racially disadvantaged children. In A. H. Passow (Ed.), *Education in depressed areas.* New York: Columbia University Press.

Coleman, J. S., et al. (1966). *Equality of educational opportunity.* Washington, DC: U.S. Government Printing Office.

Deutsch, M. (1967). Minority groups and class status as related to social and personality factors in scholastic achievement. In M. Deutsch et al. (Eds.), *The disadvantaged child.* New York: Basic Books.

Eddy, E. (1967). *Walk the white line.* Garden City, NY: Doubleday.

Frazier, E. F. (1957). *Black bourgeoisie.* New York: Free Press.

Freeman, R., Whelpton, P., & Campbell, A. (1959). *Family planning, sterility and population growth.* New York: McGraw-Hill

Fuchs, E. (1967). *Teachers talk.* Garden City, NY: Doubleday.

Gebhard, P., Pomeroy, W., Martin, C., & Christenson, C. (1958). *Pregnancy, birth and abortion.* New York: Harper & Row.

Gibson, G. (1965). Aptitude tests. *Science, 149,* 583.

Goldberg, M., Passow, A., & Justman, J. (1966). *The effects of ability grouping.* New York: Teachers College Press, Columbia University.

Harlem Youth Opportunities Unlimited. (1964). *Youth in the ghetto.* New York: HARYOU.

Henry, J. (1955). Docility, or giving the teacher what she wants. *Journal of Social Issues, 11,* 2.

Henry, J. (1959). The problem of spontaneity, initiative and creativity in suburban classrooms. *American Journal of Orthopsychiatry, 29,* 1.

Henry, J. (1963). Golden rule days: American schoolrooms. In *Culture against man.* New York: Random House.

Hollingshead, A. (1949). *Elmtown's youth.* New York: John Wiley & Sons.

Jackson, P. (1968). *Life in classrooms.* New York: Holt, Rinehart & Winston.

Kahl, J. A. (1957). *The American class structure.* New York: Holt, Rinehart & Winston.

Katz, I. (1964). Review of evidence relating to effects of desegregation on intellectual performance of Negroes. *American Psychologist, 19,* 381–399.

Kelly, H., & Thibaut, J. (1954). Experimental studies of group problem solving and process. In G. Lindzey (Ed.), *Handbook of social psychology, vol. 2.* Reading, MA: Addison-Wesley.

Kohn, H. (1967). *36 children.* New York: New American Library.

Kozol, J. (1967). *Death at an early age.* Boston: Houghton Mifflin.

Kvaraceus, W. C. (1965). *Disadvantaged children and youth: Programs of promise or pretense?* (Mimeograph). Burlingame: California Teachers Association.

Lawrence, S. (1969). *Ability grouping.* Unpublished manuscript, Harvard Graduate School of Education, Center for Educational Policy Research, Cambridge, MA.

Leacock, E. (1969). *Teaching and learning in city schools.* New York: Basic Books.

Lewin, K., Lippitt, R., & White, R. (1939). Patterns of aggressive behavior in experimentally created social climates. *Journal of Social Psychology, 10,* 271<196>299.

Lynd, H., & Lynd, R. (1937). *Middletown in transition.* New York: Harcourt, Brace & World.

MacKinnon, D. W. (1962). The nature and nurture of creative talent. *American Psychologist, 17,* 484–495.

Merton, R. K. (1957). Social theory and social structure (rev. ed.). New York: Free Press.

Moore, A. (1967). *Realities of the urban classroom.* Garden City, NY: Doubleday.

Notestein, F. (1953). Class differences in fertility. In R. Bendix & S. Lipset (Eds.), *Class, status and power.* New York: Free Press.

Preston, M., & Heintz, R. (1949). Effects of participatory versus supervisory leadership on group judgment. *Journal of Abnormal Social Psychology, 44,* 345–355.

Reissman, L. (1959). *Class in American society.* New York: Free Press.

Riessman, F. (1962). *The culturally deprived child.* New York: Harper and Row.

Riessman, F. (1965). *Teachers of the poor: A five point program* (Mimeographed). Burlingame: California Teachers Association.

Robbins, F. (1952). The impact of social climate upon a college class. *School Review, 60,* 275–284.

Rose, A. (1956). *The Negro in America.* Boston: Beacon Press.

Rosenthal, R., & Jacobson, L. (1968). *Pygmalion in the classroom.* New York: Holt, Rinehart & Winston.

Sigel, I. (1969). The Piagetian system and the world of education. In D. Elkind & J. Flavell (Eds.), *Studies in cognitive development.* New York: Oxford University Press.

Simpson, G., & Yinger, J. M. (1958). *Racial and cultural minorities.* New York: Harper and Row.

Smith, L., & Geoffrey, W. (1968). *The complexities of an urban classroom.* New York: Holt, Rinehart & Winston.

Smith, M. (1971). Equality of educational opportunity: The basic findings reconsidered. In F. Mosteller & D. P. Moynihan (Eds.), *On equality of educational opportunity.* New York: Random House.

Warner, W. L., Havighurst, R., & Loeb, M. (1944). *Who shall be educated?* New York: Harper and Row.

Wilson, A. B. (1963). Social stratification and academic achievement. In A. H. Passow (Ed.), *Education in depressed areas.* New York: Teachers College Press, Columbia University.

Lessons from Students on
Creating a Chance to Dream

▼▼▼▼▼

SONIA NIETO

> How does it come about that the one institution that is said to be the
> gateway to opportunity, the school, is the very one that is most effective
> in perpetuating an oppressed and impoverished status in society?
> (Stein, 1971, p. 178)

The poignant question above was posed in this very journal almost a quarter of a century ago by Annie Stein, a consistent critic of the schools and
a relentless advocate for social justice. This question shall serve as the
central motif of this article because, in many ways, it remains to be answered
and continues to be a fundamental dilemma standing in the way of our society's stated ideals of equity and equal educational opportunity. Annie Stein's
observations about the New York City public schools ring true today in too
many school systems throughout the country and can be used to examine
some of the same policies and practices she decried in her 1971 article.

It is my purpose in this article to suggest that successfully educating all students in U.S. schools must begin by challenging school policies and practices
that place roadblocks in the way of academic achievement for too many
young people. Educating students today is, of course, a far different and
more complex proposition than it has been in the past. Young people face in-
numerable personal, social, and political challenges, not to mention massive
economic structural changes not even dreamed about by other generations
of youth in the twentieth century. In spite of the tensions that such challenges
may pose, U.S. society has nevertheless historically had a social contract to educate *all* youngsters, not simply those who happen to be European American,
English speaking, economically privileged, and, in the current educational
reform jargon, "ready to learn."[1] Yet, our schools have traditionally failed
some youngsters, especially those from racially and culturally dominated and
economically oppressed backgrounds. Research over the past half century
has documented a disheartening legacy of failure for many students of all
backgrounds, but especially children of Latino, African American, and Native
American families, as well as poor European American families and, more re-

Harvard Educational Review Vol. 64 No. 4 Winter 1994, 392–426

cently, Asian and Pacific American immigrant students. Responding to the wholesale failure of so many youngsters within our public schools, educational theorists, sociologists, and psychologists devised elaborate theories of genetic inferiority, cultural deprivation, and the limits of "throwing money" at educational problems. Such theories held sway in particular during the 1960s and 1970s, but their influence is still apparent in educational policies and practices today.[2]

The fact that many youngsters live in difficult, sometimes oppressive conditions is not at issue here. Some may live in ruthless poverty and face the challenges of dilapidated housing, inadequate health care, and even abuse and neglect. They and their families may be subject to racism and other oppressive institutional barriers. They may have difficult personal, psychological, medical, or other kinds of problems. These are real concerns that should not be discounted. But, despite what may seem to be insurmountable obstacles to learning and teaching, some schools are nevertheless successful with young people who live in these situations. In addition, many children who live in otherwise onerous situations also have loving families willing to sacrifice what it takes to give their children the chance they never had during their own childhoods. Thus, poverty, single-parent households, and even homelessness, while they may be tremendous hardships, do not in and of themselves doom children to academic failure (see, among others, Clark, 1983; Lucas, Henze, & Donato, 1990; Mehan & Villanueva, 1993; Moll, 1992; Taylor & Dorsey-Gaines, 1988). These and similar studies point out that schools that have made up their minds that their students deserve the chance to learn do find the ways to educate them successfully in spite of what may seem to be overwhelming odds.

Educators may consider students difficult to teach simply because they come from families that do not fit neatly into what has been defined as "the mainstream." Some of them speak no English; many come from cultures that seem to be at odds with the dominant culture of U.S. society that is inevitably reflected in the school; others begin their schooling without the benefit of early experiences that could help prepare them for the cognitive demands they will face. Assumptions are often made about how such situations may negatively affect student achievement and, as a consequence, some children are condemned to failure before they begin. In a study by Nitza Hidalgo, a teacher's description of the students at an urban high school speaks to this condemnation: "Students are generally poor, uneducated and come from broken families who do not value school. Those conditions that produce achievers are somewhere else, not here. We get street people" (Hidalgo, 1991, p. 58). When such viewpoints guide teachers' and schools' behaviors and expectations, little progress can be expected in student achievement.

On the other hand, a growing number of studies suggest that teachers and schools need to build on rather than tear down what students bring to school. That is, they need to understand and incorporate cultural, linguistic, and experiential differences, as well as differences in social class, into the learning process (Abi-Nader, 1993; Hollins, King, & Hayman, 1994; Lucas et al., 1990; Moll & Díaz, 1993). The results of such efforts often provide inspiring examples of success because they begin with a belief that all students deserve a chance to learn. In this article, I will highlight these efforts by exploring the stories of some academically successful young people in order to suggest how the policies and practices of schools can be transformed to create environments in which all children are capable of learning.

It is too convenient to fall back on deficit theories and continue the practice of blaming students, their families, and their communities for educational failure. Instead, schools need to focus on where they *can* make a difference, namely, their own instructional policies and practices. A number of recent studies, for example, have concluded that a combination of factors, including characteristics of schools as opposed to only student background and actions, can explain differences between high- and low-achieving students. School characteristics that have been found to make a positive difference in these studies include an enriched and more demanding curriculum, respect for students' languages and cultures, high expectations for all students, and encouragement for parental involvement in their children's education (Lee, Winfield, & Wilson, 1991; Lucas et al., 1990; Moll, 1992). This would suggest that we need to shift from a single-minded focus on low- or high-achieving students to the conditions that create low- or high-achieving schools. If we understand school policies and practices as being enmeshed in societal values, we can better understand the manifestations of these values in schools as well. Thus, for example, "tracked" schools, rather than reflecting a school practice that exists in isolation from society, reflect a society that is itself tracked along racial, gender, and social-class lines. In the same way, "teacher expectations" do not come from thin air, but reflect and support expectations of students that are deeply ingrained in societal and ideological values.

Reforming school structures alone will not lead to substantive differences in student achievement, however, if such changes are not also accompanied by profound changes in how we as educators think about our students; that is, in what we believe they deserve and are capable of achieving. Put another way, changing policies and practices is a necessary but insufficient condition for total school transformation. For example, in a study of six high schools in which Latino students have been successful, Tamara Lucas, Rosemary Henze, and Rubén Donato (1990) found that the most crucial element is a shared belief among teachers, counselors, and administrators that all students are capable of learning. This means that concomitant changes are needed in policies and practices *and* in our individual and collective will to educate all students. Fred Newmann (1993), in an important analysis of educational restructuring, underlines this point by emphasizing that reform efforts will fail unless they are accompanied by a set of particular commitments and competencies to guide them, including a commitment to the success of all students, the creation of new roles for teachers, and the development of schools as caring communities.

Another crucial consideration in undertaking educational change is a focus on what Jim Cummins (1994) has called the "relations of power" in schools. In proposing a shift from coercive to collaborative relations of power, Cummins argues that traditional teacher-centered transmission models can limit the potential for critical thinking on the part of both teachers and students, but especially for students from dominated communities whose cultures and languages have been devalued by the dominant canon.[3] By encouraging collaborative relations of power, schools and teachers can begin to recognize other sources of legitimate knowledge that have been overlooked, negated, or minimized because they are not part of the dominant discourse in schools.

Focusing on concerns such as the limits of school reform without concomitant changes in educators' attitudes towards students and their families, and the crucial role of power relationships in schools may help rescue current reform efforts from simplistic technical responses to what are essentially moral and political dilemmas. That is, such technical changes as tinkering with the length of the school day, substituting one textbook for another, or adding curricular requirements may do little to change student outcomes unless these changes are part and parcel of a more comprehensive conceptualization of school reform. When such issues are considered fundamental to the changes that must be made in schools, we might more precisely speak about *transformation* rather than simply about reform. But educational transformation cannot take place without the inclusion of the voices of students, among others, in the dialogue.

WHY LISTEN TO STUDENTS?

One way to begin the process of changing school policies and practices is to listen to students' views about them; however, research that focuses on student voices is relatively recent and scarce. For example, student perspectives are for the most part missing in discussions concerning strategies for confronting educational problems. In addition, the voices of students are rarely heard in the debates about school failure and success, and the perspectives of students from disempowered and dominated communities are even more invisible. In this article, I will draw primarily on the words of students interviewed for a previous research study (Nieto, 1992). I used the interviews to develop case studies of young people from a wide variety of ethnic, racial, linguistic, and social-class backgrounds who were at the time students in junior or senior high school. These ten young people lived in communities as diverse as large urban areas and small rural hamlets, and belonged to families ranging from single-parent households to large, extended families. The one common element in all of their experiences turned out to be something we as researchers had neither planned nor expected: they were all successful students.[4]

The students were selected in a number of ways, but primarily through community contacts. Most were interviewed at home or in another setting of their choice outside of school. The only requirement that my colleagues and I determined for selecting students was that they reflect a variety of ethnic and racial backgrounds, in order to give us the diversity for which we were looking. The students selected self-identified as Black, African American, Mexican, Native American, Black and White American (biracial), Vietnamese, Jewish, Lebanese, Puerto Rican, and Cape Verdean. The one European American was the only student who had a hard time defining herself, other than as "American" (for a further analysis of this issue, see Nieto, 1992). That these particular students were academically successful was quite serendipitous. We defined them as such for the following reasons: they were all either still in school or just graduating; they all planned to complete at least high school, and most hoped to go to college; they had good grades, although they were not all at the top of their class; they had thought about their future and had made some plans for it; they generally enjoyed school and felt engaged in it (but they were also critical of their own school experiences and that of their peers, as we shall see); and most described themselves as successful. Although it had not been our initial intention to focus exclusively on academically successful students, on closer reflection it seemed logical that such students would be more likely to want to talk about their experiences than those who were not successful. It was at that point that I decided to explore what it was about these students' specific experiences that helped them succeed in school.

Therefore, the fact that these students saw themselves as successful helped further define the study, whose original purpose was to determine the benefits of multicultural education for students of diverse backgrounds. I was particularly interested in developing a way of looking at multicultural education that went beyond the typical "Holidays and Heroes" approach, which is too superficial to have any lasting impact in schools (Banks, 1991; Sleeter, 1991).[5] By exploring such issues as racism and low expectations of student achievement, as well as school policies and practices such as curriculum, pedagogy, testing, and tracking, I set about developing an understanding of multicultural education as anti-racist, comprehensive, pervasive, and rooted in social justice. Students were interviewed to find out what it meant to be from a particular background, how this influenced their school experience, and what about that experience they would change if they could. Although they were not asked specifically about the policies and practices in their schools, they nevertheless reflected on them in their answers to questions ranging from identifying their favorite subjects to describing the importance of getting an education. In this article, I will revisit the interviews to focus on students' thoughts about a number of school policies and practices and on the effects of racism and other forms of discrimination on their education.

The insights provided by the students were far richer than we had first thought. Although we expected numerous criticisms of schools and some concrete suggestions, we were surprised at the depth of awareness and analysis the students shared with us. They had a lot to say about the teachers they liked, as well as those they disliked, and they were able to explain the differences between them; they talked about grades and how these had become overly important in determining curriculum and pedagogy; they discussed their parents' lack of involvement, in most cases, in traditional school activities such as P.T.O. membership and bake sales, but otherwise passionate support for their children's academic success; they mused about what schools could do to encourage more students to learn; they spoke with feeling about their cultures, languages, and communities, and what schools could do to capitalize on these factors; and they gave us concrete suggestions for improving schools for young people of all backgrounds. This experience confirmed my belief that educators can benefit from hearing students' critical perspectives, which might cause them to modify how they approach curriculum, pedagogy, and other school practices. Since doing this research, I have come across other studies that also focus on young people's perspectives and provide additional powerful examples of the lessons we can learn from them. This article thus begins with "lessons from students," an approach that takes the perspective proposed by Paulo Freire, that teachers need to become students just as students need to become teachers in order for education to become reciprocal and empowering for both (Freire, 1970).

This focus on students is not meant to suggest that their ideas should be the final and conclusive word in how schools need to change. Nobody has all the answers, and suggesting that students' views should be adopted wholesale is to accept a romantic view of students that is just as partial and condescending as excluding them completely from the discussion. I am instead suggesting that if we believe schools must provide an equal and quality education for all, students need to be included in the dialogue, and that their views, just as those of others, should be problematized and used to reflect critically on school reform.

SELECTED POLICIES AND PRACTICES AND STUDENTS' VIEWS ABOUT THEM

School policies and practices need to be understood within the sociopolitical context of our society in general, rather than simply within individual schools' or teachers' attitudes and practices. This is important to remember for a number of reasons. First, although "teacher bashing" provides an easy target for complex problems, it fails to take into account the fact that teachers function within particular societal and institutional structures. In addition, it results in placing an inordinate amount of blame on some of those who care most deeply about students and who struggle every day to help them learn. That some teachers are racist, classist, and mean-spirited and that others have lost all creativity and caring is not in question here, and I begin with the assumption that the majority of teachers are not consciously so. I do suggest, however, that although many teachers are hardworking, supportive of their students, and talented educators, many of these same teachers are also burned out, frustrated, and negatively influenced by societal views about the students they teach. Teachers could benefit from knowing more about their students' families and experiences, as well as about students' views on school and how it could be improved.

How do students feel about the curriculum they must learn? What do they think about the pedagogical strategies their teachers use? Is student involvement a meaningful issue for them? Are their own identities important considerations in how they view school? What about tracking and testing and disciplinary policies? These are crucial questions to consider when reflecting on what teachers and schools can learn from students, but we know very little about students' responses. When asked, students seem surprised and excited about being included in the conversation, and what they have to say is often compelling and eloquent. In fact, Patricia Phelan, Ann Locke Davidson, and Hanh Thanh Cao (1992), in a two-year research project designed to identify students' thoughts about school, discovered that students' views on teaching and learning were remarkably consistent with those of current theorists concerned with learning theory, cognitive science, and the sociology of work. This should come as no surprise when we consider that students spend more time in schools than anybody else except teachers (who are also omitted in most discussions of school reform, but that is a topic for another article). In the following sections, I will focus on students' perceptions concerning the curriculum, pedagogy, tracking, and grades in their schools. I will also discuss their attitudes about racism and other biases, how these are manifested in their schools and classrooms, and what effect they may have on students' learning and participation in school.

Curriculum

The curriculum in schools is at odds with the experiences, backgrounds, hopes, and wishes of many students. This is true of both the tangible curriculum as expressed through books, other materials, and the actual written curriculum guides, as well as in the less tangible and "hidden" curriculum as seen in the bulletin boards, extracurricular activities, and messages given to students about their abilities and talents. For instance, Christine Sleeter and Carl Grant (1991) found that a third of the students in a desegregated junior high school they studied said that *none* of the class content related to their lives outside class. Those who indicated some relevancy cited only current events, oral history, money and banking, and multicultural content (because it dealt with prejudice) as being relevant. The same was true in a study by Mary Poplin and Joseph Weeres (1992), who found that students frequently reported being bored in school and seeing little relevance in what was taught for their lives or their futures. The authors concluded that students became more disengaged as the curriculum, texts, and assignments became more standardized. Thus, in contrast to Ira Shor's (1992) suggestion that "What students bring to class is where learning begins. It starts there and goes places" (p. 44), there is often a tremendous mismatch between students' cultures and the culture of the school. In many schools, learning starts not with what students bring to class, but with what is considered high-status knowledge; that is, the "canon," with its overemphasis on European and European American history, arts, and values. This seldom includes the backgrounds, experiences, and talents of the majority of students in U.S. schools. Rather than "going elsewhere," their learning therefore often goes nowhere.

That students' backgrounds and experiences are missing in many schools is particularly evident where the native language of most of the students is not English. In such settings, it is not unusual to see little or no representation of those students' language in the curriculum. In fact, there is often an insistence that students "speak only English" in these schools, which sends a powerful message to young people struggling to maintain an identity in the face of overpowering messages that they must assimilate. This was certainly the case for Marisol, a Puerto Rican girl of sixteen participating in my research, who said:

> I used to have a lot of problems with one of my teachers 'cause she didn't want us to talk Spanish in class and I thought that was like an insult to us, you know? Just telling us not to talk Spanish, 'cause they were Puerto Ricans and, you know, we're free to talk whatever we want, . . . I could never stay quiet and talk only English, 'cause sometimes . . . words slip in Spanish. You know, I think they should understand that.

Practices such as not allowing students to speak their native tongue are certain to influence negatively students' identities and their views of what constitutes important knowledge. For example, when asked if she would be interested in taking a course on Puerto Rican history, Marisol was quick to answer: "I don't think [it's] important. . . . I'm proud of myself and my culture, but I think I know what I should know about the culture already, so I wouldn't take the course." Ironically, it was evident to me after speaking with her on several occasions that Marisol knew virtually nothing about Puerto Rican history. However, she had already learned another lesson well: given what she said about the courses she needed to take, she made it clear that "important" history is U.S. history, which rarely includes anything about Puerto Rico.

Messages about culture and language and how they are valued or devalued in society are communicated not only or even primarily by schools, but by the media and community as a whole. The sociopolitical context of the particular city where Marisol lived, and of its school system, is important to understand: there had been an attempt to pass an ordinance restricting the number of Puerto Ricans coming into town based on the argument that they placed an undue burden on the welfare rolls and other social services. In addition, the "English Only" debate had become an issue when the mayor had ordered all municipal workers to speak only English on the job. Furthermore, although the school system had a student body that was 65 percent Puerto Rican, there was only a one-semester course on Puerto Rican history that had just recently been approved for the bilingual program. In contrast, there were two courses, which although rarely taught were on the books, that focused on apartheid and the Holocaust, despite the fact that both the African American and Jewish communities in the town were quite small. That such courses should be part of a comprehensive multicultural program is not being questioned; however, it is ironic that the largest population in the school was ignored in the general curriculum.

In a similar vein, Nancy Commins's (1989) research with four first-generation Mexican American fifth-grade students focused on how these students made decisions about their education, both consciously and unconsciously, based on their determination of what counted as important knowledge. Her research suggests that the classroom setting and curriculum can support or hinder students' perceptions of themselves as learners based on the languages they speak and their cultural backgrounds. She found that although the homes of these four students provided rich environments for a variety of language uses and literacy, the school did little to capitalize on these strengths. In their classroom, for instance, these children rarely used Spanish, commenting that it was the language of the "dumb kids." As a result, Commins states: "Their reluctance to use Spanish in an academic context also limited their opportunities to practice talking about abstract ideas and to use higher level cognitive skills in Spanish" (p. 35). She also found that the content of the curriculum was almost completely divorced from the experiences of these youngsters, since the problems of poverty, racism, and discrimination, which were prominent in their lives, were not addressed in the curriculum.

In spite of teachers' reluctance to address such concerns, they are often compelling to students, particularly those who are otherwise invisible in the curriculum. Vinh, an 18-year-old Vietnamese student attending a high school in a culturally heterogeneous town, lived with his uncle and younger brothers and sisters. Although grateful for the education he was receiving, Vinh expressed concern about what he saw as insensitivity on the part of some of his teachers to the difficulties of adjusting to a new culture and learning English:

> [Teachers] have to know about our culture. . . . From the second language, it is very difficult for me and for other people.

Vinh's concern was echoed by Manuel, a nineteen-year-old Cape Verdean senior who, at the time of the interviews, was just getting ready to graduate, the first in his family of eleven children to do so:

> I was kind of afraid of school, you know, 'cause it's different when you're learning the language. . . . It's kind of scary at first, especially if you don't know the language and like if you don't have friends here.

In Manuel's case, the Cape Verdean Crioulo bilingual program served as a linguistic and cultural mediator, negotiating difficult experiences that he faced in school so that, by the time he reached high school, he had learned enough English to "speak up." Another positive curricular experience was the theater workshop he took as a sophomore. There, students created and acted in skits focusing on their lived experiences. He recalled with great enthusiasm, for example, a monologue he did about a student going to a new school, because it was based on his personal experience.

Sometimes a school's curriculum is unconsciously disrespectful of students' cultures and experiences. James, a student who proudly identified himself as Lebanese American, found that he was invisible in the curriculum, even in supposedly multicultural curricular and extracurricular activities. He mentioned a language fair, a multicultural festival, and a school cookbook, all of which omitted references to the Arabic language and to Lebanese people. About the cookbook, he said:

> They made this cookbook of all these different recipes from all over the world. And I would've brought in some Lebanese recipes if somebody'd let me know. And I didn't hear about it until the week before they started selling them. . . . I asked one of the teachers to look at it and there was nothing Lebanese in there.

James made an effort to dismiss this oversight, and although he said that it didn't matter, he seemed to be struggling with the growing realization that it mattered very much indeed:

> I don't know, I guess there's not that many Lebanese people in . . . I don't know; you don't hear really that much . . . Well, you hear it in the news a lot, but I mean, I don't know, there's not a lot of Lebanese kids in our school. . . . I don't mind, 'cause I mean, I don't know, just I don't mind it. . . . It's not really important. It *is* important for me. It would be important for me to see a Lebanese flag.

Lebanese people were mentioned in the media, although usually in negative ways, and these were the only images of James's ethnic group that made their way into the school. He spoke, for example, about how the Lebanese were characterized by his peers:

> Some people call me, you know, 'cause I'm Lebanese, so people say, "Look out for the terrorist! Don't mess with him or he'll blow up your house!" or some stuff like that. . . . But they're just joking around, though. . . . I don't think anybody's serious 'cause I wouldn't blow up anybody's house — and they know that. . . . I don't care. It doesn't matter what people say. . . . I just want everybody to know that, you know, it's not true.

Cultural ambivalence, both pride and shame, were evident in the responses of many of the students. Although almost all of them were quite clear that their culture was important to them, they were also confronted with debilitating messages about it from society in general. How to make sense of these contradictions was a dilemma for many of these young people.

Fern, who identified herself as Native American, was, at thirteen, one of the youngest students interviewed. She reflected on the constant challenges she faced in the history curriculum in her junior high school. Her father was active in their school and community and he gave her a great deal of support for defending her position, but she was the only Native American student in her entire school in this mid-size city in Iowa. She said:

> If there's something in the history book that's wrong, my dad always taught me that if it's wrong, I should tell them that it is wrong. And the only time I ever do is if I know it's *exactly* wrong. Like we were reading about Native Americans and scalping. Well, the French are really the ones that made them do it so they could get money. And my teacher would not believe me. I finally just shut up because he just would not believe me.

Fern also mentioned that her sister had come home angry one day because somebody in school had said "Geronimo was a stupid chief riding that stupid horse." The connection between an unresponsive curriculum and dropping out of school was not lost on Fern, and she talked about this incident as she wondered aloud why other Native Americans had dropped out of the town's schools. Similar sentiments were reported by students in Virginia Vogel Zanger's (1994) study of twenty Latinos from a Boston high school who took part in a panel discussion in which they reflected on their experiences in school. Some of the students who decided to stay in school claimed that dropping out among their peers was a direct consequence of the school's attempts to "monoculture" them.

Fern was self-confident and strong in expressing her views, despite her young age. Yet she too was silenced by the way the curriculum was presented in class. This is because schools often avoid bringing up difficult, contentious, or conflicting issues in the curriculum, especially when these contradict the sanctioned views of the standard curriculum, resulting in what Michelle Fine has called "silencing." According to Fine: "Silencing is about who can speak, what can and cannot be spoken, and whose discourse must be controlled" (1991, p. 33). Two topics in particular that appear to have great saliency for many students, regardless of their backgrounds, are bias and discrimination, yet these are among the issues most avoided in classrooms. Perhaps this is because the majority of teachers are European Americans who are unaccustomed, afraid, or uncomfortable in discussing these issues (Sleeter, 1994); perhaps it is due to the pressure teachers feel to "cover the material"; maybe it has to do with the tradition of presenting information in schools as if it were free of conflict and controversy (Kohl, 1993); or, most likely, it is a combination of all these things. In any event, both students and teachers soon pick up the message that racism, discrimination, and other dangerous topics are not supposed to be discussed in school. We also need to keep in mind that these issues have disparate meanings for people of different backgrounds, and are often perceived as particularly threatening to those from dominant cultural and racial groups. Deidre, one of the young African American women in Fine's 1991 study of an urban high school, explained it this way: "White people might feel like everything's over and OK, but we remember" (p. 33).

Another reason that teachers may avoid bringing up potentially contentious issues in the curriculum is their feeling that doing so may create or exacerbate animosity and hostility among students. They may even believe, as did the reading teacher in Jonathan Kozol's 1967 classic book on the Boston Public Schools, *Death at an Early Age,* that discussing slavery in the context of U.S. history was just too complicated for children to understand, not to mention uncomfortable for teachers to explain. Kozol writes of the reading teacher:

> She said, with the very opposite of malice but only with an expression of the most intense and honest affection for the children in the class: "I don't want these children to have to think back on this year later on and to have to remember that we were the ones who told them they were Negro. (p. 68)

More than a quarter of a century later, the same kinds of disclaimers are being made for the failure to include in the curriculum the very issues that would engage students in learning. Fine (1991) found that although over half of the students in the urban high school she interviewed described experiences with racism, teachers were reluctant to discuss it in class, explaining, in the words of one teacher, "It would demoralize the students, they need to feel positive and optimistic — like they have a chance. Racism is just an excuse they use to not try harder" (p. 37). Some of these concerns may be sincere expressions of protectiveness towards students, but others are merely self-serving and manifest teachers' discomfort with discussing racism.

The few relevant studies I have found concerning the inclusion of issues of racism and discrimination in the curriculum suggest that discussions about these topics can be immensely constructive if they are approached with sensitivity and understanding. This was the case in Melinda Fine's description of the "Facing History and Ourselves" (FHAO) curriculum, a project that started in the Brookline (Massachusetts) Public Schools almost two decades ago (Fine, 1993). FHAO provides a model for teaching history that encourages students to reflect critically on a variety of contemporary social, moral, and political issues. Using the Holocaust as a case study, students learn to think critically about such issues as scapegoating, racism, and personal and collective responsibility. Fine suggests that moral dilemmas do not disappear simply because teachers refuse to bring them into the schools. On the contrary, when these realities are separated from the curriculum, young people learn that school knowledge is unrelated to their lives, and once again, they are poorly prepared to face the challenges that society has in store for them.

A good case in point is Vanessa, a young European American woman in my study who was intrigued by "difference" yet was uncomfortable and reluctant to discuss it; although she was active in a peer education group that focused on such concerns as peer pressure, discrimination, and exclusion, these were rarely discussed in the formal curriculum. Vanessa, therefore, had no language with which to talk about these issues. In thinking about U.S. history, she mused about some of the contradictions that were rarely addressed in school:

> It seems weird . . . because people came from Europe and they wanted to get away from all the stuff that was over there. And then they came here and set up all the stuff like slavery, and I don't know, it seems the opposite of what they would have done.

The curriculum, then, can act to either enable or handicap students in their learning. Given the kind of curriculum that draws on their experiences and energizes them because it focuses precisely on those things that are most important in their lives, students can either soar or sink in our schools. Curriculum can provide what María Torres-Guzmán (1992) refers to as "cognitive empowerment," encouraging students to become confident, active critical thinkers who learn that their background experiences are important tools for further learning. The connection of the curriculum to real life and their future was mentioned by several of the students interviewed in my study. Avi, a Jewish boy of sixteen who often felt a schism between his school and home lives, for instance, spoke about the importance of school: "If you don't go to school, then you can't learn about life, or you can't learn about things that you need to progress [in] your life." And Vanessa, who seemed to yearn for a more socially conscious curriculum in her school, summed up why education was important to her: "A good education is like when you personally learn something . . . like growing, expanding your mind and your views."

Pedagogy

If curriculum is primarily the *what* of education, then pedagogy concerns the *why* and *how*. No matter how interesting and relevant the curriculum may be, the way in which it is presented is what will make it engaging or dull to students. Students' views echo those of educational researchers who have found that teaching methods in most classrooms, and particularly those in secondary schools, vary little from traditional "chalk and talk" methods; that textbooks are the dominant teaching materials used; that routine and rote learning are generally favored over creativity and critical thinking; and that teacher-centered transmission models prevail (Cummins, 1994; Goodlad, 1984; McNeil, 1986). Martin Haberman is especially critical of what he calls "the pedagogy of poverty," that is, a basic urban pedagogy used with children who live in poverty and which consists primarily of giving instructions, asking questions, giving directions, making assignments, and monitoring seat work. Such pedagogy is based on the assumption that before students can be engaged in creative or critical work, they must first master "the basics." Nevertheless, Haberman asserts that this pedagogy does not work and, furthermore, that it actually gets in the way of real teaching and learning. He suggests instead that we look at exemplary pedagogy in urban schools that actively involves students in real-life situations, which allows them to reflect on their own lives. He finds that good teaching is taking place when teachers welcome difficult issues and events and use human difference as the basis for the curriculum; design collaborative activities for heterogeneous groups; and help students apply ideals of fairness, equity, and justice to their world (Haberman, 1991).

Students in my study had more to say about pedagogy than about anything else, and they were especially critical of the lack of imagination that led to boring classes. Linda, who was just graduating as the valedictorian of her class in an urban high school, is a case in point. Her academic experiences had not always been smooth sailing. For example, she had failed both seventh and eighth grade twice, for a combination of reasons, including academic and medical problems. Consequently, she had experienced both exhilarating and devastating educational experiences. Linda had this to say about pedagogy:

> I think you have to be creative to be a teacher; you have to make it interesting. You can't just go in and say, "Yeah, I'm going to teach the kids just that; I'm gonna teach them right out of the book and that's the way it is, and don't ask questions." Because I know there were plenty of classes where I lost complete interest. But those were all because the teachers just, "Open the books to this page." They never made up problems out of their head. Everything came out of the book. You didn't ask questions. If you asked them questions, then the answer was "in the book." And if you asked the question and the answer *wasn't* in the book, then you shouldn't have asked that question!

Rich, a young Black man, planned to attend pharmacy school after graduation, primarily because of the interest he had developed in chemistry. He too talked about the importance of making classes "interesting":

> I believe a teacher, by the way he introduces different things to you, can make a class interesting. Not like a normal teacher that gets up, gives you a lecture, or there's teachers that just pass out the work, you do the work, pass it in, get a grade, good-bye!

Students were especially critical of teachers' reliance on textbooks and blackboards, a sad indictment of much of the teaching that encourages student passivity. Avi, for instance, felt that some teachers get along better when they teach from the point of view of the students: "They don't just come out and say, `All right, do this, blah, blah, blah.' . . . They're not so one-tone voice." Yolanda said that her English teacher didn't get along with the students. In her words, "She just does the things and sits down." James mentioned that some teachers just don't seem to care: "They just teach the stuff. `Here,' write a couple of things on the board, `see, that's how you do it. Go ahead, page 25.' " And Vinh added his voice to those of the students who clearly saw the connection between pedagogy and caring: "Some teachers, they just go inside and go to the blackboard. . . . They don't care."

Students did more than criticize teachers' pedagogy, however; they also praised teachers who were interesting, creative, and caring. Linda, in a particularly moving testimony to her first-grade teacher, whom she called her mentor, mentioned that she would be "following in her footsteps" and studying elementary education. She added:

> She's always been there for me. After the first or second grade, if I had a problem, I could always go back to her. Through the whole rest of my life, I've been able to go back and talk to her. . . . She's a Golden Apple Award winner, which is a very high award for elementary school teachers. . . . She keeps me on my toes. . . . When I start getting down . . . she peps me back up and I get on my feet.

Vinh talked with feeling about teachers who allowed him to speak Vietnamese with other students in class. Vinh loved working in groups. He particularly remembered a teacher who always asked students to discuss important issues, rather than focusing only on learning what he called "the word's meaning" by writing and memorizing lists of words. The important issues concerned U.S. history, the students' histories and cultures, and other engaging topics that were central to their lives. Students' preference for group work has been mentioned by other educators as well. Phelan et al. (1992), in their research on students' perspectives concerning school, found that both high- and low-achieving students of all backgrounds expressed a strong preference for working in groups because it helped them generate ideas and participate actively in class.

James also appreciated teachers who explained things and let everybody ask questions because, as he said, "There could be someone sitting in the back of the class that has the same question you have. Might as well bring it out." Fern contrasted classes where she felt like falling asleep because they're just "blah," to chorus, where the teacher used a "rap song" to teach history and involve all the students. And Avi, who liked most of his teachers, singled out a particular math teacher he had had in ninth grade for praise:

> 'Cause I never really did good in math until I had him. And he showed me that it wasn't so bad, and after that I've been doing pretty good in math and I enjoy it.

Yolanda had been particularly fortunate to have many teachers she felt understood and supported her, whether they commented on her bilingual ability, or referred to her membership in a folkloric Mexican dance group, or simply talked with her and the other students about their lives. She added:

> I really got along with the teachers a lot. . . . Actually, 'cause I had some teachers, and they were always calling my mom, like I did a great job. Or they would start talking to me, or they kinda like pulled me up some grades, or moved me to other classes, or took me somewhere. And they were always congratulating me.

Such support, however, rarely represented only individual effort on the part of some teachers, but rather was often manifested by the school as a whole; that is, it was integral to the school's practices and policies. For instance, Yolanda had recently been selected "Student of the Month" and her picture had been prominently displayed in her school's main hall. In addition, she received a certificate and was taken out to dinner by the principal. Although Linda's first-grade teacher was her special favorite, she had others who also created an educational context in which all students felt welcomed and connected. The entire Tremont Elementary School had been special for Linda, and thus the context of the school, including its leadership and commitment, were the major ingredients that made it successful:

> All of my teachers were wonderful. I don't think there's a teacher at the whole Tremont School that I didn't like. . . . It's just a feeling you have. You know that they really care for you. You just know it; you can tell. Teachers who don't have you in any of their classes or haven't ever had you, they still know who you are. . . . The Tremont School in itself is a community. . . . I love that school! I want to teach there.

Vanessa talked about how teachers used their students' lives and experiences in their teaching. For her, this made them especially good teachers:

> [Most teachers] are really caring and supportive and are willing to share their lives and are willing to listen to mine. They don't just want to talk about what they're teaching you; they also want to know you.

Aside from criticism and praise, students in this study also offered their teachers many thoughtful suggestions for making their classrooms more engaging places. Rich, for instance, said that he would "put more activities into the day that can make it interesting." Fern recommended that teachers involve students more actively in learning: "More like making the whole class be involved, not making only the two smartest people up here do the whole work for the whole class." Vanessa added, "You could have games that could teach anything that they're trying to teach through notes or lectures." She suggested that in learning Spanish, for instance, students could act out the words, making them easier to remember. She also thought that other books should be required "just to show some points of view," a response no doubt to the bland quality of so many of the textbooks and other teaching materials available in schools. Avi thought that teachers who make themselves available to students ("You know, I'm here after school. Come and get help.") were most helpful.

Vinh was very specific in his suggestions, and he touched on important cultural issues. Because he came from Vietnam when he was fifteen, learning English was a difficult challenge for Vinh, and he tended to be very hard on himself, saying such things as "I'm not really good, but I'm trying" when asked to describe himself as a student. Although he had considered himself smart in Vietnam, he felt that because his English was not perfect, he wasn't smart anymore. His teachers often showered him with praise for his efforts, but Vinh criticized this approach:

> Sometimes, the English teachers, they don't understand about us. Because something we not do good, like my English is not good. And she say, "Oh, your English is great!" But that's the way the American culture is. But my culture is not like that. . . . If my English is not good, she has to say, "Your English is not good. So you have to go home and study." And she tell me what to study and how to study and get better. But some Americans, you know, they don't understand about myself. So they just say, "Oh! You're doing a good job! You're doing great! Everything is great!" Teachers talk like that, but my culture is different. . . . They say, "You have to do better."

This is an important lesson not only because it challenges the overuse of praise, a practice among those that María de la Luz Reyes (1992) has called "venerable assumptions," but also because it cautions teachers to take into account both cultural and individual differences. In this case, the practice of praising was perceived by Vinh as hollow, and therefore insincere. Linda referred to the lesson she learned when she failed seventh and eighth grade and "blew two years":

> I learned a lot from it. As a matter of fact, one of my college essays was on the fact that from that experience, I learned that I don't need to hear other people's praise to get by. . . . All I need to know is in here [pointing to her heart] whether I tried or not.

Students have important messages for teachers about what works and what doesn't. It is important, however, not to fall back on what Lilia Bartolomé (1994) has aptly termed the "methods fetish," that is, a simplistic belief that particular methods will automatically resolve complex problems of underachievement. According to Bartolomé, such a myopic approach results in teachers avoiding the central issue of why some students succeed and others fail in school and how political inequality is at the heart of this dilemma. Rather than using this or that method, Bartolomé suggests that teachers develop what she calls a "humanizing pedagogy" in which students' languages and cultures are central. There is also the problem that Reyes (1992) has called a "one-size-fits all" approach, where students' cultural and other differences may be denied even if teachers' methods are based on well-meaning and progressive pedagogy. The point here is that no method can become a sacred cow uncritically accepted and used simply because it is the latest fad. It is probably fair to say that teachers who use more traditional methods but care about their students and believe they deserve the chance to dream may have more of a positive effect than those who know the latest methods but do not share these beliefs. Students need more than such innovations as heterogeneous grouping, peer tutoring, or cooperative groups. Although these may in fact be excellent and effective teaching methods, they will do little by themselves unless accompanied by changes in teachers' attitudes and behaviors.

The students quoted above are not looking for one magic solution or method. In fact, they have many, sometimes contradictory, suggestions to make about pedagogy. While rarely speaking with one voice, they nevertheless have similar overriding concerns: too many classrooms are boring, alienating, and disempowering. There is a complex interplay of policies, practices, and attitudes that cause such pedagogy to continue. Tracking and testing are two powerful forces implicated in this interplay.

Tracking/Ability Grouping/Grades and Expectations of Student Achievement

> It is not low income that matters but low status. And status is always created and imposed by the ones on top. (Stein, 1971, p. 158)

In her 1971 article, Annie Stein cited a New York City study in which kindergarten teachers were asked to list in order of importance the things a child should learn in order to prepare for first grade. Their responses were coded according to whether they were primarily socialization or educational goals. In the schools with large Puerto Rican and African American student populations, the socialization goals were always predominant; in the mixed schools, the educational goals were first. Concluded Stein, "In fact, in a list of six or seven goals, several teachers in the minority-group kindergartens forgot to mention any educational goals at all" (p. 167). A kind of tracking, in which students' educational goals were being sacrificed for social aims, was taking place in these schools, and its effects were already evident in kindergarten.

Most recent research on tracking has found it to be problematic, especially among middle- and low-achieving students, and suggestions for detracking schools have gained growing support (Oakes, 1992; Wheelock, 1992). Nevertheless, although many tracking decisions are made on the most tenuous grounds, they are supported by ideological norms in our society about the nature of intelligence and the distribution of ability. The long-term effects of ability grouping can be devastating for the life chances of young people. John Goodlad (1984) found that first- or second-grade children tracked by teachers' judgments of their reading and math ability or by testing are likely to remain in their assigned track *for the rest of their schooling*. In addition, he found that poor children and children of color are more likely to face the negative effects of tracking than are other youngsters. For example, a recent research project by Hugh Mehan and Irene Villanueva (1993) found that when low-achieving high school students are detracked, they tend to benefit academically. The study focused on low-achieving students in the San Diego City Schools. When these students, mostly Latinos and African Americans, were removed from a low track and placed in college-bound courses with high-achieving students, they benefitted in a number of ways, including significantly higher college enrollment. The researchers concluded that a rigorous academic program serves the educational and social interests of such students more effectively than remedial and compensatory programs.

Most of the young people in my study did not mention tracking or ability grouping by name, but almost all referred to it circuitously, and usually in negative ways. Although by and large academically successful themselves, they were quick to point out that teachers' expectations often doomed their peers to failure. Yolanda, for instance, when asked what suggestions she would give teachers, said, "I'd say to teachers, 'Get along more with the kids that are not really into themselves. . . . Have more communication with them.' " When asked what she would like teachers to know about other Mexican American students, she quickly said, "They try real hard, that's one thing I know." She also criticized teachers for having low expectations of students, claiming that materials used in the classes were "too low." She added, "We are supposed to be doing higher things. And like they take us too slow, see, step by step. And that's why everybody takes it as a joke." Fern, although she enjoyed being at the "top of my class," did not like to be treated differently. She spoke about a school she attended previously where "you were all the same and you all got pushed the same and you were all helped the same. And one thing I've noticed in Springdale is they kind of teach 25 percent and they kinda leave 75 percent out." She added that, if students were receiving bad grades, teachers did not help them as much: "In Springdale, I've noticed if you're getting D's and F's, they don't look up to you; they look down. And you're always the last on the list for special activities, you know?"

These young people also referred to expectations teachers had of students based on cultural or class differences. Vanessa said that some teachers based their expectations of students on bad reputations, and found least helpful those teachers who "kind of just move really fast, just trying to get across to you what they're trying to teach you. Not willing to slow down because they need to get in what they want to get in." Rich, who attended a predominately Black school, felt that some teachers there did not expect as much as they should from the Black students: "Many of the White teachers there don't push. . . . Their expectations don't seem to be as high as they should be. . . . I know that some Black teachers, their expectations are higher than White teachers. . . . They just do it, because they know how it was for them. . . . Actually, I'd say, you have to be in Black shoes to know how it is." Little did Rich know that he was reaching the same conclusion as a major research study on fostering high achievement for African American students. In this study, Janine Bempechat determined that "across all schools, it seems that achievement is fostered by high expectations and standards" (Bempechat, 1992, p. 43).

Virginia Vogel Zanger's research with Latino and Latina students in a Boston high school focused on what can be called "social tracking." Although the students she interviewed were high-achieving and tracked in a college-bound course, they too felt the sting of alienation. In a linguistic analysis of their comments, she found that students conveyed a strong sense of marginalization, using terms such as "left out," "below," "under," and "not joined in" to reflect their feelings about school (Zanger, 1994). Although these were clearly academically successful students, they perceived tracking in the subordinate status they were assigned based on their cultural backgrounds and on the racist climate established in the school. Similarly, in a study on dropping out among Puerto Rican students, my colleague Manuel Frau-Ramos and I found some of the same kind of language. José, who had dropped out in eleventh grade, explained, "I was alone. . . . I was an outsider" (Frau-Ramos & Nieto, 1993, p. 156). Pedro, a young man who had actually graduated, nevertheless felt the same kind of alienation. When asked what the school could do to help Puerto Ricans stay in school, he said, *"Hacer algo para que los boricuas no se sientan aparte"* (Do something so that the Puerto Ricans wouldn't feel so separate) (p. 157).

Grading policies have also been mentioned in relation to tracking and expectations of achievement. One study, for example, found that when teachers de-emphasized grades and standardized testing, the status of their African American and White students became more equal, and White students made more cross-race friendship choices (Hallinan & Teixeira, 1987). In my own research, I found a somewhat surprising revelation: although the students were achieving successfully in school, most did not feel that grades were very helpful. Of course, for the most part they enjoyed receiving good grades, but it was not always for the expected reason. Fern, for instance, wanted good grades because they were one guarantee that teachers would pay attention to her. Marisol talked about the "nice report cards" that she and her siblings in this family of eight children received, and said, "and, usually, we do this for my mother. We like to see her the way she wants to be, you know, to see her happy."

But they were also quick to downplay the importance of grades. Linda, for instance, gave as an example her computer teacher, who she felt had been the least helpful in her high school:

> I have no idea about computer literacy. I got A's in that course. Just because he saw that I had A's, and that my name was all around the school for all the "wonderful things" I do, he just automatically assumed. He didn't really pay attention to who I was. The grade I think I deserved in that class was at least a C, but I got A just because everybody else gave me A's. . . . He didn't help me at all because he didn't challenge me.

She added,

> To me, they're just something on a piece of paper. . . . [My parents] feel just about the same way. If they ask me, "Honestly, did you try your best?" and I tell them yes, then they'll look at the grades and say okay.

Rich stated that, although grades were important to his mother, "I'm comfortable setting my own standards." James said, without arrogance, that he was "probably the smartest kid in my class." Learning was important to him and, unlike other students who also did the assignments, he liked to "really get into the work and stuff." He added,

> If you don't get involved with it, even if you do get, if you get perfect scores and stuff . . . it's not like really gonna sink in. . . . You can memorize the words, you know, on a test . . . but you know, if you memorize them, it's not going to do you any good. You have to *learn* them, you know?

Most of the students made similar comments, and their perceptions challenge schools to think more deeply about the real meaning of education. Linda was not alone when she said that the reason for going to school was to "make yourself a better person." She loved learning, and commented that "I just want to keep continuously learning, because when you stop learning, then you start dying." Yolanda used the metaphor of nutrition to talk about learning: "[Education] is good for you. . . . It's like when you eat. It's like if you don't eat in a whole day, you feel weird. That's the same thing for me." Vanessa, also an enthusiastic student, spoke pensively about success and happiness: "I'm happy. Success is being happy to me, it's not like having a job that gives you a zillion dollars. It's just having self-happiness."

Finally, Vinh spoke extensively about the meaning of education, contrasting the difference between what he felt it meant in the United States and what it meant in his home culture:

> In Vietnam, we go to school because we want to become educated people. But in the United States, most people, they say, "Oh, we go to school because we want to get a good job." But my idea, I don't think so. I say, if we go to school, we want a good job *also,* but we want to become a good person.
>
> [Grades] are not important to me. Important to me is education. . . . I not so concerned about [test scores] very much. . . . I just know I do my exam very good. But I don't need to know I got A or B. I have to learn more and more.
>
> Some people, they got a good education. They go to school, they got master's, they got doctorate, but they're just helping *themselves.* So that's not good. I don't care much about money. So, I just want to have a normal job that I can take care of myself and my family. So that's enough. I don't want to climb up compared to other people.

RACISM AND DISCRIMINATION

The facts are clear to behold, but the BIG LIE of racism blinds all but its victims. (Stein, 1971, p. 179)

An increasing number of formal research studies, as well as informal accounts and anecdotes, attest to the lasting legacy of various forms of institutional discrimination in the schools based on race, ethnicity, religion, gender, social class, language, and sexual orientation. Yet, as Annie Stein wrote in 1971, these are rarely addressed directly. The major reason for this may be that institutional discrimination flies in the face of our stated ideals of justice and fair play and of the philosophy that individual hard work is the road to success. Beverly Daniel Tatum, in discussing the myth of meritocracy, explains why racism is so often denied, downplayed, or dismissed: "An understanding of racism as a system of advantage presents a serious challenge to the notion of the United States as a just society where rewards are based solely on one's merits" (Tatum, 1992, p. 6).

Recent studies point out numerous ways in which racism and other forms of discrimination affect students and their learning. For instance, Angela Taylor found that, to the extent that teachers harbor negative racial stereotypes, the African American child's race *alone* is probably sufficient to place him or her at risk for negative school outcomes (Taylor, 1991). Many teachers, of course, see it differently, preferring to think instead that students' lack of academic achievement is due solely to conditions inside their homes or communities. But the occurrence of discriminatory actions in schools, both by other students and by teachers and other staff, has been widely documented. A 1990 study of Boston high school students found that while 57 percent had witnessed a racial attack and 47 percent would either join in or feel that the group being attacked deserved it, only a quarter of those interviewed said they would report a racial incident to school officials (Ribadeneira, 1990). It should not be surprising, then, that in a report about immigrant students in California, most believed that Americans felt negatively and unwelcoming toward them. In fact, almost every immigrant student interviewed reported that they had at one time or another been spat upon, and tricked, teased, and laughed at because of their race, accent, or the way they dressed. More than half also indicated that they had been the victims of teachers' prejudice, citing instances where they were punished, publicly embarrassed, or made fun of because of improper use of English. They also reported that teachers had made derogatory comments about immigrant groups in front of the class, or had avoided particular students because of the language difficulty (Olsen, 1988). Most of the middle and high school students interviewed by Mary Poplin and Joseph Weeres (1992) had also witnessed incidents of racism in school. In Karen Donaldson's study in an urban high school where students used the racism they experienced as the content of a peer education program, over 80 percent of students surveyed said that they had perceived racism to exist in school (Donaldson, 1994).

Marietta Saravia-Shore and Herminio Martínez found similar results in their ethnographic study of Puerto Rican young people who had dropped out of school and were currently participating in an alternative high school program. These adolescents felt that their former teachers were, in their words, "against Puerto Ricans and Blacks" and had openly discriminated against them. One reported that a teacher had said, "Do you want to be like the other Puerto Rican women who never got an education? Do you want to be like the rest of your family and never go to school?" (Saravia-Shore & Martínez, 1992, p. 242). In Virginia Vogel Zanger's study of high-achieving Latino and Latina Boston high school students, one young man described his shock when his teacher called him "spic" right in class; although the teacher was later suspended, this incident had left its mark on him (Zanger, 1994). Unfortunately, incidents such as these are more frequent than schools care to admit or acknowledge. Students, however, seem eager to address these issues, but are rarely given a forum in which such discussions can take place.

How do students feel about the racism and other aspects of discrimination that they see around them and experience? What effect does it have on them? In interviews with students, Karen Donaldson found three major ways in which they said they were affected: White students experienced guilt and embarrassment when they became aware of the racism to which their peers were subjected; students of color sometimes felt they needed to overcompensate and overachieve to prove they were equal to their White classmates; and students of color also mentioned that discrimination had a negative impact on their self-esteem (Donaldson, 1994). The issue of self-esteem is a complicated one and may include many variables. Children's self-esteem does not come fully formed out of the blue, but is *created* within particular contexts and responds to conditions that vary from situation to situation, and teachers' and schools' complicity in creating negative self-esteem certainly cannot be discounted. This was understood by Lillian, one of the young women in Nitza Hidalgo's study of an urban high school, who commented, "That's another problem I have, teachers, they are always talking about how we have no type of self-esteem or anything like that. . . . But they're the people that's putting us down. That's why our self-esteem is so low" (Hidalgo, 1991, p. 95).

The students in my research also mentioned examples of discrimination based on their race, ethnicity, culture, religion, and language. Some, like Manuel, felt it from fellow students. As an immigrant from Cape Verde who came to the United States at the age of eleven, he found the adjustment difficult:

> When American students see you, it's kinda hard [to] get along with them when you have a different culture, a different way of dressing and stuff like that. So kids really look at you and laugh, you know, at the beginning.

Avi spoke of anti-Semitism in his school. The majority of residents in his town were European American and Christian. The Jewish community had dwindled significantly over the years, and there were now very few Jewish students in his school. On one occasion, a student had walked by him saying, "Are you ready for the second Holocaust?" He described another incident in some detail:

> I was in a woods class, and there was another boy in there, my age, and he was in my grade. He's also Jewish and he used to come to the temple sometimes and went to Hebrew school. But then, of course, he started hanging around

with the wrong people and some of these people were in my class, and I guess they were . . . making fun of him. And a few of them starting making swastikas out of wood. . . . So I saw one and I said to some kid, "What are you doing?" and the kid said to me, "Don't worry. It's not for you, it's for him." And I said to him, "What?!"

Other students talked about discrimination on the part of teachers. Both Marisol and Vinh specifically mentioned language discrimination as a problem. For Marisol, it had happened when a particular teacher did not allow Spanish to be spoken in her room. For Vinh, it concerned teachers' attitudes about his language: "Some teachers don't understand about the language. So sometimes, my language, they say it sounds funny." Rich spoke of the differences between the expectations of White and Black teachers, and concluded that all teachers should teach the curriculum *as if they were in an all-White school,* meaning that then expectations would be high for everybody. Other students were the object of teasing, but some, including James, even welcomed it, perhaps because it at least made his culture visible. He spoke of Mr. Miller, an elementary teacher he had been particularly fond of, who had called him "Gonzo" because he had a big nose and "Klinger" after the *M.A.S.H.* character who was Lebanese. James said, "And then everybody called me Klinger from then on. . . . I liked it, kind of . . . everybody laughing at me."

It was Linda who had the most to say about racism. As a young woman who identified herself as mixed because her mother was White and her father Black, Linda had faced discrimination or confusion on the part of both students and teachers. For example, she resented the fact that when teachers had to indicate her race, they came to their own conclusions without bothering to ask her. She explained what it was like:

> [Teachers should not] try to make us one or the other. And God forbid you should make us something we're totally not. . . . Don't write down that I'm Hispanic when I'm not. Some people actually think I'm Chinese when I smile. . . . Find out. Don't just make your judgments. . . . If you're filling out someone's report card and you need to know, then ask.

She went on to say:

> I've had people tell me, "Well, you're Black." I'm not Black; I'm Black and White. I'm Black and White American. "Well, you're Black!" No, I'm not! I'm both. . . . I mean, I'm not ashamed of being Black, but I'm not ashamed of being White either, and if I'm both, I want to be part of both. And I think teachers need to be sensitive to that.

Linda did not restrict her criticisms to White teachers, but also spoke of a Black teacher in her high school. Besides Mr. Benson, her favorite teacher of all, there was another Black teacher in the school:

The other Black teacher, he was a racist, and I didn't like him. I belonged to the Black Students Association, and he was the advisor. And he just made it so obvious: he was all for Black supremacy. . . . A lot of times, whether they deserved it or not, his Black students passed, and his White students, if they deserved an A, they got a B. . . . He was insistent that only Hispanics and Blacks be allowed in the club. He had a very hard time letting me in because I'm not all Black. . . . I just really wasn't that welcome there. . . . He never found out what I was about. He just made his judgments from afar.

It was clear that racism was a particularly compelling issue for Linda, and she thought and talked about it a great deal. The weight of racism on her mind was evident when she said, "It's hard. I look at history and I feel really bad for what some of my ancestors did to some of my other ancestors. Unless you're mixed, you don't know what it's like to be mixed." She even wrote a poem about it, which ended like this:

> But all that I wonder is who ever gave
> them the right to tell me
> What I can and can't do
> Who I can and can't be
> God made each one of us
> Just like the other
> the only difference is,
> I'm darker in color.

IMPLICATIONS OF STUDENTS' VIEWS FOR TRANSFORMATION OF SCHOOLS

Numerous lessons are contained within the narratives above. But what are the implications of these lessons for the school's curriculum, pedagogy, and tracking? How can we use what students have taught us about racism and discrimination? How can schools' policies and practices be informed through dialogue with students about what works and doesn't work? Although the students in my study never mentioned multicultural education by name, they were deeply concerned with whether and in what ways they and their families and communities were respected and represented in their schools. Two implications that are inherently multicultural come to mind, and I would suggest that both can have a major impact on school policies and practices. It is important that I first make explicit my own view of multicultural education: It is my understanding that multicultural education should be *basic for all students, pervasive in the curriculum and pedagogy, grounded in social justice, and based on critical pedagogy* (Nieto, 1992). Given this interpretation of multicultural education, we can see that it goes beyond the "tolerance" called for in numerous proclamations about diversity. It is also a far cry from the "cultural sensitivity" that is the focus of many professional development workshops (Nieto,

1994). In fact, "cultural sensitivity" can become little more than a conde-scending "bandaid" response to diversity, because it often does little to solve deep-seated problems of inequity. Thus, a focus on cultural sensitivity in and of itself can be superficial if it fails to take into account the structural and in-stitutional barriers that reflect and reproduce power differentials in society. Rather than promoting cultural sensitivity, I would suggest that multicultural education needs to be understood as "arrogance reduction"; that is, as en-compassing *both* individual *and* structural changes that squarely confront the individual biases, attitudes, and behaviors of educators, as well as the policies and practices in schools that emanate from them.

Affirming Students' Languages, Cultures, and Experiences

Over twenty years ago, Annie Stein reported asking a kindergarten teacher to explain why she had ranked four of her students at the bottom of her list, not-ing that they were "mute." "'Yes,' she said, 'they have not said one word for six months and they don't appear to hear anything I say.' 'Do they ever talk to the other children?' we asked. 'Sure,' was her reply. 'They cackle to each other in Spanish all day.'" (Stein, 1971, p. 161). These young children, al-though quite vocal in their own language, were not heard by their teacher be-cause the language they spoke was bereft of all significance in the school. The children were not, however, blank slates; on the contrary, they came to school with a language, culture, and experiences that could have been important in their learning. Thus, we need to look not only at the individual weaknesses or strengths of particular students, but also at the way in which schools assign status to entire groups of students based on the sociopolitical and linguistic context in which they live. Jim Cummins addressed this concern in relation to the kinds of superficial antidotes frequently proposed to solve the problem of functional illiteracy among students from culturally and economically domi-nated groups: "A remedial focus only on technical aspects of functional illit-eracy is inadequate because the causes of educational underachievement and 'illiteracy' among subordinated groups are rooted in the systematic devalua-tion of culture and denial of access to power and resources by the dominant group" (1994, pp. 307–308). As we have seen in many of the examples cited throughout this article, when culture and language are acknowledged by the school, students are able to reclaim the voice they need to continue their edu-cation successfully.

Nevertheless, the situation is complicated by the competing messages that students pick up from their schools and society at large. The research that I have reviewed makes it clear that, although students' cultures are important to them personally and in their families, they are also problematic because they are rarely valued or acknowledged by schools. The decisions young peo-ple make about their identities are frequently contradictory and mired in the tensions and struggles concerning diversity that are reflected in our society. Schools are not immune to such debates. There are numerous ways in which students' languages and cultures are excluded in schools: they are invisible, as with James, denigrated, as in Marisol's case, or simply not known, as happened with Vinh. It is no wonder then that these young people had conflicted feelings about their backgrounds. In spite of this, all of them spoke about the strength they derived from family and culture, and the steps they took to maintain it. James and Marisol mentioned that they continued to speak their native languages at home; Fern discussed her father's many efforts to maintain their Native American heritage; Manuel made it clear that he would always consider himself first and foremost Cape Verdean. Vinh spoke movingly about what his culture meant to him, and said that only Vietnamese was allowed in the home and that his sisters and brothers wrote to their parents in Vietnamese weekly. Most of these young people also maintained solid ties with their religion and places of worship as an important link to their heritage.

Much of the recent literature on educating culturally diverse students is helping to provide a radically different paradigm that contests the equation *education = assimilation* (Trueba, 1989). This research challenges the old assumptions about the role of the school as primarily an assimilationist agent, and provides a foundation for policy recommendations that focus on using students' cultural background values to promote academic achievement. In the case of Asian Pacific American youth, Peter Kiang and Vivian Wai-Fun Lee state the following:

> It is ironic that strengths and cultural values of family support which are so often praised as explanations for the academic achievement of Asian Pacific American students are severely undercut by the lack of programmatic and policy support for broad-based bilingual instruction and native language development, particularly in early childhood education. (Kiang & Lee, 1993, p. 39)

A study by Jeannette Abi-Nader of a program for Hispanic youth provides an example of how this can work. In the large urban high school she studied, students' cultural values, especially those concerned with *familia,* were the basis of everyday classroom interactions. Unlike the dismal dropout statistics prevalent in so many other Hispanic communities, up to 65 percent of the high school graduates in this program went on to college. Furthermore, the youth attributed their academic success to the program, and made enthusiastic statements about it, including this one written on a survey: "The best thing I like about this class is that we all work together and we all participate and try to help each other. We're family!" (Abi-Nader, 1993, p. 213).

The students in my research also provided impassioned examples of the effect that affirming their languages and cultures had on them and, conversely, on how negating their languages and cultures negated a part of them as well. The attitudes and behaviors of the teachers in Yolanda's school, for example, were reflected in policies that seemed to be based on an appreciation for student diversity. Given the support of her teachers and their affirmation of her language and her culture, Yolanda concluded, "Actually, it's fun around here if you really get into learning. . . . I like learning. I like really getting my mind working." Manuel also commented on how crucial it was for teachers to become aware of students' cultural values and backgrounds. This was especially important for Manuel, since his parents were immigrants unfamiliar with U.S. schools and society, and although they gave him important moral support, they could do little to help him in school. He said of his teachers:

> If you don't know a student there's no way to influence him. If you don't know his background, there's no way you are going to get in touch with him. There's no way you're going to influence him if you don't know where he's been.

Fern, on the other hand, as the only Native American student in her school, spoke about how difficult it was to discuss values that were different from those of the majority. She specifically mentioned a discussion about abortion in which she was trying to express that for Native Americans, the fetus is alive: "And, so, when I try to tell them, they just, 'Oh, well, we're out of time.' They cut me off, and we've still got half an hour!" And Avi, although he felt that teachers tried to be understanding of his religion, also longed for more cultural affirmation. He would have welcomed, for example, the support of the one Jewish teacher at school who Avi felt was trying to hide his Jewishness.

On the contrary, in Linda's case, Mr. Benson, her English teacher, who was also her favorite teacher, provided just that kind of affirmation. Because he was racially mixed like Linda, she felt that he could relate to the kinds of problems she confronted. He became, in the words of Esteban Díaz and his colleagues, a "sociocultural mediator" for Linda by assigning her identity, language, and culture important roles in the learning environment (Díaz, Flores, Cousin, & Soo Hoo, 1992). Although Linda spoke English as her native language, she gave a wonderful example of how Mr. Benson encouraged her to be "bilingual," using what she referred to as her "street talk." Below is her description of Mr. Benson and the role he played in her education:

> I've enjoyed all my English teachers at Jefferson. But Mr. Benson, my English Honors teacher, he just threw me for a whirl! I wasn't going to college until I met this man. . . . He was one of the few teachers I could talk to . . . 'cause Mr. Benson, he says, I can go into Harvard and converse with those people, and I can go out in the street and "rap with y'all." It's that type of thing. I love it. I try and be like that myself. I have my street talk. I get out in the street and I say "ain't" this and "ain't" that and "your momma" or "wha's up?" But I get somewhere where I know the people aren't familiar with that language or aren't accepting that language, and I will talk properly. . . . I walk into a place and I listen to how people are talking and it just automatically comes to me.

Providing time in the curriculum for students and teachers to engage in discussions about how the language use of students from dominated groups is discriminated against would go a long way in affirming the legitimacy of the discourse of *all* students (Delpit, 1992). According to Margaret Gibson (1991), much recent research has confirmed that schooling may unintentionally contribute to the educational problems of students from culturally dominated groups by pressuring them to assimilate against their wishes. The conventional wisdom that assimilation is the answer to academic under-achievement is thus severely challenged. One intriguing implication is that the more students are involved in resisting assimilation while maintaining their culture and language, the more successful they will be in school. That is, maintaining culture and language, although a conflicted decision, seems to have a positive impact on academic success. In any case, it seems to be a far healthier response than adopting an oppositional identity that effectively limits the possibility of academic success (Fordham & Ogbu, 1986; Skutnabb-Kangas, 1988). Although it is important not to overstate this conclusion, it is indeed a real possibility, one that tests the "melting pot" ideology that continues to dominate U.S. schools and society.

We know, of course, that cultural maintenance is not true in all cases of academic success, and everybody can come up with examples of students who felt they needed to assimilate to be successful in school. But the question remains whether this kind of assimilation is healthy or necessary. For instance, in one large-scale study, immigrant students clearly expressed a strong desire to maintain their native languages and cultures and to pass them on to their children (Olsen, 1988). Other research has found that bilingual students specifically appreciate hearing their native language in school, and want the opportunity to learn in that language (Poplin & Weeres, 1992). In addition, an intriguing study of Cambodian refugee children by the Metropolitan Indochinese Children and Adolescent Service found that the more successful they became at modeling their behavior to be like U.S. children, the more their emotional adjustment worsened (National Coalition, 1988). Furthermore, a study of Southeast Asian students found a significant connection between grades and culture: in this research, higher grade point averages correlated with the *maintenance* of traditional values, ethnic pride, and close social and cultural ties with members of the same ethnic group (Rumbaut & Ima, 1987).

All of the above suggests that it is time to look critically at policies and practices that encourage students to leave their cultures and languages at the schoolhouse door. It also suggests that schools and teachers need to affirm, maintain, and value the differences that students bring to school as a foundation for their learning. It is still too common to hear teachers urging parents to "speak only English," as my parents were encouraged to do with my sister and me (luckily, our parents never paid attention). The ample literature cited throughout this article concerning diverse student populations is calling such practices into question. What we are learning is that teachers instead need to encourage parents to speak their *native* language, not English, at home with their children. We are also learning that they should emphasize the importance of family values, not in the rigid and limiting way that this term has been used in the past to create a sense of superiority for those who are culturally dominant, but rather by accepting the strong ethical values that all cultural groups and all kinds of families cherish. As an initial step, however, teachers and schools must first learn more about their students. Vinh expressed powerfully what he wanted teachers to know about him by reflecting on how superficial their knowledge was:

> They understand something, just not all Vietnamese culture. Like they just understand something *outside*. . . . But they cannot understand something inside our hearts.

Listen to Students

Although school is a place where a lot of talk goes on, it is not often student talk. Student voices sometimes reveal the great challenges and even the deep pain young people feel when schools are unresponsive, cold places. One of the students participating in a project focusing on those "inside the school," namely students, teachers, staff, and parents, said, "This place hurts my spirit" (Poplin & Weeres, 1992, p. 11). Ironically, those who spend the most time in schools and classrooms are often given the least opportunity to talk. Yet, as we saw in the many examples above, students have important lessons to teach educators and we need to begin to listen to them more carefully. Suzanne Soo Hoo captured the fact that educators are losing a compelling opportunity to learn from students while working on a project where students became coresearchers and worked on the question, "What are the obstacles to learning?" a question that, according to Soo Hoo, "electrified the group" (1993, p. 386). Including students in addressing such important issues places the focus where it rightfully belongs, said Soo Hoo: "Somehow educators have forgotten the important connection between teachers and students. We listen to outside experts to inform us, and consequently, we overlook the treasure in our very own backyards: our students" (p. 390). As Mike, one of the coresearchers in her project, stated, "They think just because we're kids, we don't know anything" (p. 391).

When they are treated as if they do know something, students can become energized and motivated. For the ten young people in my study, the very act of speaking about their schooling experiences seemed to act as a catalyst for more critical thinking about them. For example, I was surprised when I met Marisol's mother and she told me that Marisol had done nothing but speak about our interviews. Most of the students in the study felt this enthusiasm and these feelings are typical of other young people in similar studies. As Laurie Olsen (1988) concluded in an extensive research project in California in which hundreds of immigrant students were interviewed, most of the students were gratified simply to have the opportunity to speak about their experiences. These findings have several implications for practice, including using oral histories, peer interviews, interactive journals, and other such strategies. Simply providing students with time to talk with one another, including group work, seems particularly helpful.

The feeling that adults do not listen to them has been echoed by many young people over the years. But listening alone is not sufficient if it is not accompanied by profound changes in what we expect our students to accomplish in school. Even more important than simply *listening* is *assisting* students to become agents of their own learning and to use what they learn in productive and critical ways. This is where social action comes in, and there have been a number of eloquent accounts of critical pedagogy in action (Peterson, 1991; Torres-Guzmán, 1992). I will quote at length from two such examples that provide inspiring stories of how listening to students can help us move beyond the written curriculum.

Iris Santos Rivera wrote a moving account of how a Freirian "problem-posing" approach was used with K–6 Chicano students in a summer educational program of the San Diego Public Schools in 1975 (Santos Rivera, 1983–1984). The program started by having the students play what she called the "Complain, Moan, and Groan Game." Using this exercise, in which students dialogued about and identified problems in the school and community, the young people were asked to identify problems to study. One group selected the school lunch program. This did not seem like a "real" problem to the teacher, who tried to steer the children toward another problem. Santos Rivera writes: "The teacher found it hard to believe in the problem's validity as an issue, as the basis for an action project, or as an integrating theme for education" (p. 5). She let the children talk about it for awhile, convinced that they would come to realize that this was not a serious issue. However, when she returned, they said to her, "Who is responsible for the lunches we get?" (p. 6). Thus began a summer-long odyssey in which the students wrote letters, made phone calls, traced their lunches from the catering truck through the school contracts office, figured out taxpayers' cost per lunch, made records of actual services received from the subcontractors, counted sandwiches and tested milk temperatures, and, finally, compared their findings with contract specifications, and found that there was a significant discrepancy. "We want to bring in the media," they told the teacher (p. 6). Both the local television station and the major networks responded to the press releases sent out by the students, who held a press conference to present the facts and answer reporters' questions. When a reporter asked who had told them all this, one nine-year old girl answered, "We found this stuff out. Nobody had to tell us anything. You know, you adults give yourselves too much credit" (p. 7). The postscript to this story is that state and federal laws had to be amended to change the kinds of lunches that students in California are served, and tapes from the students in this program were used in the state and federal hearings.

In a more recent example, Mary Ginley, a student in the doctoral program at the School of Education at the University of Massachusetts and a gifted teacher in the Longmeadow (Massachusetts) Public Schools, tries to help her second-graders develop critical skills by posing questions to them daily. Their responses are later discussed during class meeting time. Some of these questions are fairly straightforward ("Did you have a good weekend?"), while others encourage deeper thinking; the question posed on Columbus Day, "Was Columbus a hero?" was the culmination of much reading and dialogue that had previously taken place. Another activity she did with her students this year was to keep a daily record of sunrise and sunset. The students discovered to their surprise that December 21 was *not* the shortest day of the year. Using the daily almanac in the local newspaper, the students verified their finding and wrote letters to the editor. One, signed by Kaolin, read (spelling in original):

> Dear Editor,
>   Acorting to our chart December 21 was not the shotest day of the year. But acorting to your paper it is. Are teacher says it happens evry year! What's going on?

As a result of this letter, the newspaper called in experts from the National Weather Service and a local planetarium. One of them said, "It's a fascinating question that [the pupils] have posed. . . . It's frustrating we don't have an adequate answer."(Kelly, 1994, p. 12). Katie, one of the students in Mary's class, compared her classmates to Galileo, who shook the scientific community by saying that the earth revolved around the sun rather than the other way around. Another, Ben, said, "You shouldn't always believe what you hear," and Lucy asserted, "Even if you're a grown-up, you can still learn from a second grader!"

In the first part of this article, I posed the question, "Why listen to students?" I have attempted to answer this question using numerous comments that perceptive young people, both those from my study and others, have made concerning their education. In the final analysis, the question itself suggests that it is only by first listening *to* students that we will be able to learn to talk *with* them. If we believe that an important basis of education is dialogue and reflection about experience, then this is clearly the first step. Yolanda probably said it best when she commented, "'Cause you learn a lot from the students. That's what a lot of teachers tell me. They learn more from their students than from where they go study."

CONCLUSION

I have often been struck by how little young people believe they deserve, especially those who do not come from economically privileged backgrounds. Although they may work hard at learning, they somehow believe that they do not deserve a chance to dream. This article is based on the notion that all of our students deserve to dream and that teachers and schools are in the best position for "creating a chance" to do so, as referred to in the title. This means developing conditions in schools that let students know that they have a right to envision other possibilities beyond those imposed by traditional barriers of race, gender, or social class. It means, even more importantly, that those traditional barriers can no longer be viewed as impediments to learning.

The students in my study also showed how crucial extracurricular activities were in providing needed outlets for their energy and for teaching them important leadership skills. For some, it was their place of worship (this was especially true for Avi, Manuel, and Rich); for others, it was hobbies (Linda loved to sing); and for others, sports were a primary support (Fern mentioned how she confronted new problems by comparing them to the sports in which she excelled: "I compare it to stuff, like, when I can't get science, or like in sewing, I'll look at that machine and I'll say, 'This is a basketball; I can overcome it' "). The schools' responsibility to provide some of these activities becomes paramount for students such as Marisol, whose involvement in the Teen Clinic acted almost like a buffer against negative peer pressure.

These students can all be characterized by an indomitable resilience and a steely determination to succeed. However, expecting all students, particularly those from subordinated communities, to be resilient in this way is an unfair burden, because privileged students do not need this quality, as the schools generally reflect their backgrounds, experiences, language, and culture. Privileged students learn that they are the "norm," and although they may believe this is inherently unfair (as is the case with Vanessa), they still benefit from it.

Nevertheless, the students in this research provide another important lesson about the strength of human nature in the face of adversity. Although they represented all kinds of families and economic and social situations, the students were almost uniformly upbeat about their future and their lives, sometimes in spite of what might seem overwhelming odds. The positive features that have contributed to their academic success, namely, caring teachers, affirming school climates, and loving families, have helped them face such odds. "I don't think there's anything stopping me," said Marisol, whose large family lived on public assistance because both parents were disabled. She added, "If I know I can do it, I should just keep on trying." The determination to keep trying was evident also in Fern, whose two teenage sisters were undergoing treatment for alcohol and drug abuse, but who nevertheless asserted, "I succeed in everything I do. If I don't get it right the first time, I always go back and try to do it again," adding, "I've always wanted to be president of the United States!" And it was evident as well in the case of Manuel, whose father cleaned downtown offices in Boston while his mother raised the remaining children at home, and who was the first of the eleven children to graduate from high school: "I can do whatever I want to do in life. Whatever I want to do, I know I could make it. I believe that strongly." And, finally, it was also clear in the case of Rich, whose mother, a single parent, was putting all three of her children through college at the same time. Rich had clearly learned a valuable lesson about self-reliance from her, as we can see in this striking image: "But let's not look at life as a piece of cake, because eventually it'll dry up, it'll deteriorate, it'll fall, it'll crumble, or somebody will come gnawing at it." Later he added, "As they say, self-respect is one gift that you give yourself."

Our students have a lot to teach us about how pedagogy, curriculum, ability grouping, and expectations of ability need to change so that greater numbers of young people can be reached. In 1971, Annie Stein expressed the wishes and hopes of students she talked with, and they differ little from those we have heard through the voices of students today: "The demands of high school youth are painfully reasonable. They want a better education, a more 'relevant' curriculum, some voice in the subject matter to be taught and in the running of the school, and some respect for their constitutional and human rights" (1971, p. 177). Although the stories and voices I have used in this article are primarily those of individual students, they can help us to imagine what it might take to transform entire schools. The responsibility to do so cannot be placed only on the shoulders of individual teachers who, in spite of the profound impact they can have on the lives of particular students, are part of a system that continues to be unresponsive to too many young people. In the final analysis, students are asking us to look critically not only at structural conditions, but also at individual attitudes and behaviors. This implies that we need to undertake a total transformation not only of our schools, but also of our hearts and minds.

NOTES

1. I recognize that overarching terms, such as "European American," "African American," "Latino," etc., are problematic. Nevertheless, "European American" is more explicit than "White" with regard to culture and ethnicity, and thus challenges Whites also to think of themselves in ethnic terms, something they usually reserve for those from more clearly identifiable groups (generally, people of color). I have a more in-depth discussion of this issue in chapter two of my book, *Affirming Diversity* (1992).
2. The early arguments for cultural deprivation are well expressed by Carl Bereiter and Siegfried Englemann (1966) and by Frank Reissman (1962). A thorough review of a range of deficit theories can be found in Herbert Ginsburg (1986).
3. "Critical thinking," as used here, is not meant in the sense that it has come to be used conventionally to imply, for example, higher order thinking skills in math and science as disconnected from a political awareness. Rather, it means developing, in the Freirian (1970) sense, a consciousness of oneself as a critical agent in learning and transforming one's reality.
4. I was assisted in doing the interviews by a wonderful group of colleagues, most of whom contacted the students, interviewed them, and gave me much of the background information that helped me craft the case studies. I am grateful for the insights and help the following colleagues provided: Carlie Collins Tartakov, Paula Elliott, Haydée Font, Maya Gillingham, Mac Lee Morante, Diane Sweet, and Carol Shea.
5. "Holidays and Heroes" refers to an approach in which multicultural education is understood as consisting primarily of ethnic celebrations and the acknowledgment of "great men" in the history of particular cultures. Deeper structures of cultures, including values and lifestyle differences, and an explicit emphasis on power differentials as they affect particular cultural groups, are not addressed in this approach. Thus, this approach is correctly perceived as one that tends to romanticize culture and treat it in an artificial way. In contrast, multicultural education as empowering and liberating pedagogy confronts such structural issues and power differentials quite directly.

REFERENCES

Abi-Nader, J. (1993). Meeting the needs of multicultural classrooms: Family values and the motivation of minority students. In M. J. O'Hair & S. Odell (Eds), *Diversity and teaching: Teacher education yearbook 1* (pp. 212–236). Fort Worth, TX: Harcourt Brace Jovanovich.

Banks, J. A. (1991). *Teaching strategies for ethnic studies* (6th ed.). Boston: Allyn & Bacon.

Bartolomé, L. (1994). Beyond the methods fetish: Toward a humanizing pedagogy. *Harvard Educational Review, 64,* 173–194.

Bempechat, J. (1992). *Fostering high achievement in African American children: Home, school, and public policy influences.* New York: ERIC Clearinghouse on Urban Education, Teachers College, Columbia University.

Bereiter, C., & Englemann, S. (1966). *Teaching disadvantaged children in the preschool.* Englewood Cliffs, NJ: Prentice Hall.

Clark, R. M. (1983). *Family life and school achievement: Why poor Black children succeed or fail.* Chicago: University of Chicago Press.

Commins, N. L. (1989). Language and affect: Bilingual students at home and at school. *Language Arts, 66,* 29–43.

Cummins, J. (1994). From coercive to collaborative relations of power in the teaching of literacy. In B. M. Ferdman, R-M. Weber, & A. G. Ramírez (Eds.), *Literacy across languages and cultures* (pp. 295–331). Albany: State University of New York Press.

Delpit, L. (1992). The politics of teaching literate discourse. *Theory into Practice, 31,* 285–295.

Díaz, E., Flores, B., Cousin, P. T., & Soo Hoo, S. (1992, April). *Teacher as sociocultural mediator.* Paper presented at the Annual Meeting of the AERA, San Francisco.

Donaldson, K. (1994). Through students' eyes. *Multicultural Education, 2*(2), 26–28.

Fine, M. (1991). *Framing dropouts: Notes on the politics of an urban public high school.* Albany: State University of New York Press.

Fine, M. (1993). "You can't just say that the only ones who can speak are those who agree with your position": Political discourse in the classroom. *Harvard Educational Review, 63,* 412–433.

Fordham, S., & Ogbu, J. (1986) Black students' school success: Coping with the "burden of acting White". *Urban Review, 18,* 176–206.

Frau-Ramos, M., & Nieto, S. (1993). "I was an outsider": Dropping out among Puerto Rican youths in Holyoke, Massachusetts. In R. Rivera & S. Nieto (Eds.), *The education of Latino students in Massachusetts: Research and policy considerations* (pp. 143–166). Boston: Gastón Institute.

Freire, P. (1970). *Pedagogy of the oppressed.* New York: Seabury Press.

Gibson, M. (1991). Minorities and schooling: Some implications. In M. A. Gibson & J. U. Ogbu (Eds.), *Minority status and schooling: A comparative study of immigrant and involuntary minorities* (pp. 357–381). New York: Garland.

Ginsburg, H. (1986). The myth of the deprived child: New thoughts on poor children. In U. Neisser (Ed.), *The school achievement of minority children: New perspectives.* Hillsdale, NJ: Lawrence Erlbaum.

Goodlad, J. I. (1984). *A place called school.* New York: McGraw-Hill.

Haberman, M. (1991). The pedagogy of poverty versus good teaching. *Phi Delta Kappan, 73,* 290–294.

Hallinan, M., & Teixeira, R. (1987). Opportunities and constraints: Black-White differences in the formation of interracial friendships. *Child Development, 58,* 1358–1371.

Hidalgo, N. M. (1991). *"Free time, school is like a free time": Social relations in City High School classes.* Unpublished doctoral dissertation, Harvard University.

Hollins, E. R., King, J. E., & Hayman, W. C. (Eds.). (1994). *Teaching diverse populations: Formulating a knowledge base.* Albany: State University of New York Press.

Kelly, R. (1994, January 11). Class searches for solstice. *Union News,* p. 12.

Kiang, P. N., & Lee, V. W-F. (1993). Exclusion or contribution? Education K–12 policy. In *The State of Asian Pacific America: Policy Issues to the Year 2020* (pp. 25–48). Los Angeles: LEAP Asian Pacific American Public Policy Institute and UCLA Asian American Studies Center.

Kohl, H. (1993). The myth of "Rosa Parks, the tired." *Multicultural Education, 1*(2), 6–10.

Kozol, J. (1967). *Death at an early age: The destruction of the hearts and minds of Negro children in the Boston Public Schools.* New York: Houghton Mifflin.

Lee, V. E., Winfield, L. F., & Wilson, T. C. (1991). Academic behaviors among high-achieving African-American students. *Education and Urban Society, 24*(1), 65–86.

Lucas, T., Henze, R., & Donato, R. (1990). Promoting the success of Latino language-minority students: An exploratory study of six high schools. *Harvard Educational Review, 60,* 315–340.

McNeil, L. M. (1986). *Contradictions of control: School structure and school knowledge.* New York: Routledge & Kegan Paul.

Mehan, H., & Villanueva, I. (1993). Untracking low achieving students: Academic and social consequences. In *Focus on Diversity* (Newsletter available from the National Center for Research on Cultural Diversity and Second Language Learning, 399 Kerr Hall, University of California, Santa Cruz, CA 95064).

Moll, L. (1992). Bilingual classroom studies and community analysis: Some recent trends. *Educational Researcher, 21*(2), 20–24.

Moll, L., & Díaz, S. (1993). Change as the goal of educational research. In E. Jacob & C. Jordan (Eds.), *Minority education: Anthropological perspectives* (pp. 67–79). Norwood, NJ: Ablex.

National Coalition of Advocates for Students. (1988). *New voices: Immigrant students in U.S. public schools.* Boston: Author.

Newmann, F. M. (1993). Beyond common sense in educational restructuring: The issues of content and linkage. *Educational Researcher, 22*(2), 4–13, 22.

Nieto, S. (1992). *Affirming diversity: The sociopolitical context of multicultural education.* White Plains, NY: Longman.

Nieto, S. (1994). Affirmation, solidarity, and critique: Moving beyond tolerance in multicultural education. *Multicultural Education, 1*(4), 9–12, 35–38.

Oakes, J. (1992). Can tracking research inform practice? *Educational Researcher, 21*(4), 12–21.

Olsen, L. (1988). *Crossing the schoolhouse border: Immigrant students and the California public schools.* San Francisco: California Tomorrow.

Peterson, R. E. (1991). Teaching how to read the world and change it: Critical pedagogy in the intermediate grades. In C. E. Walsh (Ed.), *Literacy as praxis: Culture, language, and pedagogy* (pp. 156–182). New Jersey: Ablex.

Phelan, P., Davidson, A. L., & Cao, H. T. (1992). Speaking up: Students' perspectives on school. *Phi Delta Kappan, 73,* 695–704.

Poplin, M., & Weeres, J. (1992). *Voices from the inside: A report on schooling from inside the classroom.* Claremont, CA: Claremont Graduate School, Institute for Education in Transformation.

Reissman, F. (1962). *The culturally deprived child.* New York: Harper & Row.

Reyes, M. de la Luz (1992). Challenging venerable assumptions: Literacy instruction for linguistically different students. *Harvard Educational Review, 62,* 427–446.

Ribadeneira, D. (1990, October 18). Study says teen-agers' racism rampant. *Boston Globe,* p. 31.

Rumbaut, R. G., & Ima, K. (1987). *The adaptation of Southeast Asian refugee youth: A comparative study.* San Diego: Office of Refugee Resettlement.

Santos Rivera, I. (1983–1984, October-January). Liberating education for little children. In *Alternativas* (Freirian newsletter from Río Piedras, Puerto Rico, no longer published).

Saravia-Shore, M., & Martínez, H. (1992). An ethnographic study of home/school role conflicts of second generation Puerto Rican adolescents. In M. Saravia-Shore & S. F. Arvizu (Eds.), *Cross-cultural literacy: Ethnographies of communication in multiethnic classrooms* (pp. 227–251). New York: Garland.

Shor, I. (1992). *Empowering education: Critical teaching for social change.* Chicago: University of Chicago Press.

Skutnabb-Kangas, T. (1988). Resource power and autonomy through discourse in conflict: A Finnish migrant school strike in Sweden. In T. Skutnabb-Kangas & J. Cummins (Eds.), *Minority education: From shame to struggle* (pp. 251–277). Clevedon, England: Multilingual Matters.

Sleeter, C. E. (1991). *Empowerment through multicultural education.* Albany: State University of New York Press.

Sleeter, C. E. (1994). White racism. *Multicultural Education, 1*(4), 5–8, 39.

Sleeter, C. E., & Grant, C. A. (1991). Mapping terrains of power: Student cultural knowledge vs. classroom knowledge. In C. E. Sleeter (Ed.), *Empowerment through multicultural education* (pp. 49–67). Albany: State University of New York Press.

Soo Hoo, S. (1993). Students as partners in research and restructuring schools. *Educational Forum, 57,* 386–393.

Stein, A. (1971). Strategies for failure. *Harvard Educational Review, 41,* 133–179.

Tatum, B. D. (1992). Talking about race, learning about racism: The application of racial identity development theory in the classroom. *Harvard Educational Review, 62,* 1–24.

Taylor, A. R. (1991). Social competence and the early school transition: Risk and protective factors for African-American children. *Education and Urban Society, 24*(1), 15–26.

Taylor, D., & Dorsey-Gaines, C. (1988). *Growing up literate: Learning from inner-city families.* Portsmouth, NH: Heinemann.

Torres-Guzmán, M. (1992). Stories of hope in the midst of despair: Culturally responsive education for Latino students in an alternative high school in New York City. In M. Saravia-Shore & S. F. Arvizu (Eds.), *Cross-cultural literacy: Ethnographies of communication in multiethnic classrooms* (pp. 477–490). New York: Garland.

Trueba, H. T. (1989). *Raising silent voices: Educating the linguistic minorities for the twenty-first century.* Cambridge, MA: Newbury House.

Wheelock, A. (1992). *Crossing the tracks: How "untracking" can save America's schools.* New York: New Press.

Zanger, V. V. (1994). Academic costs of social marginalization: An analysis of Latino students' perceptions at a Boston high school. In R. Rivera & S. Nieto (Eds.), *The education of Latino students in Massachusetts: Research and policy considerations* (pp. 167–187). Boston: Gastón Institute.

Promoting the Success of
Latino Language-Minority Students:
An Exploratory Study of Six High Schools

▼▼▼▼▼

TAMARA LUCAS
ROSEMARY C. HENZE
RUBÉN DONATO

In "Effective Schools for the Urban Poor," Ron Edmonds states: "All children are eminently educable, and the behavior of the school is critical in determining the quality of the education" (1979, p. 20). This way of thinking diverges from often-cited "deficit" models of education, which account for student failure by reference to certain cultural, linguistic, and socioeconomic factors in students' backgrounds, thus making a liability out of difference. Language-minority (LM) students in particular have often been blamed for their underachievement in U.S. schools.[1] By considering them "difficult" or culturally and linguistically "deprived," schools have found it easy to absolve themselves of responsibility for the education of these students. Edmonds, on the other hand, places the responsibility for quality education squarely in the hands of the schools.

This assignment of responsibility for language-minority students has had a complex legal history. In 1973 the Supreme Court held, in the *Lau v. Nichols* decision, that public schools had to provide an education comprehensible to limited English proficient (LEP) students.[2] In an attempt to equalize educational opportunities for LEP students in U.S. schools, the Court stated: "Basic English is at the very core of what public schools teach. Imposition of a requirement that, before a child can effectively participate in the education program, he must already have acquired those basic skills is to make a mockery of public education" (*Lau v. Nichols*, 1973).

The *Lau* decision has had a powerful impact on the education of language-minority students. It marked the beginning of a national interest in educational equity for LM students and provoked policymakers throughout the country to respond to the special needs of this growing student population.

Harvard Educational Review   Vol. 60   No. 3   August 1990, 315–340

After 1974, under pressure from the federal government, many states began to push school districts to develop programs for LM students. California, for example, passed a bill in 1976 mandating bilingual education in its public schools.[3] School districts in California with large numbers of LEP students were required by the state to demonstrate how they were going to serve those students. For the most part, however, school districts focused on LEP students in elementary schools and ignored the schooling of secondary LEP students.

However, secondary schools do enroll many students whose English proficiency is limited. For example, poor economic conditions in Mexico have caused large numbers of Mexican students to arrive in the Southwest, with or without their families. Political unrest and war have brought thousands of refugees to the United States from such countries as El Salvador, Nicaragua, Guatemala, Vietnam, Cambodia, Laos, and Afghanistan. Students of all ages often arrive with little or no knowledge of English. Because of wartime conditions in their countries, many students have had interrupted schooling and thus come unprepared not only in English, but also in content knowledge, basic study skills, and knowledge of school culture. Providing effective schooling for these students is particularly challenging at the secondary level, when students are expected to possess a wealth of implicit and explicit knowledge about how to be a student.

On the other hand, many immigrant students arrive in the United States with strong educational backgrounds; for example, those who have attended *"Secundaria"* in Mexico may have had higher levels of math than their U.S.-born peers. Secondary LM students, in other words, are extremely diverse, bringing with them educational, social, academic, and cultural experiences that may differ widely from those of members of the host culture. To assure academic success, schools must attend to this diversity through special programs and practices, and through increased sensitivity to students' needs. High drop-out rates, low standardized test scores, poor attendance records, and the small numbers of students going on to postsecondary education all attest to the failure of most high schools to meet the needs of this student population (See Arias, 1986; Brown & Haycock, 1984; Espinosa & Ochoa, 1986; Gingras & Careaga, 1989; Medina, 1988; Orfield, 1986; Orum, 1988; Rumberger, 1987; U.S. General Accounting Office, 1987).

Because we believe that schools are responsible for the quality of education students receive, and that given a good education, all students can achieve, we are interested in what makes some schools more successful than others. During the past fifteen years, some educational researchers have turned away from attempting to explain school and student failure and have focused instead on explaining success, producing a body of research known as the "effective schools" literature. This work, most of which comes from studies conducted in urban elementary schools, provides some insight into the attributes of successful schools, including strong leadership; high expectations of students; schoolwide staff development; parent involvement and support; recognition of students' academic success; district support; collaborative planning; collegial relationships; and sense of community (Edmonds, 1979; Purkey & Smith, 1983).

The research on effective schools is not without its detractors, however. Critics have pointed to shortcomings in the literature, citing, for example, lack of generalizability to any but elementary schools; lack of attention to the variety of student populations and community contexts; an over-emphasis on attributes and lack of sufficient attention to complex processes and interrelationships; and a top-down strategy for school improvement growing out of the "implementation of attributes" approach (see Carter & Chatfield, 1986; Rosenholtz, 1985; Rowen, Bossert, & Dwyer, 1983; Stedman, 1987; Wilson & Corcoran, 1988).

One of the most frequent criticisms is that the effective schools literature has given little attention to what makes some schools more successful than others with language-minority students. Jennifer Bell (1989) has offered several reasons for this lack of attention. First, since most of the effective schools studies were conducted in schools that were predominantly Black and White in composition, LM students were not a major factor in overall student achievement. Second, with certain exceptions, most researchers did not consider language to be an important factor in student achievement. Third, the diversity of LM students was generally considered too difficult to account for in research design. Furthermore, since the public has been so sharply divided over bilingual instruction, research on LM students in the schools has focused primarily on the role of language in instruction rather than on the effectiveness of the whole school.

Recently, however, some studies have focused on effective schooling for language-minority students. Thomas Carter and Michael Chatfield (1986) reported on characteristics of three effective bilingual elementary schools, emphasizing processes over structures and attributes. The schools they described were characterized by such factors as: a well-functioning total system producing a school climate that promotes positive student outcomes; positive leadership, usually from the formal leaders; high staff expectations for students and instructional programs; strong demand for academic performance; denial of the cultural deprivation argument and stereotypes that support it; and high staff morale.

Bruce Wilson and Thomas Corcoran (1988) report on a number of middle and secondary schools that are successful with "at risk" students, which they define as students from poor and minority backgrounds (p. 130). Since some of the schools had sizable numbers of Latino and Asian students, we can assume that some of them were language-minority students, although the authors do not discuss the language backgrounds or English proficiency of students. The common elements of these successful schools include a positive attitude toward the students, a willingness to question conventional practices, a strong and competent leadership, a highly committed teaching staff, high expectations and standards, and an emphasis on high achievement in academics.

A number of studies have examined effective instructional practices for language-minority students in elementary bilingual programs (Ramírez, 1988; Tikunoff, 1985; Wong-Fillmore, McLaughlin, Ammon, & Ammon, 1985). However, there is little research of any kind at the secondary level, and little at either the elementary or secondary level that looks beyond effective classroom instruction to the broader issues involved in effective schooling for LM students. In a critique of the ways in which the "effective schools formula" has been applied, Stedman (1987) argues for a reconceptualization of the effective schools literature, focusing on "detailed descriptions of school organization and practice" (p. 217) and on providing "concrete guidance about what to do to make a school effective" (p. 218). Ways in which good schools foster cultural pluralism need to be documented, Stedman writes, and secondary schools need to be given more attention.

The exploratory study reported here intends to narrow these gaps in the existing research and to extend our knowledge about effective schooling. The study is based on information gathered at six secondary schools that have been recognized by local, state, or federal agencies for their success in providing a quality education for LM students, not only through effective classroom instruction but also through whole-school approaches. Because previous research, such as that described above, has primarily focused on successful instructional practices for LM students, our discussion will focus its attention on the whole school rather than on classroom practices per se.

It is important to point out that there is of course no formula or prescription for success; no single combination of variables will produce an effective school. Educators cannot simply adopt the features of these six schools and expect their institutions to become successful with LM students overnight. Schools can, however, begin to work toward such success by following the lead of these schools in ways that are appropriate and realistic for their particular school settings.

We believe that the most critical element in determining whether educators can work toward success for all students is the belief that all students can succeed. In 1979, Edmonds argued that the degree to which we effectively teach "the children of the poor" depends more on our political persuasions than on the information we gain from educational research. He asserted that we already know more than enough to successfully teach all students, and that the question is whether we *want* to teach all students. Recently, Shirley Jackson (1989) made a similar assertion. Yet many educators still appear uncertain as to whether schools can significantly influence the achievement and attainment of poor and minority youths, often claiming that parents do not support their children's educational efforts and implying that therefore schools cannot be blamed for failing to educate these children (Suro, 1990). In contrast, we hope that by presenting case studies of "living examples of success" (Carter & Chatfield, 1986, p. 229), we will not only encourage educators to believe that *all* students can succeed, but also provide them with concrete knowledge of what schools can do to help them.

BACKGROUND

In 1988, an initiative was undertaken by the Southwest Center for Educational Equity, at the request of and in collaboration with the Arizona Department of Education and representatives of six Arizona school districts, to develop strategies for Arizona high schools to serve language-minority students.[4] In surveying the literature on effective schooling, we realized that little was known about successful schooling for LM students at the secondary level. To gather information for the Arizona High School Initiative, we therefore conducted an exploratory study of schools promoting the achievement of this student population. We visited five high schools in California and one in Arizona that had large populations of Latino students and that had been recognized by local, state, and/or federal agencies for excellence.[5] Because the needs of different groups of LM students vary, and because we wanted to increase comparability of student populations across schools, we decided that schools working successfully with Latino LM students in particular would be the focus of this part of the initiative.[6]

METHODS

Selection of Case Study Schools

The selection of case study schools was complicated by the lack of consensus about what constitutes an "effective" or "successful" school. After much deliberation over which criteria were the most relevant, we decided to take a two-pronged approach to site selection, using both qualitative and quantitative criteria. First, we sought nominations from a variety of people familiar with secondary schools with large numbers of language-minority students, consulting with educators at state, county, and district levels and asking them to recommend schools that they believed were successful with those students (Wilson & Corcoran, 1988). We then contacted the principals of the recommended schools to determine whether they had received any formal recognition from local, state, or federal agencies for their instructional programs for LM students and whether they could provide us with some quantitative evidence of their success — for example, average daily attendance rates, drop-out rates, numbers of Latino LM students going on to postsecondary education, and standardized test scores that compared favorably with other minority schools. While we recognize that "effectiveness is a construct, an abstraction" (Wilson & Corcoran, 1988, p. 26) and that this process did not capture the full range of possible indicators of success, we believe it enables us to select six schools which are taking identifiable, positive steps to educate LM students.

DATA COLLECTION

Data were collected at five school sites in California and one in Arizona.[7] Two to four project staff members visited each site for three days, thus providing multiple perspectives and allowing for intensive collection of information. The combined data from all six schools consisted of audiotapes and notes from structured interviews with one superintendent, two district-level bilingual program directors, six principals, six assistant principals, five school-level project and program directors, fifteen counselors, fifty-two teachers and aides, and 135 students; 124 student questionnaires (35 from newcomers and 89 from non-newcomers); fifty-four classroom observations; schoolwide observations of the six schools; and various records and documents for each school, including policies regarding LM students, special program descriptions, transcripts for students who were interviewed, and other written information that interviewees gave us. Because we wanted above all to facilitate communication, we allowed students to use either English or Spanish for interviews and questionnaires, depending upon their preference. Students whose proficiency in English was very limited would not have been able to participate had they not been given the opportunity to use Spanish. Because the study sought to understand what contributes to the success of high school LM students, we were primarily interested in obtaining information from school staff who worked extensively and effectively with these students. Assistant principals, counselors, and teachers were selected to be interviewed if they 1) worked with large numbers of Latino LEP students, and 2) were recommended by others (administrators, counselors, teachers, students) as being especially effective with, and/or knowledgeable about, these students.

At each school, we asked a counselor, or in some cases a program director, to select students for us to interview. We requested six Latino students in each of four groups — high achievers, average achievers, students who had been doing poorly but had now improved, and students who had immigrated within the last two years. We also asked that students be non-native speakers of English. Though we succeeded in interviewing an average of twenty-four Latino LM students at each school, the distinctions among high achievers, average achievers, and "turnarounds" were not at all clear. For purposes of analysis, therefore, we grouped students only as newcomers or non-newcomers. Both groups included students from grades nine through twelve.

Sixty-one percent of the students interviewed were born in Mexico. The newcomers had arrived in the United States between the ages of fourteen and eighteen, while the non-newcomers were students born in the United States and students who had entered the United States in the early and middle grades. According to the student questionnaire, 72.5 percent of the students spoke Spanish at home, while 39 percent used Spanish at school. Ninety-eight percent of the students' fathers worked in labor- or service-related jobs, while 90 percent of the mothers worked as housewives or in service-related jobs.

In the aggregate, then, the Latino students we interviewed came from working-class backgrounds. However, they represented a tremendous range of educational and cultural experiences, from those whose entire education had been in the United States to those who had attended school in several different countries before coming here. Some students, according to the questionnaire, had had interruptions of several years in their schooling due to political unrest in their countries, while others had attended continuously. Factors such as these, combined with the different cultural identities of Mexicanos, Chicanos, Nicaragüenses, and other groups, made it clear that there is no such thing as a "typical" Latino student, and that a school successful with this population would have to be sensitive to differences in students' experiences and backgrounds.

Data Analysis

Data Analysis was a recursive process which began with the design of the study. The design, influenced by previous research on effective schooling, determined who would be interviewed and what other types of data would be collected. The questions used in interviews were formulated as new issues emerged from the data. Categories for analysis, inspired at first by the effective schools literature, were continually shaped as we interviewed, observed, and gathered documents at each site. Once information gathering had ended, intensive analysis proceeded from within-site analyses to cross-site analyses:

1. Each person who visited a site wrote a report of the data that she or he collected from interviews, observations, and serendipitous encounters. These reports brought together all of the data collected by each researcher into one organized and accessible whole. Reports included information about the school context (community, school board, student body composition and ethnicity, language census), types of Latino LM students enrolled at the school, what seemed to be working based on what was reported and what we saw, and what improvements were suggested to better meet the needs of the students.
2. All individual reports about each school were then synthesized into one case study report per school to provide "a well-grounded sense of the local reality" in that setting (Miles & Huberman, 1984, p. 151).
3. The six case studies were then analyzed in order to compare perceived realities across these schools.

In this process, we developed both concrete descriptions of what we observed and categories or themes derived from the data and informed by other studies of effective schooling (see Merriam, 1988). This process resulted in highlighting eight features that existed across sites, as noted in the introduction. Although each school is unique, the eight features represent commonalities in the ways the schools were promoting success for language-minority students. Most of the study findings are derived from interviews with staff members and students — particularly when the same or similar features were mentioned by a large number of people in different schools — and from our informed observations. In many cases, the language of the findings reflects words or phrases we heard repeatedly. What we were told in interviews was also confirmed and concretized through classroom and schoolwide observation and consultation of school records and documents.

FINDINGS

School Profiles

Five of the six schools were relatively large, with 1,700 to 2,200 students. All had minority White populations, and in all but the smallest school, Latino students constituted the largest single group — more than one-third of the school population. The four schools with the larger proportions of non-White students (Nogales, Overfelt, Sweetwater, and Newcomer) also had larger proportions of non-White staff. In none of the schools, however, was the ethnicity of the staff comparable to the student population; in all of them, a much larger proportion of staff than students was White. The percentage of students participating in a school lunch program — a rough measure of their socioeconomic status — varied considerably among the six schools. At Anaheim and Artesia, fewer than 25 percent of the students received such aid, at Overfelt and Sweetwater, about 33 percent did so, and at Nogales and Newcomer 80 percent did so. Thus, socioeconomic status of students is not a feature shared by these schools overall, although as noted earlier, the Latino students whom we interviewed were largely working class.

Key Features that Promote the Success of
Language-Minority Students

Through the exploratory case studies and the analysis across cases, eight features emerged which we believe to be the most important in promoting the success of language-minority students at the six schools we visited. (A more concise version of these eight features appears in Table 1.)

1. Value is placed on the students' languages and cultures.
Rather than ignoring barriers to equality and perpetuating the disenfranchisement of minority students, the principals, administrators, counselors, teachers, and other support staff at the schools we visited celebrated diversity. They gave language minority students the message that their languages and cultures were valued and respected, thus promoting the self-esteem necessary for student achievement. They communicated this sense of value and respect in a number of concrete ways, translating the ideal into an everyday reality.

First, the ability to speak a language in addition to English was treated as an advantage rather than a liability. A number of White and Latino teachers and counselors who were not native speakers of Spanish had learned the language. Some spoke it well enough to understand some of what their students said; others had learned it well enough to teach bilingual content classes. Students commented in interviews that they appreciated efforts made by teachers to speak Spanish and were pleased to see that the teachers valued their language. One student noted that "when teachers are bilingual, it makes our learning easier. They treat us equally." Another described the school as *"una amiga bilingüe"* (a bilingual friend).

Although these high schools made English literacy a primary goal, they also encouraged students to enhance their native language skills in classes for those students who spoke Spanish. Four of the six high schools we visited offered Spanish courses for Spanish speakers. Of these, three of them offered both literacy skills instruction and advanced courses in Spanish. Advanced Placement (AP) Spanish classes at these schools gave native-Spanish-speaking students the opportunity to capitalize on their native language to obtain college credit. The principal at Nogales High School, where 89 percent of the students were Latino, had gone even further in demonstrating the value placed on Spanish. All students at this school were required to take five years of language instruction — four in English and one in Spanish. Students who passed a proficiency test in Spanish were free to take another language to fulfill the fifth year requirement; others had to take Spanish for Spanish speakers or Spanish as a second language, whichever was appropriate.

A less formal but no less effective way that educators showed respect for the students' language was to allow them to speak their native language when English language development was not the focus of instruction. Their philosophy was that nothing was gained from stifling a young person's desire to communicate in his or her primary language. Throughout the campuses of the high schools we visited, students were free to speak Spanish with each other and with school staff. The use of their native language was not restricted to informal settings. Five of the schools provided content courses in Spanish, thus giving students the opportunity to progress through the content areas while developing their English skills. They were not required to postpone taking advanced content courses until they were fluent in English.

Besides showing respect for students' native language, staff in these schools also celebrated the students' cultures. Perhaps the most transparent and readily accessible aspects of culture are customs, holidays, and overtly stated values. While many schools give lip service to these aspects of culture, for example, by celebrating *Cinco de Mayo* and serving tacos on that day, the schools we visited affirmed the customs, values, and holidays of the language-minority students' countries in deeper and more consistent ways throughout the year.

Teachers, for example, made it their business to know about their students' past experiences. Some had visited Mexican schools to better understand their students' previous educational experiences. A group of teachers from one school had observed mathematics teaching in a Mexican school. One of them said that understanding how Mexican students were taught math in Mexico made teaching them easier. He could say to students, "This is the way most of you were taught how to divide in Mexico. And that's OK. This is another way of doing it." Without denigrating what they had learned in Mexico, he would ask which way was easiest for them.

In addition, while faculty and staff were sensitive to the importance of students' language and cultures, they did not treat students simply as members

TABLE 1   *Features of High Schools That Promote the Achievement of Language-Minority Students*

1. *Value is placed on the students' languages and cultures by:*
    Treating students as individuals, not as members of a group
    Learning about students' cultures
    Learning students' languages
    Hiring bilingual staff with similar cultural backgrounds to the students
    Encouraging students to develop their primary language skills
    Allowing students to speak their primary languages except when English development is the focus of instruction or interactions
    Offering advanced as well as lower division content courses in the students' primary languages
    Instituting extracurricular activities that will attract LM students

2. *High expectations of language-minority students are made concrete by:*
    Hiring minority staff in leadership positions to act as role models
    Providing a special program to prepare LM students for college
    Offering advanced and honors bilingual/sheltered classes in content areas
    Making it possible for students to exit ESL programs quickly
    Challenging students in class and providing guidance to help them meet the challenge
    Providing counseling assistance (in the primary language if necessary) to help students apply to college and fill out scholarship and grant forms
    Bringing in representatives of colleges and minority graduates who are in college to talk to students
    Working with parents to gain their support for students going to college
    Recognizing students for doing well

3. *School leaders make the education of language-minority students a priority.* These leaders:
    Hold high expectations of LM students
    Are knowledgeable of instructional and curricular approaches to teaching LM students and communicate this knowledge to staff
    Take a strong leadership role in strengthening curriculum and instruction for all students, including LM students
    Are often bilingual minority-group members themselves
    Hire teachers who are bilingual and/or trained in methods for teaching LM students

4. *Staff development is explicitly designed to help teachers and other staff serve language-minority students more effectively.* Schools and school districts:
    Offer incentives and compensation so that school staff will take advantage of available staff development programs
    Provide staff development for teachers and other school staff in:
    – effective instructional approaches to teaching LM students, e.g., cooperative learning methods, sheltered English, and reading and writing in the content areas
    – principles of second-language acquisition
    – the cultural backgrounds and experiences of the students
    – the languages of the students
    – cross-cultural communication
    – cross-cultural counseling

5. *A variety of courses and programs for language-minority students is offered.* The programs:
    Include courses in ESL and primary language instruction (both literacy and advanced placement) and bilingual and sheltered courses in content areas

TABLE 1 *continued*

Insure that the course offerings for LM students do not limit their choices or trap
them in low-level classes by offering advanced as well as basic courses taught
through bilingual and sheltered methods

Keep class size small (20–25 students) in order to maximize interaction

Establish academic support programs that help LM students make the transition from
ESL and bilingual classes to mainstream classes and prepare them to go to college

6. *A counseling program gives special attention to language-minority students* through counselors who:

Speak the students' languages and are of the same or similar cultural backgrounds

Are informed about postsecondary educational opportunities for LM students

Believe in, emphasize, and monitor the academic success of LM students

7. *Parents of language-minority students are encouraged to become involved in their children's
education.* Schools can provide and encourage:

Staff who can speak the parents' languages

On-campus ESL classes for parents

Monthly parents' nights

Parent involvement with counselors in planning their children's course schedules

Neighborhood meetings with school staff

Early morning meetings with parents

Telephone contacts to check on absent students

8. *School staff members share a strong commitment to empower language-minority students
through education.* This commitment is made concrete through staff who:

Give extra time to work with LM students

Take part in a political process that challenges the status quo

Request training of various sorts to help LM students become more effective

Reach out to students in ways that go beyond their job requirements, for example, by
sponsoring extra-curricular activities

Participate in community activities in which they act as advocates for Latinos and
other minorities

of an undifferentiated ethnic group. They recognized students' individual strengths, interests, problems, and concerns rather than characterizing them by reference to stereotypes. The assistant principal at one school said, "Basically, Hispanic kids are no different from other kids; they want to learn. Those who fall by the wayside are those whose needs aren't being met. Who wants to fail everyday?"

Faculty and staff also knew that there is no such thing as a generic Latino LM student. Rather, people from Mexico, Nicaragua, El Salvador, Guatemala, Cuba, and other Spanish-speaking countries were known to have different histories and customs and to speak different varieties of Spanish. Mexican immigrants, Mexican Americans, and Chicanos were also recognized as different from one another, and variation among Mexican immigrants based upon socioeconomic background and educational attainment level was acknowledged. When asked to describe the Latino students at the school, one teacher responded with five categories: those who are "well off, well educated, not disenfranchised; the migrant kids who have little education; children born here of parents who have immigrated here; limited-English-proficient students who have been here ten to twelve years but have lived in insular communities and had no education in Spanish; and then Central Americans."

Respect for students' languages and cultures was communicated through support programs as well as academic programs. In some schools, special programs provided tutorial and counseling assistance. Teachers and Latino students were paired in mentoring and advocacy activities, thus increasing the sense among faculty of a personal connection with the students. Extracurricular programs involved activities that were relevant to Latino cultures. In one school, students could take a PE class called *Bailes,* in which they learned and performed dances from different regions of Mexico. In another, a student-run group published a monthly newspaper in Spanish called *El Mitotero.* Begun by a teacher, the paper was quickly "taken over" by the students themselves. They formed a committee and organized a formal club with officers and by-laws, which was then recognized by the school's student association. According to the teacher who started it, the paper is "very culturally oriented — if you understand Spanish, you might understand the words, but if you are not familiar with the local Mexican culture, you will probably miss a lot of the 'double meanings' and cultural references." One issue of the newspaper was devoted to a debate about bilingual education. The newspaper staff interviewed students and teachers and then presented both pro and con sides of the debate, the former written in Spanish and the latter in English.

A final and important way in which these high schools showed respect for the students' cultures and languages was through their staffing. Faculty members who spoke the native languages of the language-minority students in the school and shared similar cultural backgrounds not only used this skill and knowledge to improve instruction for them, but also served as role models and advocates for these students. Comments of several faculty reflect their awareness of the roles they were playing. For example, the principal at Nogales High School said:

> When we hire teachers, we try to look for the best teachers, number one, but number two and most importantly, we try to get teachers that relate to our type of kids, and number three, if we can get teachers that are from this area, that are teachers that have graduated from this high school, teachers that have had to go through these problems, the growing-up problems, the educational problems from here, and have gone out and have become successful, then we have provided role models for our kids that are essential. I think probably that's one of the reasons I'm principal. We've had all kinds of principals, but I think that the community itself has tried to hire administrators that, number one, relate to our community, and number two, have been here [for a long time]. The majority of the administration from this district is from here.

A teacher at another school said, "The students are very proud and the teachers support that. It's okay to speak Spanish, to be Mexican, not to know English." He believes that students at the school feel supported by the fact that teachers speak Spanish "in public." One student had come to him and reported with some incredulity. "Mr. W. [an Anglo] spoke Spanish to me in class!" The head counselor at the same school said:

> Parents and students see us [Latinos] in leadership positions, not just in the cafeteria or as janitors. People in the school understand problems in the community and have lived it themselves. . . . For example, I understand if a student has to stay home all week to take care of kids. . . . Parents come in because I speak Spanish and can understand their problems. I'm not from a middle-class, elite, intellectual background.

A counselor at a third school said, "I have a sensitivity to these students that comes from my family background. I'm third generation here. I know what it is to leave your roots and live in a system different from that of your parents. Maybe that's why I have an urgency to push college." Students also referred to their teachers and others at the schools as role models. When asked to tell us about a faculty member who was particularly effective, one student commented, "Ms. V. has been a good role model. She speaks many languages and inspires me." Another student said, "Mr. A. encourages students to break stereotypes by being good in chemistry, physical science, and physics."

2. High expectations of language-minority students are made concrete.
Throughout the schools we visited, people recognized the importance of high expectations for Latino LM students. Such expectations form the foundation for the program features we describe. One principal put it this way: "I firmly believe that what you give to the best kids, you give to all," while taking into account special needs and equity issues. The professional staff members in the six schools we visited not only held high expectations of their students but had also taken concrete actions to demonstrate those expectations and to help students accomplish what was expected. Some of these actions already have been mentioned. For example, when students see people like themselves who have become teachers, counselors, and principals, they learn that professions like these are attainable.

Recognizing that language-minority students do not have information that mainstream students possess, school counselors who understood students' languages and cultures helped them plan their high school programs, find information about different colleges, apply to college, fill out financial aid forms, and apply for scholarships. Counselors also communicated with parents to gain their support for their children to apply for college, understanding that if going to college is a new idea to the student, it is probably completely unfamiliar, perhaps even threatening, to the parents. As one female student noted, "At first my parents weren't wanting me to go to college, but

Mrs. C. [the counselor] convinced them that it was okay." College and university representatives were brought to the high school to talk with students. Former graduates of similar backgrounds who had gone to college were invited back to the high school to share their experiences and to encourage others to follow in their path.

In classes, teachers challenged students with difficult questions and problems. Complex ideas and materials were made more accessible to LM students through visuals, board work, group work, reading aloud, and clear and explicit class expectations. Teachers did not talk down to limited-English-proficient students in "foreigner talk," but spoke clearly, with normal intonation, explaining difficult words and concepts as needed.

In all the schools we visited, student success was recognized publicly. In one high school, achievement in a particular class was recognized through a ritual in which the principal came to the class and congratulated the student. In another school, LM students who did well in particular areas (for example, most improved or perfect attendance) were recognized at a monthly "Student of the Month" luncheon during which teachers who had nominated the students presented certificates to them and spoke briefly about the students' accomplishments. Several high schools had special assemblies for students on the honor roll, where parents were invited and recognized while the students received certificates. "It makes you want to try harder when you get an award," noted one student. Latino LM students received these forms of recognition just as other students did.

3. School leaders make the education of language-minority students a priority.
Strong instructional leadership has been cited as a key ingredient of effective schools (Carter & Chatfield, 1986; Purkey & Smith, 1983). Effective school leaders, usually principals, are described as actively coordinating curriculum; monitoring students' academic progress; having a clear mission for the school which they communicate to staff, students, and parents; holding high expectations for student achievement and promoting the same among faculty and staff. In the high schools we visited, the principals were, in addition, sincerely committed to educating LM students and knowledgeable about effective teaching approaches for this population. All but one of the principals were bilingual minority-group members themselves. Although each had a unique leadership style, they all demonstrated a strong commitment to raising the achievement levels of minority students, including LM students. Sweetwater's principal, a Latino himself, said:

> One of our major roles in this community is to develop a sense of confidence that we can compete in all areas, not just athletics, that we can go out there and be just as good as anybody else. I guess if I had a wish, I would like for the kids in the school to absolutely believe and know in their hearts that they are as good as anybody on this planet.

Steps taken by this principal to support the success of language-minority students illustrate the types of leadership that we found in these schools. Sweetwater's principal was given the authority by the district to make virtually all decisions at the school, including hiring teachers of his choice. He had initiated several changes in the education program for language-minority students. For example, all remedial classes were eliminated so that LM students would not receive "watered-down versions of content." When he came to the school, he discovered that bilingual classes were "remedial," that the school offered bilingual life science rather than biology and bilingual math rather than algebra. He quickly set out to "amend" the situation. Sections of physics, chemistry, and calculus were added along with summer sessions of geometry; the requirements for athletic participation were raised; the number of bilingual staff was increased from eight to thirty-three; the bilingual program was expanded to include advanced courses such as economics, biology II, and honors chemistry as well as lower division bilingual courses.

Although now credited with raising standardized test scores, tightening discipline, and raising the morale of students and teachers, the principal (and staff who supported his changes) encountered opposition from some staff members from the very beginning. When he eliminated the "remedial" classes in the school, for example, some teachers felt he was unrealistic; they argued that students were going to be lost in algebra. The principal recalled telling them that "students perform as well as they're expected . . . [and that] students in remedial classes in junior high school are still in remedial classes in the twelfth grade, often performing worse as time [goes] on." He believes students "will learn more in a classroom filled with students of mixed abilities than in a class composed solely of students with minimal math skills." He provided calculators for students, justifying their placement in basic algebra when others would think them more suited for remedial math: "If they're going to fail remedial math, why not have them fail basic algebra?"

We found that good leadership can and does come from program directors, department chairpersons, and teachers in high schools as well as from principals. In some schools, these individuals had taken on strong leadership roles vis-à-vis the education of LM students. At Artesia High School, for example, a separate ESL department had been formed, and it was the chair of this department who advocated most strongly for the education of LEP students. The principal at this school played a less active role in this area, though the previous principal, it should be noted, had been very active in making changes for the LM population. This example of a leader who is not a principal serves as a reminder that the strength for change does not necessarily have to come from the top. Though a strong principal who is deeply committed to the needs of LM students is certainly desirable, the principal is not the only person who can make a difference. Teachers, program coordinators, and department chairs can also take it upon themselves to be leaders in the education of LM students.

4. Staff development is explicitly designed to help teachers and other staff serve language-minority students more effectively.

As Lisa Delpit writes, "It is impossible to create a model for the good teacher without taking issues of culture and community context into account" (1988, p. 291). Teachers who are expert in the instruction of mainstream students are not necessarily effective instructors of language-minority students. For this reason, professional development was a high priority for school administrators, teachers, and other professional staff at these schools. Teachers at Nogales High School in Arizona, for example, were encouraged to get an ESL or bilingual endorsement. Teachers received a salary bonus if they held such an endorsement and incorporated ESL or bilingual methods into their curriculum plans. In addition, staff at this school and others we visited received professional development through in-service workshops and conferences. Teachers received training in the principles of second language acquisition and effective instructional approaches for teaching language-minority students, such as sheltered content, cooperative learning, and reading and writing in the content areas.[8] Teachers and other staff learned about students' cultural backgrounds and experiences. Counselors became informed about cross-cultural counseling strategies. Professional staff worked to develop their ability in the native languages of their students, enabling them to communicate more effectively with LM students and their parents.

Most important, *all* teachers and other professional staff were encouraged to participate in professional development of the sort described here, not just those who taught specific classes for this special student population. It appeared that all school staff took responsibility for teaching these students. No one expressed the attitude that one group of teachers would "take care" of LM students and that the others therefore did not need to "worry" about them. In fact, one principal had set a policy prohibiting bilingual teachers from teaching bilingual classes the entire day. He believed that bilingual teachers should teach mainstream as well as bilingual classes so they would not forget what they were preparing LM students to do.

At Anaheim High School, a five-year plan developed to improve the achievement of Latino students included a strong emphasis on staff development and teacher empowerment. When the current principal first came to Anaheim High School in 1983, she convened the ten department heads, and together they examined the effective schools literature to establish a commonality of language and philosophy before instituting changes. These teachers developed a school plan. According to the principal, "[Empowering the teachers] was the best thing I could have done. I had ten advocates for change, and the plan was theirs, not mine. . . . You can force compliance, but you can't force commitment." Later, the principal and ten department heads shared the process they had gone through with all the teachers. One of the teachers who went through the process reflected, "There is an overall drive to help kids. That's one of the unique things about Anaheim High School. That mood was set by Mrs. C., and the turn-around is now being seen." At Anaheim, staff development was conceived of as teacher-motivated, rather than the traditional top-down process. A small cadre of teachers, with the support of the principal, made it their business to learn what could be done to improve the quality of education at their school and later served as models and teachers for the rest of the staff. A similar process occurred at Artesia High School, where a strong staff development program had been developed partly as a result of the school's participation in the state's School Improvement Program.

5. A variety of courses and programs for language-minority students is offered.
Too often LM students are placed and kept in a limited selection of low-level high school courses with the rationale that their English is not proficient enough to allow them to cope with more advanced classes. Often these classes are overfilled, leaving students with few opportunities to interact with the teacher adequately (Brown & Haycock, 1984). Yet LM students, like all students, do best when they have the opportunity to take a wide range of courses, including advanced courses that challenge them intellectually.

In these high schools, those who did not yet speak or write fluent English nonetheless were given the opportunity to progress in content courses appropriate to their academic level. Educators in these high schools did not assume that English proficiency matched content knowledge or cognitive skills. They recognized the fine but critical line between programs that failed to prepare LM students for college and those that facilitated their transition to an English language curriculum while providing continuing academic challenge through a variety of bilingual and sheltered courses. If, for instance, a student from Mexico had passed fundamental math and algebra in her country and had limited proficiency in English, she was able to take a geometry class taught in Spanish or one that used sheltered English methods. Advanced-Placement Spanish offered strong Spanish speakers the opportunity to receive college credit for studying Neruda and Cervantes, just as native-English-speaking students could receive advanced credit for studying Wordsworth and Hawthorne. Bilingual economics and bilingual honors chemistry allowed those who possessed the required content-area background to move beyond basics, doing advanced work in these areas while developing their English language competence. In addition to offering a wide range of courses to LM students, two of the schools also had special programs to facilitate their transition to mainstream classes, and another had a program to identify those who qualified for participation in the school's GATE (Gifted and Talented) program.

Special programs were also in place in all the high schools to promote LM students' academic and social growth. These programs have the net effect of extending learning time through before- and after-school activities, a feature which Wilson and Corcoran believe may be the "critical difference between a mediocre school and an excellent one" (1988, p. 58). In an advocate program, teachers were paired with students as tutors and advocates. BECA (Bi-

TABLE 2   *Courses, Programs, and Activities for Language-Minority Students at Six High Schools*

Academic Courses and Programs
- *ESL:* focus on English language development.
- *Transitional ESL/Booster courses:* for students who have completed the ESL sequence but need some extra help in order to succeed in mainstream English classes.
- *Sheltered English content classes:* content classes with English language development built in (includes advanced classes).
- *Spanish-language content courses:* content classes taught in Spanish (includes advanced classes).
- *Spanish for Spanish speakers:* basic literacy and advanced Spanish skills.
- *Math and reading labs (computer-assisted instruction):* work on basic skills at individual pace.

Support Programs
Some of these programs serve only Latino and/or LM students; most include but are not limited to Latino LM students. Some focus on helping students develop advanced skills; others focus on more basic skills.*
- *Advocate Program:* Teachers volunteer to be paired with students, act as advocates and tutors. (Nogales)
- *BECA (Bilingual Excellence in Cognitive Achievement):* tutoring, career planning, multicultural awareness for Latino LM students. (Overfelt)
- *UCO (University and College Opportunity Program):* to encourage and prepare underrepresented minorities to go to college. Students are assigned to a special counselor, go on field trips to colleges. (Overfelt)
- *AVID (Advance Via Individual Determination):* college-prep program for disadvantaged students of all ethnic backgrounds. Uses peer and college tutors. One class in the program is specifically geared to LM students. (Sweetwater)
- *SAT Program, funded by the Tanner Bill:* for Latino students who have potential for academic success. Teachers are specially trained, classes are small (25 students), teachers act as mentors for 10–12 students, parents are involved. (Anaheim)
- *MESA (Math, Engineering, Science Achievement):* college-prep program for disadvantaged students of all ethnic backgrounds with emphasis on science and math. (Overfelt)
- *PLATO (Programmed Logic for Automatic Teaching Operations):* This computer-based dropout program allows students to attend school part of the day and work part-time. They use computers for individualized instruction, get career and college counseling. Students can receive regular diploma. (Sweetwater)
- *High-Risk Program:* for students who have failed a class or two and/or have attendance problems. Students are assigned to work with mentor teachers who have had training to participate. All participate voluntarily.
- *Chapter 1 program:* for students in low socioeconomic brackets who have scored below the 36th percentile on the CTBS or equivalent. Focuses on basic math and language arts and the use of computers; 20 students per class. (Anaheim)

Extracurricular Activities
- *Bailes:* a group of students who learn and perform dances from different regions of Mexico. (Anaheim)
- *La Prensa Latina:* a student journalism group that produces a Spanish-language newspaper called *El Mitotero.* (Sweetwater)

TABLE 2   *continued*

- *International Club:* a student group that sponsors events to increase intercultural awareness. (Artesia)
- *Celebration of cultural events and holidays* such as *Cinco de Mayo* by the whole school.
- *MECHA (Movimiento Estudiantil Chicano de Atzlá):* a group that represents the interests of Chicano, Mexican American, and Mexican students on college and high school campuses. (Sweetwater)
- *Sports:* soccer and baseball are emphasized over football.

---

*Schools where these programs were operating are listed in parentheses.

lingual Excellence in Cognitive Achievement) provided tutoring, career planning, and multicultural awareness for both limited and fluent English-speaking Latino students at one high school. UCO (University and College Opportunity) encouraged and prepared underrepresented minority students in another high school to go to college. The Tanner Bill Program (or "SAT Program," as it was known in one school) had a similar goal, though it targeted Latino students in particular. AVID (Advance Via Individual Determination) was a college-prep program for disadvantaged students in one high school that included one class specifically geared to LEP students. These are only a few of the special programs that either targeted or included LM students. A more complete listing appears in Table 2 along with names of the schools where the programs were offered.

6. A counseling program gives special attention to language-minority students.
In our interviews with students, one question asked them to identify the teacher or other staff member who had helped them the most. Many students referred to counselors as being key to their adjustment to the new environment and to their clarification of future goals. "At the beginning of the year," said one student, "I wasn't into school. Then I talked to Mrs. B. [a counselor] and got into it. My mom said she was proud of me." In the schools we visited, there was at least one bilingual Latino counselor who was able to communicate effectively with newcomers as well as with longer term residents and understood the sociocultural backgrounds of the students. This person was also well informed about postsecondary educational opportunities for language-minority students — scholarships, fellowships, grants — and could guide the students in getting and filling out the appropriate forms. He or she could also communicate with parents about students' successes and problems in school and the value of a college or university education.

One case we heard of involved a twelfth-grade student who lived with her aunt and uncle because her parents were in Mexico. The parents were reluctant to let their daughter, who had been accepted at a reputable college, move away from the family. The counselor took it upon herself to call the parents and talk it over with them, eventually convincing them of the wisdom of letting their daughter take this opportunity. In a school with no bilingual counselor who cared as much as this one did, this student — and presumably others like her — would have missed her opportunity and become another statistic of the low college attendance of minority students.

Simply having one or more bilingual counselors on the staff who are sensitive to students' cultures does not necessarily mean that LM students have access to that counselor, however. In talking with counselors and students, we learned about the importance of having an effective method of assigning students to counselors. Schools used a variety of methods, including assignment by class level, alphabetical order, special needs, and various combinations of these. Those that were most effective made sure that language-minority students were assigned to a counselor who could communicate with them, was knowledgeable of postsecondary opportunities for language-minority students, and was sincerely committed to helping all students succeed in school and beyond.

In the better counseling programs, case loads were relatively low, and bilingual Latino counselors were specifically designated for Latino LM students. At Sweetwater, in order to encourage counselors to guide all students toward postsecondary education, the procedures used to evaluate counselors took into account the test scores of the students with whom they worked, the number of students who applied to college, and the number of students who received college/university grants and scholarships. The head counselor said that four or five years before, they had realized that some people on the counseling staff were doing a much better job than others. They all sat down together and decided that helping students get money for college and go to college would be the priorities of the staff. The approach was later adopted for the whole district. It is a competitive approach, but "we work together. A counselor might say, 'What did you do that I didn't?'" At Artesia High School several Latino LM students indicated that their counselors worked with them on future plans, made sure they were doing well in classes, and advised them about the courses to take so they would have the option of going to a university. A College Aspiration Partnership Program (CAPP), developed by the counseling department at this high school, paired the school with several colleges and universities in the surrounding area. Language-minority students met with representatives of these institutions to learn the requirements for entry and procedures for applying for scholarships and other student support funds.

At Newcomer High, which unlike the other schools serves immigrant students for only a year before they make the transition to regular high schools, college counseling is not as large a component of the counselors' roles as helping students, many of them refugees, deal with the emotional and physical traumas they have experienced in leaving war-torn countries and coming to the United States. The counselors there, two of whom speak Spanish and one of whom speaks Chinese, see themselves as nurturers and facilitators of cultural adjustment. One of them described her roles: "I wear many hats; at times I'm a mother, a referral service to agencies, and I may have to be a co-median when needed." A student, commenting on her first day at the school, said, *"Para mi no fue tan extraño. La Señora S. me presentó a los compañeros."* ("For me it wasn't so strange. Mrs. S. introduced me to friends.") It is the counselor's job, as well as that of teachers, to acquaint students with the expectations of the school system, particularly those areas that differ from one culture to another. Students learn, for instance, that in most U.S. classrooms student participation — including asking questions of the teacher — is expected and desired and that one shows respect to Anglo teachers by making eye contact while they are speaking. In addition to dealing with cross-cultural issues, counselors at Newcomer had to be experts at referring students to appropriate agencies for medical or psychological traumas which could not be handled at the school.

We realize that for schools which are only now beginning to see an increase in language-minority and LEP populations, it may be difficult to find qualified counselors who share the students' linguistic and cultural backgrounds. Until such counselors are found and hired, however, it is advisable to at least have a counselor who speaks the students' native language, who has been trained in cross-cultural counseling techniques, and who can bring to students' attention special funding and scholarship opportunities.

7. Parents of language-minority students are encouraged to become involved in their children's education.

The parent participation feature was the least developed component of the high schools we visited. The principals, counselors, and teachers at all of the schools commented that more needed to be done to increase the schools' interaction with the parents of LM students. Yet they had taken steps to encourage parents to take an active part in their children's education. Several schools had Parent Advisory Committees that met monthly and included parents of LM students. These committees typically reached out to other parents for assistance with parent-sponsored multicultural activities. Some schools regularly sent newsletters to parents in their native languages.

Newcomer High School held a parent night once a month. Students and teachers in the school worked together to plan presentations about various aspects of the school's education program, including ways parents could help their children be better students. When we visited the high school, students were being prepared in their reading class to present to parents a play that dramatized some ways of "monitoring and motivating one's child," the topic for that month's meeting. The play was to be performed in Spanish, Chinese, Burmese, Vietnamese, Tagalog, and English. Afterwards, students would read several poems to parents — "Exile" by Pablo Neruda; "The Truth" by a student; and "The Road Not Taken" by Robert Frost. Finally, students would sing "The Impossible Dream."

The Tanner Bill program for Latino students at Anaheim High School required that the teachers and parents of participating students meet twice a month. In addition, the program coordinator held evening meetings several times a year in the neighborhoods of the students in the program. Representatives of colleges and universities in the area attended these meetings to inform parents of the college programs offered by their institutions, the entry requirements, and the scholarships and other support services available to language-minority students. Generally, the college and university representatives who attended spoke the parents' native language(s).

Nogales and Anaheim held early morning pancake breakfasts and invited parents to attend before they went to work; eight hundred people had attended Anaheim's most recent breakfast when we visited the school. Nogales also held monthly student-of-the-month breakfasts for parents and students in which a student in each department was honored, as well as an Honors Assembly each quarter in which parents were asked to stand up and be recognized with their children. More than 750 people attended the most recent Honors Assembly. Overfelt High School had a full-time community liaison who spoke Spanish and offered ESL classes for parents on the school campus. Parents of Overfelt students had also come out on weekends to paint the school. Several schools contacted parents by telephone to check on students who were absent or to inform parents when a student had become ill and was returning home. The person making the contact spoke the parents' native language.

Although we did not interview parents, comments from students indicated that many Latino parents were very supportive of their children's education. The language barrier, lack of familiarity with the U.S. educational system, and their own lack of educational experience made it difficult for some parents to help directly with homework; however, they encouraged their children in other ways to pursue the education they had not had the opportunity to receive. One student reported, "For my mom, the only thing is school. She said I could do anything; 'All I want is for you to finish school.' She pushes that I get educated. She herself dropped out and got married and regrets it. I dropped out too for awhile; it tore my mom and me apart." The theme of "becoming somebody" is a strong thread in the students' talk about their parents and their own goals for the future. "My dad is always telling me to work and study, to be somebody," said one. *"Quiero seguir estudiando para llegar a ser alguien en la vida"* ("I want to keep studying so that I can become somebody in life"), said another. These comments by students attest to the strong desire among these Latino parents to do whatever they are able to do to gain a good education for their children. The schools we visited were working hard to find ways of making the schools accessible to parents.

8. School staff members share a strong commitment to empower language-minority students through education.

The most fundamental feature of all, and the most difficult to describe in concrete terms, is the commitment we heard about from most if not all of the school staff and students we interviewed. This commitment goes beyond the value the staff places on students' languages and cultures and beyond the high expectations staff members hold for language-minority students. One can value the language and culture of a student and expect that student to be successful, yet still remain passive when it comes to promoting that student in the world. Commitment and empowerment of students involve staff members reaching out, giving extra time to further the goals of a few students, and taking part in a political process that challenges the status quo. In the words of Jim Cummins, "minority students can become empowered only through interactions with educators who have critically examined and, where necessary, challenged the educational (and social) structure within which they operate" (1989, p. 6).

Such commitment manifested itself in various ways at the schools we visited. Teachers and other staff at the schools were described as having students' best interests at heart and giving extra time and energy after school and during lunch or preparation time to counsel as well as teach them. For example, the Coordinator of Special Projects at Overfelt High School said that he had found the teachers there to be very eager to learn how to work effectively with language-minority students. He said that they considered it "a very serious endeavor" to be sensitive to the needs of such students, and that they frequently requested training of various sorts to help them become more effective. At all of the schools, students mentioned teachers who had given them special help and attention, often crediting them with providing personal counseling as well as academic support. Typical student comments included the following: "The teachers here don't just teach; they care about you" and "Teachers stay after school to explain what we didn't understand."

Activities at these schools promoted participation and empowerment of Latino students outside the classroom as well. Through participation in MECHA groups, Latino clubs, Spanish language newspapers, soccer teams, and other activities sponsored and advised by school staff, Latino students developed awareness and knowledge of their cultures and language as well as a sense of community and cooperation with other Latino and non-Latino students.[9] School staff involved in these activities took their commitment beyond the classroom to help develop students as whole people. Through the *Ballet Folklórico* group at Anaheim, for example, students not only learned and performed various Mexican dances, but also learned about the different regions in Mexico where dances originated, and presented this information in performances as well. They thus deepened their own and others' knowledge and understanding of Mexican culture and history.

Besides their work in the school setting to promote the achievement and success of Latino and other language-minority students, staff at these schools also participated in various community activities, attended meetings, and held positions in their communities through which they acted as advocates for Latinos and other minorities. An assistant principal at Nogales High School, a Latino from the community, had been the mayor of Nogales. A teacher and MECHA advisor at Sweetwater High School, also a Latino, was elected to the City Council of National City in 1989. The principal at Anaheim High School described her work to develop an advocacy base in the community through her ongoing participation in a variety of community events and activities. She had gotten support from Anaheim graduates in the community, some business people, and many parents — both Latino and Anglo — by participating in community activities herself. Some of these people had spoken out at school board meetings advocating programs and services that were crucial to the success of the district's language-minority students. Sensitive to the fact that the way certain issues are discussed can trigger negative reactions and therefore interfere with the achievement of desired goals, she worked to communicate effectively with different audiences. Above all, she said, "I have not been naïve in thinking I can do it all by myself; I spent the first year getting a sense of who supported the equity issues that I'm concerned with."

It was evident at these schools that teachers, counselors, administrators, and other staff were highly committed to promoting the success of language-minority students in school and beyond. Besides promoting the achievement of such students, they acknowledged the educational and social structures that surround the students and challenged these structures in productive ways through concrete actions such as those described above. By taking their advocacy into the community, those who held elective offices and participated in community groups challenged negative attitudes and policies that may have been creating obstacles to the improvement of education for minority groups. Those who initiated and sponsored activities to expand LM students' knowledge and understanding of their own cultures and languages helped them develop a sense of identity and community that knowledge of their own backgrounds can provide. Those who were putting their extra energy into helping students with their academic work were fighting to raise the low achievement records of language-minority students. This commitment and accompanying action provided the framework within which the attributes and processes we have described above were developed and carried out.

CONCLUSION

The eight features we have described appeared to be key to the success of language-minority students at the schools we visited. While the study was exploratory in nature, we believe it provides educators with a working model of effective education for language-minority students at the secondary level. These eight features can be thought of as a set of general recommendations, or perhaps as a checklist against which to compare other schools or programs.

Many of the key features we have described mirror features in the effective schools literature. The notions of high expectations, parent involvement, strong leadership, and staff development are common threads throughout the many studies that have been conducted. In addition, those studying schools with large numbers of minority and bilingual students found, as we did, that support services, a positive attitude toward students, and commitment to helping students achieve were crucial factors in the overall success of the schools. In these areas, our report offers further confirmation that, in order to be successful with language-minority students, high schools must place a high priority on services and attitudes that go beyond academic instruction.

But this study makes several additional contributions. The first of these is the focus on secondary schools with large numbers of LM students. Second, wherever possible, general features across schools have been operationalized through concrete examples of practices in particular schools. Much of the effective schools literature lists general attributes, but does not take the next step in describing ways of actually carrying out these broad manifestos. We have tried to provide not only food for thought but also suggestions for concrete action. Third, we have emphasized an integrated approach to secondary programs for language-minority students. The schools we visited provided strong academic preparation for these students in three areas — content knowledge and understanding, English language skills, and primary language skills. They also helped students develop their pride and identity as individuals, as members of ethnic groups, and as participants in a multicultural society by showing respect for students' languages and cultures, holding high expectations of students and acting upon them in concrete ways, guiding them in preparing for their futures, encouraging their parents to become involved in their schooling, and promoting student empowerment in school and in the larger community. This multifaceted approach manifested itself at all levels of the curriculum and throughout academic, support, and extracurricular programs at these schools.

Finally, this study strongly suggests that the diversity among students cannot simply be ignored. While the schools recognized the importance of integrating language-minority students with mainstream students and of providing equally challenging instruction for all students, they did not try to minimize differences among mainstream and Latino students or among Latino students themselves. Approaches to schooling that value linguistic and cultural diversity and that promote cultural pluralism were welcomed and explored whenever possible (see Stedman, 1987). Students' languages and cultures were incorporated into school programs as part of the effort to create a context in which all students felt valuable and capable of academic success (see Cummins, 1989).

Though this study was exploratory in nature, we hope the findings will guide further research. Many more secondary schools with large numbers of language-minority students need to be visited for longer periods of time to determine whether the features which emerged in the six schools we studied apply to other similar schools. The features themselves need to be examined in greater depth so that educators can understand them more fully and apply them in appropriate contexts. For example, a study of parent involvement in language-minority student schooling should include extensive interviews with parents themselves as well as with students and school staff. Longitudinal studies of secondary schools with large numbers of language-minority students could increase our understanding of the processes schools go through in providing and maintaining effective schooling for such students. Schools with different populations of students also need to be examined — for example, students of different ethnic and language backgrounds, students who have lived in the United States for various lengths of time, students who are immigrants, refugees, and native-born citizens. Nevertheless, the study has extended our knowledge of what makes schooling work for a rapidly growing segment of the school population. We hope that this working model will also provide inspiration and a sense of possibility to educators who are seeking an effective response to the needs of secondary language-minority students.

NOTES

1. We will use the term *language-minority (LM) students* to refer to those who come from families where a language other than English is spoken. Such students may or may not speak English fluently.
2. We will use the term *limited-English-proficient (LEP) students* to refer specifically to those language-minority students who are not yet fluent in English.
3. California State Department of Education, Assembly Bill 1329, 1976. In 1982, AB-1329 was revised as AB-507.
4. The Southwest Center for Educational Equity is funded by Title IV of the U.S. Department of Education to assist school districts in California, Arizona, and Nevada in their desegregation efforts in the areas of race, gender, and national origin.
5. Awards and recognition included a California Department of Education Distinguished School Award, a city Commendation Award, nomination as an exemplary school for the National Secondary School Recognition Program, an award for the academic achievement of the school's graduates attending a university in the state, a U.S. Department of Education Excellence in Education Award, and selection as one of the "77 Schools of the Future" by *Omni* magazine.
6. The term *Latino* is used here because it is the term that the majority of people we interviewed used to describe their own ethnicity, when speaking on a broader level than their individual countries of origin.
7. In California: Anaheim High School, Anaheim; Artesia High School, Lakewood; Newcomer High School, San Francisco; Overfelt High School, San Jose; Sweetwater High School, National City. In Arizona: Nogales High School, Nogales.
8. The term *sheltered content* refers to an approach to teaching content classes for LEP students in English in which the development of English language skills is emphasized along with content area development. Teachers use whatever means they can to make the content comprehensible and meaningful to the students: for example, simplified speech, vocabulary work, visuals, hands-on activities, and highly structured lessons (see Northcutt & Watson, 1986).
9. MECHA, or *Movimiento Estudiantil Chicano de Atzlán*, represents the interests of Chicano, Mexican American, and Mexican students on college and high school campuses.

REFERENCES

Arias, B. (1986). The context of education for Hispanic students: An overview. *American Journal of Education, 95*, 26–57.

Bell, J. (1989, February). *Merging the research on effective instruction for LEP students with effective schools' research and practice.* Paper presented at the Annual Conference of the California Association for Bilingual Education, Anaheim, CA.

Brown, P. R., & Haycock, K. (1984). *Excellence for whom?* Oakland, CA: Achievement Council.

Carter, T. P., & Chatfield, M. L. (1986). Effective bilingual schools: Implications for policy and practice. *American Journal of Education, 95*, 200–232.

Cummins, J. (1989). *Empowering minority students.* Sacramento: California Association of Bilingual Education.

Delpit, L. D. (1988). The silenced dialogue: Power and pedagogy in educating other people's children. *Harvard Educational Review, 58*, 280–298.

Edmonds, R. (1979, May 5). Effective schools for the urban poor. *Educational Leadership, 37*(1), 15–27.

Espinosa, R., & Ochoa, A. (1986). Concentration of California Hispanic students in schools with low achievement: A research note. *American Journal of Education, 95*, 77–95.

Gingras, R. C., & Careaga, R. C. (1989). *Limited-English-proficient students at risk: Issues and prevention strategies.* Silver Spring, MD: National Clearinghouse for Bilingual Education.

Jackson, S. (1989, May). Luncheon address, *Symposium on Excellence in Mathematics and Science Achievement: The Gateway to Learning in the 21st Century.* Sponsored by the Southwest Center for Educational Equity, San Francisco.

Lau v. Nichols, 414 U.S. 563, 566 (1973).

Levin, H. M. (1987). Accelerated schools for disadvantaged students. *Educational Leadership, 44*(6), 19–21.

Medina, M. (1988). Hispanic apartheid in American public education. *Educational Administration Quarterly, 24*, 336–349.

Merriam, S. B. (1988). *Case study research in education: A qualitative approach.* San Francisco: Jossey-Bass.

Miles, M. B., & Huberman, A. M. (1984). *Qualitative data analysis: A sourcebook of new methods.* Beverly Hills, CA: Sage.

Northcutt, L., & Watson, D. (1986). *SET: Sheltered English teaching handbook.* San Marcos, CA: AM Graphics and Printing.

Orfield, G. (1986). Hispanic education: Challenges, research, and policies. *American Journal of Education, 95*, 1–25.

Orum, L. S. (1988). *The education of Hispanics: Status and implications.* Washington, DC: National Council of La Raza.

Purkey, S. C., & Smith, M. S. (1983). Effective schools: A review. *The Elementary School Journal, 83*, 428–452.

Ramírez, D. (1988, April). *A comparison of structured English, immersion, and bilingual education programs: Results of a national study.* Paper presented at the Annual Meeting of the American Educational Research Association, New Orleans.

Rosenholtz, S. J. (1985). Effective schools: Interpreting the evidence. *American Journal of Education, 93*, 352–388.

Rowen, B., Bossert, S. T., & Dwyer, D. C. (1983). Research on effective schools: A cautionary note. *Educational Researcher, 12*(4), 24–31.

Rumberger, R. W. (1987). High school dropouts: A review of issues and evidence. *Review of Educational Research, 57*, 101–121.

Stedman, L. C. (1987). It's time we changed the effective schools formula. *Phi Delta Kappan, 69*, 215–224.

Suro, R. (1990, April 11). Education secretary criticizes the values of Hispanic parents. *New York Times,* pp. A1, B8.

Taylor, S. J., & Bogdan, R. (1984). *Introduction to qualitative research methods* (2nd ed.). New York: Wiley.

Tikunoff, W. (1985). *Applying significant bilingual instructional features in the classroom.* Rosslyn, VA: National Clearinghouse for Bilingual Education.

U.S. General Accounting Office. (1987). *School dropouts: Survey of local programs* (GAO/HRD-87-108). Washington, DC: Government Printing Office.

Wilson, B. L., & Corcoran, T. B. (1988). *Successful secondary schools.* New York: Falmer Press.

Wong-Fillmore, L., McLaughlin, B., Ammon, P., & Ammon, M. S. (1985). *Learning English through bilingual instruction. Final Report to the National Institute of Education.* Berkeley: University of California.

The authors wish to extend their thanks to all of the staff and students of the schools we visited. We greatly appreciated the hospitality and friendliness with which we were received and the unique perspectives which people took the time to describe to us in interviews. We also want to thank our colleagues Marie Mayen, Leticia Pérez, Huynh Dinh Te, William Tikunoff, Sau-Lim Tsang, Betty Ward, and Harriet Doss Willis for their work on various stages of this project and their support throughout. The information reported here was collected as part of a plan for providing technical assistance to Arizona secondary schools. The technical assistance project was conducted by the Southwest Center for Educational Equity, which is funded by the U.S. Department of Education, Office of Elementary and Secondary Education, under Title IV of the Civil Rights Act of 1964. The contents of this article do not necessarily reflect the views or policies of the Department of Education.

PART THREE

School Accountability and Teacher Control

A Charter to Educate or a Mandate to Train: Conflicts between Theory and Practice

▼▼▼▼▼

JOHANNA ELENA HADDEN

In a recent issue of the *Harvard Educational Review*, Abigail Brant Erdmann reflected on her teaching experiences in a democratic school.[1] It is encouraging to read about teachers working in liberating environments, where they can experience a "rebirth" without fear of retribution.[2] There are too few inspirational stories of this nature. It is also reassuring to read about positive experiences, but celebrations of transformative classrooms can sometimes be misleading. As important as such stories are, for many teachers there is another, not so pleasant, story to tell. In schools across the country, many teachers are not free to educate: to determine curriculum, to express disagreements with each other and with administration, to create and become a part of a democratic classroom. Sadly, although these teachers entered the profession with a firm belief in their charter to educate, in practice they find instead a mandate to train: to compel adherence to implicit and explicit behavioral norms; to demonstrate loyalty to business-promoted, state-sustained, traditional curricula; and to support bureaucratically imposed rules and regulations that include standardized testing and tracking. At the very least, these teachers are expected to remain silent in the face of their own ethical disagreements with the hierarchy that governs schools. At worst, they are forced to either abandon their projects or lose their positions.

In this essay, I discuss the differences between a charter to educate and a mandate to train. The charter to educate, encouraged through the theory taught at the university level and supported by research, endorses teachers as agents of change. Specifically, critical theorists such as Stanley Aronowitz and Henry Giroux argue that teachers should take a more active role in questioning what and how they teach. Aronowitz and Giroux assert that "teachers need to view themselves as public intellectuals . . . with a political project grounded in the struggle for a culture of liberation and justice."[3] The mandate to train, imposed in practice, insists that teachers be disciples of received

Harvard Educational Review Vol. 70 No. 4 Winter 2000, 524–537

wisdom and reinforce existing power relations. I illustrate the tension between the charter and the mandate with my own experiences in a working-
class elementary school. While pursuing a master's degree and teaching full
time in Utah, I found myself caught between my passion for critical education, born and nurtured at the university level, and my accountability as a
practicing teacher to a conservative system of controls. Although the references made in this article to state- and local-level mandates are specific to
Utah, they are nonetheless representative of a large number of areas in the
United States. Thus, my experience speaks to some of the difficulties that
many practitioners encounter when they attempt to bridge the gulf between
theory and practice.

AGENTS OF CHANGE OR DISCIPLES

It is an old story and one of the great paradoxes of education that teachers will
encourage the quest for new knowledge at the same time they impart accepted wisdom. In this view, educators should be guides to the unexplored
territories and teach students to think for themselves while concurrently being disciples of received values and reinforcing existing structures. There is a
basic dichotomy, discussed in the literature on critical theory, between liberatory methods designed to teach students to think for themselves and more traditional methods that frequently teach students to obey without questioning.

Critical education theorists often expect teachers to foster "cooperation,
equality, participation, and social action to redress political injustices."[4] Their
recommendations to teachers might include allowing students to determine
curricula through generative themes, "illuminating the myths supporting the
elite hierarchy of society," and distributing censored information useful for
investigating power.[5] Unfortunately, systemic constraints often prevent this
type of liberatory teaching. Entrenched practices and beliefs, reinforced
through bureaucratic regulations and sustained through state-level mandates, are frequently more conservative. Conservative theoreticians expect
practicing educators to represent conformity through patriotic citizenship,
build congruence and impart the "common culture," and model socially approved behavior and thought through reasoned disciplinary action.[6]

Critical education theorists such as Giroux and Peter McLaren support a
combination of theory and practice in order for educators to become "transformative intellectuals."[7] Richard A. Brosio explains that transformative intellectuals use critical skills to "point out what is wrong and unjust about the
present status quo, as well as to attempt an analysis of how it might be recognized widely, resisted, and hopefully overcome through collective action."[8]
However, it is often the case, as frequently lamented by critical education theorists, that the gulf between critical theory and classroom practice is enormous. Practice demands discipleship. Teachers must subscribe to and assist
in spreading dominant beliefs and ideologies. This discipleship requires the

inculcation of "basic American values" that are frequently emphasized in mandated and regulated core curricula.[9] The values that constitute the official curriculum are not neutral.[10] We do not have to travel too far back in U.S. history to understand that "basic American values" have been used as an excuse to apply force to settle economic and political questions. The concept has been used to justify slavery, the denial of equal rights for women, the containment of Native Americans on reservations, and class oppression. Social activism is emphatically discouraged because education is not supposed to be political. Education should impart the common culture, something Pepi Leistyna, Arlie Woodrum, and Stephen Sherblom see as an unnegotiated and "selective view of social reality in which difference is viewed as deviant or a deficit."[11]

The state-mandated and -regulated curriculum in Utah, for example, is not the only avenue through which the discipleship function is reinforced. Through union-bargained professional agreements that sometimes require teachers to support school and district programs, ethical disagreements with established protocol are rarely voiced.[12] Teachers and principals, in my experience, sometimes resist adopting prepackaged discipline programs, but districts that purchase these programs expect them to be enthusiastically supported.[13] A school district, for example, may impose computerized and standardized grading programs that obligate teachers to adhere to specific instructional objectives and evaluation techniques.[14] When this happens, the teachers' freedom to develop curricula and use professional judgments in establishing criteria for success are effectively curtailed.

Methods such as these, imposed from above by district or state decrees, are frequently accompanied by practices at the school level that serve to cut short transformative efforts. I have observed that too often the individual results of standardized tests are discussed openly in faculty meetings or the general results are published in Utah newspapers.[15] This tends to focus the attention of some teachers on rote memorization or fact-learning in order to raise scores. At times, traditional pedagogical techniques are recommended so that students learn the basics and leave the frills behind. Teachers are sometimes evaluated on how well they employ these techniques. Teachers and students are not to challenge these traditional practices because that implies that there is something wrong with the way teaching has been done for years.[16]

Critical education theory asks of each teacher a willingness to question such practices; however, the components of discipleship are often imposed upon classroom teachers to perpetuate ideological domination, severely limiting the potential for transformative educational practice. Nonetheless, educators sometimes try to step outside the limits imposed by mandated curricula, traditional pedagogies, and hierarchical governance structures. These educators are willing to attempt to develop a democratic classroom or school in order to exercise their charter to educate. With the help of critical theorists at some universities, these educators often find success. Sometimes they do not.

THE MANDATE TO TRAIN TRIUMPHS

I entered a master's program in 1992 after teaching in Pacific Island, rural, and city elementary and secondary schools for thirteen years. After becoming passionate about the possibilities seemingly inherent in critical pedagogy, I decided that my master's thesis research should deal with the facilitation of a more democratic culture in my classroom.[17] My project was an attempt to enhance a critical consciousness in my students and myself, and for the next year I based many of my ideas on methods advocated by Paulo Freire and Ira Shor.[18] The focus of the project was threefold. First, as a group, my students and I analyzed the overt curricula regulated through the Utah State Core Curriculum Guide and the reading text supplied by the school district.[19] The overt curriculum in our school was a written set of concepts intended to govern the forms of knowledge taught. Through criterion-referenced testing and end-of-level testing, it served to regulate teacher actions and student thought patterns. Second, my students and I also investigated and sought to identify the hidden curriculum of my classroom.[20] The hidden curriculum consisted of the underlying directives for behavior and thought found in the everyday workings of schools, with certain forms of behavior and thought rewarded while others were discouraged and sometimes punished. Third, we attempted to establish the parameters of the "null" curriculum, or what is deliberately made absent from overt curricula. The overt and hidden forms of knowledge found within many Utah school settings, including mine, and the principles under which they are selected, organized, and evaluated are value governed and represent a minute part of a much larger universe of possible forms of knowledge. That larger universe includes the legal system, working-class history, African American literature, and codes of power that make up the null curriculum.[21] My central goal, the enhancement of critical consciousness in my students and myself, required that I involve my students in the analysis of the curricula.

I was teaching a combination fifth- and sixth-grade class at the time in Winterton Elementary, Dillard School District.[22] This working-class school had recently acquired a new principal, a woman who appeared quite supportive of my ideas. However, as my students and I learned to ask and analyze whose interests would be served by the overt, hidden, and null curricula, some unanticipated consequences began to arise. The critical consciousness that was developing in my students and myself seemed to open up many areas to question. For example, we extended our analysis of the overt curriculum to school discipline plans, written dress codes, standardized tests, and university research on tracking and cooperative learning. All of us were swept up in the fervor generated by critical thinking. A small group of students, knowing that the school discipline plan was in the process of revision, decided to contribute their own proposals for consideration.

As I think back on that time, it seems that this was the turning point in an otherwise enthusiastically supported master's project. At the end of the year,

I was called into the principal's office, told that I should be more of a team player, and asked to cease involving my students in a critical study of the school discipline plan. The research was over anyway and the school year ended, so I agreed. I was to teach a full sixth-grade the next year, and I thought that it would be easy to return to the traditional and authoritarian teacher I was before my master's research. Because I had taught a combination fifth- and sixth-grade class for that year, parents of many of the fifth-grade students requested that their children be placed in my class the following year. Fourteen of the original fifteen fifth-grade students were in my class for sixth grade.

It is a somewhat striking feature of critical pedagogy, and one that is not often explored, that once young students acquire the ability and tools to analyze, they become extremely reluctant to discard them. The sixth graders I had worked with the previous year retained these critical-thinking skills and influenced my new sixth graders. Critical consciousness spread through my new classroom. I was secretly delighted, since I could not give up my own critical view of schooling. We had all gone too far and done too much to let it go now.

That September, I involved my students in planning a field trip. Although I was unaware of it at the time, this was perceived by the principal as the first step in a pattern of insubordination. Other actions on my part perceived to be insubordinate included my voicing ethical disagreements in an October faculty meeting with standardized tests being given to the fifth graders. That same month, in a computer-training session, I asked whether it was justifiable to record every single behavioral infraction in a file just because we could keep it all on disk now. In November, I advised my students about the ways that district aptitude tests were analyzed. In December, my students were given forms to take home that asked parents to assess their own child's capabilities to succeed at various tracks in the junior high. Twenty-three forms were returned, and I sat down to fill out the classroom teacher's portion of the tracking forms. Questions arose in my mind about tracking. After all, I had read Jeannie Oakes's works during my master's coursework and was aware of the research demonstrating the negative repercussions of tracking.[23] I was disgusted as well by the assumption that a teacher would know students well enough in December to rank them in a tracking program that would impact their educational and occupational futures. Obediently, I filled out the twenty-three tracking forms. Not so obediently, I ranked every student at the highest level.

A few days later I was called to the assistant principal's office to explain the forms. I told him that I had a very bright group of students, and barring any behavioral or self-esteem problems, each one of them could achieve at the highest level. He was hesitant to accept my judgment of their ability, since he was not ranking that high the students he taught at an upper-middle-class school in the foothills, an area where schools were believed to be better and the students smarter. The meeting was emotional because I felt that my professional judgment was being questioned without reason, and I was disturbed by the implication that I did not take the forms seriously. The assistant principal turned the forms over to the principal, and I was called to the main office to justify my actions.

I wish I could say that I presented a brilliant case against the tracking policy, that I referred to research and eloquently argued a sophisticated case on ethical grounds. I am ashamed to admit that I did not. I avoided the issue of ethics, fearful that it would outrage an already angry authority figure who already perceived me as "rebellious and defiant."[24] Slightly nervous about what I had done, I relied on my professional judgment that these clever and analytical sixth graders could really achieve at this level. I told the principal that if the schools did not impede their ability to critically think through the issues and lessons presented at the junior high, each and every one of them could succeed at the highest level. The principal said that the forms would be sent in to the district office, with her reservations, but she warned me that she had discussed my behavior with other administrators, and her conclusion was that it was bordering on insubordination.

As I reflected during the next few days on the threatening climate of the meeting, I looked around at each of my students and considered which ones I could rank lower if it became necessary in order for me to keep my job. I knew what tracking meant, and not only was I afraid that I might have to leave teaching over this, but somewhere in the recesses of my mind I thought I might have done something wrong by disobeying authority or expertise. All of those years of attending and teaching in public schools had effectively indoctrinated me into the hierarchy, into thinking that if authorities said I was wrong then maybe I was. However, looking at each of my students convinced me not to change their rankings. There was not one student that I was willing to downgrade to save my job. I had come to believe that each and every student could succeed if the structure and people involved in schooling did not present obstacles to impede their success. I did not seriously doubt my actions again, although I must confess that I had to make a conscious effort not to do so.

For the next week I retired to my classroom and stayed out of view and as quiet as possible. Unfortunately, three of my students received tickets for misbehavior on the school grounds during recess and they were called to the office. When they returned they informed me that they were questioned by the principal about my lessons in the classroom. Assuming that the ire of the principal was because they misbehaved at recess, the students went home and told their parents that they had gotten me into trouble. I was later informed that several parents called the school to support me and to protest the administrator's actions. Before we left school for the holidays, the principal told me that we needed to have a serious discussion about my behavior. She said that she did not want to ruin the holiday for me, so we would do this when we returned to school in January.

On January 3, 1995, I received a two-page letter of reprimand. It began:

> This letter is a written warning for serious misconduct, neglect of employ-
> ment obligations, and a pattern of insubordination resulting from your fail-
> ure to correct your repeated behavior of undermining school and district
> programs and inappropriately and unprofessionally involving students and
> parents in internal school disagreements.

The letter listed seven points. The first point stated that I had involved my students in field-trip planning without prior permission of the principal, who believed I should have gone through her in its planning; by not doing so, I was somehow guilty of "undermining the school discipline plan." The second point argued that I had told my students they did not have to follow the discipline program. Third, during the previous school year a parent had complained that I had "devastated" some unnamed student in a parent conference because I said the principal did not like him. Fourth, the letter stated, "You were questioned about evaluating all of your students identically on the teacher recommendation portion of the IBRIC Challenge Sixth Grade Evaluation Program." This is the tracking program for Dillard School District. The fifth point of the letter stated that I had told my class that I would not be back next year. The sixth point accused me of telling my students that the principal and assistant principal were "mean," resulting in parents calling the school because they did not want their "children becoming involved in the dispute" between a classroom teacher and the administration. This point also included the complaint that I had "coached" students on their part of the IBRIC. The seventh point was that a mother called the principal to support me and to say that the administration should not feel threatened when its authority is challenged. By making this a point in the letter, I think that the principal was attempting to indicate that I was not being a team player in the school's effort to present a united front to the public.

My defense: First, I did involve my students in planning the field trip, but it was not because I wished to undermine the principal's authority to make decisions. I wanted to generate enthusiasm and allow students some freedom in determining their own curriculum. Second, although I had some serious disagreements with the discipline program, I had always officially supported it. My students always did their time in the control room, which was documented. Third, I had no memory of any such parent conference, and without names or further details, I could not respond to that charge except to say that I could not recall ever discussing who liked whom in an official parent conference. Furthermore, I would never intentionally or carelessly devastate any student. Fourth, I certainly was guilty of evaluating all of my students at the highest level on the junior high tracking forms. Nothing since the original discussion about that program had changed, and I still thought my students could achieve at the highest level. Fifth, I did inform my class that I might go back to school the next year to pursue a doctorate, so I was guilty of that charge. Sixth, it was not I, but the principal, who involved my students in a dispute by interrogating them about their teacher after they received tickets on the playground. I did not tell my students that the principal and assistant principal were mean. That must have been a conclusion the students arrived at on their own. However, I did plead guilty to coaching students in self-evaluation. Seventh, the phone call came from a parent whose intention was to offer support for a teacher whom the parent thought was challenging authority. This could only be viewed as negative if those in authority actually felt threatened or challenged by questions.

In my written reply to the letter of reprimand I delineated many of those points. The reply was to serve as my resignation. It was one of the most difficult things I ever did, and something about which I will always have some regrets.[25] Although choosing to resign was painful, I felt at the time that the school environment was not supportive of my needs and those of other teachers. In fact, this incident was only one of several patterns of behavior that I viewed as characteristic of a climate of oppression. I, like many of my colleagues, often felt excluded, distrusted, and disrespected by the administration. Also, it seemed to me that I had little choice because I really was guilty of some of the points listed in the letter. Looking over the union-negotiated contract, the letter of reprimand was the first step in nonrenewal of contract if the specified behaviors did not change. The district had, according to the contract, the right to identify "job performance deficiencies," and any changes in my behavior would be "evaluated by the District," so I did not think involving the teachers' union was an option.[26] Tracking forms would be issued again the next year, and my responses would be closely examined. I believed that they would have to reflect some kind of bell curve in order to appear accurate, and I wondered what the repercussions would be if my students did not fit the curve. Since I now had serious reasons to doubt that I could ever go back to the uncritical, complacent elementary teacher I had been before my graduate education, I gave the district thirty working days to find a replacement.

Although I received a great deal of support from the parents in the community, teachers in my school remained silent. They became hesitant to express their own disagreements with administrative policies or practices. Several teachers met with me often during those days to express dismay and anger, but never came forward to publicly offer support. The strongest support I received from my colleagues came from a fellow sixth-grade teacher who informed the principal that I really did have a smart group of students. On my last day of teaching, I was told by a very good friend that she had learned from my experience not to make waves. From that day forward, she said, she would just coast into retirement.

For these teachers, and many like them who see the classroom as their career and their only option, it is important to adhere to administrative expectations and refrain from alienating their peers in the process. Many times that means simply not being visible — not drawing attention to oneself, not questioning district policy, and not leading the way with reforms. Although this inactivity can make teachers appear apathetic, their motivations may stem from realistic views of the power of hierarchy or fear of personal reprisals. For many of my colleagues, this was indeed the situation. For example, a teacher whom I had mentored two years earlier had a very difficult time understanding the conflict I experienced with my school administration. She held firmly to a deep trust that those in positions of authority do not abuse their power. Seeing authority figures as arbitrary, capricious, remiss, or even mistaken would have been a difficult conceptual step for her to take. Yet, I too had been an authority figure during her first teaching year. She felt that the entire event could come down to her making some kind of choice between authority figures, and found it easier to explain the episode as some kind of "miscommunication" between two friends. She thereafter removed herself from any discussions about it.

Parents were less hesitant to express themselves. Because of their vocal actions, which included calls to the local and state boards of education, an attorney, and the local and state PTAs, a meeting was called at the district office with the assistant superintendent. It was at this meeting that I was informed that, despite my own opinions, it was my obligation to support school and district programs, and I obviously had not done that. The assistant superintendent also told me — and I have come to regard this statement as the most crucial part of the entire meeting — "Although you are obviously an exceptional teacher, this letter [of reprimand] indicates deficiencies as an employee."[27]

That statement alone illustrates the conflict between the charter to educate and the mandate to train. It was not enough that I had strong parental support, or that my evaluations had always been high. I had crossed the boundary from being simply a disciple of the system to an agent of change. That journey was one of the most rewarding but hurtful journeys of my life. My project in critical pedagogy did not result in a transient critical consciousness, a way of thinking about issues that was left behind once the project was completed. It really did have a lasting impact on me. But my attempts to integrate the critical theory I had learned in my course work at the university with my practice in the classroom met with extreme disapproval from the system and cost me my job.

CONCLUSION

My experience is not an isolated example.[28] It is not simply an anomaly in the record of public schooling. Nor is it simply a reflection of the conservative culture in which I was teaching. My experience could have taken place in many other areas of the country and in other types of schools. Frequently, critical education researchers who teach prospective and practicing teachers know only too well how difficult it is to encourage a link between critical theory and practice. When critical education theorists discuss the charter to educate, they lament the fact that critical education theory does not inform practice. But despite the faith of some progressives that cultural norms, cemented ideologies, or even the workplace are subservient to the process of schooling, education does not operate in a vacuum, independent of existing economic, political, or social conditions.[29]

Even maneuvering within the confines of mandated curricula, recommended pedagogies, or traditional governance procedures can seem to challenge the status quo. The simple maneuvering itself can appear threatening to administrators tenaciously protecting their authority. At a conference I once attended, an educational researcher stated that all the teacher needs to do in this case is teach what he or she wants and then lie to the principal when asked about what is going on behind the closed door. This researcher's view ignores the fact that, throughout the learning process, students and teachers undergo intellectual, emotional, or psychological changes that extend beyond the classroom. Most importantly, the view that it may be necessary to lie to the principal implicitly acknowledges the constraints established by the mandate to train.

Discipleship is never complete. It saturates the atmosphere of many public schools, but it does not always dominate the behavior and thinking of the human beings that occupy those schools. Teachers do have some room to maneuver within the limitations imposed by mandated curricula, testing, and other administrative dictates. However, the key phrase here is *within the limitations imposed*. Critical education that falls outside those confines has the potential to disturb or disrupt conventional and cherished ideas about the political neutrality of education. Teachers who attempt to break down the barriers established by the status quo are placing themselves at some risk of disciplinary action.

Nonetheless, some teachers have been willing to risk being fired, or to receive letters of reprimand or accusations of insubordination in order to teach against the grain. Another group of teachers has been trained to passively accept and often wholeheartedly believe that whatever comes down from on top is in some sense superior to what those on the bottom can devise. Then there are those teachers who have not questioned hierarchical authority or their role in it, and thus may be more likely to support bureaucratic institutions than to challenge them. These teachers frequently support the maintenance and reinforcement of bureaucratic, hierarchical, social, political, and economic power structures. The enforcement process does not have to work perfectly, with precision, and without exception. Even Machiavelli maintained that threats need only be carried to fruition once in a generation to serve as a mechanism of control for the normally law-abiding and authority-respecting citizen.[30] The example of one teacher in a building being removed from a position for not following administrative dictates will discourage many others for a long time from attempting such foolishness.

This discussion is not meant to lead to a sense of cynicism. There are classrooms and schools like the one about which Abigail Brant Erdmann writes.

There are abundant examples of teachers and principals taking up the call to transform education; however, as a result we face accusations of occupying positions on the lunatic fringe, or experiencing cancellation of our transformative projects, or even suffering the loss of occupation. Those of us who would wish to see more schools transformed into democratic places, similar to the one in which Erdmann teaches, might consider backing up critical educational research with political action on behalf of those who take that research seriously and of other transformative educators who, while not involved in academia, are committed to making schools more participatory or democratic.[31] Attending school board or faculty meetings might be a beginning. Offering complimentary letters or letters of recommendation for the district files of classroom teachers whose work we respect, or providing them avenues of pursuit at the university level are ways of showing support. At the very least, it would be reasonable to refrain from blaming the practitioner for not making changes unless it is something over which the practitioner has ultimate and unquestioned control. Practicing teachers may neglect social activism because they have authentic economic or political concerns, as did many of my colleagues. Criticisms are better directed at those in authority who insist on discipleship and the mandate to train at the expense of the charter to educate.

There are few stories about democratic schools like the one described by Erdmann, and those stories are important since they indicate what is possible. Still, it is important to realize how rigid and imposing some schools can be. Without recognizing that positive and inspirational stories are the exception, the impetus for action may be diluted. Sadly, for some of the teachers and students who occupy authoritarian schools, education can be a dreary, austere, or boring phase of life. For critical teachers who want to make democratic change in authoritarian environments, it can seem as if they receive little to no support from administrators or parents. For their students, schooling is only tolerated because it is compulsory. I can remember when my elder brother, Kenneth, told me, "Everybody has to serve their time." That is an attitude we must do everything within our power to change.

I, like many teachers, entered the field of education with high ideals and a firm commitment to educating. Also, like many teachers, I found myself on an endless treadmill of training students to unquestioningly accept overt and hidden measures of control. In my case, the treadmill ended when I realized that I had been putting the interests of the institution ahead of the interests of my students. I found myself no longer being able to do that. I made a choice to leave that school, and to this day I still don't know if it was the best one. My choice cost me a job I deeply loved, but remaining would have cost my love of my career. When faced with a dilemma of this nature, ultimately there can be no comfortable decision. Nor can there be, strictly speaking, a correct one. Critical pedagogy alone cannot resolve this conflict. For me, the only genuine transgression would have been to remain silent.

NOTES

1. Abigail Brant Erdmann, "Middle-Age Teaching: A Time of Vitality," *Harvard Educational Review, 68* (1998), 583–587.
2. Erdmann, "Middle-Age Teaching," p. 584.
3. Stanley Aronowitz and Henry A. Giroux, *Postmodern Education: Politics, Culture, and Social Criticism* (Minneapolis: University of Minnesota Press, 1991), p. 108.
4. Michael W. Apple and Landon E. Beyer, eds., *The Curriculum: Problems, Politics, and Possibilities* (Albany: State University of New York Press, 1988), p. 346. There is an extensive literature on critical educational theory and its practical applications. For an excellent collection on this theme, see Pepi Leistyna, Arlie Woodrum, and Stephen A. Sherblom, eds., *Breaking Free: The Transformative Power of Critical Pedagogy* (Cambridge, MA: Harvard Educational Review, 1996). Powerful critiques of critical pedagogy are offered in Carmen Luke and Jennifer Gore, eds., *Feminisms and Critical Pedagogy* (New York: Routledge, 1992).
5. These and many other aspects of desocialization are described in Ira Shor, *Freire for the Classroom: A Sourcebook for Liberatory Teaching* (Portsmouth, NH: Boynton/Cook, 1987), pp. 14–15.
6. William J. Bennett, *Our Children and Our Country* (New York: Simon & Schuster, 1988), p. 47. See also Connaught Marshner, ed., *A Blueprint for Education Reform* (Chicago: Free Congress Research and Education Foundation, 1984).
7. This view of teachers as "transformative intellectuals" is expressed in Aronowitz and Giroux, *Postmodern Education,* see especially pp. 108–109. See also Henry Giroux and Peter McLaren, eds., *Critical Pedagogy, the State, and Cultural Struggles* (Albany: State University of New York Press, 1989), p. xiii.
8. Richard A. Brosio, *A Radical Democratic Critique of Capitalist Education* (New York: Peter Lang, 1994), p. 526.
9. *Utah State Core Curriculum Guide* (Salt Lake City: Utah State Office of Education, 1988), Introduction.
10. *Utah State Core,* p. Fiii, states, "A primary goal for all students and teachers is increasing their ability to be more productive" and to foster the "development of the means whereby the essential processes, values, and capabilities undergirding our society can be perpetuated." Of the 120 core objectives taught in economics in fifth and sixth grades, for instance, only two of them represent alternative economic systems. This does serve to perpetuate a particular set of values.
11. Leistyna, Woodrum, and Sherblom, *Breaking Free,* p. 3.
12. The assistant superintendent of the school district used the word "support" when he discussed a teacher's responsibility (personal communication, February 13, 1995).
13. At one time, several school districts in Utah adopted the book by Lee Canter, with Marlene Canter, *Assertive Discipline: A Take Charge Approach for Today's Educator* (Santa Monica, CA: Canter and Associates, 1976), as their official discipline program. Many have recently discarded that requirement.
14. In my last year of teaching, our school was selected to pilot a computer grading system developed within the school district. Each objective taught had to be correlated with individual objectives for that grade level that were taken from the official core curriculum. Despite objections that the program did not allow teachers to reward improvement or effort, and that it did not provide for easy access to objectives from other grade levels, at the end of the test year we were informed that the program was to be adopted district-wide. We were told bluntly that we had better get used to it. I have since heard that the district is marketing the program to other districts.
15. Standardized scores are averaged by school and published in newspapers in Utah. Those of individual classrooms are sometimes scrutinized in faculty meetings, and teachers are told on which areas they should focus their efforts.

16. When critical pedagogues reject the banking concept of education as described by Paulo Freire in *Pedagogy of the Oppressed* (New York: Continuum, 1993), they are challenging extant power relations. Those power relations, and the canons and methods that support them, are considered by some to be neutral, superior, and universal, and any challenge to them may be viewed as suspect. See especially, Allan Bloom, *The Closing of the American Mind* (New York: Simon & Schuster, 1987); Diane Ravitch, *The Troubled Crusade* (New York: Basic Books, 1983); and Chester E. Finn, "National Standards: A Plan for Consensus," *Teachers College Record, 91,* No. 1 (Fall 1989), 3–9.

17. Rarely have journals reported on the use of critical pedagogy with young children. One notable exception is Paul Skilton Sylvester, "Elementary School Curricula and Urban Transformation," *Harvard Educational Review, 64* (1994), 309–331.

18. I used ideas found in Freire, *Pedagogy of the Oppressed,* and in three books by Ira Shor: *Freire for the Classroom; Critical Teaching and Everyday Life* (Boston: South End Press, 1980); and *Empowering Education: Critical Teaching for Social Change* (Chicago: University of Chicago Press, 1992).

19. The district-mandated basal reader was *I Touched the Sun* (Lexington, MA: D. C. Heath, 1989).

20. See Michael W. Apple, ed., *Cultural and Economic Reproduction in Education* (Boston: Routledge & Kegan Paul, 1982); Michael W. Apple and Lois Weis, eds., *Ideology and Practice in Schooling* (Philadelphia: Temple University Press, 1983); Henry Giroux, *Theory and Resistance in Education* (South Hadley, MA: Bergin & Garvey, 1983); and Gail McCutcheon, "Curriculum and the Work of Teachers," in *The Curriculum: Problems, Politics, and Possibilities,* ed. Michael W. Apple and Landon E. Beyer (Albany: State University of New York Press, 1988).

21. Eliot Eisner, *The Educational Imagination: On the Design and Evaluation of School Programs* (New York: Macmillan, 1979). Eisner argues that neglecting the null curriculum in schools can be dangerous for many students because "ignorance is not simply a neutral void; it has important effects on the kinds of options one is able to consider, the alternatives that one can examine, and the perspectives from which one can view a situation or problem" (p. 83). On "codes of power" see Lisa Delpit, "The Silenced Dialogue: Power and Pedagogy in Educating Other People's Children," *Harvard Educational Review, 58* (1988), 280–298.

22, Names of the school and district have been changed for confidentiality.

23. Jeannie Oakes, "Tracking in Mathematics and Science Education: A Structural Contribution to Unequal Schooling," in *Class, Race, and Gender in American Education,* ed. Lois Weis (Albany: State University of New York Press, 1988).

24. Earlier that week I was informed by a colleague that the principal told her I was getting "rebellious and defiant."

25. Absent my income, we had to sell our house and move in with my parents. My two children were uprooted from schools they both loved, our community of friends was left behind, and I walked away from the one thing I believed I could do really well. A year later, however, I was able to procure a part-time job-share situation in a more progressive school district.

26. The 1994–1995 Professional Agreement of the negotiated contract between the County School District and the Education Association states that "Progress by the employee in correcting the job performance deficiencies and satisfactorily performing his/her duties will be evaluated by the District."

27. This quote is taken from my notes of the meeting written immediately afterward.

28. The most notable case of this sort is that of Jonathan Kozol, who wrote about his experiences in *Death at an Early Age* (New York: Penguin Books, 1985).

29. The point is made by Martin Carnoy and Henry M. Levin, *Schooling and Work in the Democratic State* (Stanford, CA: Stanford University Press, 1985), pp. 16–18.

30. Niccolo Machiavelli, *The Prince and The Discourses* (New York: Modern Library, 1950), p. 400. Machiavelli states that "not more than ten years should lapse . . . unless some case occurs that recalls the punishment to their memory and revives the fear in their hearts, the delinquents will soon become so numerous that they cannot be punished without danger."

31. George H. Wood describes schools where "traits such as a commitment to community and a desire to participate, values such as a sense of justice, equality, or liberty, skills of interpretation, debate, and compromise, habits of reflection, study, examining multiple perspectives" are encouraged. Implementing critical education theory and critical pedagogy are not the only ways to approach these objectives. See George H. Wood, *Schools that Work: America's Most Innovative Public Education Program* (New York: Plume, 1992), p. xxiii.

The author wishes to thank the Marriner S. Eccles Fellowship committee for their generous gift, which provided time to work on this essay. Thanks are also due to Harvey Kantor, Andrew Gitlin, and Audrey Thompson for comments on an earlier draft, and to *HER* editors Adriana Katzew and Frances Shavers for all their work on this manuscript.

Organizational Control in
Secondary Schools

▼▼▼▼▼

RICHARD M. INGERSOLL

O ver the past decade, both educational researchers and policymakers have increasingly focused on the degree of organizational control over teachers and their work in schools. For researchers, a continuing interest in the nature and impact of schools, as opposed to the characteristics of students or staffs, has led to increasing attention to the organizational structure of schools and, in particular, to the degree of administrative control or faculty autonomy found in schools. For policymakers, the growing national interest in site-based management, school choice, and educational restructuring has led to increasing attention to the nature and consequences of decisionmaking and management within schools.

Although the subject of organizational control in schools has become of great interest and importance, it is marked by substantial disagreement over the degree to which schools and teachers are controlled. This article examines the two most prominent and contradictory viewpoints on organizational control in schools.

Traditionally, studies of both teachers' working conditions and the organizational structure of schools have found schools to be an unusual type of modern organization and teaching an unusual type of occupation. Schools, researchers have argued, exhibit an exceptional degree of "structural looseness" compared to most organizations, because of the incompatibility between educating children and formal bureaucratization (Bidwell, 1965; Dreeben, 1973; Lortie, 1969, 1975). Among those who study occupations, work, and organizations in general, this theme has been reformulated and made the core of one of the more prominent contemporary perspectives within this interdisciplinary field. This perspective focuses on organizations characterized by an inordinate lack of coordination, control, consensus, and accountability. Researchers have created a colorful vocabulary to describe these settings, maintaining that schools are the archetype of such "loosely coupled systems" and "organized anarchies" (Cohen, March, & Olsen 1972; March & Olsen, 1976; Meyer & Scott, 1983; Weick, 1976, 1984).

Harvard Educational Review Vol. 64 No. 2 Summer 1994, 150–172

As a result, until very recently, the conventional wisdom among both organizational and educational researchers has been that schools are highly decentralized organizations, and that teaching, although in many ways not a self-regulating profession, is characterized by a great deal of workplace autonomy and discretion (Firestone, 1985; Stevenson & Baker, 1991; Tyler, 1988).

Beginning in the early 1980s, the subject of school organization and management became of increasing importance in a second arena — that of educational policy and reform. While the research community differed over the implications of loose structuring for school and teacher performance, those participating in the policy and reform debate tended, initially, to assume that a lack of coordination and control in schools has been a major factor in the educational crisis. A number of national studies and reports concluded that school problems are, to an important extent, a result of inadequacies in the classroom performance of teachers. The target of scrutiny and, ultimately, blame from this perspective was typically the ability, the training, or the motivation of individual teachers. Successful reform, these critics have argued, must, therefore, focus on greater accountability, higher standards, top-down state controls, national goals, and a general "tightening of the ship" (Bacharach, 1990; Goodlad, 1985; Kirst 1989; National Commission on Excellence in Education, 1983; Weis, Altbach, Kelly, Petrie, & Slaughter, 1989; Wise, 1979).

There is, however, a second view of school organization, which is antithetical to the traditional "loose-schools" perspective. This viewpoint is also perennially popular, but among a different group of education reformers, policymakers, and researchers. Schools are not too decentralized, those in this group hold, but exactly the opposite. They argue that highly bureaucratized school systems have become stultifying, rigid, and unresponsive, and that schools have become the epitome of the modern centralized undemocratic bureaucracy (Conley & Cooper, 1991; Sergiovanni & Moore, 1989).

More than one version of this anti-bureaucracy viewpoint has appeared. One version concentrates on community and client control and makes the argument that local constituencies and parents do not have adequate input into their children's and communities' schools. As Katz (1972) suggested over twenty years ago, this theme resurfaces on a regular basis in U.S. education. For instance, in the late 1960s and early 1970s, numerous reform groups sought to reform schools by implementing community control (Borman & Spring, 1984; Fantini, Gittell, & Magat, 1979; Ravitch, 1974; Rogers, 1968) or by institutionalizing increased student input into school affairs (Kozol, 1967). More recently, advocates of school "choice" reforms have adopted the same arguments and rhetoric — that is, that powerful central school boards deny parents any voice in their children's education. Ironically, this version of school decentralization often advocates reform measures similar to those offered by the traditional loose-schools viewpoint. For instance, the objective of much of the choice movement is often to *increase* the accountability of schools and teachers by shifting substantial control from school staffs to parents and communities (Clune & Witte, 1990).

Nevertheless, community control is often confused with a different and newer version of the anti-bureaucracy viewpoint. Over the past several years, reformers and researchers alike have extended and applied this critique specifically to the working conditions of teachers. The focus of this group is the impact of the bureaucratic structure of schools on teachers and teaching. In this view, public schools in particular are far too often based on an archaic nineteenth-century factory model of organization. Such schools, they argue, unduly disempower, de-professionalize, and de-motivate teachers. Hence, in this view, schools and teachers are already overly controlled and overly constrained — a situation that is both dissatisfying to teachers and a source of school inefficiency and ineffectiveness (Bacharach, Bauer, & Shedd, 1988; Corcoran, Walker, & White, 1988; Johnson, 1990; Rosenholtz, 1989; Shedd & Bacharach, 1991). Typically, this viewpoint advocates forms of decentralization, such as school-based management, that are designed to increase the authority, autonomy, and professionalism of teachers (Carnegie Forum, 1986; Holmes Group, 1986; Weis et al., 1989).

As a result of these changes in both the policy and research realms, there is now considerable debate over the degree to which teachers are subject to organizational control. Underlying much of this debate are contradictory images of the manner in which schools are organized. The traditional loose-schools perspective portrays schools as organized anarchies and finds school faculties to be overly autonomous and to lack sufficient accountability. The newer disempowerment perspective portrays schools as top-down bureaucracies and finds school faculties to lack sufficient influence over school operations. Both of these perspectives show substantial empirical support, offer policy agendas, and have fostered numerous reform measures. But, although many have drawn attention to the dissimilarity of these two polar perspectives (see, for example, Kirst, 1989; Rowan, 1990), there has been little effort to explain the simultaneous presence of contradictory images of organizational control in schools, and little effort to test empirically which viewpoint is more valid.

In this article, I address this contradiction by empirically examining nationally representative data on the levels, distribution, and variations of organizational control, centralization, and decentralization in secondary schools. The data come from the 1987–1988 Schools and Staffing Survey (SASS), a nationally representative survey of school teachers and administrators conducted by the National Center for Education Statistics (NCES), the statistical agency of the U.S. Department of Education.

The major argument of this article is that assessing control in schools depends on the issues examined, the valuative criteria used, the level of analysis chosen, and the schools investigated. I show that the differing conclusions of each of the two contradictory viewpoints largely derive from implicit differences in their emphases and in their assumptions concerning how to assess organizational control in schools. My objective is to empirically ground the debate and offer a more elaborated and refined view of organizational control in schools. This investigation draws particular attention to a neglected but important dimension — that is, who controls the key social, sorting, and behavioral activities and decisions occurring within schools.

After examining differences in the influence and control exercised by teachers over different sets of activities within schools, the analysis proceeds to the question of evaluating these levels of control and assessing the extent to which schools are or are not decentralized or centralized organizations. To do so, I directly compare the control reportedly exercised by faculties with that exercised by both principals and central boards over key activities within schools.

Finally, the analysis turns to an examination of the extent to which control varies among different kinds of schools. I specifically address the question: In what types of schools do faculty have the greatest and the least say and what proportion of the teaching force works in each of these different types of schools?

DATA AND METHODS

The Schools and Staffing Survey is one of the largest and most comprehensive data sources available on the organizational structure and character of schools. This survey was conducted to remedy the lack of nationally representative data on the staffing, occupational, and organizational characteristics of schools.[1] The U.S. Census Bureau collected the data for NCES in 1988 from a random sample, stratified by state, sector, and school level. The survey consisted of separate questionnaires for the principals of the schools sampled, for administrators of the central school or governing board of each sample school, and for faculty within each sample school. Within each school, from three to twenty teachers (average of four) were randomly sampled, depending on level, size, and sector of the school. The response rate was quite high: 86 percent for public school teachers; 79 percent for private school teachers; 94 percent for public school administrators; and 79 percent for private school administrators. All the data reported here are weighted to be representative of the national population of teachers and schools in 1988.[2]

This analysis focuses on secondary schools serving grades seven through twelve, including both junior and senior high schools. The sample contains 24,480 teachers and principals from 5,292 schools. Approximately 17 percent of the school sample (889) is in the private sector. Because private schools are usually smaller than public schools, approximately 9 percent of these teachers (2,158) are employed in the private sector.

In the debate over school organization, different analysts and observers have focused on a wide variety of different units of analysis (e.g., students, parents, teachers, administrators, school boards, state agencies) and different levels of analysis (e.g., classrooms, schools, districts, states).

The topic, however, that lies at the crux of the debate as to whether schools are organizationally centralized or decentralized, and that provides the focus of this investigation, is the relative degree of control exercised by faculty and administrators over school activities and decisions. Therefore, the units of analysis in this study are schools rather than individuals in schools. The data represent either school-level responses, as in the case of information collected from administrators, or schoolwide averages, as in the case of information collected from teachers. Aggregating individual-level data in the latter case, of course, underemphasizes diversity within schools, but it allows the empirical analysis to narrow its focus to the topic of interest — the levels, distribution, and variations of organizational control.[3]

Measures of Organizational Control in Schools

Control is measured in this investigation by both teachers' and administrators' reports of their influence or control over a range of decisions and policies within schools.

The teacher questionnaire obtained data on teachers' influence or control over decisions and policies concerning nine important educational activities within schools. These questions focused on both teachers' influence over school policies, such as those concerned with curriculum and discipline, and their control over activities within classrooms, such as selecting teaching materials and methods. The questionnaire items used a six-point scale from "none" to "a great deal" or "complete control."

The principal questionnaire obtained data on the relative influence of central school administrative or governing boards, school principals (or headmasters in private schools), and teachers. School principals were asked to evaluate the influence of these groups over decisions and policies concerned with three key areas within schools: faculty hiring, establishing curriculum, and student discipline policy. As before, respondents evaluated these influence levels on a six-point scale from "none" to "a great deal."

Although respondents' reports of organizational characteristics, such as the distribution of control, are one of the most commonly used sources of information in organizational research, it is necessary to acknowledge several limitations inherent to such data. Researchers have long noted the difficulties in obtaining reliable and valid information about control and influence in organizations (Pfeffer, 1981). Most methods for assessing these phenomena in social settings are confronted with questions concerning both respondent candor and accuracy. The approach used here treats organization members as informants of conditions in their organizational settings. One of the advantages of this approach is that the information comes from those who most closely experience it. Because such data represent members' perceptions, however, these responses are, by definition, not objective assessments, but, rather, subjective attributions. Respondents may have different experiences and perspectives; hence, wide variation in their perceptions can be expected.

One means of addressing these limitations is by using data from a range of respondents representing different roles and perspectives in the organization. In this case, SASS provides data from both a random sample of teachers and from the principal of each school. Each group can be expected to have different perspectives on school characteristics, and neither perspective may be more valid in an absolute sense. Indeed, as the analysis to follow indicates, in the two instances in which both teachers and principals were asked the same question about teachers' influence over school curriculum and discipline, there is disagreement. On the other hand, there is consistency in the two sets of responses when compared across activities and across schools. This investigation will focus on these comparisons, and thus attempt to take advantage of the strengths of each group's point of view. For instance, because teachers are closer to the educational process itself, this analysis will use their reports to compare teacher control across different types of key educational and teaching activities. Principals, on the other hand, are further removed from the details of the educational process and more involved with overall organizational activities. Hence, their reports will be used to discern the relative influence exercised by different groups and the overall hierarchical distribution of control in schools. The analysis begins with an examination of teachers' reported control in schools.

TEACHER CONTROL OF THE EDUCATIONAL CORE

Assessments of organizational control typically focus on two critical questions: First, what are the key processes and activities within an organization? Second, which groups or members control decisions and policies concerned with these activities?

Research on the organization of schools, whether representing the traditional loose-schools perspective or the newer disempowerment perspective, commonly subscribes to what has been labelled the "zone view" of school structure. In this view, school processes and activities are divided into separate classroom and schoolwide zones (Lortie, 1969, 1975; Tyler 1988). The zone view of schools is an adaptation of the traditional core/structure framework commonly used by those who study work and organizations in general (Pfeffer, 1982). This framework subdivides organizations into a technical core — the site of productive activities — and an administrative structure — the site of managerial activities. In educational research, core and structure have been translated into classroom and schoolwide zones, respectively. The technical or productive core of school organizations is deemed to lie in the classroom, defined as the site of teaching and educational activities. On the other hand, the administrative structure is labelled as the schoolwide zone, defined as the site of managerial, coordination, planning, and resource allocation activities.

Where the two perspectives of school control differ is in deciding which is the most important zone and set of activities to emphasize. The traditional loose-schools perspective typically emphasizes the educational or classroom zone. Hence, when these researchers analyze how centralized or decentralized schools are, they commonly focus on how much influence and autonomy teachers have, or alternatively, how much control administrators have over educational matters within classrooms. They find that teachers have high levels of discretion over issues of classroom instruction and, typically, conclude that teachers are autonomous and schools decentralized (Firestone, 1985; Lortie, 1975; Meyer & Scott, 1983).

The newer disempowerment perspective, on the other hand, does not deny that teachers have substantial autonomy over issues of classroom instruction. Those who hold this point of view instead draw attention to the importance of the schoolwide zone. They hold that teachers ought to have input into a school's allocation, planning, and strategic policies. Hence, when analyzing how centralized or decentralized schools are, they commonly ask how much say faculties have or, alternatively, how much influence administrators have over important schoolwide policies. They find little faculty influence and much administrative discretion over policy, resource allocation, and planning; hence, they have concluded that schools are overly centralized (Bacharach et al., 1988; Conley & Cooper, 1991; Rosenholtz 1989; Shedd & Bacharach, 1991).

The different conclusions of the two groups of researchers partly result from their different emphases. Each draws attention to different types of activities and different levels of analysis. But, notably, both agree on the existing division of labor and control within schools: "Schools are marked by a 'traditional influence pattern' in which decisions are differentiated by locale and position. . . . Administrators make strategic decisions outside of classrooms and teachers make operational decisions inside of classrooms" (Conley, 1991, pp. 237–238).

Moreover, and central to the point, both groups of researchers accept a narrow view of the educational or productive core of schools. When it comes to operationalizing the latter concept, most researchers assume that the most fundamental educational processes are limited to the classroom and most emphasize academic instruction. This focus, however, underemphasizes some of the most important educational activities that occur within classrooms and across schools.

Beginning with classic education theory (Dewey, 1902/1974; Durkheim, 1925/1961; Sorokin, 1927; Waller, 1932), continuing through Parsons (1959) and related educational researchers (e.g., Dreeben, 1968; Henry, 1965; Jackson, 1968), and including more recent revisionist and critical analysts of schools (Apple, 1982; Bourdieu & Passeron, 1977; Bowles & Gintis, 1976;

Giroux, 1982), investigators have long held that the major purpose of educational organizations lies in their social and institutional functions. Moreover, some have argued that this social role is expanding, as schools are being increasingly called upon to accept tasks once solely reserved for parents, churches, and communities (Coleman & Hoffer, 1987). Current research on effective schools, for instance, has concluded that one of the most important indicators of the successful school is the presence and transmission of a "shared moral order" (Bryk, Lee, & Smith, 1990; Grant, 1988; Kirst, 1989).

According to this view, the most important task of schools is the production of citizens and the reproduction of social order. This task involves two overlapping activities — socialization and sorting. The first involves the inculcation of societal norms, beliefs, behaviors, and roles. The second involves differentiation or the reproduction of societal patterns of stratification. This line of education theory draws attention to the idea that what students learn in schools is governed as much by school social relations as by the content of the official curriculum. Much of this social dimension is implicit, informal, and unstated, prompting observers often to use the term "hidden curriculum" (Giroux, 1982) to refer to the norms, values, and behaviors transmitted to students.

Despite this larger theoretical context, however, much empirical research in education, including that concerned with school control, adopts a far narrower focus — classroom academic instruction and, by extension, student academic performance, as measured on mass-produced standardized tests. Academic instruction and achievement are, of course, integrally related to the socialization and sorting processes in schools. Because of this emphasis on academic instructional activities, however, researchers usually have not directly specified, nor examined, the behavioral and normative dimensions of school educational processes. As a result, these social activities have secondary empirical status.

For example, research on school control invariably focuses on the degree of teacher autonomy or administrative control over key instructional decisions, such as the selection of course textbooks and materials, the choice of classroom curricular topics, and the determination of teaching methods used in classrooms. In contrast, such research rarely focuses on who controls key socialization and sorting decisions. Researchers typically underemphasize the extent to which teachers shape the criteria by which students are tracked into ability groups, or the extent to which teachers have input into whether the school even uses tracking in the first place — one of the most fundamental social decisions schools face. Likewise, there has been little emphasis on the extent to which teachers influence or control their schools' boundaries of permissible student behavior for issues such as student attendance, smoking, language use, evaluation, and expulsion.

Examination of the area of student discipline is one of the more glaring omissions in research on school control. Decisions concerning student discipline are among the most fundamental in schools. In the first place, without the maintenance of some degree of discipline and order, educational processes cannot proceed at all. Yet, student discipline is not simply a necessary prerequisite for the adequate enactment of instructional activities: Discipline is, at heart, an issue concerning which and whose set of norms are to dominate school life. Typically, discipline involves conflict between competing behavioral and moral codes, which often revolve around issues of class and race (Apple, 1982; Bowles & Gintis, 1976; Giroux, 1982; Grant, 1988). Research on school control should ask the crucial question, who makes the decisions concerned with disciplinary aspects of the social order in schools?

In order to offer both a broader and more elaborated view of the organizational control of key educational processes in schools, the analysis below will examine the degree to which teachers exercise control over important educational activities, both in classrooms and schoolwide, and will distinguish how these levels of control vary across both the social and instructional dimensions of the educational core.

There are, of course, a wide array of activities that could be included under the rubric of these core dimensions. SASS provides measures of a selected set of key activities representing each dimension. The social dimension is represented by decisions concerned with setting and enforcing norms and rules for student behavior, selecting criteria and means for tracking students, and determining programs for socializing and standardizing teacher behavior. Representing the instructional dimension are decisions concerned with designing, establishing, and implementing the curriculum.

Table 1 displays the percentage of schools in which teachers, on average, reported themselves to have substantial influence or control over the decisions or policies listed.

Several features are readily apparent from this table. First, the conventional zone view initially appears to be correct in that teachers report substantial influence over a number of instructional activities. It is also clear, however, that teachers' levels of control vary widely and that these variations depend on the dimension examined. In contrast, fewer school faculties report having substantial influence over either shaping the tracking policy, determining discipline policy for students, or making faculty in-service training decisions — all social functions.[4]

Moreover, there is a clear difference between teachers' control within classrooms and teachers' control over school policies. Teachers report far higher levels of control at the classroom level. Indeed, it is *only* in reference to instruction within classrooms, the traditional focus of much research, that a majority of school faculties report substantial control.

Even in this already delimited area of teacher control, however, there are other sources of constraint, which are overlooked in most analyses of organizational control in schools. Traditional research on school control has argued that, regardless of overall school curriculum policy, teachers are able, in reality, to exercise wide latitude and discretion over the curriculum within their classrooms. In this view, the decoupling of administrative structure and

TABLE 1 *Percentage of Schools in Which, on Average, Teachers Report Having a Great Deal of Influence or Complete Control over Selected Activities*

Activities	Percentage (n = 5,292)
Social Dimension	
Setting school policy on grouping students in classes by ability	8
Determining faculty in-service programs	8
Determining school discipline policy	11
Disciplining students in classrooms	42
Mean Percentage for Social Dimension	17
Instructional Dimension	
Establishing school curriculum	15
Selecting classroom texts and materials	44
Selecting classroom content and topics	51
Selecting classroom teaching techniques	80
Determining classroom homework levels	85
Mean Percentage for Instructional Dimension	55

Note: Teachers are defined as having a "great deal of influence" or "complete control" if the school's mean score was greater than five on a scale of one to six.

technical core results in teacher control over educational processes: that is to say, "behind the closed doors of their classrooms," teachers largely teach what they choose.

This view, however, overlooks the network of power relations that exist between teachers in classrooms and administrators in schools. Decisions concerned with classroom activities are neither independent of, nor of equal import to, decisions concerned with school policies. In extensive fieldwork associated with this research, I have found the classroom and administrative zones to be highly connected, not loosely coupled (Ingersoll, 1993, forthcoming). For instance, in most schools, a number of classroom instructional decisions are, as indicated in Table 1, commonly delegated to teachers. These decisions, however, are often subsidiary to, largely nested within, and predetermined by higher order decisions not under the control of teachers. Typically, teachers are delegated responsibility for implementation, execution, and enforcement, but do not exercise actual control over the conception and determination of larger policies and decisions. The parameters of teachers' classroom activities are effectively set by larger school policies — standardized curricula, tracking criteria, testing programs, attendance requirements, evaluation procedures, student behavioral rules, disciplinary infraction codes, and teacher workplace rules. Hence, even in the domain of apparent teacher control — classroom instruction — teachers' choices and discretion are far more circumscribed than has been acknowledged in much research on school organization.

THE HIERARCHICAL DISTRIBUTION OF CONTROL

Establishing the set of activities within schools upon which to focus, and determining levels of faculty influence over them, are necessary first steps in assessing organizational control in schools. However, it is also necessary to evaluate these levels. That is, what constitutes high or low levels of teacher control? On what basis is a setting labelled as centralized or decentralized? Organizational control, it must be remembered, is a relative concept, and the researchers must always pose the question, "Compared to what?" Close examination of the research on organizational control in schools reveals that each of the two polar perspectives, the loose-schools view and the new disempowerment view, assumes a very different standard of comparison.

The traditional perspective compares schools to the rational-bureaucratic ideal of organization, often known as the machine model of organization. In comparison to this ideal, schools are found to be highly decentralized (Conley, 1991; Meyer & Scott, 1983). In contrast, the newer disempowerment view commonly compares schools to a different standard — the ideal of the professional organization. This second standard is also a traditional ideal, but one that is, in important ways, diametrically opposite to the rational-bureaucratic model. While the bureaucratic machine model is synonymous with centralized control, the professional model of organization is synonymous with decentralization (Friedson, 1973; Pfeffer, 1982; Rowan, 1990). Hence, it is not surprising that the disempowerment viewpoint comes to a quite different conclusion from that of the loose-schools viewpoint — that is, that schools are highly centralized (Bacharach et al., 1988; Rosenholtz, 1989; Shedd & Bacharach, 1991; see Figure 1).

Given their different standards of comparison, both viewpoints may well be correct. However, actually empirically testing either of these comparisons is difficult. In fact, school researchers rarely do so — their comparisons are largely based on hypothetical ideals of bureaucratic or professionalized workplaces (Conley, 1991; Meyer & Scott, 1983). However, mere assertions that organizations are overly centralized or decentralized are scarcely sufficient. The analysis below offers one means of empirically testing these comparisons.

A closer look reveals that the relative influence of employees and management lies at the heart of the concepts of organizational control, centralization, and decentralization. Indeed, one of the key criteria distinguishing professions from other kinds of work, and the bureaucratic model from the professional model of organization, is the distribution of control between these two groups (Friedson, 1973, 1984). In other words, a key distinction in

FIGURE 1   *The Comparison of Schools with Other Organizations*

Type of Organization	*Distribution of Control*
Traditional Loose-Schools Perspective	
Rational Bureaucracy	Centralized
Educational Bureaucracy	Decentralized
New Disempowerment Perspective	
Professional Organization	Decentralized
Educational Bureaucracy	Centralized

any organization is whether decisions concerned with technical and production processes are controlled from the administrative center, or whether these are delegated to employees and, hence, are decentralized. We would expect employees to have far less control than management in rationalized, bureaucratized workplaces and, alternatively, we would expect employees to have influence approaching that of management in decentralized, debureaucratized, or professionalized settings. Therefore, for evaluating a school's organization, a key question is: Which group has more influence over important core educational activities, administrators or faculty? In other words, is there a hierarchical distribution of control within schools?

It is possible to provide an answer to this question by turning to the SASS data on the relative control of school central boards, school principals, and school faculties. Table 2 displays the percentage of schools in which principals reported each group, including themselves, to have a great deal of influence. The survey focused on a selected set of three key activities, which represent the instructional and social dimensions of the educational core and the administrative zone.

The results present a picture of intraorganizational centralization in schools, at least from the viewpoint of principals. For each of these key activities within schools, principals lie at the top of the hierarchy. For these three important activities, principals clearly view themselves as the most powerful actors and teachers as the least powerful actors within schools.

Especially striking is the principal/faculty gap over control of decisions concerned with establishing school curricula. Although teachers are traditionally thought to exercise high levels of control over many aspects of school instruction, and although the data in Table 1 suggest that teachers themselves believe that this is true for several specific activities, principals report that teachers have relatively little control over the overall school curricular program. According to principals, less than a quarter of high school faculties have a great deal of actual influence over decisions concerning the establishment of the curriculum in their schools. Moreover, even though a compari-

TABLE 2   *Percentage of Schools in Which Principals Report that Faculties, Boards, or Principals Have a Great Deal of Influence over Selected Activities*

Activities	Percentage (n = 5,292)
Hiring New Full-Time Teachers	
Faculties	2
Boards	27
Principals	57
Setting School Discipline Policy	
Faculties	18
Boards	31
Principals	52
Establishing School Curriculum	
Faculties	23
Boards	24
Principals	31
Overall Mean Percentage for 3 Activities	
Faculties	14
Boards	27
Principals	47

Note: A score of six on a scale from one to six equals "a great deal of influence."

son of Tables 1 and 2 indicates that principals report teachers to be more frequently empowered regarding the overall curriculum than teachers themselves do, principals nevertheless report teachers to be less frequently influential than themselves over these activities.

Hence, if we accept the comparison of teachers' and administrators' reports of control as a valid criterion of the degree of centralization or professionalization in schools, this analysis suggests that for several key sets of decisions concerned with both core and administrative activities, teachers are highly de-professionalized and schools highly centralized.

It is also clear, however, that this assessment depends on the level of analysis chosen. Changing the focus from the intraorganizational to the interorganizational level yields a very different picture. That is, if we focus on the interface between principals and central boards rather than on the interface between teachers and administrators, schools appear quite autonomous. Principals report more influence than their central boards for all three activities — suggesting interorganizational decentralization — a finding to which I will return later.

VARIATIONS IN CONTROL AMONG SCHOOLS

In this investigation, I have argued that assessment of organizational control in schools depends on the activities examined and the valuative criteria used. In addition, the degree of control may also depend on the schools investigated. It is necessary to determine if the levels of control and of hierarchy we have assessed do truly represent general trends. In other words, are schools generally similar in terms of control, or do particular types of schools stand out?

Previous research suggests that there are, in fact, important differences in the organizational character and conditions of schools, and that these differences are related to the context of the school, its community setting, and the type of students enrolled (Anderson, 1982; Pallas, 1988; Rowan et al., 1991). Differences in public and private sectors, in particular, have been the focus of a number of investigations of school organization; most studies have concluded that private schools are far more decentralized than public schools (Chubb & Moe, 1990).

Most of this research has been concerned with assessing the effects of school organization and control on school performance. However, there has been little analysis of the extent of differences in control among different types of schools, and of the proportion of schools as a whole that can be described as centralized or decentralized. The discussion below turns to these questions.

Analysis of the SASS data indicates that, consistent with much previous research, among the most significant predictors of school control are school sector and school size (Choy, Medrich, Henke, & Bobbitt, 1992). Tables 3 and 4 provide an illustration of these differences for both teacher control over the educational core and for school hierarchy. Each table presents a typology of organizational control in schools based upon both the public/private distinction and school enrollment.

On one end of the scale lie the larger, public secondary schools. These schools employ over half (55%) of all secondary school teachers in the United States. On average, 24 percent of the students in these schools are from poor families (i.e., eligible for the Federal Free Lunch Program) and 27 percent are from minority families.

On the other end of the scale lie the smaller, private secondary schools. These schools employ only 5 percent of secondary school teachers in the United States. On average, 11 percent of the students in these schools are from poor families and 16 percent are from minority families.

As expected, Table 3 shows that reported teacher control of the educational core varies widely among the different types of schools. Moreover, within each school type, teachers report similarly wide differences in their control over the two dimensions of the educational core.

Larger, public schools lie on the most centralized end of the scale. In almost half of these schools, teachers on average report having high control over decisions within the instructional dimension. On the other hand, teach-

TABLE 3   *Percentage of Schools in Which, on Average, Teachers Report Having a Great Deal of Influence or Complete Control over Selected Activities*

Activities	Public Schools		Private Schools	
	Larger (n=1,839)	Smaller (n=1,094)	Larger (n=114)	Smaller (n=459)
Social Dimension				
Setting school policy on grouping students in classes by ability	1	7	17	25
Determining faculty in-service programs	3	9	11	17
Determining school discipline policy	3	13	9	32
Disciplining students in classrooms	30	50	61	59
Mean Percentage for Social Dimension	9	20	25	33
Instructional Dimension				
Establishing school curriculum	5	19	23	37
Selecting classroom texts and materials	26	61	55	52
Selecting classroom content and topics	34	63	67	64
Selecting classroom teaching techniques	79	82	93	80
Determining classroom homework levels	87	88	86	77
Mean Percentage for Instructional Dimension	46	63	65	62

Note: Smaller school size for both private and public here refers to those schools with student enrollments of less than or equal to 350. Larger school size refers to schools with student enrollments greater than 650. Data for schools with enrollments between 351 and 650 is not displayed. Teachers are defined as having a "great deal of influence" or "complete control" if the school's mean score was greater than five on a scale of one to six.

ers report having equivalent control over decisions in the social dimension in less than one-tenth of these schools.

Smaller, private secondary schools lie on the least centralized end of the scale. It is striking, however, that even in this elite group, while, on average, teachers in over two-thirds of the schools report having substantial control over instructional activities, teachers in only a third of the schools report substantial faculty control over the social dimension of the core.

TABLE 4   *Percentage of Schools in Which Principals Report that Faculties, Boards, or Principals Have a Great Deal of Influence over Selected Activities*

Activities	Public Schools		Private Schools	
	Larger (n=1,839)	Smaller (n=1,094)	Larger (n=114)	Smaller (n=459)
Hiring New Full-Time Teachers				
Faculties	3	2	6	4
Boards	29	30	5	17
Principals	52	51	82	78
Setting School Discipline Policy				
Faculties	14	17	23	28
Boards	37	30	12	17
Principals	45	47	76	70
Establishing School Curriculum				
Faculties	17	22	38	32
Boards	32	20	11	12
Principals	21	29	63	57
Overall Mean Percentage for 3 Activities				
Faculties	11	14	22	21
Boards	33	27	9	15
Principals	39	42	74	68

Note: Smaller school size for both private and public here refers to those schools with student enrollments of less than or equal to 350. Larger school size refers to schools with student enrollments greater than 650. Data for schools with enrollments between 351 and 650 is not displayed. A score of six on a scale from one to six equals "a great deal of influence."

Hence, across a wide range of schools, the degree of teacher control depends on the activities examined. As before, two different pictures of teacher control emerge, depending on whether one focuses on the instructional or social dimension of the educational core of schools — a distinction under-emphasized in most research on school organization. Although there are wide differences in control among different types of schools, for the vast majority, including private schools, important social decisions are highly centralized.

Table 4 turns to differences in the hierarchical ranking reported by principals for teachers, principals, and boards across the different school types. Especially striking are the overall differences in the hierarchy between public and private schools. In the first place, far more private school principals perceive themselves to be highly influential than do public school principals. For instance, averaging over the three activities examined, over two-thirds of the principals in private schools view themselves as having a great deal of influence, versus less than half of public school principals.

The primary source of this difference between private and public sectors appears to be the relative influence of school governing boards. Not surprisingly, these groups are far more often reported to be influential in the public sector. This finding seems to be a zero-sum pattern, that is, a trade-off: principals are more often influential and boards less often influential in private than public schools.

Moreover, as in the data from the teacher survey, there are distinct public/private differences in reports of faculty influence. On average, almost a quarter of the private school respondents report their faculties to have high influence, in contrast to about one-sixth of public school respondents. But, notably, in both sectors, faculty are perceived to have substantial control less often than school principals. These results further erode the argument that private schools are decentralized. That is, although it is true that private school teachers are perceived to be more frequently influential than their public counterparts, they are still, nevertheless, less often influential than their principals.

In sum, just as in the data on teacher control of the educational core displayed in Table 3, these results bring to light the overwhelming extent of school centralization and teacher deprofessionalization across the population of secondary schools. Although there are wide differences, the vast majority of schools, including private schools, are reported to have a high degree of internal organizational control for these key activities. But the data also highlight an important distinction noted earlier: assessments of control depend on the level of analysis examined. The results suggest that both public and private schools are centralized at the intraorganizational level, but that both are decentralized at the interorganizational level.

This distinction between the control exercised by teachers and that of both levels of administration clarifies an important issue underlying two different versions of the disempowerment viewpoint of school control and different models of site-based management and school decentralization: Does the locus of disempowerment in schools lie with teachers, or with teachers and their principals alike? Or, alternatively, does the locus of administrative control lie with central school boards, or with building principals?

Research on public school control suggests two possible answers to these questions. One stream of research, which focuses on the intraorganizational level, argues that it is primarily teachers within public schools who lack control (Bacharach et al., 1988; Corcoran et al., 1988). Another version focuses on the interorganizational level, arguing that public schools lack autonomy and that their staffs — that is, principals and teachers alike — are constrained by overbearing school boards (Borman & Spring, 1984; Chubb & Moe, 1990; Rogers 1968).

The analysis here suggests that the latter view is oversimplified. To be sure, it is true that if we focus solely on the interface between principals and their governing boards, public schools are more often constrained by their boards than are private schools. Nevertheless, public school principals still perceive themselves to be in control more often than their boards. The one exception is control of curriculum in larger public schools. In other words, although school boards are more powerful in the public sector, principals do not report themselves to be the beleaguered, constrained, middle managers depicted in many popular accounts.

Moreover, if we focus on the intraorganizational level, it becomes clear that principals are far more often in control than their faculties, in both public and private schools. Hence, the data suggest that in the majority of schools in this country, the locus of disempowerment lies with teachers, and the locus of empowerment lies with building principals.

CONCLUSION

The issue of organizational control in schools has become a topic of great importance, but there is still significant disagreement over the degree to which schools and teachers are controlled. My argument has been that distinguishing the degree of control in schools depends on the activities focused upon, the valuative criteria used, the level of analysis chosen, and the schools investigated. I have shown that the differing conclusions of the current prominent and contradictory viewpoints of school control largely derive from implicit differences in their emphases, and in their assumptions concerning how to assess organizational control in schools. The objective of this investigation has been to ground the debate empirically and to offer a more elaborated and refined view of organizational control in schools by examining nationally representative data on organizational centralization and decentralization in secondary schools.

Such an approach has its limits. This analysis relies on respondents' perceptions of organizational control as recorded in survey questionnaires. These data provide neither a means of capturing the social organization of power and influence, nor the actual mechanisms whereby control operates in schools. On the other hand, statistical analysis of survey data on a broad range and large number of teachers and school sites allows us to make generalizations concerning broad patterns in the reported distribution of control in schools and to establish appropriate comparisons of control across schools. As a result, this analysis highlights several overlooked aspects of the overall levels, distribution, and variations of organizational control across a wide range of schools.

First, this investigation draws attention to the importance of the often overlooked, but crucial, social, behavioral, and tracking activities within the core of schools. The data suggest that it is for those activities that are most fundamentally social — where the educational process involves the transmission of values, behaviors, and norms — that schools exhibit the greatest degree of internal organizational control.

This finding has implications for current trends in educational reform. School restructuring and decentralization efforts, for example, usually focus on expanding teacher input into either instructional activities, such as curricular innovation, or into administrative activities, such as hiring and budget allocation (David, 1989). In contrast, reforms rarely focus on a similar expansion of teacher influence over the social functions of schools — one of the most telling sites of centralized control.

Second, this analysis draws attention to the importance of empirically testing evaluations of whether schools are/are not centralized bureaucracies, or are/are not professionalized settings. This investigation offers one empirical means of evaluating the degree of organizational control in schools — the comparison of teachers' and administrators' reported influence over decisions representing a range of key activities within schools. This criterion illuminates the extent to which teachers are deprofessionalized and, in contrast, principals are relatively influential actors.

Third, this investigation draws attention to the extent to which assessments of control depend on the level of analysis chosen. The results suggest that both public and private schools are centralized at the intraorganizational level, but that both are decentralized at the interorganizational level.

These findings also have implications for reform. School restructuring, site-based management, and decentralization efforts often confound teacher empowerment and principal empowerment. Is it teachers, principals, or school staffs as a whole that need to be empowered? The data suggest that these three options need to be carefully distinguished.

Finally, this analysis draws attention to the degree to which organizational control varies across different kinds of schools. Larger public schools are frequently characterized by lower levels of reported teacher control than smaller private schools. Even in this latter group, however, faculty are infrequently reported by either themselves or by their principals to have substantial control over crucial social decisions. The data suggest that private schools are, in important ways, not particularly decentralized or professionalized settings, in contrast to much current thinking.

This finding also has implications for reform. For instance, school choice reforms often hold up private schools as examples to be emulated by public schools. Given private schools' relatively lower salary levels, relatively higher teacher turnover rates (Choy et al., 1992), and, as this analysis shows, high levels of internal organizational control, it may be premature to assume these are sites of superior teaching conditions.

In sum, the objective of this study has been to counter some of the oversimplifications and clarify some of the contradictions prevalent in much of the thinking on the organization of private and public secondary schools in the United States. My aim has been to offer a more elaborated view of the extent of organizational control in schools — how it is distributed across actors and to what degree it varies across different kinds of schools. Such clarification is necessary because of the crucial importance of the organizational structure of schools to the performance and well-being of teachers and students, a conclusion increasingly accepted by many in the realms of both research and policy in education.

Presently we need a more detailed and refined investigation into the nature of organizational control in schools, one that asks: By what forms and mechanisms is teachers' work controlled? How does this control vary across different organizational issues and in different kinds of school settings? Beyond establishing the degree and forms of control, future research must then turn to the larger question of the consequences of control. What impact does the distribution of control have on how schools function? In what ways do the degrees and forms of organizational control in schools affect the lives and behaviors of students and teachers within them?

If schools are to be improved, teaching must be improved. But in order to improve teaching, we must first better understand how the work of teachers is currently organized and with what consequences.

NOTES

1. SASS data tapes, survey questionnaires, and user's manuals are available from NCES, U.S. Department of Education, 555 New Jersey Ave., Washington, DC 20208-5641. For information concerning the survey design and sample estimation of SASS, see Kaufman (1991). For an extensive report that summarizes the items used in this investigation and provides an overview of the entire survey, see *Schools and Staffing in the U.S.: A Statistical Profile, 1987–88* (Choy, Medrich, Henke, & Bobbitt, 1992).

2. Throughout, this analysis uses data weighted to compensate for the over- and under-sampling resulting from the complex, stratified survey design. Each observation is weighted by the inverse of its probability of selection in order to obtain unbiased estimates of population parameters.

3. The data used in this investigation are multi-level. They represent responses collected from both individual teachers within schools and from administrators of those schools. There has been a great deal of debate concerning the appropriate level of analysis for such data (e.g., Bidwell & Kasarda, 1980; Pfeffer, 1982; Rowan, Raudenbush, & Kang, 1991). As a result, several multi-level statistical techniques and packages have been recently developed specifically to capitalize on the nested or hierarchical nature of such data (see, for example, Bryk & Raudenbush, 1992).

    Background analyses for this investigation using all three approaches (individual-, school-, and multi-level) indicate that there are not appreciable differences in their results for the questions addressed here. As a result, this investigation will be couched at a school level of analysis, because that level most closely matches the level of the research questions addressed. School-wide conditions are represented by both principals' reports and the means of teachers' reports for those schools. Teacher weights were used in aggregating the teacher scores. School weights were used in the analysis proper.

    This investigation, however, does not assume that schools are uniform entities. As in many previous analyses of school organization (e.g., Lee, Dedrick, & Smith, 1991; Pallas, 1988), diversity exists across teachers within schools for teachers' reports of organizational conditions, but these reports are only weakly related to commonly measured teacher characteristics (e.g., gender, race, experience, education, subject taught, salary). This suggests there is both actual variation in control among teachers within schools and also some degree of measurement error.

    Background analysis also indicates substantial variation among schools for the items of interest here. This variation suggests that control is also a collective property of schools. The levels, distribution, and variations of this organizational control provide the focus of this investigation.

4. In-service programs — that is, in-school development and training programs for faculty — are examples of school activities that can be classified in more than one manner. Here, I have classified in-service as a social issue because many such programs are designed as a means to socialize and standardize teacher behavior (Rowan, 1990). Indeed, researchers have traditionally assigned great importance to the role of teacher training in the normative control of teachers (e.g., Lortie, 1975).

REFERENCES

Anderson, C. (1982). The search for school climate: A review of the research. *Review of Educational Research, 52,* 368–420.

Apple, M. (1982). *Education and power.* Boston: Routledge & Kegan Paul.

Bacharach, S. (1990). *Education reform: Making sense of it all.* Boston: Allyn & Bacon.

Bacharach, S., Bauer, S., & Shedd, J. (1988). The learning workplace: The conditions and resources of teaching. In National Education Association (Ed.), *Conditions and resources of teaching* (pp. 8–40). Washington, DC: National Education Association.

Bidwell, C. (1965). The school as a formal organization. In J. March (Ed.), *Handbook of organizations* (pp. 973–1002). Chicago: Rand McNally.

Bidwell, C., & Kasarda, J. (1980). Conceptualizing and measuring the effects of school and schooling. *American Journal of Education, 89,* 401–431.

Borman, K., & Spring, J. (1984). *Schools in central cities.* New York: Longman.

Bourdieu, P., & Passeron, J-C. (1977). *Reproduction: In education, society and culture.* Beverly Hills, CA: Sage.

Bowles, S., & Gintis, H. (1976). *Schooling in capitalist America.* New York: Basic Books.

Bryk, A., Lee, V., & Smith, J. (1990). High school organization and its effects on teachers and students: An interpretive summary of the research. In W. H. Clune & J. F. Witte (Eds.), *Choice and control in American education: Vol. 1. The theory of choice and control in education.* New York: Falmer Press.

Bryk, A., & Raudenbush, S. (1992). *Hierarchical linear models for social and behavioral research.* Newbury Park: Sage.

Carnegie Forum on Education and the Economy. (1986). *A nation prepared: Teachers for the 21st century.* New York: Author.

Choy, S., Medrich, E., Henke, R., & Bobbitt, S. (1992). *Schools and staffing in the U.S.: A statistical profile, 1987–88.* Washington, DC: National Center for Education Statistics.

Chubb, J. E., & Moe, T. (1990). *Politics, markets and America's schools.* Washington, DC: Brookings Institution.

Clune, W. H., & Witte, J. F. (Eds.). (1990). *Choice and control in American education: Vol. 1. The theory of choice and control in education.* New York: Falmer Press.

Cohen, M., March, J., & Olsen, J. (1972). A garbage can theory of organizational decision making. *Administrative Science Quarterly, 17,* 1–25.

Coleman, J., & Hoffer, T. (1987). *Public and private schools: The impact of communities.* New York: Basic Books.

Conley, S. (1991). Review of research on teacher participation in school decision making. In G. Grant (Ed.), *Review of research in education* (pp. 225–266). Washington, DC: American Educational Research Association.

Conley, S., & Cooper, B. (1991). *The school as a work environment: Implications for reform.* Boston: Allyn & Bacon.

Corcoran, T., Walker, L., & White, J. L. (1988). *Working in urban schools.* Washington, DC: Institute for Educational Leadership.

David, J. (1989). Synthesis of research on school-based management. *Educational Leadership, 46*(8), 45–52.

Dewey, J. (1974). *The child and the curriculum.* Chicago: University of Chicago Press. (Original work published 1902)

Dreeben, R. (1968). *On what is learned in school.* Reading, MA: Addison-Wesley.

Dreeben, R. (1973). The school as a workplace. In R. W. Travers (Ed.), *Second handbook of research on teaching* (pp. 450–473). Chicago: Rand McNally.

Durkheim, E. (1961). *Moral education: A study in the theory and application of the sociology of education* (Trans. by E. K. Wilson & H. Schnurer). New York: Free Press. (Original work published 1925)

Fantini, M., Gittell, M., & Magat, R. (1979). *Community control and the urban school.* New York: Praeger.

Firestone, W. (1985). The study of loose coupling: Problems, progress, and prospects. In A. Kerckhoff (Ed.), *Research in the sociology of education and socialization* (vol. 5, pp. 3–30). Greenwich, CT: JAI Press.

Friedson, E. (1973). *The professions and their prospects.* Beverly Hills, CA: Sage.

Friedson, E. (1984). The changing nature of professional control. *Annual Review of Sociology, 10,* 1–20.

Giroux, H. (1982). *Ideology, culture and the process of schooling.* Philadelphia: Temple University Press.

Goodlad, J. (1985). Structure, process and an agenda. In K. Rehage (Ed.), *The ecology of school renewal* (pp. 1–19). Chicago: University of Chicago Press.

Grant, G. (1988). *The world we created at Hamilton High.* Cambridge, MA: Harvard University Press.

Henry, J. (1965). *Culture against man.* New York: Vintage.

Holmes Group. (1986). *Tomorrow's teachers.* East Lansing, MI: Author.

Ingersoll, R. (1993). Loosely coupled organizations revisited. *Research in the Sociology of Organizations, 11,* 81–112.

Ingersoll, R. (2003). *Who controls teachers' work? Power and accountability in America's schools.* Cambridge, MA: Harvard University Press.

Jackson, P. (1968). *Life in classrooms.* New York: Holt, Rinehart, & Winston.

Johnson, S. M. (1990). *Teachers at work.* New York: Basic Books.

Katz, M. (1972). *Class, bureaucracy and schools.* New York: Vintage.

Kaufman, S. (1991). *1988 Schools and Staffing Survey sample design and estimation.* Washington, DC: National Center for Education Statistics.

Kirst, M. (1989). Who should control the schools. In T. J. Sergiovanni & J. Moore (Eds.), *Schooling for tomorrow* (pp. 62–88). Boston: Allyn & Bacon.

Kozol, J. (1967). *Death at an early age.* Boston: Houghton-Mifflin.

Lee, V., Dedrick, R., & Smith, J. (1991). The effect of the social organization of schools on teachers' efficacy and satisfaction. *Sociology of Education, 64,* 190–208.

Lortie, D. (1969). The balance of control and autonomy in elementary school teaching. In A. Etzioni (Ed.), *The semi-professions and their organizations: Teachers, nurses and social workers* (pp. 1–53). New York: Free Press.

Lortie, D. (1975). *School teacher.* Chicago: University of Chicago Press.

March, J., & Olsen, J. (1976). *Ambiguity and choice in organizations.* Bergen, Norway: Universitetsforlaget.

Meyer, J., & Scott, W. R. (1983). *Organizational environments: Ritual and rationality.* Beverly Hills, CA: Sage.

National Commission on Excellence in Education. (1983). *A nation at risk: The imperative for educational reform.* Washington, DC: Government Printing Office.

Pallas, A. (1988). School climate in American high schools. *Teachers College Record, 89,* 541–543.

Parsons, T. (1959). The school class as a social system: Some of its functions in American society. *Harvard Educational Review, 29,* 297–318.

Pfeffer, J. (1981). *Power in organizations.* Marshfield, MA: Pitman.

Pfeffer, J. (1982). *Organizations and organization theory.* Marshfield, MA: Pitman.

Ravitch, D. (1974). *The great school wars.* New York: Harper.

Rogers, D. (1968). *110 Livingston Street.* New York: Vintage.

Rosenholtz, S. (1989). *Teacher's workplace: The social organization of schools.* New York: Longman.

Rowan, B. (1990). Commitment and control: Alternative strategies for the organizational design of schools. In C. Cazden (Ed.), *Review of research in education* (vol. 16, pp. 353–389). Washington, DC: American Educational Research Association.

Rowan, B., Raudenbush, S., & Kang, S. J. (1991). Organizational design in high schools: A multilevel analysis. *American Journal of Education, 99,* 238–260.

Sergiovanni, T. J., & Moore, J. (1989). *Schooling for tomorrow.* Boston: Allyn & Bacon.

Shedd, J., & Bacharach, S. (1991). *Tangled hierarchies.* San Francisco: Jossey-Bass.

Sorokin, P. (1927). *Social and cultural mobility.* New York: Harper & Row.

Stevenson, D., & Baker, D. (1991). State control of the curriculum and classroom instruction. *Sociology of Education, 64,* 1–10.

Tyler, W. (1988). *School organization.* New York: Croom Helm.

Waller, W. (1932). *The sociology of teaching.* New York: Wiley.

Weick, K. (1976). Educational organizations as loosely coupled systems. *Administrative Science Quarterly, 21,* 1–19.

Weick, K. (1984). Management of organizational change among loosely coupled elements. In P. Goodman (Ed.), *Change in organizations* (pp. 375–409). San Francisco: Jossey-Bass.

Weis, L., Altbach, P., Kelly, G., Petrie, H., & Slaughter, S. (1989). *Crisis in teaching.* Albany: State University of New York Press.

Wise, A. (1979). *Legislated learning: The bureaucratization of the American classroom.* Berkeley: University of California Press.

Support for this project was provided through a Research Fellowship jointly sponsored by the National Science Foundation and the National Center for Education Statistics, and administered by the American Educational Research Association. A previous version of this article was presented at the Annual Meeting of the American Sociological Association in August 1993.

Getting to Scale with Good Educational Practice

▼▼▼▼▼

RICHARD F. ELMORE

THE PROBLEM OF SCALE IN EDUCATIONAL REFORM

Why do good ideas about teaching and learning have so little impact on U.S. educational practice? This question, I argue, raises a central problem of U.S. education: A significant body of circumstantial evidence points to a deep, systemic incapacity of U.S. schools, and the practitioners who work in them, to develop, incorporate, and extend new ideas about teaching and learning in anything but a small fraction of schools and classrooms. This incapacity, I argue, is rooted primarily in the incentive structures in which teachers and administrators work. Therefore, solving the problem of scale means substantially changing these incentive structures.

Changing the Core: Students, Teachers, and Knowledge

The problem of scale in educational innovation can be briefly stated as follows: Innovations that require large changes in the core of educational practice seldom penetrate more than a small fraction of U.S. schools and classrooms, and seldom last for very long when they do. By "the core of educational practice," I mean how teachers understand the nature of knowledge and the student's role in learning, and how these ideas about knowledge and learning are manifested in teaching and classwork. The "core" also includes structural arrangements of schools, such as the physical layout of classrooms, student grouping practices, teachers' responsibilities for groups of students, and relations among teachers in their work with students, as well as processes for assessing student learning and communicating it to students, teachers, parents, administrators, and other interested parties.

One can think of schools as generally representing a standard set of solutions to these problems of how to manage the core. Most teachers tend to think of knowledge as discrete bits of information about a particular subject and of student learning as the acquisition of this information through processes of repetition, memorization, and regular testing of recall (e.g., Cohen, 1988). The teacher, who is generally the center of attention in the classroom,

Harvard Educational Review   Vol. 66   No. 1   Spring 1996, 1–26

initiates most of the talk and orchestrates most of the interaction in the classroom around brief factual questions, if there is any discussion at all.

Hence, the teacher is the main source of information, defined as discrete facts, and this information is what qualifies as knowledge. Often students are grouped by age, and again within age groups, according to their perceived capabilities to acquire information. The latter is generally accomplished either through within-class ability groups or, at higher grade levels, through "tracks," or clusters of courses for students whom teachers judge to have similar abilities. Individual teachers are typically responsible for one group of students for a fixed period of time. Seldom working in groups to decide what a given group of students should know or how that knowledge should be taught, teachers are typically solo practitioners operating in a structure that feeds them students and expectations about what students should be taught. Students' work is typically assessed by asking them to repeat information that has been conveyed by the teacher in the classroom, usually in the form of worksheets or tests that involve discrete, factual, right-or-wrong answers (Elmore, 1995).

At any given time, there are some schools and classrooms that deliberately violate these core patterns. For example, students may initiate a large share of the classroom talk, either in small groups or in teacher-led discussions, often in the context of some problem they are expected to solve. Teachers may ask broad, open-ended questions designed to elicit what students are thinking and how they are thinking, rather than to assess whether they have acquired discrete bits of information. Students' work might involve oral or written responses to complex, open-ended questions or problems for which they are expected to provide explanations that reflect not only their acquisition of information, but also their judgments about what kinds of information are most important or appropriate. Students may be grouped flexibly according to the teacher's judgment about the most appropriate array of strengths and weaknesses for a particular task or subject matter. Teachers may share responsibility for larger groups of students across different ages and ability levels and may work cooperatively to design classroom activities that challenge students working at different levels. In other words, students' learning may be assessed using a broad array of tasks, problems, mediums of expression, and formats.

In characterizing these divergences from traditional educational practice, I have deliberately avoided using the jargon of contemporary educational reform — "teaching for understanding," "whole language," "heterogeneous grouping," "team teaching," "cooperative learning," "authentic assessment," etc. I have done this because I do not want to confuse the problems associated with the implementation of particular innovations with the more general, systemic problem of what happens to practices, by whatever name, that violate or challenge the basic conventions of the core of schooling. The names of these practices change, and the intellectual traditions associated with particular versions of the practices ebb and flow. But, the fundamental problem remains: Attempts to change the stable patterns of the core of schooling, in the fundamental ways described above, are usually unsuccessful on anything more than a small scale. It is on this problem that I will focus.

Much of what passes for "change" in U.S. schooling is not really about changing the core, as defined above. Innovations often embody vague intentions of changing the core through modifications that are weakly related, or not related at all, to the core. U.S. secondary schools, for example, are constantly changing the way they arrange the schedule that students are expected to follow — lengthening or shortening class periods, distributing content in different ways across periods and days, increasing and decreasing class size for certain periods of the day, etc. These changes are often justified as a way to provide space in the day for teachers to do a kind of teaching they wouldn't otherwise be able to do, or to develop a different kind of relationship with students around knowledge.

However, the changes are often not explicitly connected to fundamental changes in the way knowledge is constructed, nor to the division of responsibility between teacher and student, the way students and teachers interact with each other around knowledge, or any of a variety of other stable conditions in the core. Hence, changes in scheduling seldom translate into changes in the fundamental conditions of teaching and learning for students and teachers. Schools, then, might be "changing" all the time — adopting this or that new structure or schedule or textbook series or tracking system — and never change in any fundamental way what teachers and students actually do when they are together in classrooms. I am not interested, except in passing, in changes that are unrelated to the core of schooling, as I have defined it above. My focus is on that narrower class of changes that directly challenge the fundamental relationships among student, teacher, and knowledge.

In some instances, such as the high-performance schools described by Linda Darling-Hammond (in press), a whole school will adopt a dramatically different form of organization, typically by starting from scratch rather than changing an existing school, and that form of organization will connect with teaching practices that are dramatically different from those traditionally associated with the core of schooling. At any given time there may be several such model schools, or exemplars of good practice, but as a proportion of the total number of schools, they are always a small fraction. In other words, it is possible to alter organization and practice in schools dramatically, but it has thus far never been possible to do it on a large scale.

The closer an innovation gets to the core of schooling, the less likely it is that it will influence teaching and learning on a large scale. The corollary of this proposition, of course, is that innovations that are distant from the core will be more readily adopted on a large scale. I will later develop some theoretical propositions about why this might be the case.

The problem of scale is a "nested" problem. That is, it exists in similar forms at different levels of the system. New practices may spring up in isolated classrooms or in clusters of classrooms within a given school, yet never move to most classrooms within that school. Likewise, whole schools may be created from scratch that embody very different forms of practice, but these schools remain a small proportion of all schools within a given district or state. And finally, some local school systems may be more successful than others at spawning classrooms and schools that embody new practices, but these local systems remain a small fraction of the total number in a state.

The problem of scale is not a problem of the general resistance or failure of schools to change. Most schools are, in fact, constantly changing — adopting new curricula, tests, and grouping practices, changing schedules, creating new mechanisms for participation in decisionmaking, adding or subtracting teaching and administrative roles, and myriad other modifications. Within this vortex of change, however, basic conceptions of knowledge, of the teacher's and the student's role in constructing knowledge, and of the role of classroom- and school-level structures in enabling student learning remain relatively static.

Nor is the problem of scale a failure of research or of systematic knowledge of what to do. At any given time, there is an abundance of ideas about how to change fundamental relationships in the core of schooling, some growing out of research and demonstration projects, some growing directly out of teaching practice. Many of these ideas are empirically tested and many are based on relatively coherent theories of student learning. We might wish that these ideas were closer to the language and thought processes of practitioners, and that they were packaged and delivered better, but there are more ideas circulating about how to change the core processes of schooling than there are schools and classrooms willing to engage them. There are always arguments among researchers and practitioners about which are the most promising ideas and conflicting evidence about their effects, but the supply of ideas is there. The problem, then, lies not in the supply of new ideas, but in the demand for them. That is, the primary problem of scale is understanding the conditions under which people working in schools seek new knowledge and actively use it to change the fundamental processes of schooling.

Why Is the Problem of Scale Important to Educational Reform?

Two central ideas of the present period of U.S. educational reform raise fundamental, recurring problems of U.S. education. One idea is that teaching and learning in U.S. schools and classrooms is, in its most common form, emotionally flat and intellectually undemanding and unengaging; this idea is captured by that famous, controversial line from *A Nation at Risk*: "a rising tide of mediocrity" (National Commission on Excellence in Education, 1983). This is a perennial critique of U.S. education, dating back to the first systematic surveys of educational practice in the early twentieth century and confirmed by contemporary evidence.[1] One recent survey characterized typical classroom practice this way:

No matter what the observational perspective, the same picture emerges. The two activities involving the most students were being lectured to and working on written assignments. . . . Students were working alone most of the time, whether individually or in groups. That is, the student listened as one member of a class being lectured, or the student worked individually on a seat assignment. . . . In effect, then, the modal classroom configurations which we observed looked like this: the teacher explaining or lecturing to the total class or a single student, occasionally asking questions requiring factual answers; the teacher, when not lecturing, observing or monitoring students working individually at their desks; students listening or appearing to listen to the teacher and occasionally responding to the teacher's questions; students working individually at their desks on reading or writing assignments; and all with little emotion, from interpersonal warmth to expressions of hostility. (Goodlad, 1984, p. 230)

Every school can point to its energetic, engaged, and effective teachers; many students can recall at least one teacher who inspired in them an engagement in learning and a love of knowledge. We regularly honor and deify these pedagogical geniuses. But these exceptions prove the rule. For the most part, we regard inspired and demanding teaching as an individual trait, much like hair color or shoe size, rather than as a professional norm. As long as we consider engaging teaching to be an individual trait, rather than a norm that might apply to any teacher, we feel no obligation to ask the broader systemic question of why more evidence of engaging teaching does not exist. The answer to this question is obvious for those who subscribe to the individual trait theory of effective teaching: few teachers are predisposed to teach in interesting ways. Alternatively, other explanations for the prevalence of dull, flat, unengaging teaching might be that we fail to select and reward teachers based on their capacity to teach in engaging ways, or that organizational conditions do not promote and sustain good teaching when it occurs.

The other central idea in the present period of reform is captured by the slogan, "all students can learn." What reformers seem to mean by this idea is that "all" students — or most students — are capable of mastering challenging academic content at high levels of understanding, and the fact that many do not is more a testimonial to how they are taught than to whether they are suited for serious academic work. In other words, the slogan is meant to be a charge to schools to make challenging learning available to a much broader segment of students than they have in the past. The touchstone for this critique is consistent evidence over the last two decades or so that U.S. students do reasonably well on lower level tests of achievement and cognitive skill, but relatively poorly on tests that require complex reasoning, inference, judgment, and transfer of knowledge from one type of problem to another (National Center for Education Statistics, 1993).

It is hard to imagine a solution to this problem of the distribution of learning among students that does not entail a solution to the first problem of increasing the frequency of engaging teaching. Clearly, getting more students to learn at higher levels has to entail some change in both the way students are taught and in the proportion of teachers who are teaching in ways that cause students to master higher level skills and knowledge. It is possible, of course, that some piece of the problem of the distribution of learning can be solved by simply getting more teachers to teach more demanding academic content, even in boring and unengaging ways, to a broader population of students. But, at some level, it seems implausible that large proportions of students presently disengaged from learning academic content at high levels of understanding will suddenly become more engaged if traditional teaching practices in the modal U.S. classroom remain the norm. Some students overcome the deadening effect of unengaging teaching through extraordinary ability, motivation, or family pressure. Other students, however, require extraordinary teaching to achieve extraordinary results. The problem of scale, then, can be seen in the context of the current reform debate as a need to change the core of schooling in ways that result in most students receiving engaging instruction in challenging academic content.

This view of educational reform, which focuses on changing fundamental conditions affecting the relationship of student, teacher, and knowledge, might be criticized as being either too narrow or too broad. My point in focusing the analysis wholly on the core of schooling is not to suggest that teaching and learning can be changed in isolation from an understanding of the contextual factors that influence children's lives. Nor is it to suggest that the object of reform should be to substitute one kind of uniformity of teaching practice for another. Rather, my point is that most educational reforms never reach, much less influence, long-standing patterns of teaching practice, and are therefore largely pointless if their intention is to improve student learning. I am interested in what is required before teaching practice can plausibly be expected to shift from its modal patterns toward more engaging and ambitious practices. These practices might be quite diverse. They might involve creative adaptations and responses to the backgrounds, interests, and preferences of students and their families. And they might be wedded in interesting ways to solutions to the multitude of problems that children face outside of school. But the fundamental problem I am interested in is why, when schools seem to be constantly changing, teaching practice changes so little, and on so small a scale.

THE EVIDENCE

The central claims of my argument, then, are that the core of schooling — defined as the standard solutions to the problem of how knowledge is defined, how teachers relate to students around knowledge, how teachers relate to other teachers in the course of their daily work, how students are grouped for purposes of instruction, how content is allocated to time, and how students' work is assessed — changes very little, except in a small proportion of schools and classrooms where the changes do not persist for very long. The changes that do tend to "stick" in schools are those that are most distant from the core.

The Progressive Period

To evaluate these claims, one would want to look at examples where reformers had ideas that challenged the core of schooling and where these ideas had time to percolate through the system and influence practice. One such example is the progressive period, perhaps the longest and most intense period of educational reform and ferment in the history of the country, running from roughly the early teens into the 1940s. What is most interesting about the progressive period, as compared with other periods of educational reform, is that its aims included explicit attempts to change pedagogy, coupled with a relatively strong intellectual and practical base. Noted intellectuals — John Dewey, in particular — developed ideas about how schools might be different, and these ideas found their way into classrooms and schools. The progressive period had a wide agenda, but one priority was an explicit attempt to change the core of schooling from a teacher-centered, fact-centered, recitation-based pedagogy to a pedagogy based on an understanding of children's thought processes and their capacities to learn and use ideas in the context of real-life problems.

In a nutshell, the progressive period produced an enormous amount of innovation, much of it in the core conditions of schooling. This innovation occurred in two broad forms. One was the creation of single schools that exemplified progressive pedagogical practices. The other was an attempt to implement progressive pedagogical practices on a large scale in public school systems. In discussing these two trends, I draw upon Lawrence Cremin's *The Transformation of the American School* (1961), which provides a detailed review of progressive education.

The single schools spawned by the progressive movement represented an astonishing range of pedagogical ideas and institutional forms, spread over the better part of four decades. In their seminal review of pedagogical reform in 1915, *Schools of To-Morrow*, John and Evelyn Dewey documented schools ranging from the Francis Parker School in Chicago to Caroline Pratt's Play School in New York, both exemplars of a single founder's vision. While these schools varied enormously in the particulars of their curricula, activities, grade and grouping structures, and teaching practices, they shared a common aim of breaking the lock of teacher-centered instruction and generating high levels of student engagement through student-initiated inquiry and group activities. Furthermore, these schools drew on a common wellspring of social criticism and prescription, exemplified in John Dewey's lecture, *The School and Society* (1899). According to Cremin, *The School and Society* focused school reform on shifting the center of gravity in education "back to the child. His natural impulses to conversation, to inquiry, to construction, and to expression were . . . seen as natural resources . . . of the educative process" (1961, pp. 118–119). Also included in this vision was the notion that school would be "recalled from isolation to the center of the struggle for a better life" (p. 119).

This dialectic between intellect and practice continued into the 1920s and 1930s, through the publication of several books: William Heard Kilpatrick's *Foundations of Method* (1925), an elaboration of Dewey's thinking about the connection between school and society; Harold Rugg and Ann Schumaker's *The Child-Centered School* (1928), another interpretive survey of pedagogical practice like Dewey's *Schools of To-Morrow*; and Kilpatrick's *The Educational Frontier* (1933), a restatement of progressive theory and philosophy written by a committee of the National Society of College Teachers of Education (Cremin, 1961, pp. 216–229). Individual reformers and major social educational institutions, such as Teachers College and the University of Chicago, designed and developed schools that exemplified the key tenets of progressive thinking.

One example illustrates the power of this connection between ideas and institutions. In 1915, Abraham Flexner, the father of modern medical education, announced his intention to develop a model school that would do for general education what the Johns Hopkins Medical School had done for medical education. He wrote an essay called "A Modern School" (1917), a blueprint for reform describing a school that embodied major changes in curriculum and teaching. It was designed to serve as a laboratory for the scientific study of educational problems. In 1917, Teachers College, in collaboration with Flexner and the General Board of Education, opened the Lincoln School, which became a model and a gathering place for progressive reformers, a major source of new curriculum materials, and the intellectual birthplace of many reformers over the next two decades. The school survived until 1948, when it was disbanded in a dispute between its parents' association and the Teachers College administration (Cremin, 1961, pp. 280–291).

The second form of innovation in the progressive period, large-scale reforms of public school systems, drew on the same intellectual base as the founding of individual schools. A notable early example was the Gary, Indiana, school district. The Gary superintendent in 1907 was William Wirt, a former student of John Dewey at the University of Chicago. Wirt initiated the "Gary Plan," which became the leading exemplar of progressive practice on a large scale in the early progressive period. The key elements of the Gary Plan were "vastly extended educational opportunity" in the form of playgrounds, libraries, laboratories, machine shops, and the like; a "platoon system" of grouping, whereby groups of children moved *en masse* between classrooms and common areas, allowing for economies in facilities; a "community" system of school organization in which skilled tradespeople from the community played a role in teaching students; and a heavily project-focused curriculum (Cremin, 1961, pp. 153–160).

In 1919, Winnetka, Illinois, hired Carleton Washburn of the San Francisco State Normal School as its superintendent. Washburn launched a reform agenda based on the idea of individually paced instruction, where the "common essentials" in the curriculum were divided into "parcels," through which each student advanced, with the guidance of teachers, at his or her own pace. As students mastered each parcel, they were examined and moved on to the next. This individualized work was combined with "self-expressive" work in which students were encouraged to develop ideas and projects on their own, as well as group projects in which students worked on issues related to the community life of the school. Over the next decade, the Winnetka plan was imitated by as many as 247 other school districts, but with a crucial modification. Most districts found the practice of tailoring the curriculum to individual students far too complex for their tastes, so they organized students into groups to which they applied the idea of differential progress. In this way, a progressive reform focused on individualized learning led to the development of what is now called tracking (Cremin, 1961, pp. 295–298).

A number of cities, including Denver and Washington, DC, undertook massive curriculum reform projects in the late 1920s and early 1930s. These efforts were extraordinarily sophisticated, even by today's relatively rarefied standards. Typically, teachers were enlisted to meet in curriculum revision committees during regular school hours, and outside experts were enlisted to work with teachers in reformulating the curriculum and in developing new teaching practices. In Denver, Superintendent Jesse Newlon convinced his school board to appropriate $35,500 for this process. Denver became a center for teacher-initiated and -developed curriculum, resulting in the development of a monograph series of course syllabi that attained a wide national circulation. The resulting curriculum changes were sustained in Denver over roughly two decades, when they were abandoned in the face of growing opposition to progressive pedagogy (Cremin, 1961, pp. 299–302; Cuban, 1984, pp. 67–83). In Washington, DC, Superintendent Frank Ballou led a pared-down version of the Denver curriculum revision model: Teacher committees chaired by administrators met after school, without the support of outside specialists. Despite these constraints, the process reached large numbers of teachers in both Black and White schools in the city's segregated system (Cuban, 1984, pp. 83–93).

Larry Cuban concluded in *How Teachers Taught: Constancy and Change in American Classrooms, 1890–1980*, his study of large-scale reforms of curriculum and pedagogy in the late-progressive period, that progressive practices, defined as movement away from teacher-centered and toward student-centered pedagogy, "seldom appeared in more than one-fourth of the classrooms in any district that systematically tried to install these varied elements" (Cuban, 1984, p. 135). Even in settings where teachers made a conscious effort to incorporate progressive practices, the result was more often than not a hybrid of traditional and progressive, in which the major elements of the traditional core of instruction were largely undisturbed:

> The dominant pattern of instruction, allowing for substantial spread of these hybrid progressive practices, remained teacher centered. Elementary

and secondary teachers persisted in teaching from the front of the room, deciding what was to be learned, in what manner, and under what conditions. The primary means of grouping for instruction was the entire class. The major daily classroom activities continued with a teacher telling, explaining, and questioning students while the students listened, answered, read, and wrote. Seatwork or supervised study was an extension of these activities. (Cuban, 1984, p. 137)

The fate of the progressive movement has been well documented. As the language of progressivism began to permeate educational talk, if not practice, the movement began to lose its intellectual edge and to drift into a series of empty clichés, the most extreme of which was life adjustment education. Opposition to progressivism, which had been building through the twenties, came to a crescendo in the forties. The movement was increasingly portrayed by a skeptical public and press in terms of its most extreme manifestations — watered-down content, a focus on children's psychological adjustment at the expense of learning, and a preoccupation with self-expression rather than learning. Abraham Flexner, looking back on his experiences as a moderate progressive, observed that "there is something queer about the genus 'educator'; the loftiest are not immune. I think the cause must lie in their isolation from the rough and tumble contacts with all manner of men. They lose their sense of reality" (Cremin, 1961, p. 160).

The particular structure that educational reform took in the progressive period, though, is deeply rooted in American institutions and persists to this day. First, contrary to much received wisdom, intellectuals found ways to express their ideas about how education could be different in the form of real schools with structures and practices that were radically different from existing schools. There was a direct and vital connection between ideas and practice, a connection that persists up to the present, though in a much diluted form. But this connection took the institutional form of single schools, each an isolated island of practice, connected by a loosely defined intellectual agenda that made few demands for conformity, and each a particular, precious, and exotic specimen of a larger genus. So the most vital and direct connections between ideas and practice were deliberately institutionalized as separate, independent entities, incapable of and uninterested in forming replicates of themselves or of pursuing a broader institutional reform agenda.[2] A few exceptions, like the Lincoln School, were deliberately designed to influence educational practice on a larger scale, but the exact means by which that was to happen were quite vague. For the most part, progressive reformers believed that good ideas would travel, of their own volition, into U.S. classrooms and schools.

Second, where public systems did attempt to change pedagogical practice on a large scale, often using techniques that would be considered sophisticated by today's standards, they succeeded in changing practice in only a small fraction of classrooms, and then not necessarily in a sustained way over time. Sometimes, as in the case of Washburn's strategy of individualizing instruction in Winnetka, as the reforms moved from one district to another they became sinister caricatures of the original. The district-level reforms produced impressive tangible products, mostly in the form of new curriculum materials that would circulate within and outside the originating districts. The connection to classroom practice, however, was weak. Larry Cuban likens this kind of reform to a hurricane at sea — "storm-tossed waves on the ocean surface, turbulent water a fathom down, and calm on the ocean floor" (Cuban, 1984, p. 237).

Third, the very successes of progressive reformers became their biggest liabilities as the inevitable political opposition formed. Rather than persist in Dewey's original agenda of influencing public discourse about the nature of education and its relation to society through open public discussion, debate, and inquiry, the more militant progressives became increasingly like true believers in a particular version of the faith and increasingly isolated from public scrutiny and discourse. In this way, the developers of progressive pedagogy became increasingly isolated from the public mainstream and increasingly vulnerable to attack from traditionalists.

The pattern that emerges from the progressive period, then, is one where the intellectual and practical energies of serious reformers tended to turn inward, toward the creation of exemplary settings — classrooms or schools — that embodied their best ideas of practice, producing an impressive and attractive array of isolated examples of what practice *could* look like. At the same time, those actors with an interest in what would now be called systemic change focused on developing the tangible, visible, and material products of reform — plans, processes, curricula, materials — and focused much less, if at all, on the less tangible problem of what might cause a teacher to teach in new ways, if the materials and support were available to do so. These two forces produced the central dilemma of educational reform: We can produce many examples of how educational practice could look different, but we can produce few, if any, examples of large numbers of teachers engaging in these practices in large-scale institutions designed to deliver education to most children.

Large-Scale Curriculum Development Projects

Another, more recent body of evidence on these points comes from large-scale curriculum reforms of the 1950s and 1960s in the United States, which were funded by the National Science Foundation (NSF). In their fundamental structure, these reforms were quite similar to the progressive reforms, although much more tightly focused on content. The central idea of these curriculum reforms was that learning in school should resemble, much more than it usually does, the actual processes by which human beings come to understand their environment, culture, and social settings. That is, if students are studying mathematics, science, or social science, they should actually engage in activities similar to those of serious practitioners of these disciplines and, in the process, discover not only the knowledge of the subject, but also the thought processes and methods of inquiry by which that knowledge is constructed. This view suggested that construction of new curriculum for schools should proceed by bringing the best researchers in the various subjects together with school teachers, and using the expertise of both groups to devise new conceptions of content and new strategies for teaching it. The earliest of these projects was the Physical Sciences Study Committee's (PSSC) high school physics curriculum, begun in 1956. Another of these was the Biological Sciences Curriculum Study (BSCS), begun in 1958. A third was Man: A Course of Study (MACOS), an ambitious social science curriculum development project, which began in 1959, but only received its first substantial funding from the Ford Foundation in 1962 and NSF support for teacher training in 1969 (Dow, 1991; Elmore, 1993; Grobman, 1969; Marsh, 1964). These were among the largest and most ambitious of the curriculum reform projects, but by no means the only ones.

From the beginning, these curriculum reformers were clear that they aimed to change the core of U.S. schooling, and their aspirations were not fundamentally different from the early progressives. They envisioned teachers becoming coaches and coinvestigators with students into the basic phenomena of the physical, biological, and social sciences. Students' work was to focus heavily on experimentation, inquiry, and study of original sources. The notion of the textbook as the repository of conventional knowledge was to be discarded, and in its place teachers were to use carefully developed course materials and experimental apparatus that were keyed to the big ideas in the areas under study. The object of study was not the assimilation of facts, but learning the methods and concepts of scientific inquiry by doing science in the same way that practitioners of science would do it.

The curriculum development projects grew out of the initiatives of university professors operating from the belief that they could improve the quality of incoming university students by improving the secondary school curriculum. Hence, university professors tended to dominate the curriculum development process, often to the detriment of relations with the teachers and school administrators who were expected to adopt the curricula once they were developed and tested in sample sites. The projects succeeded to varying degrees in engaging actual teachers in the development process, as opposed to simply having teachers field-test lessons that had already been developed.

Teachers were engaged in one way or another at the developmental stage in all projects, but were not always codevelopers. In PSSC, a few teachers judged to be talented enough to engage the MIT professors involved in the project were part of the development process; the main involvement of teachers came at the field-testing stage, but their feedback proved to be too voluminous to accommodate systematically in the final product (Marsh, 1964). In MACOS, one school in the Boston area was a summer test site, and teachers were engaged in the curriculum project relatively early in the process of development. Later versions of the curriculum were extensively tested and marketed in schools throughout the country (Dow, 1991).

By far the most ambitious and systematic involvement of teachers as co-developers was in BSCS. BSCS was designed to produce three distinct versions of a secondary biology curriculum (biochemical, ecological, and cellular), so that schools and teachers could have a choice of which approach to use. The development process was organized into three distinct teams, each composed of equal numbers of university professors and high school biology teachers. Lessons or units were developed by a pair composed of one professor and one secondary teacher, and each of these units was reviewed and critiqued by another team composed of equal partners. After the curriculum was developed, the teachers who participated in development were drafted to run study groups of teachers using the curriculum units during the school year, and the results of these study groups were fed back into the development process. Interestingly, once the curriculum was developed, NSF abandoned funding for the teacher study groups. NSF's rationale was that the teachers had accomplished their development task, but this cut-off effectively eliminated the teacher study groups, potentially the most powerful device for changing teaching practice (Elmore, 1993; Grobman, 1969).

Evaluations of the NSF-sponsored curriculum development projects generally conclude that their effects were broad but shallow. Hundreds of thousands of teachers and curriculum directors were trained in summer institutes. Tens of thousands of curriculum units were disseminated. Millions of students were exposed to at least some product or by-product of the various projects. In a few schools and school systems, teachers and administrators made concerted efforts to transform curriculum and teaching in accord with the new ideas, but in most instances the results looked like what Cuban (1984) found in his study of progressive teaching practices: A weak, diluted, hybrid form emerged in some settings in which new curricula were shoehorned into old practices, and, in most secondary classrooms, the curricula had no impact on teaching and learning at all. While the curriculum development projects produced valuable materials that are still a resource to many teachers and shaped peoples' conceptions of the possibilities of secondary science curriculum, their tangible impact on the core of U.S. schooling has been negligible (Elmore, 1993; Stake & Easely, 1978).

Most academic critics agree that the curriculum development projects embodied a naive, discredited, and badly conceived model of how to influence teaching practice. The model, if there was one, was that "good" curriculum and teaching practice were self-explanatory and self-implementing. Once teachers and school administrators recognized the clearly superior ideas embodied in the new curricula, they would simply switch from traditional textbooks to the new materials and change long-standing practices in order to improve their teaching and the chances of their students succeeding in school.

What this model overlooked, however, was the complex process by which local curricular decisions get made, the entrenched and institutionalized political and commercial relationships that support existing textbook-driven curricula, the weak incentives operating on teachers to change their practices in their daily work routines, and the extraordinary costs of making large-scale, long-standing changes of a fundamental kind in how knowledge is constructed in classrooms. In the few instances where the advocates for the curriculum development projects appeared to be on the verge of discovering a way to change practice on a large scale — as in the BSCS teacher study groups, for example — they failed to discern the significance of what they were doing because they saw themselves as developers of new ideas about teaching and not as institution-changing actors.

The structural pattern that emerges from the large-scale curriculum development projects is strikingly similar to that of the progressive period. First, the ideas were powerful and engaging, and they found their way into tangible materials and into practice in a few settings. In this sense, the projects were a remarkable achievement in the social organization of knowledge, pulling the country's most sophisticated thinkers into the orbit of public education and putting them to work on the problem of what students should know and be able to do. Second, the curriculum developers proved to be inept and naive in their grasp of the individual and institutional issues of change associated with their reforms. They assumed that a "good" product would travel into U.S. classrooms on the basis of its merit, without regard to the complex institutional and individual factors that might constrain its ability to do so. Third, their biggest successes were, in a sense, also their biggest failures. Those few teachers who became accomplished teachers of PSSC physics, BSCS biology, or MACOS approaches to social studies only served to confirm what most educators think about talent in the classroom. A few have it, but most do not. A few have the extraordinary energy, commitment, and native ability required to change their practice in some fundamental way; most others do not. The existence of exemplars, without some way of capitalizing on their talents, only reinforces the notion that ambitious teaching is an individual trait, not a professional expectation.

What Changes?

Critiques of this argument posit that U.S. schools have changed in fundamental ways over the last one hundred years, and that focusing on the fate of what I have characterized as "good" classroom practice gives a biased picture. To be sure, schools have changed massively over the last century. David Cohen argues, for example, that in the critical period of the early twentieth century, when the secondary school population increased four-fold in three decades, massive institutional changes were necessary to accommodate newly arrived students. Larger, more complex schools, a more differentiated curriculum, and grading and retention practices designed to hold adolescents out of the labor force were just a few of those changes (Powell, Farrar, & Cohen, 1985). Vocational education emerged in the post–World War I era as a mechanism to bind schools more closely to the economy and to provide a more differentiated curriculum for a diverse student body. Kindergartens emerged on a large scale in the 1940s and 1950s, extending the period of life children were in school and altering the relationship between the family and school in important ways. The equity-based reforms of the 1960s and 1970s revealed the limits of earlier approaches to equality of opportunity, and new programs addressed the needs of students from disadvantaged backgrounds, many with physical and learning problems, and who spoke native languages other than English. In brief, this critique states that we face a much different educational system now than we did in the early decades of the twentieth century, and that these changes have surely had a significant impact on how teachers teach and how students learn.

I am inclined to agree with those who take an institutional perspective on educational change. In a nutshell, this argument states that it is possible, indeed practically imperative, for institutions to learn to change massively in their surface structures while at the same time changing little at their core (Cuban, 1990; March & Olsen, 1989; Meyer & Rowan, 1978; Tyack & Cuban, 1995; Tyack & Tobin, 1994). Institutions use their structures to buffer and assimilate the changing demands of a political and social order that is constantly in flux — they add new programs, they develop highly visible initiatives that respond to prevailing opinions in the community, they open new units in the organization to accommodate new clients, they mobilize and organize public opinion by creating new governance structures. But the gap between these institutional structures and the core patterns of schooling is slippery and elusive: The core of schooling remains relatively stable in the face of often massive changes in the structure around it. Schools legitimize themselves with their various conflicting publics by constantly changing external structures and processes, but shield their workers from any fundamental impact of these changes by leaving the core intact. This accounts for the resilience of practice within the context of constant institutional change.

THE ROLE OF INCENTIVES

Nested within this broad framework of institutional and political issues is a more specific problem of incentives that reforms need to address in order to get at the problem of scale. Institutional structures influence the behavior of individuals in part through incentives. The institution and its political context help set the values and rewards that individuals respond to within their daily work life. But individual values are also important. As David Cohen (1995) cogently argues in his discussion of rewards for teacher performance, incentives mobilize individual values; that is, individual values determine to some degree what the institution can elicit with incentives. For example, if teachers or students do not value student academic performance, do not see the relationship between academic performance and personal objectives, or do not believe it is possible to change student performance, then it is hard to use incentives to motivate them to action that would improve performance.

Thus, individual acts like the practice of teaching in complex institutional settings emanate both from incentives that operate on the individual and the individual's willingness to recognize and respond to these incentives as legitimate. Individual actions are also a product of the knowledge and the competence that the individual possesses. As Michael Fullan has argued, schools routinely undertake reforms for which they have neither the institutional nor the individual competence, and they resolve this problem by trivializing the reforms, changing the language they use, and modifying superficial structures around the practice, but without changing the practice itself (Fullan, 1982; Fullan & Miles, 1992). Individuals are embedded in institutional structures that provide them with incentives to act in certain ways, and they respond to these incentives by testing them against their values and their competence.

One way of thinking about the aforementioned evidence is that it demonstrates a massive failure of schools to harness their institutional incentives to the improvement of practice. I think this failure is rooted not only in the design of the institutions, but also in a deep cultural norm about teaching that I referred to earlier: that successful teaching is an individual trait rather than a set of learned professional competencies acquired over the course of career.

Both the progressive reformers and the curriculum reforms of the 1950s and 1960s focused on connecting powerful ideas to practice, developing exemplars of good practice and attracting true believers. These efforts largely failed, often in very interesting and instructive ways, to translate their ideas into broad-scale changes in practice. A very large incentive problem is buried in this strategy: Reform strategies of this kind rely on the intrinsic motivation of individuals with particular values and competencies — and a particular orientation toward the outside world — to develop and implement reforms in schools.

These intrinsically motivated individuals are typically highly engaged in the world outside of their workplace, and hence come in contact with the opportunities presented by new practices. They are usually willing to invest large amounts of their own time in learning new ways to think about their practice and in the messy and time-consuming work of getting others to cooperate in changing their practice. And, perhaps most importantly, they see their own practice in a broader social context, and see certain parts of that social context as having authority over how they practice. Progressive teachers and school-builders, for example, saw themselves as participants in a broad movement for social reform and were willing to evaluate their own work in terms of its consistency with the goals of that reform (Tyack & Hansot, 1982). Some teachers who were directly involved in the curriculum reform projects formed an identity as science or math teachers affiliated with professional organizations that had authority and influence over their practice.

The problem of incentives is that these individuals are typically a small proportion of the total population of teachers. The demands required by this kind of ambitious, challenging, and time-consuming work seems at best formidable, and at worst hopelessly demanding. Friedrich Engels once said that the problem with socialism is that it spoils too many good evenings at home, and one could say the same about the reform of educational practice.

Ambitious and challenging practice in classrooms thus occurs roughly in proportion to the number of teachers who are intrinsically motivated to question their practice on a fundamental level and look to outside models to improve teaching and learning. The circumstantial evidence suggests that, at the peak of reform periods, this proportion of teachers is roughly 25 percent of the total population, and that it can decrease to considerably less than that if the general climate for reform is weak (Cuban, 1990). Our most successful and ambitious strategies of reform, then, embody incentive structures that can mobilize, at most, roughly one-fourth of the total population of teachers.

Given this interpretation of the evidence, then, it is possible to see the enormous power of a cultural norm that describes successful teaching as an individual attribute rather than a body of deliberately acquired professional knowledge and skills. If what a teacher does is based wholly or largely on individual traits, then it is highly unlikely that the incentive structures of schools could alter the proportion of teachers willing to engage in ambitious practice, other than changing the composition of the teaching force.

It is also possible to see the perverse incentives buried in typical reform strategies. The first step serious reformers typically take involves gathering up the faithful and concentrating them in one place in order to form a cohesive community of like-minded practitioners. In the case of the progressives, reformers started schools that embodied their ideas; in the case of the curriculum projects, reformers identified early adopters of their new curricula as exemplars of success. This strategy immediately isolates the teachers who are most likely to change from those who are least likely to embrace reform. This dynamic creates a social barrier between the two, virtually guaranteeing that the former will not grow in number and the latter will continue to believe that exemplary teaching requires extraordinary resources in an exceptional environment.

One can see vestiges of this perverse incentive structure in the design of current school reform movements. These reforms typically begin with a few teachers in a building and nurture a distinctive identity among those teachers, or they construct a new school from scratch and recruit teachers who are highly motivated to join the faculty. Both strategies guarantee the isolation of the small fraction of teachers who are willing to engage in change from the majority who find it an intimidating and threatening prospect, and are likely to instigate a conflict between the two groups of teachers that renders the scaling up of this reform highly unlikely.

Without some fundamental change in the incentive structure under which schools and teachers operate, we will continue more or less indefinitely to repeat the experience of the progressives and the curriculum reformers. Like our predecessors, we will design reforms that appeal to the intrinsic values and competencies of a relatively small proportion of the teaching force. We will gather these teachers together in ways that cut them off from contact and connection with those who find ambitious teaching intimidating and unfeasible. We will demonstrate that powerful ideas can be harnessed to changes in practice in a small fraction of settings, but continue to fail in moving those practices beyond the group of teachers who are intrinsically motivated and competent to engage in them.

WORKING ON THE PROBLEM OF SCALE

What might be done to change this self-reinforcing incentive structure? Probably the first step is to acknowledge that social problems of this complexity are not amenable to quick, comprehensive, rational solutions. Fundamental changes in patterns of incentives occur not by engaging in ambitious, discontinuous reforms, but rather by pushing hard in a few strategic places in the system of relations surrounding the problem, and then carefully observing the results. My recommendations will be of this sort.

Furthermore, it seems important to continue to do what has yielded success in the past and to continue to do it with increasing sophistication. I have argued that the most successful part of the progressive and curriculum reform strategies was the creation of powerful connections between big ideas with large social implications and the micro-world of teaching practice. The progressives succeeded in creating versions of educational reform that both exemplified progressive ideals and embodied concrete changes in the core of schooling. Likewise, the curriculum reformers succeeded in harnessing the talent of the scientific elite to the challenge of secondary school curriculum and teaching.

This connection between the big ideas and the fine grain of practice in the core of schooling is a fundamental precondition for any change in practice. Capacity to make these connections waxes and wanes, and probably depends too heavily on the idiosyncrasies of particular individuals with a particular scientific or ideological ax to grind. One could imagine doing a much better job of institutionalizing the connection between big ideas and teaching practice. Examples might include routine major national curriculum reviews composed of groups with equal numbers of school teachers and university researchers, or a national curriculum renewal agenda that targeted particular parts of teaching and curriculum for renewal on a regular cycle. The more basic point, however, is that preserving the connection between big ideas and teaching practice, embodied in earlier reform strategies, is an essential element in tackling the problem of scale.

With these ideas as context, I offer four main proposals for how to begin to tackle the problem of scale. Each grows out of an earlier line of analysis in this article, and each embodies an argument about how incentives should be realigned to tackle the problem of scale.

1. Develop strong external normative structures for practice.

The key flaw in earlier attempts at large-scale reform was to rely almost exclusively on the intrinsic commitment of talented and highly motivated teachers to carry the burden of reform. Coupled with strong cultural norms about good teaching being an individual trait, this strategy virtually guarantees that good practice will stay with those who learn and will not travel to those who are less predisposed to learn. One promising approach, then, is to create strong professional and social normative structures for good teaching practice that are external to individual teachers and their immediate working environment, and to provide a basis for evaluating how many teachers are approximating good practice at what level of competence.

I use the concept of external normative structures, rather than a term like standards, because I think these structures should be diverse and need to be constructed on different bases of authority in order to be useful in influencing teaching practice. The category of external structures could include formal statements of good practice, such as content and performance standards developed by professional bodies like the National Council of Teachers of Mathematics. External structures might also include alternative credentialling systems, such as the National Board for Professional Teaching Standards.

But strong external structures could also include less imposing and more informal ways of communicating norms of good practice. For example, curriculum units designed to demonstrate more advanced forms of practice could be accompanied by videotapes of teachers engaging in these practices and then disseminated through teacher organizations. These external normative structures can be hooked to internal systems of rewards for teachers — salary increments for staff development related to changes in practice, release time to work on curriculum or performance standards, time to develop curriculum units that embody particular approaches to teaching, or opportunities to engage in demonstration teaching. There is no particular requirement for unanimity, consistency, or "alignment" among these various external structures, only that they embody well-developed notions of what it means for teachers to teach and students to learn at high levels of competency in a given area. The important feature of these structures is not their unanimity or consistency, which is probably illusory anyway, but the fact that the structures are external to the world in which teachers work, they form teachers' ideas about practice, and they carry some form of professional authority.

Why is the existence of external norms important? Because it institutionalizes the idea that professionals are responsible for looking outward at challenging conceptions of practice, in addition to looking inward at their values and competencies. Good teaching becomes a matter for public debate and disagreement, for serious reflection and discourse, for positive and negative feedback about one's own practices. Over time, as this predisposition to look outward becomes more routinized and ingrained, trait theories of teaching competence should diminish. Teachers would begin increasingly to think of themselves as operating in a web of professional relations that influence their

299

daily decisions, rather than as solo practitioners inventing practice out of their personalities, prior experiences, and assessments of their own strengths and weaknesses. Without external normative structures, teachers have no incentive to think of their practice as anything other than a bundle of traits. The existence of strong external norms also has the effect of legitimating the proportion of teachers in any system who draw their ideas about teaching from a professional community, and who compare themselves against a standard external to their school or community. External norms give visibility and status to those who exemplify them.

2. Develop organizational structures that intensify and focus, rather than dissipate and scatter, intrinsic motivation to engage in challenging practice.

The good news about existing reform strategies is that they tend to galvanize commitment among the already motivated by concentrating them in small groups of true believers who reinforce each other. The bad news is that these small groups of self-selected reformers apparently seldom influence their peers. This conclusion suggests that structures should, at a minimum, create diversity among the energetic, already committed reformers and the skeptical and timid. But it also suggests that the unit of work in an organization that wants to change its teaching practice should be small enough so that members can exercise real influence over each others' practice. Certain types of structures are more likely than others to intensify and focus norms of good practice: organizations in which face-to-face relationships dominate impersonal, bureaucratic ones; organizations in which people routinely interact around common problems of practice; and organizations that focus on the results of their work for students, rather than on the working conditions of professionals. These features can be incorporated into organizations, as well as into the composition of their memberships.

Heather Lewis, an accomplished practitioner of school change with the Center for Collaborative Education in New York City, has argued that we will solve the problem of scaling-up by scaling-down.[3] By this, I think she means that more ambitious teaching practice is more likely to occur in smaller schools, where adults are more likely to work collaboratively and take common responsibility for students. Teachers in schools with a tighter sense of mutual commitment, which arguably comes with smaller size, are more likely to exert influence on each other around norms of good practice than are teachers in anonymous organizations in which bureaucratic controls are the predominant mechanism of influence.

The problem is that there is so little structural variation in U.S. public education that we have little conception of what kinds of structures would have this intensifying and focusing effect. The first job of structural reform should be to create more variation in structure — more small schools, more schools organized into smaller sub-units, more structures that create stronger group norms inside larger schools, more ways of connecting adventurous teachers with their less ambitious and reflective colleagues — but not structures that isolate the true believers from the skeptical and the timid. In the absence of such structures, there will be no connective tissue to bind teachers together in a relationship of mutual obligation and force them to sort out issues of practice. Organizational forms that intensify and focus group norms, without nesting them in some system of external norms of good practice, will simply perpetuate whatever the prevailing conventional wisdom about practice happens to be in a given school.

3. Create intentional processes for reproduction of successes.

One of the major lessons from past large-scale reforms is their astounding naiveté about how to get their successes to move from one setting to another. The progressives seemed to think that a few good exemplars and a few energetic superintendents pursuing system-wide strategies of reform would ignite a conflagration that would consume all of U.S. education. If any social movement had the possibility of doing that, it was the progressive movement, since it had, at least initially, a high degree of focus, a steady supply of serious intellectual capital, and an infrastructure of committed reformers. But it did not succeed at influencing more than a small fraction of schools and classrooms. The curriculum reformers thought that good curriculum models would create their own demand, an astoundingly naive idea in retrospect, given what we know about the limits within which teachers work, the complex webs of institutional and political relationships that surround curriculum decisions, and the weak incentives for teachers to pay attention to external ideas about teaching practice.

This is not so much a failure of a theory of how to reproduce success as the absence of a practical theory that takes account of the institutional complexities that operate on changes in practice. I am skeptical that such a theory will emerge without serious experimentation, since I know of no clear a priori basis on which to construct such a theory. I suggest five theories that might serve as the basis for experimentation with processes designed to get exemplary practices to scale.

Incremental Growth. The usual way of thinking about increases in scale in social systems is incremental growth. For example, according to the incremental growth theory, the proportion of teachers teaching in a particular way would increase by some modest constant each year, until the proportion approached 100 percent. This model implies a fixed capacity for training a given number of teachers per year in an organization.

The problems with this model are not difficult to identify. The idea that new practice "takes" after a teacher has been trained is highly suspect. The notion that a fixed number of teachers could be trained to teach in a given way by circulating them through a training experience seems implausible, although it is probably the way most training programs are designed. Teaching practice is unlikely to change as a result of exposure to training, unless that training also brings with it some kind of external normative structure, a network of social relationships that personalize that structure, and supports interaction around problems of practice. The incremental model, if it is to work, needs a different kind of specification, which I will call the cumulative model.

Cumulative Growth. The cumulative growth model suggests that "getting to scale" is a slower, less linear process than that described by the incremental model. It involves not only creating interventions that expose teachers to new practices, but also monitoring the effects of these interventions on teaching practice. When necessary, processes may be created to compensate for the weaknesses of initial effects. Cumulative growth not only adds an increment of practitioners who are exposed to a new practice each year, but also involves a backlog of practitioners from previous years who may or may not have responded to past training. This problem requires a more complex solution than simply continuing to provide exposure to new practice at a given rate. It might require, for example, the creation of professional networks to support the practice of teachers who are in the process of changing their practice, or connecting the more advanced with the less advanced through some sort of mentoring scheme.

Discontinuous Growth. Another possibility is a sharply increasing, or discontinuous, growth model. This could occur through a process like a chain letter, in which an initial group of teachers learned a new kind of practice, and each member of that group worked with another group, and so on: The rate of growth might go, for example, from x, to 10x, to 100x, to 1000x, etc.

This discontinuous growth model shares the same problem with the incremental growth model, but on a larger scale. As the number of teachers exposed to new practices increases, so too does the backlog of teachers for whom the initial intervention was inadequate, eventually reaching the point at which this accumulation of teachers overwhelms the system. It also seems likely that the discontinuous growth model would create serious quality control problems. As growth accelerates, it becomes more and more difficult to distinguish between teachers who are accomplished practitioners of new ways of teaching, and those who are accomplished at making it appear as though they have mastered new ways of teaching.

In all the examples of growth models so far, teachers operate in a system of relationships that provides training and support, but not as members of organizations called schools. In addition to these three models that construct training and support around teachers, two additional models treat teachers as practitioners working in schools.

Unbalanced Growth. One of these models is the unbalanced growth model. This extends and modifies the standard model of innovation in education: collecting true believers in a few settings. Whereas the standard model socially isolates true believers from everyone else, virtually guaranteeing that new practices do not spread, versions of the unbalanced growth model correct for these deficiencies. A version of unbalanced growth might involve concentrating a critical mass of high-performing teachers in a few schools, with an explicit charge to develop each other's capacities to teach in new ways. The growth of new practice would be "unbalanced" initially because some schools would be deliberately constructed to bring like-minded practitioners together to develop their skills. Such schools might be called "pioneer" schools or "leading edge" schools to communicate that they are designed to serve as places where new practices are developed, nurtured, and taught to an ever-increasing number of practitioners. Over time, these schools would be deliberately staffed with larger proportions of less accomplished practitioners and teachers not yet introduced to new models of practice. The competencies developed in the high-performing organizations would then socialize new teachers into the norms of good practice.

The main problem with this model is that it goes against the grain of existing personnel practices in most school systems. Teaching assignments are typically made through collectively bargained seniority and/or principal entrepreneurship, rather than on the basis of a systematic interest in using schools as places to socialize teachers to new practice. Younger teachers are typically assigned to schools with the largest proportions of difficult-to-teach children, and spend their careers working their way into more desirable assignments. Principals who understand and have mastered the assignment system often use it to gather teachers with whom they prefer to work. In order for the unbalanced growth model to work, a school system would have to devise some deliberate strategy for placing teachers in settings where they would be most likely to develop new skills. Teachers, likewise, would have to be willing to work in settings where they could learn to develop their practice as part of their professional responsibility.

Cell Division, or Reproduction. The other model of growth that treats teachers as practitioners working in schools is the cell division, or reproduction, model. This model works from the analogy of reproductive biology. Rather than trying to change teaching practice by influencing the flow of teachers through schools, as in the unbalanced growth model, the cell division model involves systematically increasing the number and proportion of schools characterized by distinctive pedagogical practices.

The cell division model works by first creating a number of settings in which exemplary practitioners are concentrated and allowed to develop new approaches to teaching practice. Then, on a more or less predictable schedule, a number of these practitioners are asked to form another school, using the "genetic material" of their own knowledge and understanding to recruit a new cadre of teachers whom they educate to a new set of expectations about practice. Over time, several such schools would surface with strong communities of teachers invested in particular approaches to teaching.[4]

The reproduction model elicits more systematic thinking about what constitutes evidence of the "spread" of good teaching practice. Given the slipperiness of attempts to "replicate" successful programs or practices from one setting to another, the idea of getting to scale should not be equated with the exact replication of practices that work in one setting to others. For example, when we reproduce as human beings, children are not identical replicates of parents; rather, each child is a new human being with a distinctive personality that may bear a family resemblance to the mother and father. Children from the same family differ quite dramatically from each other, even though they may share certain common traits. The reproduction model broadens notions of evidence by allowing for the dissemination of good teaching practices with "family resemblances" in different settings. It causes us to look at the fundamental process by which practices are chosen for reproduction, while others are bypassed or significantly modified. It also prompts us to reproduce "family resemblances" in such a way as to have a meaningful impact on practice rather than merely promoting assimilation of symbols that do not go to the core.

These alternative models of growth each embody an explicit practical theory of how to propagate or reproduce practice. They also have a transparent logic that can be understood and adapted by others for use in other settings. More such theories, and more documented examples of how they work in use, should help in understanding how to get to scale with good educational practice.

4. Create structures that promote learning of new practices and incentive systems that support them.

Reformers typically make very heroic and unrealistic assumptions about what ordinary human beings can do, and they generalize these assumptions to a wide population of teachers. Cremin (1961) made the following observation about progressive education:

> From the beginning progressivism cast the teacher in an almost impossible role: [she] was to be an artist of consummate skill, properly knowledgeable in [her] field, meticulously trained in the science of pedagogy, and thoroughly imbued with a burning zeal for social improvement. It need hardly be said that here as elsewhere . . . the gap between the real and the ideal was appalling. (p. 168)

Likewise, the curriculum reformers appeared to assume that teachers, given the existence of clearly superior content, would simply use the new curricula and learn what was needed in order to teach differently. Missing from this view is an explicit model of how teachers engage in intentional learning about new ways to teach. According to Fullan and Miles (1992), "change involves learning and . . . all change involves coming to understand and to be good at something new" (p. 749). While knowledge is not deep on this subject, the following seem plausible: teachers are more likely to learn from direct observation of practice and trial and error in their own classrooms than

304

they are from abstract descriptions of new teaching; changing teaching practice even for committed teachers, takes a long time, and several cycles of trial and error; teachers have to feel that there is some compelling reason for them to practice differently, with the best direct evidence being that students learn better; and teachers need feedback from sources they trust about whether students are actually learning what they are taught.

These conditions accompany the learning of any new, complicated practice. Yet, reform efforts seldom, if ever, incorporate these conditions. Teachers are often tossed headlong into discussion groups to work out the classroom logistics of implementing a new curriculum. They are encouraged to develop model lessons as a group activity and then sent back to their classrooms to implement them as solo practitioners. Teachers are seldom asked to judge if this new curriculum translates well into concrete actions in the classroom, nor are they often asked to participate as codesigners of the ideas in the first place. The feedback teachers receive on the effects of their practice usually comes in the form of generalized test scores that have no relationship to the specific objectives of the new practice. In other words, the conditions under which teachers are asked to engage in new practices bear no relationship whatsoever to the conditions required for learning how to implement complex and new practices with success. Why would anyone want to change their practice under such conditions?

A basic prerequisite for tackling the problem of scale, then, is to insist that reforms that purport to change practice embody an explicit theory about how human beings learn to do things differently. Presently, there are few, if any, well-developed theories that meet this requirement, although I have sketched out a few above. Furthermore, these theories have to make sense at the individual and at the organizational level. That is, if you ask teachers to change the way they deal with students and to relate to their colleagues differently, the incentives that operate at the organizational level have to reinforce and promote those behaviors. Encouragement and support, access to special knowledge, time to focus on the requirements of the new task, time to observe others doing it — all suggest ways in which the environment of incentives in the organization comes to reflect the requirements of learning.

These four basic principles constitute departures from previous strategies of broad-scale reform, and they address fundamental problems of previous strategies. It is unlikely that teachers or schools will respond to the emergence of new practices any differently than they have in the past if those practices are not legitimated by norms that are external to the environment in which they work every day. It is unlikely that teachers who are not intrinsically motivated to engage in hard, uncertain work will learn to do so in large, anonymous organizations that do not intensify personal commitments and responsibilities. It is unlikely that successful practices will spontaneously reproduce themselves just because they are successful, in the absence of structures and processes based on explicit theories about how reproduction occurs. And it is unlikely that teachers will be successful at learning new practices if the organizations in which they work do not embody some explicit learning theory in the way they design work and reward people.

Each of these principles presents a formidable agenda for research and practice. The magnitude of the task suggests that we should not expect to see immediate large-scale adoption of promising new practices. It also suggests that progress will come from an explicit acknowledgment that the problems of scale are deeply rooted in the incentives and cultural norms of the institutions, and cannot be fixed with simple policy shifts or exhortations from people with money. The issue of getting to scale with good educational practice requires nothing less than deliberately creating and reproducing alternatives to the existing flawed institutional arrangements and incentives structures.

NOTES

1. See, for example, Lawrence Cremin's (1961, p. 157) reference to Randolf Bourne's critique of the "artificiality and dullness" of U.S. classrooms, published in *The New Republic* in 1915.
2. Dewey's own ambivalence about the connection between the exemplary practices developed in laboratory schools and the broader world of practice can be seen in his reflections on the University of Chicago Lab School:

    As it is not the primary function of a laboratory to devise ways and means that can at once be put to practical use, so it is not the primary purpose of this school to devise methods with reference to their direct application in the graded school system. It is the function of some schools to provide better teachers according to present standards; it is the function of others to create new standards and ideals and thus to lead to a gradual change in conditions. (quoted in Cremin, 1961, p. 290n)

3. Remarks at Project Atlas Forum on Getting to Scale, April 3, 1995.
4. This is, in fact, the model used by the Central Park East Elementary School in New York City to create two other elementary schools to serve parents and children who could not be accommodated in the original school.

REFERENCES

Cohen, D. (1988). Teaching practice: Plus que ça change . . . In P. Jackson (Ed.), *Contribution to educational change: Perspectives on research and practice* (pp. 27–84). Berkeley, CA: McCutcheon.

Cohen, D. (1995). Rewarding teachers for student performance. In S. Fuhrman & J. O'Day (Eds.), *Rewards and reforms: Creating educational incentives that work*. San Francisco: Jossey-Bass.

Cremin, L. (1961). *The transformation of the American school*. New York: Knopf.

Cuban, L. (1984.) *How teachers taught: Constancy and change in American classrooms, 1890–1980*. New York: Longman.

Cuban, L. (1990). Reforming again, again, and again. *Educational Researcher, 19*(1), 3–13.

Darling-Hammond, L. (forthcoming). Reward and reform: Creating educational incentives that work. In S. Fuhrman & J. O'Day (Eds.), *Restructuring schools for high performance*. San Francisco: Jossey-Bass.

Dewey, J. (1899). *The school and society*. Chicago: University of Chicago Press.

Dewey, J., & Dewey, E. (1915). *Schools of to-morrow.* New York: E. P. Dutton.

Dow, P. (1991). *Schoolhouse politics: Lessons from the Sputnik era.* Cambridge, MA: Harvard University Press.

Elmore, R. (1993*). The development and implementation of large-scale curriculum reforms* (Paper prepared for the American Association for the Advancement of Science). Cambridge, MA: Harvard Graduate School of Education, Center for Policy Research in Education.

Elmore, R. (1995). Teaching, learning, and school organization: Principles of practice and the regularities of schooling. *Educational Administration Quarterly, 31,* 355–374.

Flexner, A. (1917). A modern school. In *Publications of the General Education Board* (Occasional papers, No. 3). New York: General Education Board.

Fullan, M. (1982). *The meaning of education change.* New York: Teachers College Press.

Fullan, M., & Miles, M. (1992). Getting reform right: What works and what doesn't. *Phi Delta Kappan, 73,* 744–752.

Goodlad, J. (1984). *A place called school.* New York: McGraw-Hill.

Grobman, A. (1969). *The changing classroom: The role of the biological sciences curriculum study.* New York: Doubleday.

Kilpatrick, W. H. (1925). *Foundations of method: Informal talks on teaching by William Heard Kilpatrick.* New York: Macmillan.

Kilpatrick, W. H. (1933). *The educational frontier.* New York: Century Company.

March, J., & Olsen, J. (1989). *Rediscovering institutions: The organizational basis of politics.* New York: Free Press.

Marsh, P. (1964). *The physical sciences study committee: A case history of nationwide curriculum development, 1956–1961.* Unpublished doctoral dissertation, Harvard University Graduate School of Education, Cambridge, MA.

Meyer, J., & Rowan, B. (1978). The structure of educational organizations. In M. Meyer (Ed.), *Environments and organizations* (pp. 78–109). San Francisco: Jossey-Bass.

National Center for Education Statistics. (1993). *NAEP 1992 Mathematics Report Card for the nation and the states: Data from the national and trial state assessments.* Washington, DC: U.S. Department of Education.

National Commission on Excellence in Education. (1983). *A nation at risk: The imperative for educational reform.* Washington, DC: U.S. Department of Education.

Powell, A., Farrar, E., & Cohen, D. (1985). *The shopping mall high school.* Boston: Houghton Mifflin.

Rugg, H. A., & Shumaker, A. (1928). *The child-centered school.* Chicago: World Book.

Stake, R., & Easely, J. (1978). Case studies in science education. In *The case reports,* vol. 1 & 2. Washington, DC: U.S. Government Printing Office.

Tyack, D., & Cuban, L. (1995). *Tinkering toward Utopia: Reflections on a century of public school reform.* Cambridge, MA: Harvard University Press.

Tyack, D., & Hansot, E. (1982). *Managers of virtue: Public school leadership in America, 1820–1980.* New York: Basic Books.

Tyack, D., & Tobin, W. (1994). The "grammar" of schooling: Why has it been so hard to change? *American Educational Research Journal, 31,* 453–479.

About the Contributors

Cynthia Ballenger is a teacher and a member of the Brookline Teacher-Researcher Seminar. She is also a researcher at the Chèche Konnen Center for Science Education Reform. She is editor of *Making Thinking Visible* (2003), a collection of articles by members of the Brookline Teacher-Researcher Seminar, and author of *Teaching Other People's Children* (1999).

Marilyn Cochran-Smith is a professor of education and director of the doctoral program in curriculum and instruction at Boston College. Her research and writing center around teacher education and teacher research, as well as issues of diversity in schools and universities. She is coauthor of "Sticks, Stones, and Ideology: The Discourse of Reform in Teacher Education" in *Educational Researcher* (with K. Fries, 2001) and of "Relationships of Knowledge and Practice: Teacher Learning in Communities" in *Review of Research in Education* (with S. Lytle, edited by A. Iran-Nejad and C. D. Pearson, 1999). She is also editor of the *Journal of Teacher Education* and president-elect of the American Educational Research Association.

Christine Cziko is academic coordinator of the MUSE Program at the Graduate School of Education, University of California, Berkeley. Her professional interests include preservice teacher education and adolescent literacy. She is coauthor of *Reading for Understanding: A Guide to Improving Reading in Middle and High School Classrooms* (with R. Schoenbach, C. Greenleaf, and L. Hurwitz, 1999).

Lisa D. Delpit, executive director and eminent scholar at the Center for Urban Education and Innovation at Florida International University in Miami, is interested in improving urban education, particularly for children of color, and in the perspectives and aspirations of teachers of color. Her recent publications include *The Skin That We Speak: Thoughts on Language and Culture in the Classroom* (coedited with J. Kilgour Dowdy, 2002) and *The Real Ebonics Debate* (coedited with T. Perry, 1998). She received a MacArthur Fellowship in 1990 and the Horace Mann Humanity Award in 2003.

Rubén Donato is an associate professor and chair of Educational Foundations, Policy, and Practice at the School of Education at the University of Colorado at Boulder. His primary research interest is the history of American education. He is author of *The Other Struggle for Equal Schools: Mexican Americans during the Civil Rights Era* (1997) and a number of articles on the historical experiences of Mexican Americans in U.S. public schools.

Richard F. Elmore is the Gregory R. Anrig Professor of Educational Leadership at the Harvard Graduate School of Education and a senior research fellow with the Consortium for Policy Research in Education. His research focuses on the effects of federal, state, and local education policy on schools and classrooms. He is author of "Bridging the Gap between Standards and Achievement" (2002) and "Building a New Structure for School Leadership" in *American Education* (2000).

Cynthia L. Greenleaf is director of research and codirector of the Strategic Literacy Initiative at WestEd in Oakland, California. Her studies combine research and practice with secondary teachers to promote a higher level of literacy for diverse youth. She is coauthor of "Ever Newer Ways to Mean: Authoring Pedagogical Change in Secondary Subject-Area Classrooms" in *New Literacies for New Times: Bakhtinian Perspectives on Language, Literacy and Learning for the 21st Century* (with M. Katz, edited by S. W. Freedman and A. F. Ball, in press) and of *Reading for Understanding: A Guide to Improving Reading in Middle and High School Classrooms* (with R. Schoenbach, C. Cziko, and L. Hurwitz, 1999).

Johanna Elena Hadden is an instructor at Montana State University in Billings. Her primary research interests are social policy, educational history, state theory, and teachers' work. She is coauthor, with A. Gitlin, of "Educative Research: Acting on Power Relations in the Classroom" in *International Action Research: A Casebook for Educational Reform* (edited by S. Hollingsworth, 1997).

Rosemary C. Henze is an associate professor in the Linguistics and Language Development Department at San Jose State University in California. Her professional interests include language maintenance, school leadership, and racist education. Her most recent publications are "How Real Is Race? Using Anthropology to Make Sense of Human Diversity" in *Phi Delta Kappan* (2003) and *Leading for Diversity: How School Leaders Promote Positive Interethnic Relations* (2002).

Richard M. Ingersoll is an associate professor of education and sociology at the University of Pennsylvania. His research is concerned with the character of elementary and secondary schools as workplaces, teachers as employees, and teaching as a job. He has published articles and books that include *Who Controls Teachers' Work? Power and Accountability in America's Schools* (2003) and "The Problem of Underqualified Teachers in American Secondary Schools" in *Educational Researcher* (1999).

Tamara Lucas, associate professor in the Department of Educational Foundations at Montclair State University in New Jersey, has devoted her career to issues of equity and quality in the education of culturally and linguistically diverse students. She is coauthor of *Educating Culturally Responsive Teachers: A Coherent Approach* (with A. M. Villegas, 2002) and author of *Into, Through, and Beyond Secondary School: Critical Transitions for Immigrant Youths* (1997).

Faye L. Mueller is a professor at the College of San Mateo in California. Her professional interests are secondary and college reading, professional development, and assessment and evaluation. She is coauthor of *Portraits of Exemplary Literacy Practices* (with S. Chow, N. Filby, and K. Tyner, 1995).

Sonia Nieto, professor of education at the University of Massachusetts, Amherst, is interested in multicultural education, the education of Latinos in the United States, teacher education, and Puerto Rican children's literature. She is author of *What Keeps Teachers Going?* (2003) and *The Light in Their Eyes* (1999), and editor of *Puerto Rican Children in U.S. Schools* (2002).

Suzanne Plaut is an advanced doctoral student at the Harvard Graduate School of Education, where she is also a research assistant for the Alliance on Gender, Culture,

and School Practice and a former board member of the *Harvard Educational Review.*
She has worked as an English teacher and literacy specialist in both public and private
secondary schools. Plaut's research examines how students experience and express
confusion, and how teachers perceive and respond to it, while students are learning
persuasive writing.

Ray C. Rist is a senior evaluation officer in the Operations Evaluation Department of
the World Bank. His current areas of interest are the uses of evaluation in public sector management, and building results-based management systems in developing
countries. A former teacher at Johns Hopkins, Cornell, and George Washington universities, he is coauthor of "Building Results-Based Monitoring and Evaluation Systems: Assessing Developing Countries' Readiness" in *Zeitschrift für Evaluation* (with J.
Kusek, 2002) and coeditor of *International Atlas of Evaluation* (with J-E. Furubo and R.
Sandahl, 2002).

Ruth Schoenbach is codirector of the Strategic Literacy Initiative at WestEd in Oak-
land, California. Her work centers around professional development program design.
She is coauthor of *Reading for Understanding: A Guide to Improving Reading in Middle and
High School Classrooms* (with C. Greenleaf, C. Cziko, and L. Hurwitz, 1999).

Nancy S. Sharkey is an advanced doctoral student at the Harvard Graduate School of
Education and a former board member of the *Harvard Educational Review.* She is part
of a research team exploring how and why teachers and principals use student
achievement data to inform instructional practice. She previously worked in the Education Policy Center of the Urban Institute on projects including a study of the effects
of changes in Title I legislation on Title I schools. A former sixth-grade math and science teacher, her research endeavors are grounded in classroom experience.